Mastering Windows 36

The ultimate guide to designing, delivering, and managing architectures for Windows 365 Cloud PCs

Christiaan Brinkhoff

Sandeep Patnaik

Morten Pedholt

BIRMINGHAM—MUMBAI

Mastering Windows 365

Group Product Manager: Pavan Ramchandani

Publishing Product Manager: Prachi Sawant

Content Development Editor: Sujata Tripathi

Technical Editor: Arjun Varma

Copy Editor: Safis Editing

Project Coordinator: Ashwin Dinesh Kharwa

Proofreader: Safis Editing

Indexer: Subalakshmi Govindhan

Production Designer: Prashant Ghare

DevRel Marketing Coordinator: Marylou D'Mello

First published: September 2023

Production reference: 2210923

Published by Packt Publishing Ltd.

Grosvenor House

11 St Paul's Square

Birmingham

B3 1RB

ISBN 978-1-83763-796-6

www.packtpub.com

"I'd like to thank my wife, Natasja, and my beautiful kids, Nila and Mason, for supporting me and allowing me to pursue my passion while finalizing this book! Building the future of Windows as part of Windows 365 while also writing a book has been intense but also very satisfying. Building products is important; however, ensuring the product is explained both from a technical and visual perspective is even more important. I hope you enjoy reading this book and it gives you superpowers so you can do your job even better!"

– Christiaan Brinkhoff

"I would like to express my deepest gratitude to the people who have made this book possible. To my mother, Swarajya Lakshmi, who taught me to be a learn-it-all and to be unbounded in my thinking. To my father, Balamukunda, for teaching me the importance of perseverance and for being my voice of reason and source of inspiration. To my spouse, Soumya, who has been an unwavering supporter of my dreams and passions. To my daughter, Siya, who kept me on track with my writing schedule and motivated me throughout the writing process. To my baby son, Sohum, whose playful presence lights up my days. To my aunt, Pramila, a brilliant author whose books ignited my own writing journey. To my furry friend, Max, for being so understanding during the long hours of writing. Their love, support, and encouragement have been invaluable in bringing this book to life. It is an immense honor and privilege to be able to share this book with all of you, not only because it empowers readers to master Windows 365 but also because it tells the story behind the product and its creation. Your support and readership mean the world to me as an author. My greatest hope is that this book brings you understanding, inspiration, and enlightenment on Windows 365."

– Sandeep Patnaik

"It requires a lot of time and dedication to write a book like this and keep the latest Microsoft Cloud technologies such as Windows 365 at the front of your mind. I couldn't have done this without support from my fiancée, Lykke, and my son, Aske. Thanks for always supporting me in whatever I decide to do, such as becoming a Microsoft MVP, and giving me time to organize and participate in community events. I hope you as a reader will find the content of this book understandable and useful so you can manage Windows 365 like a pro!"

– Morten Pedholt

Forewords

Windows 365 redefines personal computing by bringing the elasticity of the cloud to every Windows customer, on any device. Our vision is an experience where moving between the cloud and edge is as seamless and unnoticeable as switching between Wi-Fi and 5G.

This hybrid compute model, across CPU, GPU, NPU, and Azure, enables users to access their Windows desktops and applications from anywhere, on any device, with the same familiar interface and functionality they have come to rely on. As we look forward, our team is rapidly innovating to make our Windows 365 experiences even more powerful and secure, all while providing access to cutting-edge AI features.

AI is driving the largest technology shift of this generation. The possibilities across industries – healthcare, finance, education, and tech – and even in our homes are endless. Together, we have the privilege to witness and participate in something that will change the very fabric of how we live our lives. Windows 365 provides a flexibility of compute that enables rich, new cloud and AI experiences.

It is within this exciting realm of innovation where AI, the cloud, and clients come together that *Mastering Windows 365* finds its purpose.

From the newly announced Windows Copilot to the ability for any developer to create a Windows 11 AI plugin, AI is revolutionizing how we interact with our computers, and Windows 365 is here to help you use AI to deliver an unparalleled level of efficiency and productivity to your businesses.

Christiaan, Sandeep, and Morten have combined their expertise in *Mastering Windows 365* to make deploying and maintaining Windows 365 environments simple and easy. Through these pages, you will discover how to leverage the power of AI to automate routine tasks, optimize resource allocation, and deliver an exceptional user experience. You will gain a deep understanding of the underlying architecture, security considerations, and strategies for successful adoption. Moreover, this book serves as a compass for navigating the evolving landscape of cloud computing, offering guidance on hybrid environments, data management, and integration with other cloud services.

Ultimately, *Mastering Windows 365* is a comprehensive guide that will enable you to make the most of emerging new technologies and usher in a new era for your employees, clients, and customers. I hope you enjoy the journey as much as I did.

Panos Panay

EVP and Chief Product Officer, Windows and Devices, Microsoft

Windows 365 has been on the market for two years and we have seen tremendous customer adoption for the product. When we initially built the product, we targeted six core scenarios we believed would be a good fit for Windows 365: data security, developers, **bring your own PC (BYOPC)**, temporary workforces, remote employees, and mergers and acquisitions. Two years in, we can confirm those target use cases are the right ones. We have also identified new use cases that are driving adoption, such as government and frontline.

I have personally met with over one hundred customers since the launch of Windows 365. Some of them are fully deployed, some of them are expanding beyond their first purchase for new use cases and personas, and some of them are running pilots.

Many of the customers that I have talked to have on-premises VDI; they are migrating to Windows 365 for its simplicity, seamless integration with management, security, identity and compliance products in Microsoft 365, reduction in total cost of ownership, and improvement in sustainability. I also talk to an increasingly large number of customers that are not VDI customers. They are adopting the Cloud PC concept and purchasing Windows 365 to replace their physical PCs because of the unique benefits of Cloud PCs, for example, OpEx versus CapEx, fast provisioning, restore points, and upsizing/downsizing. In fact, one of the largest Windows 365 customers has converted their entire PC fleet into Cloud PCs a year ago and has loved the experience of running Windows in the cloud.

Microsoft believes the future of Windows is in the cloud. We want the Windows experience that you all love to be available on any device. Imagine a future of Windows that's powered by and optimized for AI; imagine a purpose-built Windows device that can dynamically scale to the cloud, using Azure as a co-processor. We are just getting started with Windows 365. This book will help you to master Windows 365 and prepare yourself for a new generation of Windows that is cloud powered.

Ken Pan

CVP, Windows 365 and AVD, Microsoft

The innovation engine that drives the Windows in the cloud experience

Innovation can take many forms; as technology providers and product people, it's often difficult to put what we're building in context. And for many of us, we have a clear preference for the kinds of product areas we work on. When we develop products to meet the diverse needs of our customers, we are thoughtful in how we innovate. Consider that there are three core types of innovation: disruptive, evolutionary, and revolutionary. Let's walk through some examples of these types of innovation.

Consider the case of LCD televisions; while the act of watching screen-based entertainment remained the same, LCD televisions built on existing technological frameworks and material advancements to deliver a new device type that made the act of consuming new content better. This is a great example of an evolutionary advancement in televisions. The internet is an example of a revolutionary advancement. It's changed how we buy, learn, and communicate with each other in a fundamental way. It has created new markets and significantly expanded others. The modern electrical vehicle is a disruptive technology. Consider 15 years ago the three leading US-based automakers were Chrysler, Ford, and Chevy. As of the time of this writing, Telsa's market capitalization is around four times the size of all of these manufacturers combined. Tesla disrupted the market by offering new value, direct-to-consumer sales, and the ability to attach services to the sale after the initial purchase.

Let's discuss the forces that are shaping the innovation happening in the cloud virtualization world. The shift to hybrid work creates new opportunities, but it also creates new challenges. Things look different when the IT team isn't down the hall from employees who need help. New employees need to be onboarded, distributed teams need to be connected, specialized workloads need to be enabled, and new projects need to be scaled up. IT needs to not only get employees set up and supported but it also needs to be prepared to respond to rapidly changing environments while still maintaining business continuity. And, while managing this, IT also needs to ensure they are keeping their estate secure and meeting ever-changing regulatory requirements.

It is a challenge to address these needs with agility without overburdening IT, letting costs get out of control, sacrificing productivity, or compromising security. The changing nature of work is creating a tremendous opportunity for all of us in the virtualization market. Today, we can deliver Windows to users in three ways: on a physical device, through AVD, and through Windows 365. When you think about the innovation framework we discussed earlier, we can talk about our approach to delivering a Windows cloud experience that innovates in response to the changing nature of work.

AVD is a cloud VDI product that was a natural evolution from traditional on-premises VDI. Cloud VDI provides a PaaS-based management plane and the ultimate flexibility in compute, storage, density, and location. We think about AVD as our "any" offering – any compute and storage combination, any location, and any supported OS. Admins that are familiar with deploying and managing traditional VDI will find AVD a huge step forward that brings the reach and capabilities of Azure to bear on addressing their virtualization needs.

Windows 365 is a truly revolutionary innovation. The Cloud PC gives us an opportunity to create a **Software as a Service**, or **SaaS**, offering that redefines the user experience and can be managed by an endpoint administrator using the same tools, baselines, and processes as a traditional PC. A Cloud PC can be provisioned with Zero Touch, and the security principles are based on Zero Trust, and users can immediately be productive with Zero Ramp. We affectionately refer to Windows 365 as the "zero" offering.

Scott Manchester

VP of Product Management, Windows 365 and AVD, Microsoft

Product Quotes

We've asked our other Windows Cloud Experiences group engineering leaders at Microsoft if they wanted to share inspirational quotes about how they see the future. Here goes…

"With its seamless integration of cloud computing and desktop virtualization, Windows 365 is the ultimate computing experience that lets you access your Windows experience from anywhere, on any device. This is not just an evolution of Windows; it's a revolution that empowers you to be more productive, secure, and flexible than ever before, with the cloud as your ally."

Bhavya Chopra, Principal Group Product Manager

"Workplaces are shifting to be more hybrid, with more colleagues around the world and greater opportunity for each person to work wherever they will be more productive. The cloud-based personal computing revolution led by Windows 365, which is a key enabler of this change, makes it possible to connect with the resources and people you need, just as if you were in a physical office together."

Deb Dubrow, Principal Group Product Manager

"Just over three years ago, we embarked on a journey to reshape the essence of computing, crafting a cloud-based PC with Windows 365 that redefines our digital limits. As we look ahead, we see the future of computing being freed from the physical boundaries of the devices in front of us."

Phil Gerity, Partner Group Product Manager

"Having worked in virtualization for a while, it has always felt like you need to learn how to fly a plane before experiencing the magic of flight. Windows 365 offers a first-class passenger seat that gets you off the ground in minutes, drinking champagne as you soar through the clouds to places you've never been before!"

Tristan Scott, Principal Group Product Manager

"Windows 365 aims to be the best expression of the Windows experience. It is where the Windows user environment, familiar administration, and the advantages of the Azure cloud come together. Concepts such as flexibility, mobility, reliability, and elasticity now apply in new ways. It's an exciting future and there is lots more to come."

Randy Cook, PM Architect

Contributors

About the authors

Christiaan Brinkhoff works as a Principal Program Manager and Community Lead for Windows 365 and AVD at Microsoft. In his role at Microsoft, he works on features such as the Windows 365 app, Switch, and Boot. Christiaan is also an author and inventor. His mission is to drive innovation while bringing Windows 365, Windows, and Microsoft Intune closer together, lead the Windows 365 and AVD MVP programs, and drive new community efforts around virtualization to empower Microsoft customers in leveraging new cloud virtualization scenarios. Christiaan joined Microsoft in 2018 as part of the FSLogix acquisition. He has also been rewarded with the Microsoft MVP, Citrix CTP, and VMware vExpert community achievements for his continued support in the EUC community.

Sandeep Patnaik is a virtualization veteran with nearly two decades of experience in the industry. He has shipped multiple billion-dollar products and cloud services for Microsoft to a global user base including Windows, AVD, and Windows 365. His contributions have earned him multiple patents in this field. Currently, he leads a stellar team that is responsible for building the product strategy for Windows 365 and AVD services and shaping the future of user experiences for these services.

Morten Pedholt works as a cloud architect for a consulting company in Denmark where he advises on and implements Microsoft virtual desktop solutions to customers around the world. Morten started his journey as a consultant over 8 years ago, when he started with managing client devices but quickly found a passion for virtual device management. Today, Windows 365 and Azure Virtual Desktop are the main areas that are being focused on, alongside Microsoft Intune. Because of all the community activities Morten has done over the past few years, he received the Microsoft MVP award in the category of Windows 365 in March 2022.

About the reviewers

Sune Thomsen is based in Denmark, and he's a Windows 365 (Windows and Devices for IT) MVP with over 19 years of IT experience. He has spent at least a decade specializing in client management via Microsoft Configuration Manager and Intune, and he's currently helping enterprise customers with their cloud journey. He's working as a consultant for a small consulting company called Mindcore. Prior to joining Mindcore, Sune gained 10 years of experience in the engineering industry, managing and deploying various Microsoft solutions and projects. Sune is passionate about community work. Besides blogging and speaking at tech events, he's also an official contributor within the Windows 365 Community and the Modern Endpoint Management LinkedIn group.

I'd like to thank my wife and the kids for always supporting me and allowing me to dedicate so much private time to the community. Reviewing this book has been a tremendous honor and an educational journey – thank you Christiaan, Sandeep, and Morten for giving me this fantastic opportunity.

Dominiek Verham lives in Brunssum, the Netherlands. He has over 20 years of experience in IT working in all kinds of technical roles focused on Microsoft products. In 2017, Dominiek transitioned from Microsoft server products to endpoints, creating images for a variety of customers in different sectors using MDT. In the same year, he began his journey with the various Microsoft cloud products, such as Microsoft Intune, AVD, Windows 365, and related products such as Nerdio. He is passionate about sharing his knowledge and personal experiences with the community via his blog and presentations. Dominiek has been a Microsoft MVP for Windows 365 (Windows and Devices for IT) as well as a Nerdio NVP since 2022.

First of all, I would like to thank my wife, Myrna, and my daughter, Mila, for allowing me to invest a lot of private time in my community efforts. I would like to thank the authors of this book, Christiaan, Sandeep, and Morten, for giving me this opportunity. It was a great honor and a fun experience! And, last but not least, I want to thank the very active community! It's amazing to see all of the great content on different social media platforms.

Ola Ström is a Windows 365 MVP based in Sweden with over 10 years of experience in Microsoft Intune and cloud-based device management. Ola decided to focus on Intune rather than catching up with more senior peers who specialized in on-premises products. Since Ola loves making life easier for both IT administrators and users, Windows 365 became a natural next step for him.

Ola currently works as the Chief Technical Architect within the device segment at Knowledge Factory, a specialist unit with the Nordic Microsoft partner Advania. In this position, he helps customers on their journey to the modern workplace.

Ola loves sharing his knowledge and findings with the community, both through his blog and speaking at tech events.

First, I would like to thank Christiaan, Sandeep, and Morten for giving me this terrific opportunity to review the book. It has been a great honor and something I am really proud of being part of. I would also like to thank my girlfriend, Emma, because she has put up with me and supported me in dedicating big parts of our summer vacation to reviewing this book. And finally, a big thank you to the Windows 365 community.

Table of Contents

Part 2: Implementing and Managing Cloud PCs

2

Architecture   25

3

Deploying Cloud PCs   57

4

Managing Cloud PCs 125

Part 3: Accessing, Securing, and Analyzing Cloud PCs

5

Accessing Cloud PCs   195

6

Securing Cloud PCs   259

7

Analyzing, Monitoring, and Troubleshooting Cloud PCs   323

Part 4: Extending Windows 365 with Partner Solutions

8

Windows 365 Partner Solutions   369

9

Community Experts Hall of Fame   409

Index   417

Other Books You May Enjoy   428

Preface

Windows 365 Cloud PC is a revolutionary cloud-based computing solution that offers users a seamless and secure Windows experience from virtually any device.

The goal of this book is to help you understand, deploy, manage, secure, and optimize Windows 365 Cloud PCs effectively.

This comprehensive book takes you on an illuminating journey through the evolving landscape of Windows 365 cloud computing, delving into the core concepts, deployment intricacies, management strategies, and advanced capabilities of this cutting-edge technology.

Prepare to embark on a tour into the realm of Windows cloud computing and witness the unfolding evolution of Windows as it becomes fueled by the synergy of Intune, cloud, and AI technologies. Authored by luminaries from the Windows 365 product group and a distinguished Microsoft MVP, this book offers invaluable insights into the intricacies of Windows 365 – its functionalities, features, partner add-value solutions, and best practices. With a wealth of experience, these experts are poised to illuminate the path to the next generation of cloud computing, affording you a rare opportunity to grasp this cutting-edge technology from those embedded within the industry.

We hope you enjoy it!

Who this book is for

This book is for IT administrators, architects, consultants, and **Chief Information Officers** (**CIOs**) who want to leverage and design Windows 365 Cloud PCs effectively. This book is also for anyone who would like to move their Windows endpoints to the cloud with ease. A basic understanding of modern management based on Microsoft Intune and Microsoft 365 products is required.

What this book covers

Chapter 1, Introduction to Windows 365, provides everything you need to know first before jumping into the deployment of Windows 365 Cloud PCs. What is Windows 365 and what are Cloud PCs? What are the different product and licensing versions? How is Windows 365 different than Azure Virtual Desktop and any other virtualization solution on the market? These are a few of the topics we will handle in the chapter. Let's go and read!

Chapter 2, Architecture, covers things related to designing and creating good Windows 365 architecture. You will get a better understanding of what you, as an IT administrator, will have to manage and focus on.

Chapter 3, Deploying Cloud PCs, is the start of the real deal, the hands-on part where we will guide you through the nuts and bolts of deploying Windows 365 Enterprise, including the new Windows 365 Frontline solution. We will be explaining the basics, tips, and tricks, and all the latest new components available as part of the Windows 365 service.

Chapter 4, Managing Cloud PCs, teaches you all the necessary steps in order to manage your Cloud PCs via the Microsoft Intune portal. We will also go over the features that make your life as an IT admin much easier.

Chapter 5, Accessing Cloud PCs, explores how to access your Cloud PC, and how to take advantage of different features such as Windows 365 Boot and Switch. Furthermore, you will also be guided through how to enable some security features.

Chapter 6, Securing Cloud PCs, explains how you can secure the connection and content with **digital rights management (DRM)** such as lock-down features and more to ensure your Cloud PC is secure.

Chapter 7, Analyzing, Monitoring, and Troubleshooting Cloud PCs, covers everything about analyzing and monitoring Windows 365 Cloud PCs. You will get to know the built-in analyzing solution and how to utilize all the data that is available to be able to analyze your environment efficiently, including tips and tricks on how to troubleshoot in your Windows 365 environment.

Chapter 8, Windows 365 Partner Solutions, talks about the value that Windows 365 partner solutions are contributing. Each partner solution adds a layer on top of the existing Windows 365 service that supports new and more use cases.

Chapter 9, Community Experts – Hall of Fame, introduces some of the greatest minds in the Windows 365 community.

To get the most out of this book

To get the most out of this book, it's good to have a base-level understanding of Microsoft Intune and Microsoft 365 cloud services, and such. This is not required, however, as you'll learn all you need to know in this book!

Conventions used

There are a number of text conventions used throughout this book.

`Code in text`: Indicates code words in text, database table names, folder names, filenames, file extensions, pathnames, dummy URLs, user input, and Twitter handles. Here is an example: "This makes the environment more secure than ever because you no longer have something that is exposing itself to port `3389`."

Bold: Indicates a new term, an important word, or words that you see onscreen. For instance, words in menus or dialog boxes appear in **bold**. Here is an example: "Click on the **Options** menu in the upper-left corner, expand **My Services**, and select **DaaS** "

> **Tips or important notes**
> Appear like this.

Get in touch

Feedback from our readers is always welcome.

General feedback: If you have questions about any aspect of this book, email us at `customercare@packtpub.com` and mention the book title in the subject of your message.

Errata: Although we have taken every care to ensure the accuracy of our content, mistakes do happen. If you have found a mistake in this book, we would be grateful if you would report this to us. Please visit `www.packtpub.com/support/errata` and fill in the form.

Piracy: If you come across any illegal copies of our works in any form on the internet, we would be grateful if you would provide us with the location address or website name. Please contact us at `copyright@packt.com` with a link to the material.

If you are interested in becoming an author: If there is a topic that you have expertise in and you are interested in either writing or contributing to a book, please visit `authors.packtpub.com`.

Share Your Thoughts

Once you've read *Mastering Windows 365*, we'd love to hear your thoughts! Scan the QR code below to go straight to the Amazon review page for this book and share your feedback.

https://packt.link/r/1837637962

Your review is important to us and the tech community and will help us make sure we're delivering excellent quality content.

Download a free PDF copy of this book

Thanks for purchasing this book!

Do you like to read on the go but are unable to carry your print books everywhere? Is your eBook purchase not compatible with the device of your choice?

Don't worry, now with every Packt book you get a DRM-free PDF version of that book at no cost.

Read anywhere, any place, on any device. Search, copy, and paste code from your favorite technical books directly into your application.

The perks don't stop there, you can get exclusive access to discounts, newsletters, and great free content in your inbox daily

Follow these simple steps to get the benefits:

1. Scan the QR code or visit the link below

https://packt.link/free-ebook/978-1-83763-796-6

2. Submit your proof of purchase

3. That's it! We'll send your free PDF and other benefits to your email directly

Part 1:
Understanding the Basics of
Windows 365

This part of the book serves as an introduction to Windows 365 and Cloud PCs. It explains the various product and licensing options, highlights the distinctions between Windows 365 and other virtualization solutions on the market, and outlines the supported endpoints. By the end of this part, you will have gained a comprehensive understanding of Windows 365 and its features.

This part contains the following chapter:

- *Chapter 1, Introduction to Windows 365*

1

Introduction to Windows 365

In this chapter, we will introduce you to Windows 365. We will explore the fundamentals to help you understand the product in preparation for the other more technical chapters in the book. We highly recommend reading through this chapter fully.

We're extremely excited to kick off this first chapter, in which we will cover the following subjects:

- The Windows 365 vision – moving from buying computers to buying computing
- What is Windows 365 and what is a Cloud PC?
- Windows 365 Business and Enterprise
- Windows 365 Government
- Windows 365 Frontline
- Windows 365 and Azure Virtual Desktop – the differences
- Windows 365-supported regions
- Windows 365 licensing requirements
- Windows Copilot – bringing the power of AI to Windows 11
- Microsoft Intune
- Windows Autopatch
- Microsoft Dev Box
- Supported endpoints

Let's kick off this first chapter with some interesting research information. As we emerge from the COVID-19 pandemic and shift into a new world of hybrid work, organizations will need to adopt digital solutions to keep their employees connected and collaborating, whether they are working from home, at the office, or anywhere in between. Now is probably the most complicated time to be an IT admin, and some of the reasons for this are as follows:

- In recent surveys, 57% of remote employees plan to shift to hybrid work, whereas 51% are considering working remotely permanently

- 68% of companies report experiencing a breach due to the exploitation of an endpoint in 2021

- 67% of IT professionals feel overwhelmed by trying to manage remote work

Windows 365 can help solve these challenges for your business:

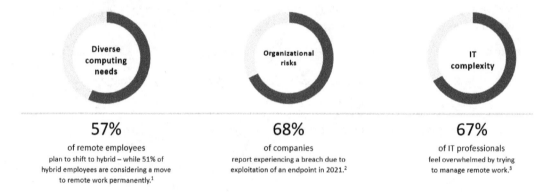

Figure 1.1 – Hybrid work market analysis

The Windows 365 vision – moving from buying computers to buying computing

> *"With Windows 365, we're creating a new category: the Cloud PC. Just like applications were brought to the cloud with SaaS, we are now bringing the operating system to the cloud..."*
>
> *– Satya Nadella, CEO, Microsoft*

During the launch of Windows 365 back in July 2021, Microsoft's CEO, Satya Nadella, shared this quote about bringing Windows to the cloud, blurring the lines between Windows today and in the future. The vision outlined a rich set of features, which has also been explained by our senior leaders, who contributed to the foreword of this book.

The following features illustrate the vision and ambitions of Windows 365 and outline the main differences in end user experiences that are unique to Windows 365:

- The **Windows 365 app** enables users to start their Windows 365 Cloud PC session from the taskbar or **Start** menu with a personal Windows experience and different end user actions to reboot, rename, restore, and troubleshoot the Cloud PC without IT admin interaction.

- **Windows 365 Boot** makes it possible for users to log directly into their Cloud PC from the initial Windows 11 logon screen. This direct-to-Cloud solution provides a Windows look and feel experience without any visible client for the end user. It is also a great solution for scenarios with shared users, such as shift workers.

- **Windows 365 Switch** makes it possible to easily move between the local and Cloud PC from the Windows 11 Task View desktops feature. It works seamlessly, directly from within the Windows 11 shell, by either swiping with your fingers, using a mouse, or keyboard interaction.

- **Windows 365 Offline** makes it possible to remain productive when there is a disconnect. With Offline mode, you enable a user to work in Windows 365 without disruption if the internet connection goes down. When the internet connection comes back online, the Cloud PC will automatically re-enable itself with the changes made on your offline Cloud PC synced.

Ultimately, Windows is moving to the cloud. We will move from buying computers to buying computing, where Windows performance will no longer be capped by the physical processing hardware on your endpoint but by a combination of your local and Cloud PC.

What is Windows 365 and what is a Cloud PC?

Windows 365 is the world's first Cloud PC service that's designed for your hybrid work needs. Windows 365 is a premium cloud service from Microsoft that securely streams your personalized Windows desktop, apps, and content from the Microsoft cloud (Microsoft Azure) to any device, anywhere. It is a revolutionary technology where both the IT admin and end user experiences are fundamentally different from traditional **virtual desktop infrastructure** (**VDI**) and Cloud VDI. It combines the best of Windows, Azure, and Microsoft 365 to deliver simplified IT and modern end user experiences – providing an easy on-ramp for both existing and new customers.

A Cloud PC is the end user's personal computer in the cloud that is optimized, scalable, and has high availability for a familiar Windows desktop experience. It's hosted in the Windows 365 service and is accessible from anywhere, on any device. Windows 365 is a hybrid local and cloud **operating system** (**OS**) that brings new possibilities to organizations of all sizes.

Figure 1.2 – Windows 365 illustration

With Windows 365, organizations can choose whether a PC, with its locally installed OS, or a Cloud PC, with its cloud-based OS, is the best fit for a particular user or role in the organization. In some cases, a user may benefit from having both a local OS and a cloud OS and choosing the one for the job.

Windows 365 is designed for organizations of all sizes that need highly secure and agile hybrid work solutions. These solutions are valuable for elastic workforces, distributed employees, and specialized workloads that require versatile compute and storage capabilities, accessible on any device.

IT administrators can swiftly scale and resize Cloud PCs to meet the changing needs of their users so that they have the compute power and storage they need, with predictable costs. Hybrid work use cases can be supported effectively with Windows 365. Let's add some fun. We asked ChatGPT to write a poem about Windows 365 to test what the general idea about it is in the industry.

Asking ChatGPT to write a poem

Here's a poem about Windows 365:

Windows 365, a tool so fine

Bringing Windows, Office, and peace of mind

In the cloud it resides, with ease to find

A comprehensive platform, of a new kind

Gone are the days, of software to buy

Now, it's a subscription, that never runs dry

Always up-to-date, no need to pry

With Windows 365, your work takes flight

Collaboration made simple, with Teams in sight;

Video calls, chats, and file sharing, all in one sight

working together, now it feels just right

And when it comes to security, have no fright

Windows 365 has got you, day and night

Protecting your data, making it just right

So rest easy, knowing your information's in sight

Windows 365, a tool for the modern day

Making work easier, in every single way

So join the revolution, and get on the way

To a future bright, with Windows 365!

Windows 365 Business and Enterprise

Before jumping straight into the editions of Windows 365, we'd like to make you aware of recent product name changes around **Azure Active Directory** becoming **Microsoft Entra ID**. Most of the screenshots in this book will be listed as Azure AD, as the book was written in the middle of the name change, and not all product pages in, for example, Microsoft Intune and Windows 365 received those changes.

Please use the following table to convert from the old names to the new ones moving forward:

Old name	New name
Azure Active Directory	Microsoft Entra ID
Azure Active Directory join	Microsoft Entra join
Hybrid Active Directory join	Hybrid Microsoft Entra join
Azure AD Conditional Access	Microsoft Entra Conditional Access
Azure AD tenant	Microsoft Entra tenant
Azure AD account	Microsoft Entra account
Azure AD Connect	Microsoft Entra Connect

Table 1.1 – Azure AD becomes Microsoft Entra

Windows 365 is available in two editions – **Windows 365 Business** and **Windows 365 Enterprise**.

Windows 365 is a solution that aims to offer benefits to businesses of various sizes, ranging from small enterprises to large corporations. Companies can purchase subscriptions through `windows365. com` by using credit cards or other local payment methods supported in their country.

The Windows 365 Business Edition caters to the needs of small and medium-sized organizations, with up to 300 users. It offers a straightforward approach to purchasing, deploying, and administering Cloud PCs. Business owners can easily manage their company's Cloud PCs using the Windows 365 Business Admin Portal.

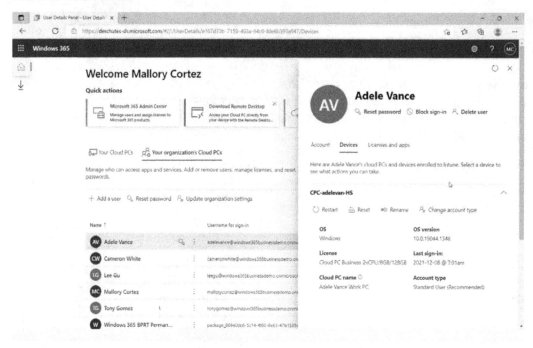

Figure 1.3 – Windows 365 Business Admin Portal

Windows 365 Enterprise is for organizations that want to manage their Cloud PCs with Microsoft Intune and take advantage of integrations with other Microsoft services, such as **Azure Active Directory** (**Azure AD**) and Microsoft Defender for Endpoint:

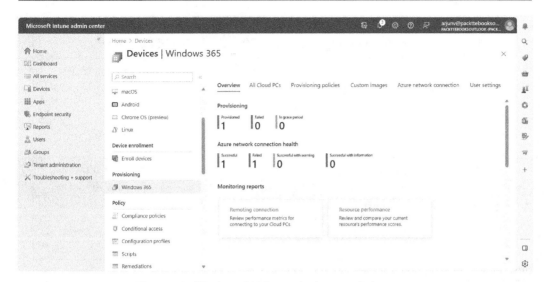

Figure 1.4 – Windows 365 Enterprise Intune admin center

We've now explained the high-level differences between Windows 365 Business and Enterprise. Let's take a bit of a deeper dive and go over a cheat sheet table explaining both services in more detail:

	Windows 365 Business	Windows 365 Enterprise
Domain join	Azure AD join with **Virtual Network (VNet)** is not supported.	Azure AD join with VNet is supported. Azure AD join without VNet is supported. Hybrid Azure AD join with VNet is supported.
Purchase channel support	Microsoft 365 Admin Center or the Azure AD portal.	Microsoft 365 Admin Center or the Azure AD portal.
License portal	There are no licensing pre-requirements to buy and deploy Windows 365 Business. Other features, such as device management, can be used if users are licensed for Microsoft Intune.	Users must be licensed for Windows 10 or 11 Enterprise (when available), Microsoft Intune, and Azure AD P1.
Seat limit	300 seats per tenant	No limits

Provisioning	Provisioning is simpler through the use of default configurations. Cloud PCs are automatically set up with a Gallery image.	Provisioning can be tailored to meet the needs of the organization. Admins choose network and user permissions and assign a policy to the Azure AD group. Cloud PCs are set up with Gallery images or custom images.
Policy management	Not supported	**Group Policy Objects (GPOs)** and Intune MDM policy are supported
Monitoring	Not supported	Reporting with Endpoint Analytics Monitoring and operational health alerts
Universal Print	Not supported	Supported
End user management	Users are able to troubleshoot, reset, restart, and rename their Cloud PCs on the Windows 365 home page	Users are able to troubleshoot, restart, restore, and rename their Cloud PCs on the Windows 365 home page
Conditional Access	Policies in Conditional Access can be deployed only from Azure AD. Requires an Azure AD P1 license.	Policies in Conditional Access can be deployed from Azure AD or the Intune admin center.
Security baselines	Not supported	Dedicated security baselines can be edited and deployed by using Microsoft Intune
Microsoft Defender for Endpoint	Supported if the customer separately has the requisite E5 license.	Integration with Defender for Endpoint. If the customer has an E5 license, all Cloud PCs will respond to Defender for Endpoint policies and show up in MDE dashboards.

Table 1.2 – Windows 365 Business and Windows 365 Enterprise comparison

In the next section, we will be talking about Windows 365 for governments.

Windows 365 Government

Today, governments use some Microsoft cloud services such as Microsoft Office and Microsoft Azure as they comply with special certifications that are required to work with US governments. Now, Microsoft has ensured that Windows 365 also meets the required certifications.

This allows governments to extend their Windows devices into the cloud with the newest functionality and technology based on top of the newest version of Windows 11 installed on powerful and secure Cloud PCs.

Windows 365 Government gives federal governments, government agencies, and public entities the opportunity to support the hybrid world we live in today by creating Cloud PCs just like it would for any other organization. This is currently restricted to governments in the United States; however, governments outside the United States can apply to get approval to use the service.

Windows 365 Government is provided in two versions – **Government Community Cloud (GCC)** comes with support for *FedRAMP High*, *DFARS,* and *DISA Level 2 Security Requirements*, and complies with *CJIS, IRS 1075*. The second version is **Government Community Cloud High (GCC High)**, which supports *FedRAMP High*, *ITAR*, and *DFARS*. All of these are security and compliance certifications that a provider needs to have to fulfill the requirements about structure and standardization that governments require.

For governments to get started with Windows 365, they must contact Microsoft directly or an approved partner.

At the publication of this book, there are some features for Windows 365 Government that are not supported in GCC or GCCH. Here are a few:

- Unified dashboard
- Support for endpoint analytics in GCCH
- Windows 365 alerting in Microsoft Intune for Cloud PCs
- Windows 365 Security Baseline
- Conversion of Windows 365 licenses to higher licenses
- User feedback in Windows 365 Web Client and End User portal
- RDP Shortpath for public networks
- Multimedia redirection
- Resize Cloud PCs
- Virtualization-based workloads

- Windows 365 Frontline

- Microsoft Dev Box

- Citrix HDX Plus for Windows 365

The following figure shows an overview of how Windows 365 can help US governments:

Figure 1.5 – How Windows 365 can help government workforces

Now we know how Windows 365 can help US governments, let's take a look at what the differences are between Windows 365 and Azure Virtual Desktop.

Windows 365 Frontline

Windows 365 Frontline allows frontline workers and shift work employees to experience the benefits of Windows in the cloud by extending the power of Cloud PCs. A single Windows 365 Frontline license supports up to three Cloud PCs, which can be used by any employee if only one employee per license is active at any given time. This means that instead of purchasing Windows 365 Frontline for every employee, you only need to purchase the number of licenses required to support the maximum number of concurrent active users.

Let's say you have shift workers, and you purchase 10 licenses for Windows 365 Frontline with a Cloud PC configuration of 2 vCPU/8 GB/128 GB. With 10 licenses, up to 30 Cloud PCs can be provisioned, which can be significantly more affordable for your business than normal Windows 365 licenses!

Figure 1.6 – One Windows 365 Frontline license supports three Cloud PCs

Windows 365 Frontline is an ideal solution for organizations of any size that employ shift workers, seasonal staff, or part-time employees who need access to a computing device only during their shifts. It's designed to help you securely equip more employees with Cloud PCs when they need them, boosting employee satisfaction and productivity without the need to equip everyone with their own device.

Windows 365 and Azure Virtual Desktop – the differences

Windows 365 is designed with simplicity in mind, enabling users to enjoy the advantages of customized Cloud PCs without needing extensive VDI or Azure knowledge. The pricing is predictable; it is billed per user, per month to make cost management easy. Windows 365 is an ideal solution for customers who are not extensively experienced in VDI or virtualization, or who prefer the convenience of a fixed-cost per-user subscription model. Azure Virtual Desktop offers a high level of flexibility, catering to organizations that have virtualization experience. Its customizable features, consumption-based pricing model, and support for remote app streaming and multi-session virtual machines make it a viable option for low-usage cases.

The following table summarizes the key differences between Windows 365 and Azure Virtual Desktop:

Cloud PC – Windows 365	Cloud VDI – Azure Virtual Desktop
Optimized for experience	Optimized for flexibility
Windows 10 or Windows 11 personalized desktop	Windows 10, Windows 11, or Windows Server multi-session or personal desktops
Complete end-to-end Microsoft service	Remote app streaming
Requires Modern Desktop knowledge	Requires VDI and Azure infra knowledge
One-stop administration in Microsoft Intune (Enterprise Edition) Direct self-service model (Business Edition)	Full control over configuration and management via the Azure portal
Windows 365 Boot and Switch	Not supported
Predictable per-user pricing	Pay for what you use

Table 1.3 – Windows 365 and Azure Virtual Desktop differences

Windows 365 license requirements

Before you can get started with deploying Cloud PCs for your users, they will need a Windows 365 license. There are multiple licenses for Windows 365; each license contains the hardware configuration of the Cloud PC that will be created – for example, if a user needs a Cloud PC with 4 vCPU, 16 GB RAM, and 128 GB hard drive space, the license will be named as *Windows 365 [Edition] 4 vCPU, 16 GB, 128 GB*. The *[Edition]* part of the license name will change depending on the Windows 365 edition you wish to deploy.

The following table shows all the current Windows 365 SKU licenses available. All the licenses are available for the Business, Enterprise, and Government Editions:

VM/OS disk size	Example scenarios	Applications
2 vCPU/4 GB/256 GB 2 vCPU/4 GB/128 GB 2 vCPU/4 GB/64 GB	Mergers and acquisitions, short-term and seasonal, customer services, **bring your own device** (**BYOD**), work from home	Microsoft 365 Apps, Microsoft Teams (audio-only), Outlook, Excel, PowerPoint, OneDrive, Adobe Reader, Edge, line-of-business app(s), Defender support
2 vCPU/8 GB/256 GB 2 vCPU/8 GB /128 GB	BYOD, work from home, market researchers, government, consultants	Microsoft 365 Apps, Microsoft Teams, Outlook, Excel, Access, PowerPoint, OneDrive, Adobe Reader, Edge, line-of-business app(s), Defender support
4 vCPU/16 GB/512 GB 4 vCPU /16 GB /256 GB 4 vCPU /16 GB /128 GB	Finance, government, consultants, healthcare services, BYOD, work from home	Microsoft 365 Apps, Microsoft Teams, Outlook, Excel, Access, PowerPoint, Power BI, Dynamics 365, OneDrive, Adobe Reader, Edge, line-of-business app(s), Defender support, nested virtualization support; Windows Subsystem for Linux/Android, Hyper-V, Defender support
8 vCPU /32 GB /512 GB 8 vCPU /32 GB /256 GB 8 vCPU /32 GB /128 GB	Software developers, engineers, content creators, design and engineering workstations	Microsoft 365 Apps, Microsoft Teams, Outlook, Access, OneDrive, Adobe Reader, Edge, Power BI, Visual Studio Code, line-of-business app(s), nested virtualization support; Windows Subsystem for Linux/Android, Hyper-V, Defender support

Table 1.4 – Windows 365 SKUs

The license pre-requirement for Windows 365 Business, Enterprise, and Government Editions are different. This means that before the users are eligible to use one of the Windows 365 licenses, they must have other licenses assigned. The available Windows 365 editions are covered next, along with their pre-required licenses.

Windows 365 Business license pre-requirements

Windows 365 Business licensing is extremely simple, as everything is cloud-only based, and all required licenses are included with the purchase. Customers can purchase Windows 365 Business licenses directly from `admin.microsoft.com`. Simply provide a credit card number to get started and become productive in a matter of minutes. Licenses are limited to 300 users per license type. Current Microsoft 365 customers must complete their purchase through the Microsoft 365 admin center. To purchase Windows 365 Business licenses, contact your Global administrator or Billing administrator.

Once a license has been assigned, IT administrators and users must go to `Windows365.microsoft.com`, set up their account without a domain, and provision and manage their Cloud PCs.

If you want to utilize the option to enable Intune on your Cloud PC deployed with Windows 365 Business, your users will need Microsoft Intune and Azure AD Premium P1 in order to get it to work. If you have bought a Windows 365 Business license with *Windows Hybrid Benefit*, then the users will also need a Windows 10/11 license.

Windows 365 Enterprise license pre-requirements

Each user must be licensed with Windows 10 Enterprise or Windows 11 Enterprise, Microsoft Intune, and Azure AD Premium P1. Each license can be bought individually as a single license, but you might find a license bundle with all three requirements to be a better fit for your organization by purchasing one of the following licensing bundles:

- Microsoft 365 F3
- Microsoft 365 E3
- Microsoft 365 E5
- Microsoft 365 A3
- Microsoft 365 A5
- Microsoft 365 Education Student Use Benefit
- Microsoft Business Premium

Although all the preceding licensing bundles give access to Microsoft Intune and Azure AD Premium P1, not all licenses are available for every company to use. Microsoft 365 A3, A5, and Education Student Use Benefit are for educational organizations only, such as schools. Microsoft 365 Business Premium has a limit of 300 licensed users; if you need more than 300 licenses, you will have to buy Microsoft 365 F3, E3, or E5.

Customers can purchase Windows 365 directly from `https://windows365.com/` or from their account representative. They can then provision and manage their Cloud PCs using Microsoft Intune, which works seamlessly with Windows 365 Enterprise.

Windows 365 Enterprise can be licensed separately with the Windows E3 or E5 license. Note that these licenses have Qualifying Operating System requirements. If a customer doesn't have a qualifying license already and wants Windows 365 Enterprise, they can go to the Windows 11 Enterprise page (`https://www.microsoft.com/licensing/product-licensing/windows`) or the Microsoft 365 page (`https://www.microsoft.com/microsoft-365/business/compare-all-microsoft-365-business-products`) to learn more and purchase the plan that's right for them.

Windows 365 Government license requirements

Just like Windows 365 Enterprise, governments who want to use Windows 365 Government must have their users licensed with Windows 10/11 Enterprise, Microsoft Intune, and Azure AD Premium P1 to be compliant. Governments also have the option to purchase these licenses through bundles.

Bundles that include the required licenses for Windows 365 Government are as follows:

- Microsoft 365 G3
- Microsoft 365 G5

You will be able to purchase any of the Windows 365 Business or Enterprise licenses alongside these bundles directly within the Microsoft 365 admin portal or by contacting your preferred cloud partner. If you are buying as a government, you need to contact the Microsoft account team you are assigned or any approved partner to purchase Windows 365 Government licenses.

Windows 365-supported regions

Windows 365 uses Microsoft's data center capacity worldwide to deploy Cloud PCs in many regions, with many more to come. The region where you can deploy your Cloud PCs depends on two aspects – the availability of Windows 365 for purchase and the Windows 365 edition you are deploying. The good news is that Windows 365 can be purchased in all 195 countries (as of the publication of this book).

Windows 365 Business Cloud PCs' region depends on the organization's billing address. These Cloud PCs will be provisioned in the same region as the organization's Exchange data location.

Windows 365 Enterprise allows the IT team to select a geography and region to provision Cloud PCs. This is particularly useful for companies that have employees working in various parts of the world, as it allows for more precise management and planning of resources.

The Windows 365 Government Edition is limited to United States-based governments, government agencies, and public entities, therefore Government Cloud PCs can be deployed to the *US Gov Virginia* and *US Gov Arizona* Azure regions.

Windows Copilot – bringing the power of AI to Windows 11

Windows Copilot is an AI assistant that helps you complete tasks, find information, and connect with your favorite apps. You can access Windows Copilot by clicking on the button next to the search bar on your taskbar, or by saying "*Hey Copilot*" if you have a microphone enabled. Windows Copilot will then appear as a sidebar on the right side of your screen, where you can type or speak your queries and commands.

Windows Copilot is not just a search engine or a voice assistant. It is also a smart helper that can assist you with your work and projects. Windows Copilot can rewrite, summarize, or explain the content on your screen, making it easier to understand and communicate. It can also help you adjust your settings, take screenshots, snap windows, and personalize your desktop. Windows Copilot can even generate creative content for you, such as poems, stories, code, essays, songs, and graphic art.

Windows Copilot is designed to be your personal assistant on Windows 11. It can help you save time, reduce stress, and achieve more. Whether you are working, studying, or having fun, Windows Copilot is always ready to help you with a simple click or a voice command. Try it out today and see how Windows Copilot can make your Windows experience better than ever.

Figure 1.7 – Windows Copilot

In the next section, we will explain Microsoft Intune and its importance in relation to Windows 365 Enterprise.

Microsoft Intune

Microsoft Intune is a cloud-based endpoint management solution that manages user access and simplifies app and device management across your devices, which can be Windows devices (such as Cloud PCs), physical PCs, mobile phones, tablets, and other devices.

Microsoft Intune operates completely from the Microsoft cloud, meaning that the control plane is 100% cloud-based to allow customers to manage endpoints without having to deploy them in any local infrastructure. This benefits Windows 365 as Cloud PCs are delivered from the cloud as well. Through the Intune admin center portal, IT administrators can control features and settings for physical PCs and Windows 365 Cloud PCs, as well as Android Enterprise, iOS/iPadOS, macOS, ChromeOS, and Linux. It integrates with other services, including Azure AD, VPN solutions, partners such as Citrix, and other technologies.

If you still have an on–premises Configuration Manager environment, Microsoft Intune also supports co-management, which lets you connect both on-premises domain-joined PCs with Intune – all from one single pane of glass experience. With one console to rule them all, no matter where you are in your journey to Windows 365 Cloud PC, Intune has got you covered!

> **Note**
> Microsoft Intune was previously known as Microsoft Endpoint Manager. The rebrand was announced at Microsoft Ignite 2022.

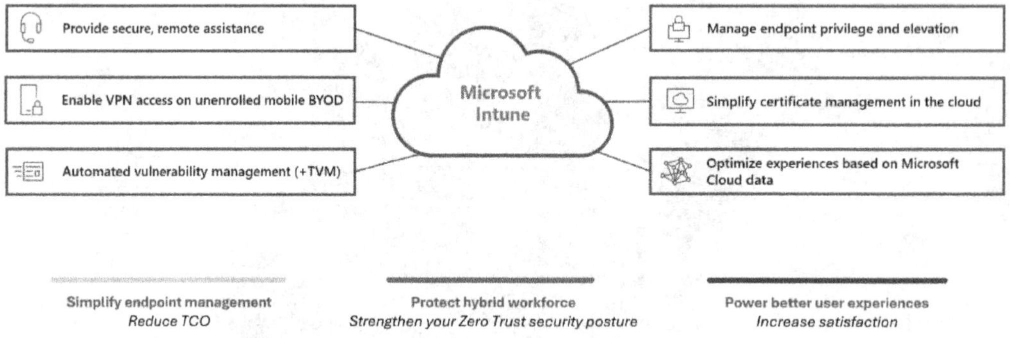

Figure 1.8 – Microsoft Intune services

Windows Autopatch

Windows Autopatch is a new Microsoft cloud service that is included within your existing Windows and Microsoft E3/E5 subscriptions. Windows Autopatch moves the burden of your IT department managing Windows devices and patches every month after Patch Tuesday to Microsoft. You can think of it as Windows-Updates-as-a-Service. Windows Autopatch is not the same as **Windows Update for Business** (**WUfB**). New and enhanced cloud service components are combined with WUfB to deliver Windows Autopatch.

In essence, Windows Autopatch automates the planning and deployment process of Windows updates for Windows 10 and Windows 11 completely, as well as for Microsoft 365 Apps for Enterprise, Microsoft Edge, and Microsoft Teams. Not only does this simplify the management of your Cloud and physical PCs but it also mitigates the risk of having security vulnerabilities entering your environment, which ultimately increases the productivity of your users.

The great thing about this service is that it seamlessly integrates with Windows 365 Enterprise during the provisioning policy process, which we will explain later in the book.

In the following diagram, we can visualize what Windows Autopatch can deliver in terms of benefits to your business, as well as what the requirements are:

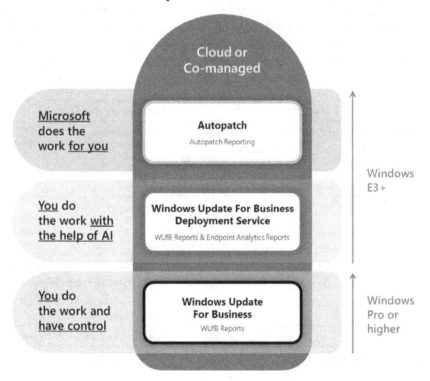

Figure 1.9 – Windows Autopatch

Microsoft Dev Box

Microsoft Dev Box is a cloud service for developers, delivered from Microsoft Azure. It requires you to have an Azure subscription to start utilizing the service. With Microsoft Dev Box, you will be able to create Cloud PCs that provide your developers with preconfigured environments that are ready to code for specific projects.

IT administrators will be able to manage all the project environments inside the Microsoft Azure portal. It is easy to get started and to deploy and scale new and existing Microsoft Dev Box environments. It also comes with a project management role, which allows project managers to manage and deploy Dev Boxes for their developers.

A Dev Box is like a Cloud PC and is built on top of Windows 365 technology. This means that developers with a Dev Box will be able to execute certain actions such as restart, restore, troubleshoot, and more. Even though Dev Boxes are deployed from the Microsoft Azure portal, they are directly integrated into Microsoft Intune just like Cloud PCs. IT administrators will be able to manage and control security and much more, just like on your physical devices, which simplifies the overall management of all your devices.

You might be thinking about when and where Microsoft Dev Box is more suited to a certain solution rather than using Windows 365 or Azure Virtual Desktop, as these platforms might also be suitable to be used for some developers. Compared to Windows 365 and Azure Virtual Desktop solutions, Microsoft Dev Box takes it a step further for bigger projects where developers are able to get cloud machines configured directly into a project environment with all the necessary tools for the developer and organizational project managers to support big and complicated coding projects.

	Windows 365 Cloud PC	**Microsoft Dev Box**
Targeted audience	Information workers, knowledge workers, Frontline workers	Developers
Optimized for	Long-running, single-session, persistent, multi-use	Project-based, task-focused, temporary
Create, update, delete	Admin	Developer
Environment	IT-defined	Team-defined
Access	Windows 365 app, Windows 365 web client, and Remote Desktop apps	Developer portal (secondary: Windows 365 app, Windows 365 web client, and Remote Desktop apps)
Management	Microsoft Intune	Microsoft Azure, Microsoft Intune
Billing	Microsoft 365	Microsoft Azure

SKU size	2, 4, 8 core	4, 8, 16, 32 core
	4, 8, 16, 32 GB RAM	16, 32, 64, 128 GB RAM
	64, 128, 256, 512 GB storage	256, 512 GB, 1 TB, 2TB storage
	Standard SSD	Premium SSD

Table 1.5 – Comparing Windows 365 Cloud PC and Microsoft Dev Box offerings

Supported endpoints

Users can access Windows 365 Cloud PCs and even control them using the Windows 365 app, Windows 365 web client, or the Microsoft Remote Desktop app.

There are client apps available for all popular platforms, including Windows, macOS, iOS, Android, Linux, and the web.

These clients can be used across different types of devices and form factors, such as desktops, tablets, smartphones, and even TVs.

Users can use one or more devices of their choice to connect to their Cloud PC. Further details about endpoint setup and optimizations are covered in *Chapter 5* later in the book.

Summary

This first chapter has now come to an end. We hope you learned a lot about the basics of Windows 365, the different versions, the vision, and how other Microsoft cloud services such as Intune and Autopatch extend the offering.

We hope you are excited to take a deeper look at Windows 365 as, in the next chapter, we will cover the architecture and other design best practices to refine your knowledge before we jump straight into the deployment chapter. Let's go!

Questions

At the end of each chapter, we ask three questions to help you evaluate your learning and challenge yourself as well. Here are the first three questions:

1. What are the benefits of using a Cloud PC instead of a traditional PC?
2. How can you access your Cloud PC from different devices and locations?
3. What are the different plans and prices for a Windows 365 Cloud PC?

Further reading

Please continue your learning journey while going through the other chapters. If you want to learn more about the subjects covered in this chapter, you can visit any of the following online resources:

- *The Microsoft Windows 365 Licensing Resources website*, which introduces the new Windows 365 editions, features, and pricing for Cloud PCs (`https://www.microsoft.com/licensing/product-licensing/windows-365`)

- *Windows 365 official product documentation*: The official Microsoft documentation for Windows 365 Enterprise and Windows 365 Business (`https://learn.microsoft.com/windows-365`)

- Additional market research and insights on modern work:

  - *"2022 Work Trend Index: Annual Report,"* Microsoft Corporation

  - *"The Cost of Data Breach Report,"* The Ponemon Institute, 2021

  - *"IT Trends Report: Remote Work Drives Priorities in 2021,"* JumpCloud, 2021

Part 2: Implementing and Managing Cloud PCs

The second part of the book is dedicated to designing and creating a Windows 365 architecture that prioritizes disaster recovery and business continuity. It covers the various components that are managed by both Microsoft and the customer, as well as RBAC roles and delegation. Additionally, this part provides guidance on deploying Windows 365, including information on Cloud PC sizes and performance, geography and region settings, networking configuration, and custom image creation. This part concludes with details on managing Cloud PCs through the Microsoft Intune portal, including moving them to another region, language settings, configuration policies, application deployment, and backup and restoration. By the end of this part, you will have gained the ability to create a solution, deploy Cloud PCs, and effectively manage them.

This part contains the following chapters:

- *Chapter 2, Architecture*
- *Chapter 3, Deploying Cloud PCs*
- *Chapter 4, Managing Cloud PCs*

2
Architecture

In this chapter, we will go one level deeper into the technical details of Windows 365. We will go over the architecture specifics as well as the different cloud services Microsoft manages as part of Windows 365. If you are an engineer at heart, this is the chapter that you will like. You will learn everything about the architecture and background components being used. This will help you with configuring the cloud service, as well as potential optimizations and troubleshooting efforts.

Alongside this, we will also take a deep dive into connectivity, disaster recovery, and delegation. I'm sure you will appreciate this chapter before jumping into the more hands-on part of this book!

In this chapter, we will be covering the following subjects:

- Windows 365 architecture
- The components that Microsoft manages and the components the customer manages
- Identity – Azure Active Directory
- Network dataflow
- Co-management
- Business continuity and disaster recovery
- RBAC roles and delegation

Windows 365 architecture

Before explaining the Windows 365 architecture, we want to jump back in time. Originally, Windows 365 was built under the internal project codename Project Deschutes (Self-Managed), and the architecture diagram was called **Host-On-Behalf-Of** (**HOBO**). This type of architecture means that all the components of the virtual machine and Cloud PC services run in a Microsoft-managed subscription and are managed on behalf of the customer.

In the early days of Windows 365, some of the components couldn't function individually when not a part of a single Azure subscription, for example, Azure Virtual Desktop service components. All these things are, of course, fixed and running inside Microsoft's own managed environment.

As you can see in the following image, Windows 365 uses **Azure Virtual Desktop** (**AVD**) as a control plane service. The services mentioned in the Windows 365 services section are developed specifically for Windows 365 as part of the SaaS-based cloud offering. One notable difference is where the user's profile is stored. While AVD stores user profiles in FSLogix containers, Windows 365 stores them directly in Cloud PCs. These profiles are synced and backed up with OneDrive.

Windows 365 is a complete SaaS service that securely delivers your personalized Windows desktop, apps, settings, and content from the Microsoft cloud to any device. An offering like this from Microsoft is unique as Microsoft generated a completely new category of computing for it called Cloud PC (as opposed to a physical PC).

This means that it's an end-to-end solution where customers can leverage the power of a computer from the cloud, with the same management tools to manage physical and Cloud PCs (e.g., Microsoft Intune admin center).

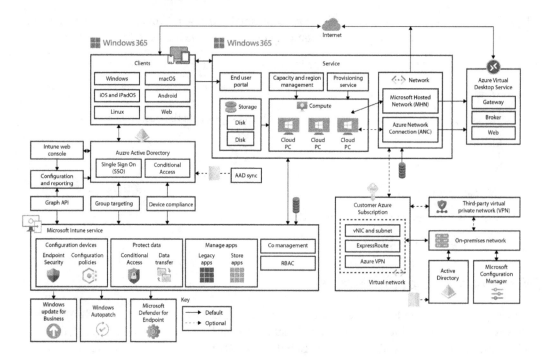

Figure 2.1 – Windows 365 service architecture

You can download the diagram here – *Windows 365 high-level architecture diagram | Microsoft Learn* (https://learn.microsoft.com/windows-365/enterprise/high-level-architecture)

The components that Microsoft manages and the components the customer manages

Microsoft has done a great job with Windows 365 by simplifying the creation of Cloud PCs for users. Both IT management and the end user experience are very simple to learn about and use. Getting started with deploying Cloud PCs is just a few clicks away and the scalability is very powerful in comparison with Azure Virtual Desktop. Even though the Windows 365 service is almost a plug-and-play solution, there are a few things you as an organization must manage yourself.

Depending on your domain and network configuration, you can either go full cloud with **Azure AD join (AADJ)** together with hosted networks or go for **hybrid Azure AD join (HAADJ)**. The following table helps you clarify the level of responsibility per service component. We have also added Azure Virtual Desktop as a comparison on the right side to help reflect the differences.

Responsibility	Windows 365	Azure Virtual Desktop
Identity	MANAGED BY CUSTOMER	MANAGED BY CUSTOMER
End user devices (mobile and PCs)	MANAGED BY CUSTOMER	MANAGED BY CUSTOMER
Application security	MICROSOFT OR CUSTOMER	MANAGED BY CUSTOMER
Operating systems	*MICROSOFT OR CUSTOMER	MANAGED BY CUSTOMER
Deployment configuration	MICROSOFT OR CUSTOMER	MANAGED BY CUSTOMER
Network controls	MICROSOFT OR CUSTOMER	MANAGED BY CUSTOMER
Virtualization control plane	MICROSOFT	MICROSOFT
Physical hosts	MICROSOFT	MICROSOFT
Physical network	MICROSOFT	MICROSOFT
Physical datacenter	MICROSOFT	MICROSOFT
*via Microsoft Autopatch	SaaS	PaaS

Figure 2.2 – Responsibilities per Windows 365 and AVD service

In the next chapter, we will switch from responsibilities to service components, to explain each of them to ensure you understand the basics of the service.

Identity – Azure Active Directory

Azure AD user identities are used everywhere – from logging in to Microsoft 365 to logging in to Windows OS, and it's no different in Windows 365. A user needs an identity to get and connect to a Cloud PC. A user identity can be created in one of two places: **Azure Active Directory** (**Azure AD**) or **Active Directory** (**AD**). If a user is created in AD, the identity must be synchronized to Azure AD before the user can be assigned a Cloud PC and login. You will be able to synchronize users with **Azure AD Connect Sync** or **Azure AD Connect Cloud Sync**. We will not into these two synchronization options in depth, but in general, if you need to synchronize devices from AD to Azure AD, you can't use Azure AD Connect Cloud Sync as it does not support it. When a user exists in both AD and Azure AD, it is what we define as a hybrid user identity.

When a user is created in Azure AD, we define it as a cloud-only user. A cloud-only user does not have any integration into the traditional server infrastructure as we have known it for decades. User management can be simpler when we have Cloud PCs created in Azure AD instead of AD. If the user doesn't need to have integration into the traditional server infrastructure, the general recommendation is to create the user as cloud-only in Azure AD.

Networking controls – virtual network connection

When you define the configuration for your Cloud PCs, you will have to choose what network the Cloud PCs are going to be connected to. There are two options, *Microsoft Hosted Network* and *Azure Network Connection*. Choosing Microsoft Hosted Network will simplify things in terms of network management because Microsoft will host and manage the network for you. There is, however, no option for a site-to-site VPN connection, so you'll need to have a software VPN solution installed on the Cloud PCs if you want them to reach your server infrastructure.

Azure Network Connection is a self-hosted network solution, meaning you'll need an Azure subscription with a virtual network within. This requires more planning in terms of IP scope and network firewall rules, and maybe a site-to-site VPN configuration if the server infrastructure is in a place other than Microsoft Azure.

We will be explaining how to set up an Azure network connection to your own on-premises and/or private cloud environments in the next chapter!

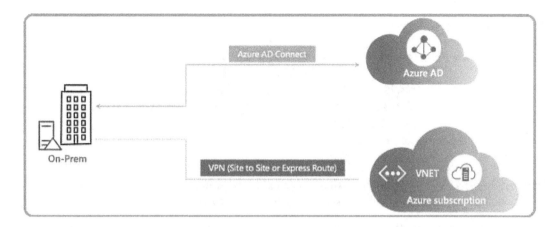

Figure 2.3 – Azure AD – on-premises architecture

In the next section, we are going to explain how you can deploy apps and secure your Cloud PCs.

Deployment configuration – Intune app deployment and security

Once a Cloud PC has been provisioned, the Cloud PC usually needs some kind of configuration to work as intended. This could be some specific settings inside Windows or an application that needs to be present in order for the user to get started working. No matter what kind of configuration the user needs, it's a good idea to secure Cloud PCs just like physical devices with Microsoft Defender for Endpoint and other security products. You, as an administrator, are responsible for configuring and installing applications and securing your Cloud PCs. Luckily, it's not very difficult to do. Cloud PCs are integrated directly into Microsoft Intune, and you can manage them alongside your physical devices. All the time and configuration that is put into physical devices can also be applied to Cloud PCs. This makes configuring and securing your Windows 365 environment very easy to implement.

User profiles

User profiles within Windows 365 are delivered as part of the cloud service, meaning OneDrive, Enterprise State Roaming, and the high availability of your managed disks delivered with high redundancy, including multiple restore points included in all licenses. Cloud PCs don't use FSLogix profile containers, as they are designed for non-persistent environments, most likely based on multi-session operating systems. In traditional **Virtual Desktop Infrastructure** (**VDI**) deployments, all kinds of complex solutions have been used to bring the physical and virtual worlds together. Within Windows 365, we don't have this challenge as we work with personal profiles and leverage other technology to modernize a user profile while also making personal documents available across all devices.

Networking dataflow

Even though a Cloud PC is quite like a physical PC, the main difference is a Cloud PC is a virtual device that the user connects to over the internet. This brings a whole new layer of network connectivity compared to physical devices. It's important to understand how a connection from the user's physical device to the Cloud PC is established. There are also some requirements that must be in place to ensure the best connectivity for the end user. In this section, you will get to know the essentials of network dataflow in the Windows 365 service.

When a user connects to their Cloud PC, they don't connect like users normally connect in a **Remote Desktop Services** (**RDS**) environment. The connection from the user's physical device to the Cloud PC is established by utilizing what's called *reverse connect transport*.

Reverse connect transport uses outbound connectivity from the physical device to the Windows 365 infrastructure that is managed by Microsoft. The connection with the reverse connect transport is initiated over HTTPS port 443. This is a big difference compared to traditional RDS where the connection is established over TCP listeners. This makes the environment more secure than ever because you no longer have something that is exposing itself to port 3389. The traditional port 3389 is unsecured as there's no encryption applied or other TLS/SSL enhancements such as with *reverse connect transport*.

Connection security

All connections between the physical client and Cloud PC are initiated over a secure connection powered by **Transport Layer Security** (**TLS**) 1.2 to the Windows 365 backend infrastructure.

TLS is a global standard that is used to encrypt data being sent over the internet. That way, potential hackers can't see the data being sent back and forth.

To secure the connection between the client and the Cloud PC after the connection is up and running, the **Remote Desktop Protocol** (**RDP**) establishes a nested TLS connection between the physical client and the Cloud PC by utilizing a certificate from the Cloud PC that is self-generated.

Reverse Connect
Disable all inbound traffic

Encryption
Secures all traffic

Network

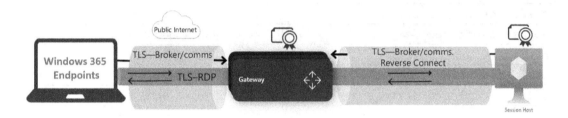

Figure 2.4 – Windows 365 network flow

The next section is all about the service URLs needed to connect to Windows 365.

Required URLs

For the connection to be established, there must be certain URLs allowed on the client network that the user is connected to and, likewise, the network the Cloud PC is connected to must allow specific outbound URLs. Be aware there are different URLs for the Azure public cloud and Azure cloud for governments. See the following tables to find the URL requirements.

The Azure **Virtual Network(s)** (**VNet(s)**) you create for Windows 365 is required to have outbound TCP access to the underlying services we use as part of the firewall rules in the customer's Azure subscription.

Are you using Azure Firewall? You can now add the following tag to your rules that include all the required URLs listed in *Table 2.4* in a more convenient way than listing them separately. If you use third-party firewalls, you would still have to add them separately:

Rule	Type	Tag name	Protocol	TLS
Windows 365 FQDNs	FQDN Tag	Windows365	HTTP: 80, HTTPS: 443	Not recommended

Table 2.1 – Windows 365 network table

In the following tables, you will find a snippet of what URLs and ports need to be open to communicate with the Windows 365 service.

Find the full list of all the required Windows 365 URLs at `https://aka.ms/W365URLs` and the Microsoft Intune URLs at `https://aka.ms/MEMURLs`:

URL	Outbound TCP Port	Purpose
`Login.microsoftonline.com`	443	Microsoft Online Services authentication
`*.wvd.microsoft.com`	443	Service Traffic
`*.Servicebus.windows.net`	443	Troubleshooting data
`Go.microsoft.com`	443	Microsoft FWLinks
`Aka.ms`	443	URL shortener
`Learn.microsoft.com`	443	Documentation
`Privacy.microsoft.com`	443	Privacy statement
`Query.prod.cms.rt.microsoft.com`	443	Client updates (only Windows clients)
`Login.microsoftonline.us`	443	Microsoft Online Services authentication
`*.wvd.azure.us`	443	Service Traffic
`*.Servicebus.usgovcloudapi.net`	443	Troubleshooting data
`Go.microsoft.com`	443	Microsoft FWLinks
`Aka.ms`	443	URL shortener
`Learn.microsoft.com`	443	Documentation
`Privacy.microsoft.com`	443	Privacy statement
`Query.prod.cms.rt.microsoft.com`	443	Client updates (only Windows clients)
`Login.microsoftonline.com`	443	Microsoft Online Services authentication
`*.wvd.microsoft.com`	443	Service traffic
`*.prod.warm.ingest.monitor.core.windows.net`	443	Agent traffic (Azure Monitor)
`Gcs.prod.monitoring.core.windows.net`	443	Agent traffic (AzureCloud)
`Catalogartifact.azureedge.net`	443	Azure marketplace
`Kms.core.windows.net`	1688	Windows activation
`Azkms.core.windows.net`	1688	Windows activation
`mrsglobalsteus2prod.blob.core.windows.net`	443	Agent and SXS stack updates

`wvdportalstorageblob.blob.core.windows.net`	443	Azure portal support
`169.254.169.254`	80	Azure instance metadata service endpoint
`168.63.129.16`	80	Cloud PC health monitoring
`oneocsp.microsoft.com`	80	Certificates
`http://www.microsoft.com`	80	Certificates

Table 2.2 – Cloud PC network URL requirements in the Azure public cloud

The following table shows the required Azure cloud network URL for the US Government.

URL	Outbound TCP Port	Purpose
`Login.microsoftonline.us`	443	Microsoft Online Services authentication
`*.wvd.azure.us`	443	Service traffic
`*.prod.warm.ingest.monitor.core.usgovcloudapi.net`	443	Agent traffic (Azure Monitor)
`gcs.monitoring.core.usgovcloudapi.net`	443	Agent traffic (AzureCloud)
`kms.core.usgovcloudapi.net`	1688	Windows activation
`mrsglobalstugviffx.blob.core.usgovcloudapi.net`	443	Agent and SXS stack updates
`wvdportalstorageblob.blob.core.usgovcloudapi.net`	443	Azure portal support
`169.254.169.254`	80	Azure instance metadata service endpoint
`168.63.129.16`	80	Cloud PC health monitoring
`ocsp.msocsp.com`	80	Certificates

Table 2.3 – Cloud PC network URL requirements in the Azure cloud for the US Government

Bandwidth requirements

Having enough bandwidth from the physical device is important to ensure a fast and responsive experience. The amount of minimum required bandwidth is different depending on what task the user will perform on their Cloud PC. It's hard to give an exact number, but in the following table, you can find the recommended ranges for some general tasks and some more specific Microsoft Teams tasks.

Task	Default mode	H.264/AVC 444 Mode	Description
Idle	0.3 Kpbs	0.3 Kbps	No activity onscreen
Microsoft Word	100-150 Kbps	200-300 Kbps	Typing, copy/pasting in Microsoft Word
Microsoft Excel	150-200 Kbps	400-500 Kbps	Typing, copy/pasting, editing multiple cells
Microsoft PowerPoint	4-4.5 Mbps	1.6-1.8 Mbps	Typing, copy/pasting, editing slide animations
Web browsing	6-6.5 Mbps	0.9-1 Mbps	Browsing a website with static and animated pictures
Windows Image Gallery	3.3-3.6 Mbps	0.7-0.8 Mbps	Browsing, rotating, editing
Video playback	7.5-8.5 Mbps	2.5-3.1 Mbps	Watching 30 FPS video

Table 2.4 – Recommended bandwidth for general tasks on a Cloud PC

In each of the following scenarios, network quality plays a critical role. It is essential to ensure the availability of adequate bandwidth to deliver the desired quality of service. Please note that full HD (1080p) video is not supported:

Task	Recommended bandwidth
Peer-to-peer audio calling	30 kbps
Peer-to-peer audio calling and screen sharing	130 kbps
Peer-to-peer quality video calling 360p at 30 FPS	500 kbps
Peer-to-peer HD quality video calling 720p at 30 FPS	1.2 Mbps
Group video calling	500 kbps (upload) 1 Mbps (download)

Table 2.5 – Recommended bandwidth for Microsoft Teams tasks on a Cloud PC

Optimizing the connection with RDP Shortpath

When a user connects with reverse connect transport to their Cloud PC, they will, by default, use WebSocket (TCP) as the transport protocol. Windows 365 supports **User Datagram Protocol (UDP)** connection instead of TCP by utilizing RDP Shortpath. This feature is enabled by default on all newly provisioned Cloud PCs and no configuration is needed on the physical device. There are, however, some network requirements that need to be in place for the user to have a UDP connection. If the RDP Shortpath connection fails for some reason, the connection will automatically fall back to use WebSocket.

There is a big difference in the connection experience if the user is using UDP over TCP. TCP is a connection-oriented protocol that is built on a three-way handshake. This basically means when a package is sent, there is validation going on between the physical client and the Cloud PC.

UDP just sends its packages without any validation. This removes a lot of checks back and forth, and this way, the response time between the physical client and the Cloud PC is much faster. The user experience will be significantly better with UDP because of the low latency, and everything on the remote connection, such as moving the mouse, will be smoother.

You can see the flow outlined in the following diagram, showcasing the value of RDP Shortpath and the TLS-RDP encryption flow.

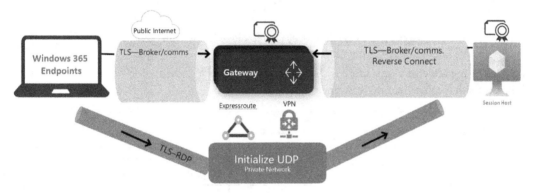

Figure 2.5 – RDP Shortpath – network flow

There are two types of UDP connections that can be established between the physical client and the Cloud PC. Only one type of UDP connection can be used at once. The connections are called **direct connection (STUN)** and **indirect connection (TURN)**.

STUN is used to establish a direct UDP connection. For this connection type to work, the physical device and Cloud PC must be able to connect to each other through a public IP address and negotiate ports. Most physical clients don't know their public IP address because they most likely sit behind a **Network Address Translation (NAT)** gateway device. If a STUN connection is unable to be established, it will automatically try a TURN connection.

TURN is an extension of STUN; it uses an indirect UDP connection. This connection relays traffic through an intermediate server between the physical client and the Cloud PC. Using TURN means the public IP address and port are known in advance, which can be allowed through the firewall and other network devices. If a TURN connection is unable to be established, it will automatically fall back to a TCP-based reverse connect transport connection, which is known as WebSocket.

Learn about the networking flow and routes being used in the following diagram.

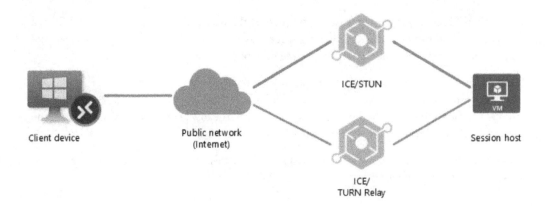

Figure 2.6 – ICE/TURN Relay flow to Cloud PC (session host)

In the following table, you find more firewall and other technical information needed to configure RDP Shortpath for the client network the physical PC is connected to.

Name	Source Port	Destination	Destination Port	Protocol
RDP Shortpath Server Endpoint	Any	Public IP of NAT Gateway or firewall	1024-65535 (default 49152-65535)	UDP
STUN/TURN UDP	Any	20.202.0.0/16	3478	UDP
STUN/TURN TCP	Any	20.202.0.0/16	443	TCP

Table 2.6 – Client network requirements for RDP Shortpath

It's not only the client network that needs to have firewall rules added, but the Cloud PC network also needs to have specific rules allowed. Following is an overview of this.

Name	Source Port	Destination	Destination Port	Protocol
RDP Shortpath Server Endpoint	Any	Any	1024-65535 (default 49152-65535)	UDP
STUN/TURN UDP	Any	20.202.0.0/16	3478	UDP
STUN/TURN TCP	Any	20.202.0.0/16	443	TCP

Table 2.7 – Cloud PC network requirements for RDP Shortpath

User connection flow

When a user initiates a connection to their Cloud PC, there are certain steps that will be checked and ensured before the connection can be established. The connection will always start with the WebSocket connection sequence flow. If the physical client detects RDP Shortpath is possible, it will initiate a new connection flow to utilize UDP instead of TCP. To increase the likelihood of a UDP connection, follow these recommendations:

- Enable UPnP on home routers
- Enable IPv6 connectivity or Teredo
- Avoid using force tunneling configurations
- Avoid using double NAT or **Carrier-Grade-NAT (CGN)** configurations
- Avoid using cloud packet inspection services
- Avoid using TCP-based VPN solutions

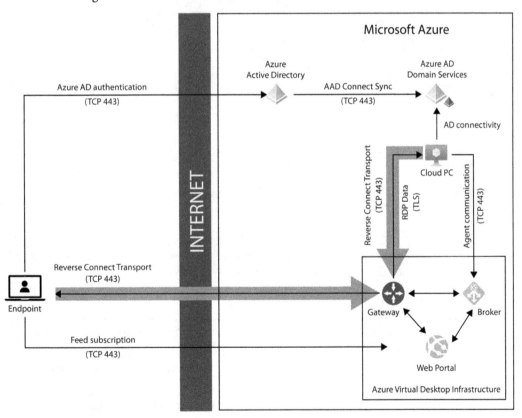

Figure 2.7 – Azure Virtual Desktop network connections

When a user connects to their Cloud PC, there is a specific connection flow that is initiated. Following is a table with the connection steps for WebSocket.

Connection step	Connection step description
1	User opens a supported Windows 365 connection client such as the Windows 365 APP.
2	The user authenticates to Azure AD.
3	When the user opts to connect to the Cloud PC, it will establish a secure TLS 1.2 connection to the closest gateway and pass the connection information.
4	The gateway validates the request and tells the broker to locate the Cloud PC.
5	The broker uses the previously persistent communication channel to create a connection.
6	The Remote Desktop stack from the Cloud PC initiates a connection secured with TLS 1.2 to the same gateway as the client.
7	The gateway starts relaying data between the physical client and the Cloud PC that established the reverse connect transport.
8	The client and Cloud PC now start the RDP handshake and get a connection established.

Table 2.8 – WebSocket connection flow

The connection steps for when using RDP Shortpath to get a faster and better connection are almost the same as using WebSocket, just with a few more steps:

Connection step	Connection step description
1	The Cloud PC enumerates all network interfaces
2	The Remote Desktop Services (TermService) Windows service allocates UDP sockets on each interface and stores IP:Port in the candidate table as a local candidate.
3	Terminal Service uses each UDP socket to try reaching the STUN server on the internet by sending a UDP packet to port 3478.
4	If the packet gets to the STUN server, it replies with a public IP and port. This information is stored on the candidate table as a reflexive candidate.
5	The Cloud PC uses all the candidates to establish reverse connect transport to pass the candidate list to the physical client device.
6	Once the physical client receives the candidate list, it starts gathering its own candidate list like the Cloud PC and sends it back to the Cloud PC.

7	After both devices have exchanged their candidate lists, both devices will try to connect using the collected data. If STUN fails because it's blocked, a connection attempt is made by using TURN.
8	The client then establishes a secure connection using TLS over reliable UDP with the Cloud PC and initiates RDP Shortpath Transport.
9	Once RDP Shortpath Transport is being used, all **Dynamic Virtual Channels** (**DVCs**), including remote graphics, input, and device redirection move to the new transport.

Table 2.9 – RDP Shortpath connection flow

Co-management

Co-management is a feature of Microsoft Intune/Configuration Manager that allows IT admins to use both Intune and Configuration Manager concurrently for Windows 10 and Windows 11 management. It combines your existing on-premises Configuration Manager environment with the cloud using Intune and other Microsoft 365 cloud services such as Windows 365. You can choose whether Configuration Manager or Intune is the management authority for the seven different workload groups.

As part of Endpoint Manager, co-management uses cloud features, including conditional access. You keep some tasks on-premises while running other tasks in the cloud with Intune.

Business continuity and disaster recovery

Business continuity and disaster recovery (**BCDR**) are critical components of any organization's risk management strategy. Disruptions can occur at any time, whether it's due to natural disasters, cyber-attacks, or other unexpected events, and without proper planning and preparation, the consequences can be catastrophic. Business continuity is the process of maintaining essential business operations during a disruption, while disaster recovery is the process of restoring critical IT systems and infrastructure after an outage. Both are essential for ensuring that organizations can recover quickly and minimize the impact of an unexpected event.

As you are aware, BCDR can be a daunting task, particularly when it comes to user desktops. Broadly speaking, the process of business continuity planning involves four key aspects: assessment, planning, capability validation, and communication. Experts from various fields, including compute, storage, applications, network, and user data, must come together to determine the course of action in the event of device, power, or network failures, among other things. After a plan is agreed upon, it can take several months or even years to build and test the system. Finally, the prospect of executing a disaster recovery protocol can be daunting because it is often complicated and must be implemented during times of high stress and pressure.

Built on Microsoft's BCDR principles, Windows 365 provides highly dependable Cloud PCs with a financially guaranteed **Service-Level Agreement** (**SLA**). If there is an in-zone Azure compute fabric failure, the Cloud PCs are automatically restored within a short **Recovery Time Objective** (**RTO**) of under 10 minutes, and a **Recovery Point Objective** (**RPO**) that is almost zero. Windows 365 Cloud PCs are also designed to automatically recover from any underlying regional or zone failures, maintaining an RPO of approximately zero. This level of reliability provides peace of mind to customers that their critical data and operations will remain available, even in the face of unexpected disruptions.

Organizations can utilize Windows and Microsoft 365 solutions and features alongside Windows 365, to benefit from enhanced resilience of user data and context. Active/active data resilience ensures that user data remains accessible through OneDrive, even during a Windows 365 outage. The automated disaster recovery process includes OneDrive, OneDrive for Business, and OneDrive with Known Folder Move, further reinforcing the continuity of user data in the event of an outage. These features offer organizations a heightened level of confidence in the resilience of their user data and context.

Building a successful BCDR strategy requires a thoughtful partnership between you and Microsoft. At a high level, the BCDR strategy encompasses the following:

- High availability of the Windows 365 service and dependent components

- Regular backup and immediate recovery of Windows 365 Cloud PC

- The resiliency of user data

- Recovery of the user's endpoint or the availability of an alternate endpoint

In the next section, we will take a deep dive into the service URLs that are needed to connect to Windows 365!

Windows 365 service availability

Windows 365 is designed with resiliency and recoverability in mind, taking into account the likelihood of hardware failure, human error, and software bugs in the underlying infrastructure and processes. The availability of Windows 365 is dependent on the availability of its numerous microservices as well as several Azure and Microsoft 365 services. Azure's virtualization technology ensures extensive redundancy, providing a reliable level of availability. This means that various services such as Azure AD, Azure Virtual Desktop, Azure Compute, Azure Storage, and Azure Networking have a robust architecture that is designed to be highly resilient, which ultimately enables the Windows 365 service to be highly available.

The Windows 365 management service comprises the Microsoft Intune admin center (`https://intune.microsoft.com`) and the Cloud PC end user portal (`https://windows365.microsoft.com`). It has a highly available, regionally redundant architecture with a 99.99% uptime target. So, if the service is down, the recovery objectives are an RTO of <6 hours and an RPO of <30 minutes.

During a Management Service outage, users cannot access their Cloud PC sessions via the end user portal, but they can still access them through a native app (for example, the Microsoft Remote Desktop app), a browser bookmark of a Cloud PC session, or using the Azure Virtual Desktop web client (`https://rdweb.wvd.microsoft.com/webclient/index.html`).

Windows 365 Cloud PC backup and recovery

By now, we know that Windows 365 offers highly resilient Cloud PCs with 99.9% availability, 99.999999999% (11 9s) data object resiliency, and automated in-zone disaster recovery. While uncommon, in-zone failures can cause disruptions to Cloud PC operations, including **virtual Network Adapter** (**vNIC**), compute, storage plane, and compute power failures. Azure automatically detects compute failures and moves the user's workload to another resource in the same zone, causing minimal disruption. If there is a failure in the storage system, the recovery process initiates automatically because of the redundancy in the storage system, eliminating the need for point-in-time recovery.

There are cases where automated recovery may not be enough. In such cases, a point-in-time restore of Windows 365 Cloud PCs can save the day. The point-in-time restore feature is useful when there is a problem with a Cloud PC that can't be resolved within the device, or maybe the device isn't reachable. These circumstances can occur through things such as user error, failed updates, and mistaken management actions, as well as malware and ransomware. Step-by-step instructions on how to set up a point-in-time restore for Cloud PCs are covered in *Chapter 4*.

Azure is divided into regions – each in a different geography. Each region has multiple Availability Zones, which are separate locations that provide redundant power, cooling, and networking. Windows 365 is supported in every Azure region that has multiple zones.

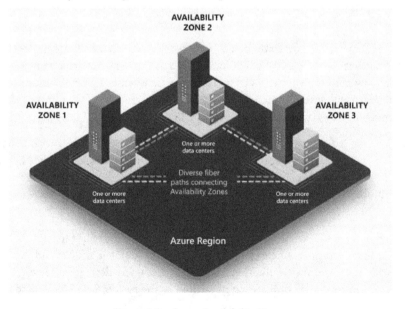

Figure 2.8 – Azure Availability Zones

Windows 365 Cloud PCs are distributed across the zones within a region for each customer. Azure employs various techniques to ensure reliability within each zone, such as monitoring compute and seamlessly moving workloads to alternate resources within the zone in the event of a disruption. Cloud PCs benefit from the reliability advantages provided to all Azure workloads. Furthermore, in the event of a zone failure, each Cloud PC can recover to a different zone within the same region that has available capacity.

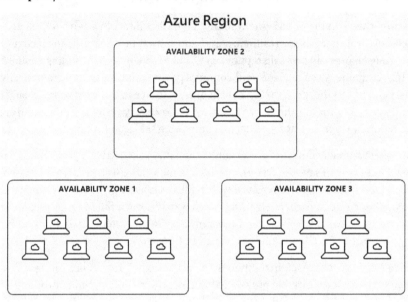

Figure 2.9 – Windows 365 Cloud PCs are distributed across the zones within a region

We'd like to address some of the most common questions we've received regarding Windows 365 BCDR. Firstly, there is a concern about the cost of adding cross-zone point-in-time restore to Windows 365 Cloud PCs. There is no need to worry about an increase in price when using this solution as this feature is included as standard with every Cloud PC, with no additional charge. At the time of publication of the book, Windows 365 doesn't support cross-region BCDR.

Secondly, customers have been asking about the process of enabling this feature. The good news is that there is no need to enable anything because cross-zone point-in-time restore is already automatically enabled and available on every Cloud PC. This means that customers can take advantage of this feature without any additional setup or configuration.

Lastly, customers have been curious about the difficulty level of recovering a Cloud PC during an outage and what they need to learn to do so. The answer is that they don't need to learn anything new. If they know how to use point-in-time restore, they can easily initiate a restore and the cross-zone restore feature will kick in automatically. This means that customers don't need to worry about any complicated recovery procedures or learning new tools, as the system will take care of everything for them.

In summary, the cross-zone point-in-time restore feature for Windows 365 Cloud PCs is included as standard, automatically enabled, and requires no additional learning or configuration. This makes it a cost-effective and user-friendly solution for disaster recovery.

Now, let us see how this works. If a zone outage occurs and users are unable to access their Cloud PC, initiating a restore through Windows 365 will trigger an automatic search for available capacity in another zone within the same region. Windows 365 will detect that the physical Azure resource where the Cloud PC is provisioned is not available and will initiate the restoration process in another zone. This ensures that users can access their Cloud PC even if there is an outage in their original zone.

The following diagram shows how Availability Zones work as a service offering with Windows 365 in case of a zone outage.

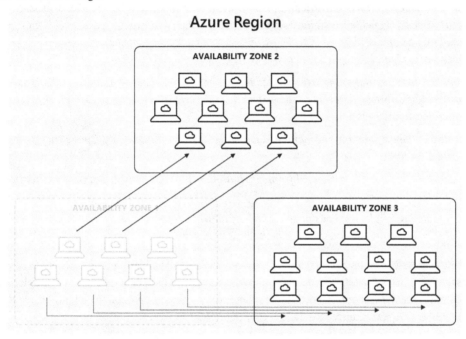

Figure 2.10 – Windows 365 Cloud PCs are distributed across Availability Zones

Point-in-time restore automatically restores a Cloud PC in a new zone with capacity during a zone outage. There are two advantages of a Cloud PC being restored to a zone in the same region – the user experience and Cloud PC performance remain the same and there is no need to fail back to the original zone after all zones are restored.

User profile data resiliency

The good news is that Microsoft understands the intricate nature of cloud computing and anticipates potential issues and therefore, has designed its cloud services to prioritize reliability. By utilizing a combination of sophisticated software and less complex physical infrastructure, data resiliency and redundancy are built into the services, providing high availability to customers. Regardless of any service failures, essential customer data remains safe and unaffected.

Here's a snippet from Microsoft (source: `https://learn.microsoft.com/compliance/assurance/assurance-data-resiliency-overview`) on how its services have been designed around these five data resiliency principles:

1. *There is critical and non-critical data. Non-critical data (for example, whether a message was read) can be dropped in rare failure scenarios. Critical data (for example, customer data such as email messages) should be protected at extreme cost. As a design goal, delivered mail messages are always critical, and things like whether a message has been read is non-critical.*

2. *Copies of customer data must be separated into different fault zones or as many fault domains as possible (for example, datacenters, accessible by single credentials (process, server, or operator)) to provide failure isolation.*

3. *Critical customer data must be monitored for failing any part of Atomicity, Consistency, Isolation, Durability (ACID).*

4. *Customer data must be protected from corruption. It must be actively scanned or monitored, repairable, and recoverable.*

5. *Most data loss results from customer actions, so allow customers to recover on their own using a GUI that enables them to restore accidentally deleted items.*

By adhering to these principles and conducting rigorous testing and validation, Windows 365 is capable of surpassing customers' expectations for business continuity and disaster recovery. For example, even in the face of significant disruptions such as complete zone or region outages, the Cloud PC OS disks exhibit 99.999999999% resilience to data loss over the course of a year.

Windows 365 seamlessly integrates with Windows features and Microsoft 365 services and provides several advantages to data resiliency. When used with OneDrive, OneDrive for Business, and OneDrive with **Known Folder Move**, a feature that roams your Windows profile data (My Documents, Desktop, Pictures, etc.), Windows 365 users can access their data across both physical and cloud-based PCs, as well as having Active/Active cross-region user data resilience that is shared across all authenticated workspaces. Additionally, Known Folder Move provides user context portability and cross-region resilience, with a **Recovery Time Objective (RTO)** and **Recovery Point Objective (RPO)** of 0. Each of these tools offers protection against corruption, accidental deletion, and the ability to version the data and therefore restore it to a previous snapshot.

Windows settings on a Cloud PC can be backed up using Windows backup as well as Enterprise State Roaming. These settings are available for a work or school account only if allowed by IT:

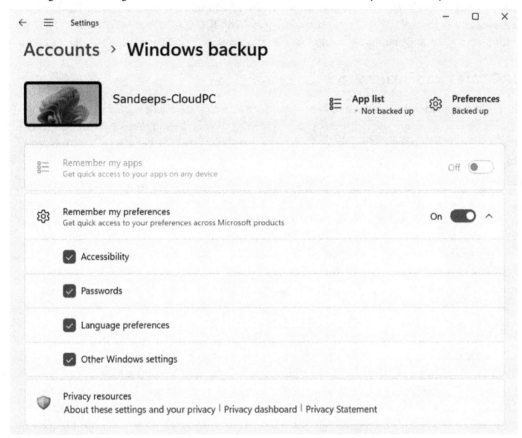

Figure 2.11 – Backup options in Windows 11

User endpoint availability

Continuity of endpoints is also integral to a BCDR strategy. It could be as simple as providing a user with an alternative supported device or as complicated as providing the user with detailed instructions on how to restore their local device, their network, and in rare cases, to help restore a failed hard drive. Each organization's situation is unique and so is each user's situation – especially in this new world of distributed and remote work.

This concludes the BCDR section. In the next section, we are going to explain RBAC delegation and more!

RBAC roles and delegation

To administrate a Windows 365 environment, you will need administrative permissions. This is where **role-based access control (RBAC)** roles come into play. With RBAC roles, you will be able to manage specific permissions and actions for each IT user that needs to support your Windows 365 solution.

RBAC roles and structure

This might not be the first time you've heard about RBAC roles; it's also a widely used permission system in Microsoft Azure subscriptions and in Azure AD. When looking inside Azure AD RBAC roles, we will find a Windows 365 dedicated role. So, what is the difference between using RBAC roles from Azure AD and Microsoft Intune?

With RBAC roles in Microsoft Intune, you'll be able to choose specific a permission/action for every single aspect. An example of this is that you can turn off the resize feature for some specific administrative users but still give them permission to act on other features. By using RBAC roles in Azure AD, you will only be able to grant access to the whole service instead of features. For example, the *Windows 365 administrator* role in Azure AD gives administrative users access to all aspects of Windows 365; you will not be able to prevent users from restarting Cloud PCs. If a user has both RBAC roles from Azure AD and Microsoft Intune, the role with the most permissions will be the role that counts.

Scope tags

While we are talking about administrative permission, we can't forget scope tags. Scope tags are used to limit/determine which objects an administrative user can see in Microsoft Intune. An example of this could be an administrative user that has permission to see and manage all configuration profiles in Intune but shouldn't have access to manage one specific configuration profile. We can then create a scope tag that can be added to the configuration profile and only members of that scope tag are able to manage it. There are a lot of elements in Intune that support scope tags. When we go into more configuration in other chapters, there will be options where we can add scope tags. We will be using the built-in scope tag called **Default**. We won't be going into more depth with scope tags from here, and we will not use any custom-created scope tags in our deployments in this book.

Now we know what scope tags are, let's get back to RBAC roles. Following is an example of some permissions for Cloud PC-specific actions you will be able to delegate to the administrative users in Microsoft Intune.

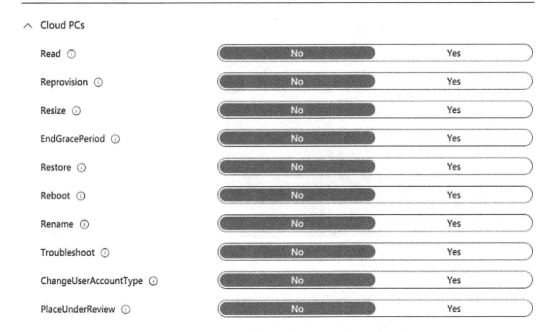

Figure 2.12 – Example of some Cloud PC-specific permissions

In the next section, we will go into delegated roles and how you can customize them.

Custom roles

There are already some built-in Windows 365 roles defined and ready to be used. This will help you get started with delegating permission to administrative users. Microsoft Intune has the following built-in roles for Windows 365:

- **Cloud PC Administrator**: Gives read and write access to all Cloud PC features within the **Cloud PC** blade

- **Cloud PC Reader**: Gives read access to all Cloud PC features within the **Cloud PC** blade

In the following screenshot, you will find all the available Microsoft Intune roles to configure to delegate access to your IT administrators and helpdesk users.

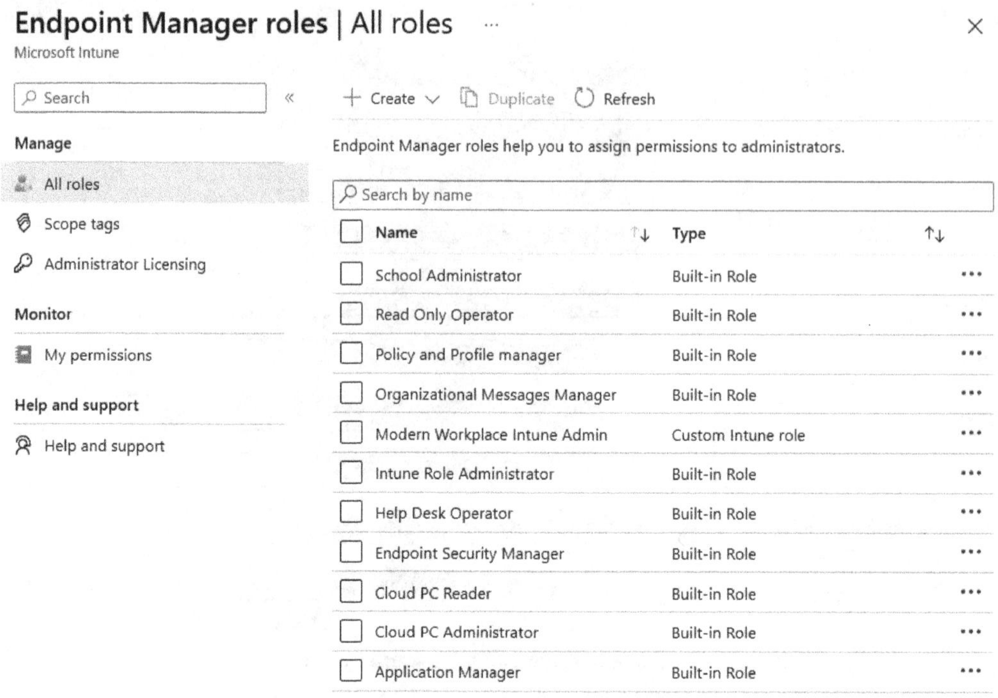

Figure 2.13 – Cloud PC Administrator and Cloud PC Reader are two built-
in roles in Microsoft Intune for Windows 365 management

You might find the built-in roles good enough for your environment and situation, but there is an option to create a custom role for Windows 365. It gives you the ability to design and structure who should have access and what actions the given person can perform.

To create a new custom Windows 365 role, you'll need to have **Global Administrator** or **Intune Service Administrator** assigned to your administrative account. Once that is done, log in to the Microsoft Intune portal. From there, navigate to **Tenant Administration** in the panel to the left and choose **Roles**. You will now be able to see all the built-in roles. This Is also where you will be able to create a new custom role.

As an example, let's create a new custom role that allows administrative users to resize Cloud PCs. An important thing to mention is administrative users must have access to Intune objects to use any of the Windows 365 roles such as resize, for example, Reader access to managed devices in Intun:.

1.   Start by clicking on **Create** and then select **Windows 365 role**.

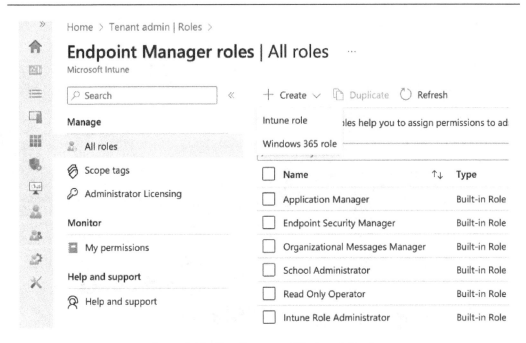

Figure 2.14 – Creating a new Windows 365 role

2. Give the new role a name and description. This role will be able to resize Cloud PCs, therefore it's included in the name to provide better awareness of the role.

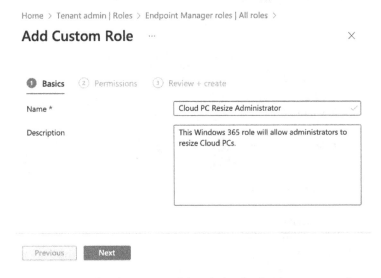

Figure 2.15 – Set the name and description for the new custom role

3. Select the permissions you want the custom role to have.

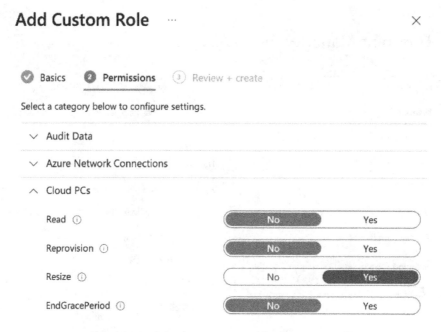

Figure 2.16 – Selecting permissions for the custom role

4.   Next, you will be able to review the custom role you have defined. Once done, select **Create**.

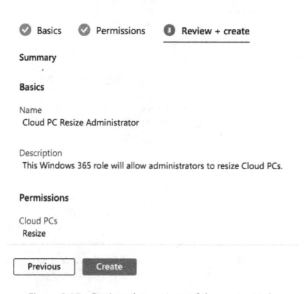

Figure 2.17 – Review the settings of the custom role

5. Once the creation is complete, you will see the new role with the other roles in Microsoft Intune. The next step is to assign the role to a group of users. Choose the role you want to assign:

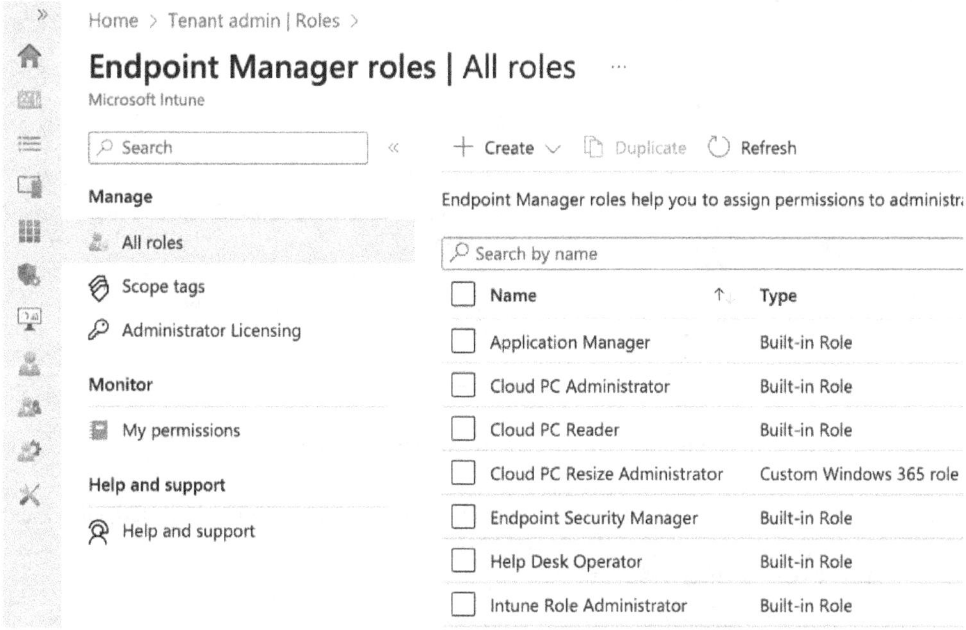

Figure 2.18 – Overview of custom roles in Intune

6. Select **Assignments** in the panel to the left and click on **Assign**.

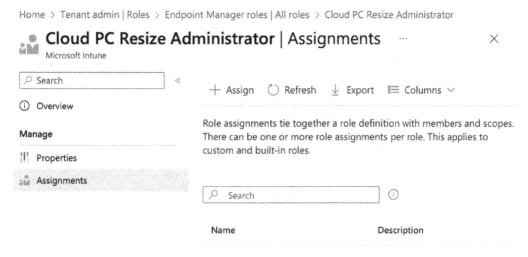

Figure 2.19 – Custom role assignment

7. Give your assignment a name and description. Once done, click **Next**.

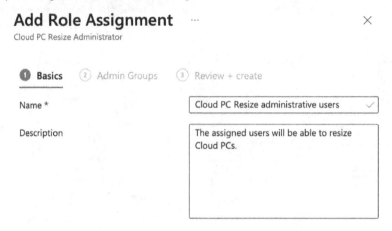

Figure 2.20 – Adding a custom role assignment

8. Select a group with the users you want to have the role permissions. Once selected, click **Next**.

Figure 2.21 – Custom role assignment group selection

You are now able to review the assignment settings you just set. Once you have reviewed the settings, click **Create**.

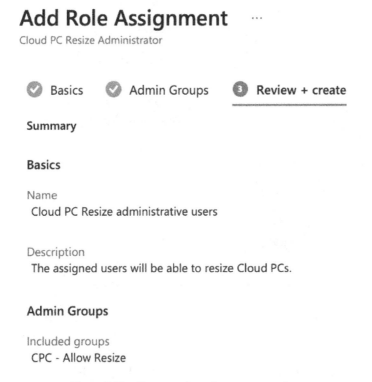

Figure 2.22 – Custom role assignment overview

The creation of the Windows 365 custom role is now done. There are many permission areas to choose from and there are plenty of options to structure and design the administrative roles in your environment as you want to.

This was an example of some of the permission areas that are available for managing Windows 365.

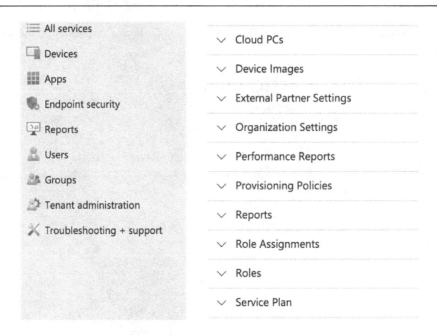

Figure 2.23 – Overview of Windows 365 permissions

After covering Windows 365 permissions, it's now time to take a deeper dive into Azure Privileged Identity Management.

Adding an additional security layer with Azure PIM

Having an administrative role assigned only when the user needs it to perform a certain task is more secure than having the role assigned all the time. With **Azure Privileged Identity Management (Azure PIM)** organizations can add the next level of security and awareness on top of their Microsoft 365 environment, including Windows 365.

Azure PIM has built-in capabilities you might be familiar with when working with other Microsoft products. With Azure PIM, you are able to force multi-factor authentication before a user is able to activate the desired role, which will help you set up the approval flow. These are two important features that ensure you only let correctly validated people into your environment.

Azure PIM integrates directly into the Microsoft portfolio. The product directly supports integration with Azure AD roles, Azure AD groups, and Azure subscriptions. You will need to select an Azure AD group when assigning an RBAC role for Windows 365. This means to integrate it into Azure PIM, you'll have to select **Add your desired group** in **Azure AD Groups** under **Azure PIM**. Once the integration is done, simply assign the user as **Eligible assignments** under the Azure AD group.

To utilize Azure PIM, administrative users will need an Azure AD Premium P2 license. This license is included in some of the available license bundles, such as Microsoft E5.

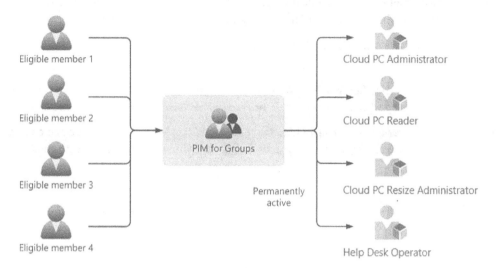

Figure 2.24 – Azure PIM – overview

This wraps up the last section of this RBAC chapter. Let's jump over to the summary!

Summary

We hope you're getting warmed up now, as this architecture-focused chapter comes to an end. We've explained what services are cloudified as part of the Windows 365 architecture section, what services are Microsoft-managed, and what is still your responsibility as a customer. We've also taken a deep dive into the different connectivity layers and options to optimize your network connectivity from the endpoint to your Cloud PC.

In the next chapter, we will go into overdrive mode and start explaining how you can implement and manage Cloud PCs yourself. We're pretty sure that it will be the chapter you will like the most!

Questions

At the end of each chapter, there are three questions you can use to evaluate your learning and challenge yourself. The questions for this chapter are as follows:

1. What is the most important component Windows 365 manages on behalf of the customer that is unique to the service – and there is no other solution doing so on the market?
2. What network port and protocol are used when using Windows 365?
3. For which scenarios is RDP Shortpath important?

Further reading

During your learning journey while going through the other chapters, if you want to learn more about the subjects covered in this chapter, you can do so by visiting the following websites:

- *Test your Microsoft and Windows 365 connectivity via* `https://connectivity.office.com/`

- *Service health in the Microsoft 365 admin center is a great tool to detect potential service issues, including their scope of impact* (`https://admin.microsoft.com/#/servicehealth`)

- *Windows 365 network requirements | Microsoft Learn:* `https://learn.microsoft.com/windows-365/enterprise/requirements-network?tabs=enterprise%2Cent`

3
Deploying Cloud PCs

In this chapter, we will get started with the real deal, the hands-on part where we will guide you through the nuts and bolts of deploying Windows 365. We will explain how you can deploy Windows 365 Cloud PCs and more!

We will also explain how you can enable new features such as Windows 365 Boot and Windows 365 Frontline for your users, application delivery settings, and more!

In this chapter, we will cover the following subjects:

- The deployment process
- The size and performance of Cloud PCs
- Geography and region settings
- Configuring networking
- The Windows 365 Network Health service
- Purchasing and assigning licenses
- Provisioning Cloud PCs
- Provisioning Windows 365 Frontline Cloud PCs
- Creating custom images
- Configuring Windows 365 Boot
- Migrating to Windows 365 – profiles and data
- Enabling Windows Autopatch

The deployment process

Windows 365 is remarkably simple to deploy. For **Hybrid Azure AD Join (HAADJ)**, it is required to bring in an Azure subscription for the domain controller (Kerberos) connection. This is to support legacy applications or other backend services that require this type of authentication.

If you are ready to go cloud-native, you can go straight up to **Azure AD Join (AADJ)** and bring in Azure AD only without the need for an Azure subscription or a domain controller! This makes it possible to provision Cloud PCs without a required infrastructure component. For Windows 365 Enterprise, you will only need licenses and Microsoft Intune administrator credentials and you are all set!

We recommend that customers use AADJ if possible. Moving from HAADJ to AADJ does require a re-provisioning of the user's Cloud PC:

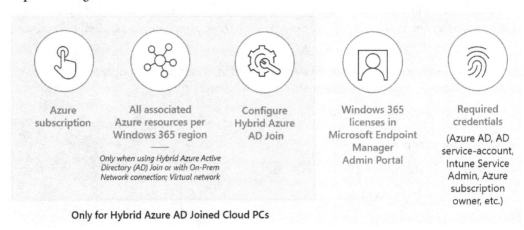

Figure 3.1 – Cloud PC deployment steps

In the following table, you can find all the licenses available for Windows 365 as of today. As you can see, we've got a variety of licenses for different sorts of scenarios.

We recommend testing your licenses based on your workloads. When you use a Cloud PC as a replacement for your physical PC, you should start converting the number of CPU/cores into the Cloud PC vCPU/RAM size as a recommended starting point:

VM/OS disk size	Example scenarios	Recommended apps
2 vCPU/4 GB/256 GB 2 vCPU/4 GB/128 GB 2 vCPU/4 GB/64 GB	Mergers and acquisitions, short-term and seasonal, customer services, Bring Your Own PC, and working from home	Microsoft 365 Apps, Microsoft Teams (audio only), Outlook, Excel, PowerPoint, OneDrive, Adobe Reader, Edge, line-of-business app(s), Defender support
2 vCPU/8 GB/256 GB 2 vCPU/8 GB /128 GB	Bring Your Own PC, working from home, market researchers, government, and consultants	Microsoft 365 Apps, Microsoft Teams, Outlook, Excel, Access, PowerPoint, OneDrive, Adobe Reader, Edge, line-of-business app(s), and Defender support
4 vCPU/16 GB/512 GB 4 vCPU/16 GB/256 GB 4 vCPU/16 GB/128 GB	Finance, government, consultants, healthcare services, Bring-Your-Own-PC, and working from home	Microsoft 365 Apps, Microsoft Teams, Outlook, Excel, Access, PowerPoint, Power BI, Dynamics 365, OneDrive, Adobe Reader, Edge, line-of-business app(s), Nested Virtualization support, Windows Subsystem for Linux/Android, Hyper-V, and Defender support
8 vCPU/32 GB/512 GB 8 vCPU/32 GB/256 GB 8 vCPU/32 GB/128 GB	Software developers, engineers, content creators, design, and engineering workstations	Microsoft 365 Apps, Microsoft Teams, Outlook, Access, OneDrive, Adobe Reader, Edge, Power BI, Visual Studio Code, line-of-business app(s), Nested Virtualization support, Windows Subsystem for Linux/Android, Hyper-V, and Defender support

Table 3.1 – Windows 365 Cloud PC recommended licenses

Per the license scenario, you will gain a certain level of performance benefits. You can use the following graph as a reference to architect the right set of licenses to achieve the performance your users need:

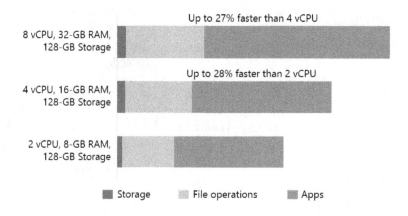

Figure 3.2 – Relative performance of Cloud PCs

In the next section, we will cover the regional availability of Windows 365.

Geography and region settings

Windows 365 uses Microsoft's data center capacity worldwide to deploy Cloud PCs in several regions, with many more to come. The region in which you can deploy your Cloud PCs depends on two factors – the availability of Windows 365 for purchase and the Windows 365 edition you are deploying.

As of September 2023, Windows 365 can be purchased in the countries and regions listed as follows (for current information, please refer to the official Microsoft website: `https://learn.microsoft.com/windows-365/enterprise/requirements?tabs=enterprise%2Cent#supported-azure-regions-for-cloud-pc-provisioning`):

Continent	Countries
Africa	Algeria, Angola, Benin, Botswana, Burkina Faso, Burundi, Cabo Verde, Cameroon, Central African Republic, Chad, Comoros, Congo, Congo (DRC), Côte d'Ivoire, Djibouti, Egypt, Equatorial Guinea, Eritrea, Eswatini (formerly Swaziland), Ethiopia, Gabon, Gambia, Ghana, Guinea, Guinea-Bissau, Kenya, Lesotho, Liberia, Libya, Madagascar, Malawi, Mali, Mauritania, Mauritius, Mayotte, Morocco, Mozambique, Namibia, Niger, Nigeria, Réunion, Rwanda, Sao Tome and Principe, Senegal, Seychelles, Sierra Leone, Somalia, South Africa, South Sudan, St Helena – Ascension - Tristan da Cunha, Sudan, Tanzania, Togo, Tunisia, Uganda, Zambia, and Zimbabwe
Asia	Afghanistan, Bahrain, Bangladesh, Bhutan, Brunei, Cambodia, China, Hong Kong SAR, India, Indonesia, Iraq, Israel, Japan, Jordan, Kazakhstan, Kuwait, Kyrgyzstan, Laos, Lebanon, Malaysia, Maldives, Mongolia, Myanmar, Nepal, Oman, Pakistan, Palestinian Authority, Philippines, Qatar, the Republic of Korea (South Korea), Saudi Arabia, Singapore, Sri Lanka, Taiwan, Tajikistan, Thailand, Timor-Leste, Turkey, Turkmenistan, the United Arab Emirates, Uzbekistan, Vietnam, and Yemen
Europe	The Åland Islands, Albania, Andorra, Austria, Belarus, Belgium, Bosnia and Herzegovina, Bulgaria, Croatia, Cyprus, Czech Republic, Denmark, Estonia, the Faroe Islands, Finland, France, Germany, Gibraltar, Greece, Guernsey, Hungary, Iceland, Ireland, the Isle of Man, Italy, Jan Mayen, Jersey, Kosovo, Latvia, Liechtenstein, Lithuania, Luxembourg, Malta, Moldova, Monaco, Montenegro, Netherlands, North Macedonia, Norway, Poland, Portugal, Romania, Russia, San Marino, Serbia, Slovakia, Slovenia, Spain, Svalbard, Sweden, Switzerland, Ukraine, United Kingdom, and Vatican City
North America	American Samoa, Canada, the Cayman Islands, Greenland, Mexico, Puerto Rico, United States, the US Outlying Islands, and the US Virgin Islands
Oceania	Australia, Fiji, French Polynesia, Guam, Kiribati, the Marshall Islands, Micronesia, Nauru, New Caledonia, New Zealand, Niue, Norfolk Island, the Northern Mariana Islands, Palau, Papua New Guinea, the Pitcairn Islands, Samoa, the Solomon Islands, Tokelau, Tonga, Tuvalu, Vanuatu, and Wallis and Futuna
South America	Argentina, Bolivia, Brazil, Chile, Colombia, Ecuador, the Falkland Islands, French Guiana, Guyana, Paraguay, Peru, Suriname, Uruguay, and Venezuela

Table 3.2 – Windows 365-supported regions

Note

Microsoft Online Services are not available in Cuba, the Democratic People's Republic of Korea (North Korea), Iran, Sudan, and Syria.

Windows 365 Business-supported regions

Windows 365 Business Cloud PCs' availability for purchase and the Cloud PC's region depend on your organization's billing address. However, the billing address country does not guarantee that the Cloud PC will be in that country. The Cloud PC will be set up in the nearest supported location with available capacity, regardless of whether it is in the same country as the billing address. If there is no capacity available in that location, the Cloud PC will be provisioned in the closest available region.

To check what data location has been detected for your organization, log in as administrator on `https://admin.microsoft.com` and go to **Settings | Org settings** in the menu panel to the left. From here, choose **Organization profile**. This will display some new options to choose from. Select **Data location**. You will now be able to see the detected location based on your organization's address. Windows 365 Cloud PCs will be created in the same location as Microsoft Exchange:

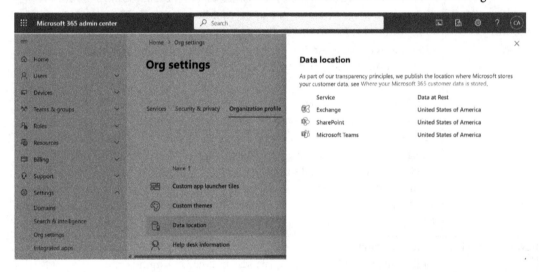

Figure 3.3 – Organization's data location

Windows 365 Enterprise-supported regions

Windows 365 Enterprise allows the IT department to select a geography and region to provision Cloud PCs into. This is particularly useful for companies that have employees working in various parts of the world, as it allows for more precise management and planning of resources. These options are available when creating a Cloud PC provisioning policy in **Microsoft Intune admin center** (`https://intune.microsoft.com`):

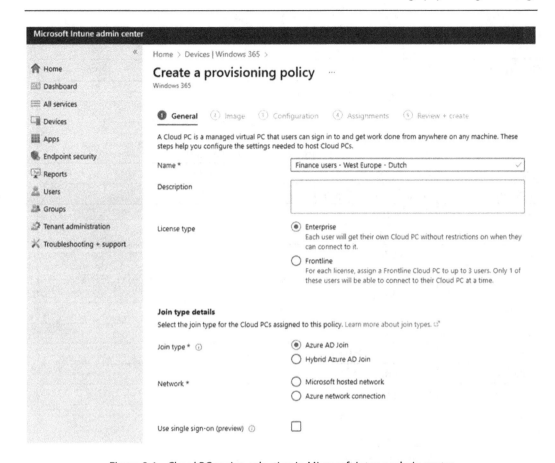

Figure 3.4 – Cloud PC region selection in Microsoft Intune admin center

On the page shown in the preceding screenshot, once you select a **Geography** option, the region defaults to **Automatic (Recommended)**. If it is absolutely necessary, you have the option to select a specific region.

The following geographies and regions are available to choose from:

Geography	Region
Asia	East Asia or Southeast Asia
Australia	Australia East
Canada	Canada Central
European Union	North Europe, West Europe, or Sweden Central
France	France Central
Germany	Germany West Central
India	Central India
Japan	Japan East
Norway	Norway East
South America	Brazil South (restricted – request your commercial executive to engage the deal manager for an exception)
South Korea	Korea Central
Switzerland	Switzerland North
UAE	UAE North, Qatar
United Kingdom	UK South
US Central	Central US or South Central US
South Africa	South Africa North
US East	East US or East US 2
US West	West US 2 (restricted, contact support) or West US 3

Table 3.3 – Windows 365 Enterprise available regions

Windows 365 Government-supported regions

The Windows 365 Government edition is limited to US-based government bodies, government agencies, and public entities, and therefore government customers have these two regions to choose from:

- US Gov Virginia
- US Gov Arizona

Windows 365 and data protection

Microsoft's Data Protection Addendum (`https://aka.ms/DPA`) defines the company's duties and responsibilities regarding the processing and safeguarding of customer data, professional services data, and personal data by its products and services. Windows 365 is a Microsoft Core Online Service and therefore, the cloud service portion of Windows 365 complies with the control standards and frameworks laid by the **System and Organization Controls** (**SOC**) for service organizations. Windows 365 has **SSAE 18 SOC 1 Type II** and **SSAE 18 SOC 2 Type II** attestations.

Microsoft's default setting is to keep customer data at rest within the geography where the Windows 365 tenant is deployed. However, if a customer provisions Windows 365 Cloud PCs within the same tenant to various available geographies, then for each Cloud PC, Microsoft will store Cloud PC customer data at rest within the respective geography.

Windows 365 is also compliant with the **General Data Protection Regulation** (**GDPR**) and the **California Consumer Privacy Act** (**CCPA**) which provide users in the European Union and California, respectively, with the rights to delete, access, and receive their personal information. The CCPA provides additional disclosures and protections against discrimination for data transfers classified as **sales**. You can read more about these at `http://aka.ms/gdpr` and `http://aka.ms/ccpa`.

Data Subject Requests (**DSRs**) made by Windows 365 Enterprise customers will only apply to data within the associated Azure AD tenant where the Windows 365 account is deployed. Windows 365 users who create an Azure subscription should be aware that it will be treated as an Azure AD tenant and DSRs will only be applicable to data within the tenant. Moreover, if an Azure subscription created using a Windows 365 account is deleted, it will not have any impact on the actual Windows 365 account. As mentioned earlier, DSRs executed within the Azure subscription will be confined to the scope of the tenant.

Configuring networking

Choosing which network a Cloud PC should be created on is an important step. Microsoft Hosted Network is the most simple and straightforward way to get your Cloud PCs up and running, and there are no setup requirements to use Microsoft Hosted Network. With **Azure Network Connection** (**ANC**), you can oversee maintaining the network for your Cloud PC platform. By using ANC, you bring your own network and can establish a connection between existing network infrastructure and newly created Cloud PCs.

ANC is required if you want to use **Active Directory (AD) as a hybrid identity** setup for your Cloud PCs, as it needs a stable connection to an on-premises or Cloud-based Active Directory domain to complete the setup.

There is a limit of a maximum of 10 ANCs for each tenant. You'll have to contact Microsoft support if you want more than 10 ANCs in your Windows 365 environment.

Prerequisites

To start configuring ANC in your Windows 365 environment, you'll need one of the following built-in roles. If you have configured a custom role with privilege to ANC, you can use that as well:

- Global Administrator
- Intune Administrator
- Windows 365 Administrator

Besides access to Intune, the same administrative account must be assigned the reader role within the Azure subscription to which the virtual network is assigned.

If you want to create an ANC with support for HAADJ, you'll have to get an account that is able to join computers to the domain. It's highly recommended to create a service account for that purpose.

Creating a virtual network in Azure

Now we have covered the requirements, let's look at how we can create a connection between a virtual network in an Azure subscription and the Windows 365 environment.

Let's go ahead and create a virtual network in Azure. If you already have an existing virtual network in Azure you would like to use, you can skip this part.

Start by going to `https://portal.azure.com/` and create a new virtual network. It's quite straightforward. You can use all the default settings, but take care that you aren't overlapping the address space with an existing one you are already using:

1. Start by logging in to `https://portal.azure.com`.
2. Start the creation of a new virtual network. From here, choose the **Resource group** option and the name of the virtual network. When these have been defined, choose **Next**.

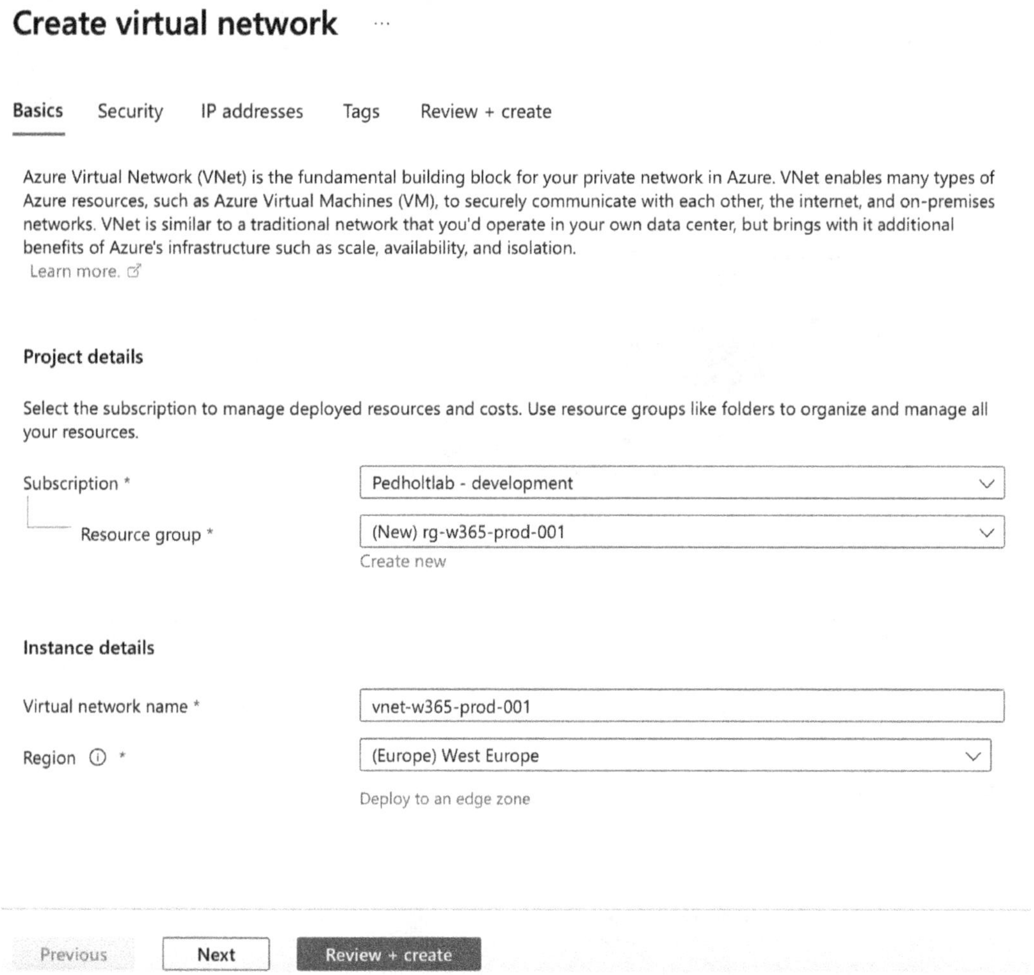

Create virtual network   ...

Basics   Security   IP addresses   Tags   Review + create

Azure Virtual Network (VNet) is the fundamental building block for your private network in Azure. VNet enables many types of Azure resources, such as Azure Virtual Machines (VM), to securely communicate with each other, the internet, and on-premises networks. VNet is similar to a traditional network that you'd operate in your own data center, but brings with it additional benefits of Azure's infrastructure such as scale, availability, and isolation.
Learn more. ☐

Project details

Select the subscription to manage deployed resources and costs. Use resource groups like folders to organize and manage all your resources.

Subscription * | Pedholtlab - development   ∨ |

Resource group * | (New) rg-w365-prod-001   ∨ |
                          Create new

Instance details

Virtual network name * | vnet-w365-prod-001 |

Region ⓘ * | (Europe) West Europe   ∨ |
                          Deploy to an edge zone

| Previous | | **Next** | | Review + create |

Figure 3.5 – Virtual network creation basic information

3. There are some security features you can enable on the virtual network. These features are optional, but Azure Firewall should be considered if no other firewall solution is deployed. When you are ready, click on **Next.**

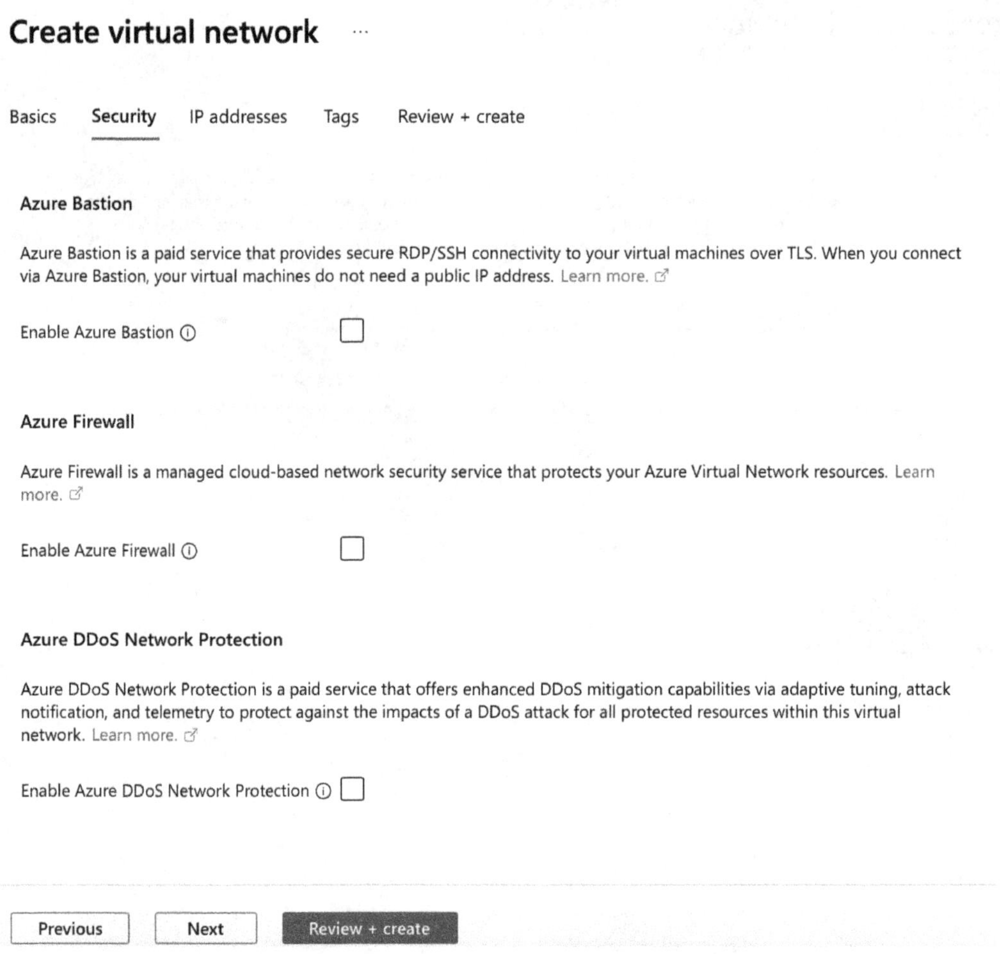

Create virtual network   ...

Basics   **Security**   IP addresses   Tags   Review + create

Azure Bastion

Azure Bastion is a paid service that provides secure RDP/SSH connectivity to your virtual machines over TLS. When you connect via Azure Bastion, your virtual machines do not need a public IP address. Learn more. ☐

Enable Azure Bastion ⓘ   ☐

Azure Firewall

Azure Firewall is a managed cloud-based network security service that protects your Azure Virtual Network resources. Learn more. ☐

Enable Azure Firewall ⓘ   ☐

Azure DDoS Network Protection

Azure DDoS Network Protection is a paid service that offers enhanced DDoS mitigation capabilities via adaptive tuning, attack notification, and telemetry to protect against the impacts of a DDoS attack for all protected resources within this virtual network. Learn more. ☐

Enable Azure DDoS Network Protection ⓘ ☐

| Previous | Next | Review + create |

Figure 3.6 – Virtual network creation security

4. Now the IP address range and subnets must be defined. Once these have been defined, click on **Next**.

Create virtual network   ...

Basics   Security   **IP addresses**   Tags   Review + create

Configure your virtual network address space with the IPv4 and IPv6 addresses and subnets you need. Learn more ☐

Define the address space of your virtual network with one or more IPv4 or IPv6 address ranges. Create subnets to segment the virtual network address space into smaller ranges for use by your applications. When you deploy resources into a subnet, Azure assigns the resource an IP address from the subnet. Learn more ☐

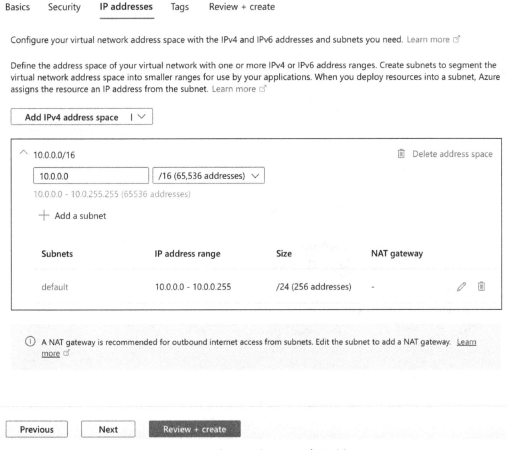

Figure 3.7 – Virtual network creation | IP addresses

5.   Next, we can add any Azure tags that might be required for your organization. We will leave it as is in this case. Click on **Next**.

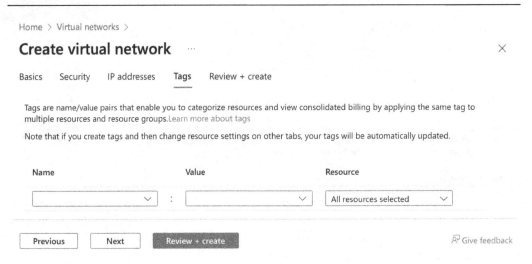

Figure 3.8 – Virtual network | Azure tags selection

6. We are now able to see an overview of the entire configuration of the new virtual network. When you have reviewed this, click on **Create**.

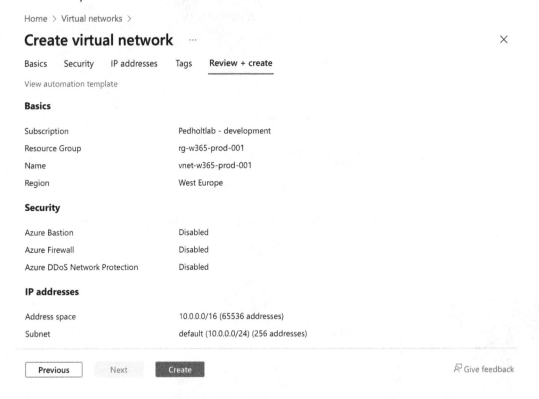

Figure 3.9 – Virtual network creation | settings review

Now that the virtual network has been created, we can start looking at how we create an ANC in Intune. We will look at the configuration for both an AADJ and HAADJ network connection.

Setting up an AADJ ANC

Let's have a look at how to configure an ANC for AADJ Cloud PC device:

1. Start by going to **Microsoft Intune | Devices | Windows 365 | Azure network connection**. From here, click on **+ Create** and select **Azure AD Join**:

Figure 3.10 – Creating an ANC in Windows 365 overview

2. Fill out the required information such as the display name of the connection, the virtual network, and the subnet you would like to integrate with Windows 365. Once that is done, click on **Next**.

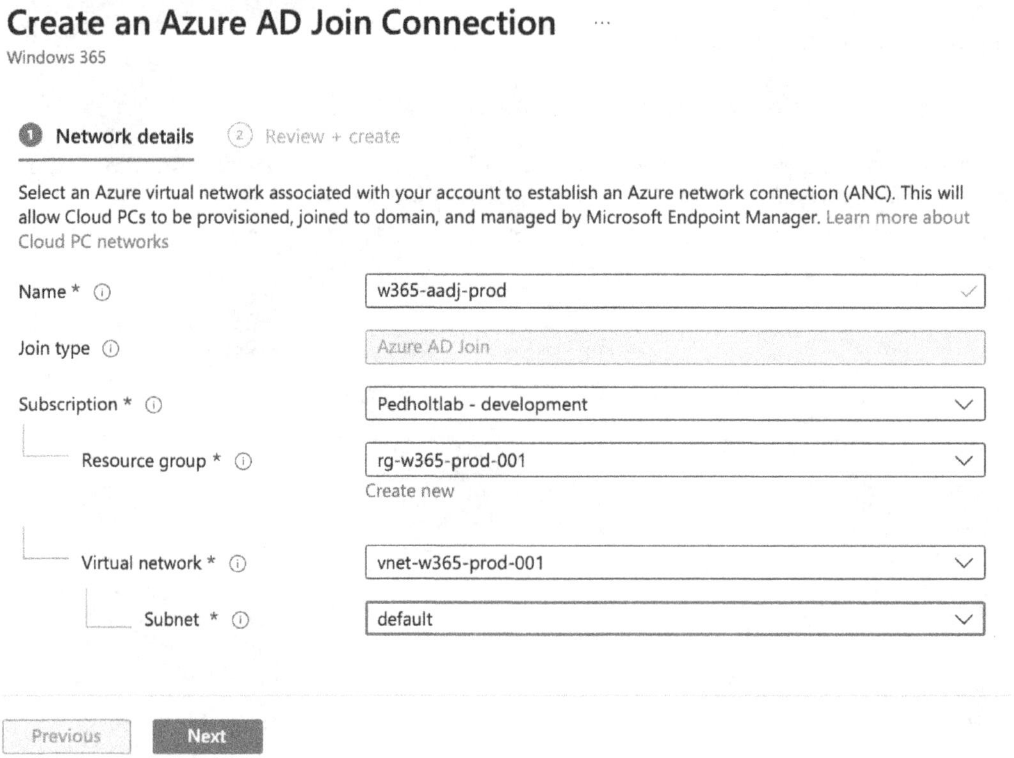

Create an Azure AD Join Connection   ...
Windows 365

1 Network details   (2) Review + create

Select an Azure virtual network associated with your account to establish an Azure network connection (ANC). This will allow Cloud PCs to be provisioned, joined to domain, and managed by Microsoft Endpoint Manager. Learn more about Cloud PC networks

Name * ⓘ	w365-aadj-prod ✓
Join type ⓘ	Azure AD Join
Subscription * ⓘ	Pedholtlab - development ⌄
Resource group * ⓘ	rg-w365-prod-001 ⌄
	Create new
Virtual network * ⓘ	vnet-w365-prod-001 ⌄
Subnet * ⓘ	default ⌄

Previous   Next

Figure 3.11 – Creating an AADJ ANC | network details

3. Review the information you have filled in. When you are ready, click **Review + create**:

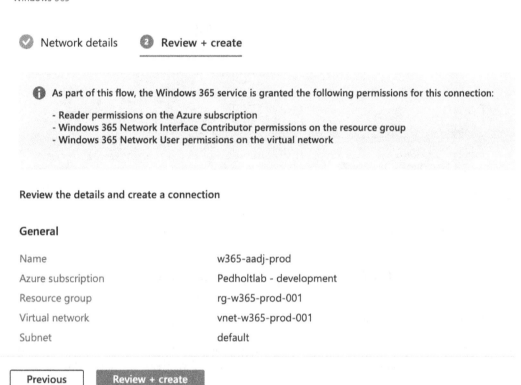

Create an Azure AD Join Connection ...
Windows 365

✓ Network details   ② **Review + create**

ⓘ As part of this flow, the Windows 365 service is granted the following permissions for this connection:

- Reader permissions on the Azure subscription
- Windows 365 Network Interface Contributor permissions on the resource group
- Windows 365 Network User permissions on the virtual network

Review the details and create a connection

General

Name	w365-aadj-prod
Azure subscription	Pedholtlab - development
Resource group	rg-w365-prod-001
Virtual network	vnet-w365-prod-001
Subnet	default

Previous   Review + create

Figure 3.12 – Creating an AADJ ANC | settings review

Once the ANC has been created, you are now done and should be able to view the connection in the ANC overview. You can now use that virtual network in your provisioning policy.

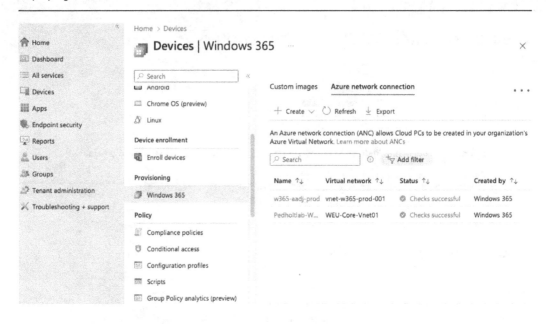

Figure 3.13 – Windows 365 ANC network overview

Setting up a HAADJ ANC

A HAADJ network connection is a bit trickier to set up than the previous one. We must ensure the virtual network we are using has a connection with the domain we are trying to join. Once we are sure about that, let's go ahead and create a connection:

1. Visit **Microsoft Intune | Windows 365 | Azure network connection**. From here, click on **+ Create** and select **Hybrid Azure AD Join**.

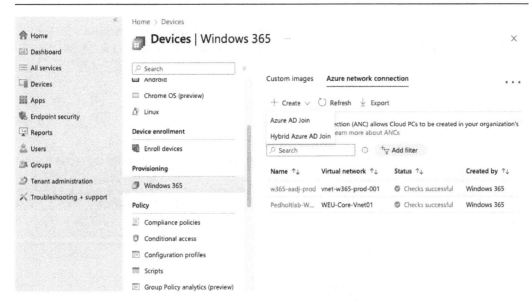

Figure 3.14 – Creating a HAADJ ANC in Windows 365 | overview

2. Provide the required information such as the display name of the connection, the virtual network, and the subnet you would like to integrate with Windows 365. Click **Next**.

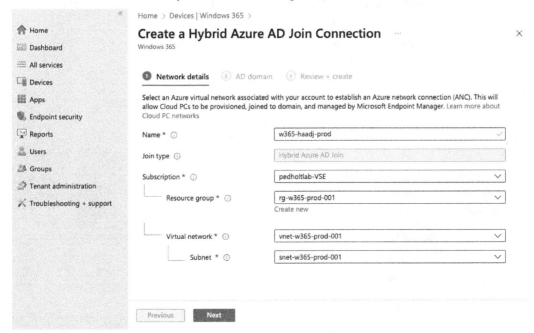

Figure 3.15 – Creating a HAADJ ANC | network details

3.   Type the domain name you want the Cloud PCs to join. The **Organization Unit** field is optional. Type in the AD username and password for your domain-joined service account. Once done, click **Next**:

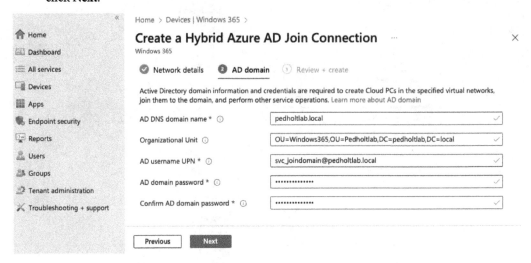

Figure 3.16 – Creating a HAADJ ANC | domain details

4.   Review the settings provided and click on **Review + create**. The connection will now be established:

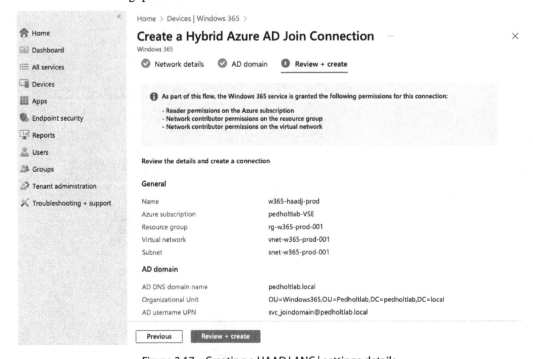

Figure 3.17 – Creating a HAADJ ANC | settings details

Once the creation is done, you can view the connection in the ANC overview. You will now be able to use that virtual network in your provisioning policy.

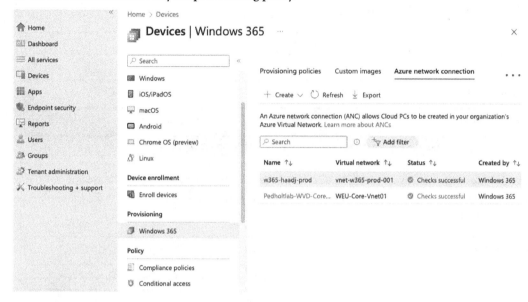

Figure 3.18 – Windows 365 ANC network overview

Let's look at how health checks work with ANC. This is an important feature that helps you get an overview to see whether there are any warnings or errors for any of your network connections.

Automatic health checks

After an ANC has been created, health checks are automatically performed once every 6 hours. The health check itself can take up to 30 minutes.

The health checks on a virtual network are done automatically by creating a virtual machine within the target virtual network. After the health check is done, the virtual machine and **Network Interface Card** (**NIC**) are removed. Everything is done behind the scenes by Microsoft, so you don't have to handle anything in these checks.

One thing to be aware of if you are using Azure Locks on your virtual network is that the Windows 365 service will not be able to delete the NIC that is created to do the health checks. If that is the case, over time, you'll see a lot of NICs being stuck in your virtual network, and you must remove them yourself.

Once the connection is established, the Windows 365 service will be granted access to the Azure subscription and the selected virtual network. These permissions mustn't be deleted after provisioning as this will result in a failed health check:

Access Level	Role Assignment	Identity
Subscription	Reader	Windows 365
Resource Group	Network Contributor	Windows 365
Virtual Network	Network Contributor	Windows 365

Table 3.4 – Windows 365 role assignment in an Azure subscription

Several things will be checked during health checks. The following series of tables show what services will be checked. This will also give you an overview of what the return statuses mean for the services and in the ANC overview.

Service check	Task check description
Active Directory DNS	Validates the provided domain name of Active Directory
Active Directory Domain Join	Domain joining a dummy device in Active Directory
Endpoint connectivity	Ensures connectivity to the required URLs is allowed
Azure Active Directory synchronization	Validates that Azure AD Sync is enabled and synchronization has been performed in the last 90 minutes
Azure subnet IP address usage	Checks whether there are available IPs within the subnet of the connected ANC
Azure tenant readiness	Checks whether the Azure subscription is ready to use without any blockers for Windows 365 needing to be integrated
Azure virtual network	Validates the selected virtual network is in a Windows 365-supported region
App permission for an Azure subscription	Validates the required permission for the Windows 365 service
App permission for an Azure Resource Group	Validates the required permission for the Windows 365 service
App permission on the Azure virtual network	Validates the required permission for the Windows 365 service
The environment and configuration are ready	The infrastructure running the Windows 365 service is healthy

Intune enrollment restrictions	Checks whether Windows enrollments are allowed within Microsoft Intune
Localization language package	Validates that the Microsoft operating system and language packages are available for download
UDP connectivity	Checks whether the network configuration allows utilization of UDP

Table 3.5 – Supported health checks

In the following table, you can find the health check statuses and what they mean.

Health check status	Status description
Passed	The health check has successfully passed.
Warning	The health check failed. The service might still work for a period: please resolve the issue and run a new check.
Error	The health check failed. Please resolve the issue and run a new check.

Table 3.6 – Health check status overview

In the following table, you can find the ANC statuses and what they mean.

ANC status	Status description
Running checks	Health checks are currently running
Checks successful	All health checks have passed successfully
Checks successful with warnings	One or more health checks have failed with a Warning status
Checks failed	One or more health checks have failed with an Error status

Table 3.7 – Azure network connection status overview

Now we have been through the checks, we will now look at how to manually trigger a health check.

Manually triggering a health check

A health check can be manually triggered if the ANC status fails or has a warning:

1. This can be done by logging in to **Microsoft Intune | Devices | Windows 365 | Azure network connection**.

2. Click on the status message. From here, you can select **Retry**.

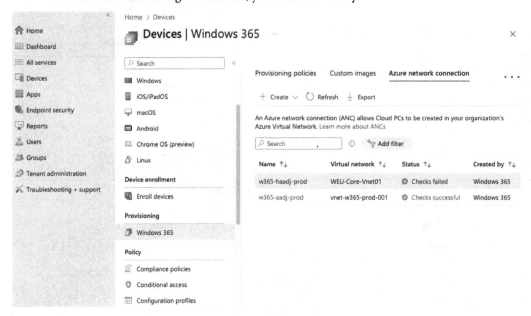

Figure 3.19 – Health check failed for the ANC connection

3. From here, you can select **Retry**. In the following screenshot, you can see how many checks the health service proactively runs as part of the HAADJ Cloud PCs.

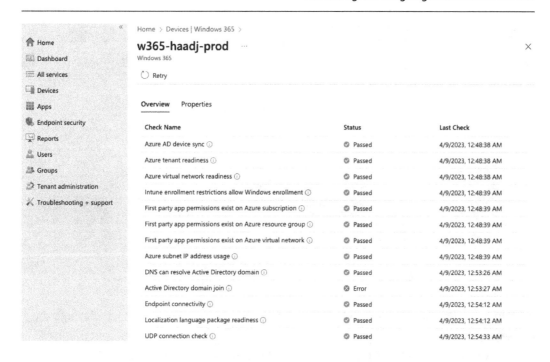

Figure 3.20 – Failed health check where the Retry button is available

In the next chapter, we will cover all you need to know about how to provision a Cloud PC.

Purchasing and assigning Windows 365 licenses

You can perform this step before or after the provisioning process. However, to provision a Cloud PC, you will have to purchase a Windows 365 license. Assigning licenses works the same as for other Microsoft 365 products.

We've also recently introduced a new licensing offering via **Windows 365 Frontline**, which allows you to share one license with three more users for the same personal Windows experience at a reduced price.

You can purchase and assign the licenses using either of these methods:

1. Via the Microsoft Admin Center portal for individual users at `admin.microsoft.com`.

2. Select the Windows 365 product license you want to purchase, meaning **Enterprise**, **Frontline**, or **Business**.

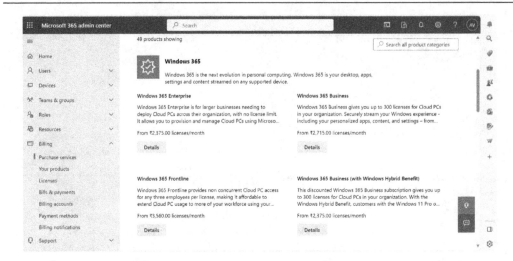

Figure 3.21 – Purchasing Windows 365 licenses in Microsoft 365 admin center

3. Once you have selected the right license size for your Cloud PC, you can go through the Microsoft 365 license purchase flow.

4. Once you are all ready, via the Azure AD admin center portal via the Azure portal based on group-based licensing at `portal.azure.com`.

5. We recommend you use group-based license assignments for more flexibility when you have multiple users consuming the same license. This makes it easier to provision new Cloud PCs, as you will only have to add your user inside the right Azure AD group.

6. Another best practice is to assign the same Azure AD for licensing as well to your provisioning policy. This way, by adding a user to the group, both the license and Cloud PC will be provided automatically!

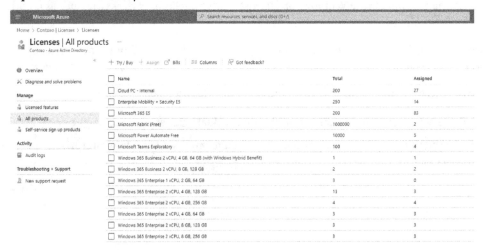

Figure 3.22 – Viewing available licenses in the Microsoft Azure portal

Provisioning Cloud PCs

Provisioning a Cloud PC starts from Microsoft Intune admin center. Everything, from the provisioning of the Cloud PC to assigning applications, everything happens via this portal:

1. Go to **Microsoft Intune admin center** in your browser:

Figure 3.23 – The Intune dashboard

2. Go to **Devices | Provisioning | Windows 365** and go to **Provisioning policies**.

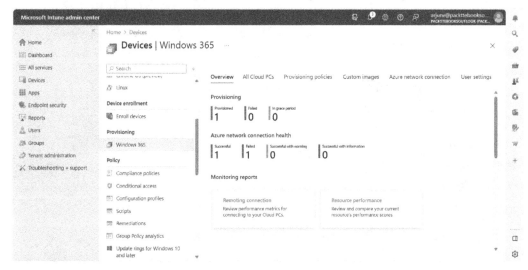

Figure 3.24 – Cloud PC overview

3.   Click on + **Create policy**.

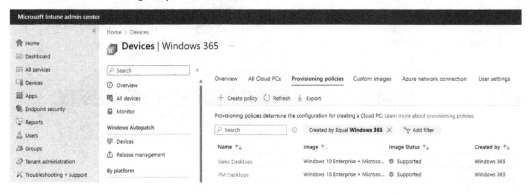

Figure 3.25 – Overview of configured provisioning policies

4.   Start by naming your provisioning policy and choosing a license type. In this example, we will choose **Enterprise**.

> **Note**
>
> You can name it based on your department name + location + language. As this is an initial step, it may be convenient to structure the policy in a certain set way.

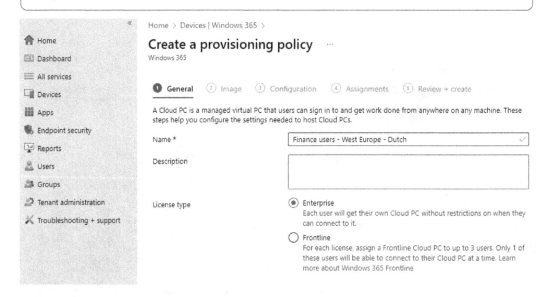

Figure 3.26 – Defining the general settings for the provisioning policy

5. Select your preferred **Join type**. Choose the **Region** and **Network** options that you want to use to deploy your Cloud PCs. Select whether you want to enable **Single Sign-On (SSO)** as the end user client experience. For this creation, we will use AADJ and Microsoft hosted network. Once done, click on **Next**.

> **Note**
>
> If you want to connect to your own on-premises network or another public cloud or private cloud data center, make sure to select the Azure network via the **Other** option during the provisioning policy configuration.

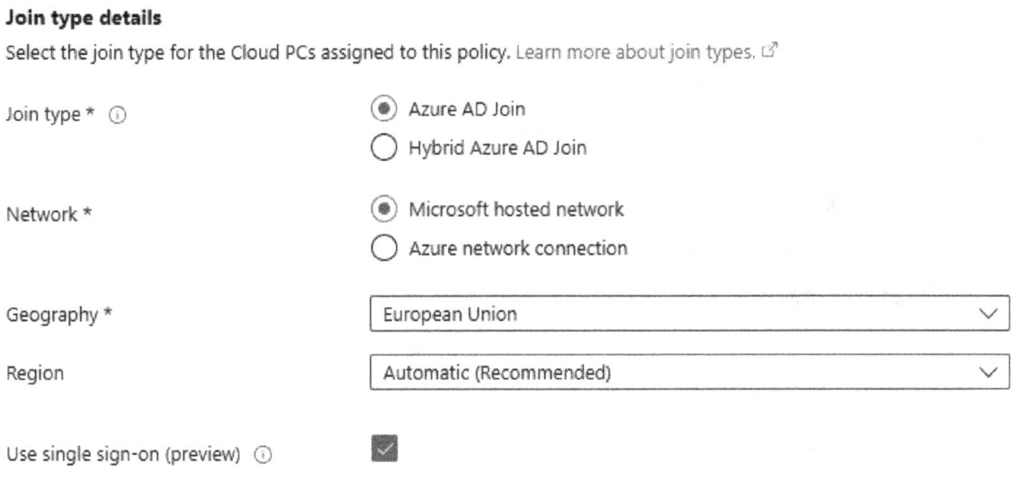

Join type details

Select the join type for the Cloud PCs assigned to this policy. Learn more about join types. ⬀

Join type * ⓘ	◉ Azure AD Join
	○ Hybrid Azure AD Join
Network *	◉ Microsoft hosted network
	○ Azure network connection
Geography *	European Union ⌄
Region	Automatic (Recommended) ⌄
Use single sign-on (preview) ⓘ	☑

Figure 3.27 – Provisioning policy join type and network selection

6. Select the Windows image version you would like to use. We recommend customers use the gallery images with Microsoft 365 apps, Microsoft Teams optimizations, multimedia redirection, and other settings pre-installed. Click on **Next** once selected.

> **Note**
>
> You are also able to use custom images. Make sure to pre-load your images via Azure – as a managed image or via Shared Image Gallery.

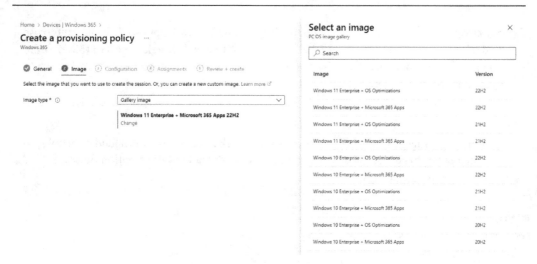

Figure 3.28 – Selecting the image type in the provisioning policy

7.   In the next section, start selecting the operating system and regional language settings.

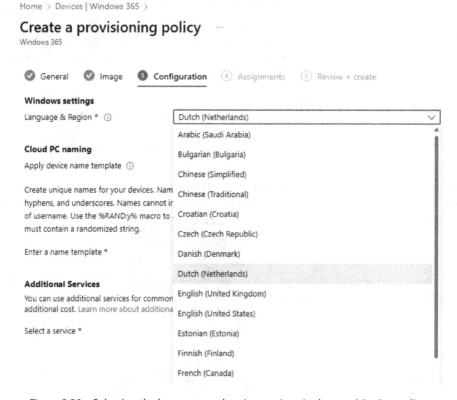

Figure 3.29 – Selecting the language and region settings in the provisioning policy

8. To create a Cloud PC naming template to use when naming all Cloud PCs that are provisioned with this policy, select **Apply device name template**. When creating the template, follow these rules:

    - Names must be between 5 and 15 characters.

    - Names can contain letters, numbers, and hyphens.

    - Names can't include blank spaces.

    - Use the `%USERNAME:X%` macro to add the first X letters of the username (optional).

    - Use the `%RAND:Y%` macro to add a random string of numbers, where Y equals the number of digits to add. Y must be 5 or more. Names must contain a randomized string (required).

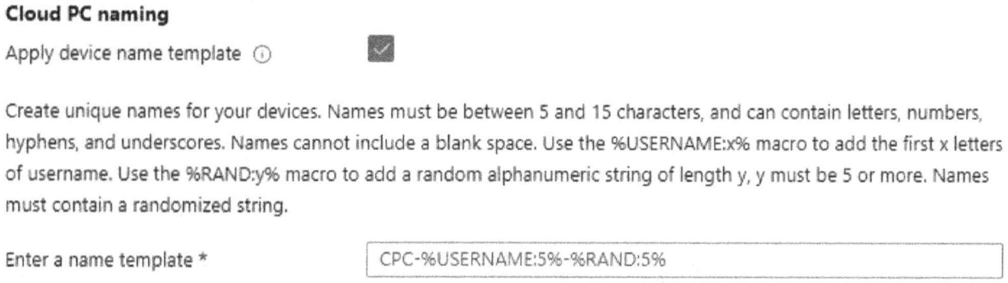

Cloud PC naming

Apply device name template ⓘ

Create unique names for your devices. Names must be between 5 and 15 characters, and can contain letters, numbers, hyphens, and underscores. Names cannot include a blank space. Use the %USERNAME:x% macro to add the first x letters of username. Use the %RAND:y% macro to add a random alphanumeric string of length y, y must be 5 or more. Names must contain a randomized string.

Enter a name template *   CPC-%USERNAME:5%-%RAND:5%

Figure 3.30 – Defining a Cloud PC naming template in the provisioning policy

9. The other option is to enable Windows Autopatch to have Microsoft take care of the Windows updates/patches of the Cloud PCs you are provisioning. We will cover how to enable Autopatch later in this chapter. When ready, click on **Next**.

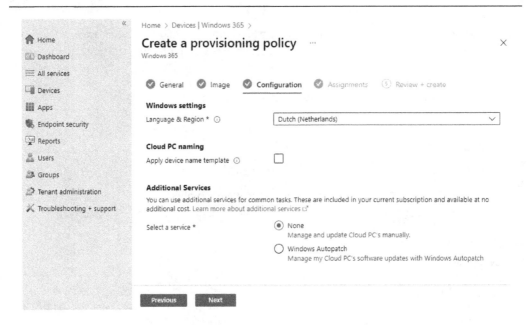

Figure 3.31 – Configuring the language and Autopatch

10. Assign the provisioning policy to an Azure AD Group. Users in this group need to have a Windows 365 license assigned. Choose **Next**.

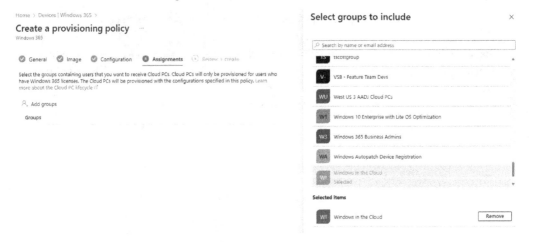

Figure 3.32 – Assigning a provisioning policy to a group of users

11. Once you have validated the settings you configured via the summary, click on **Create** to start the Cloud PC provisioning process. It takes around 30-40 minutes to finalize the provisioning of Cloud PCs.

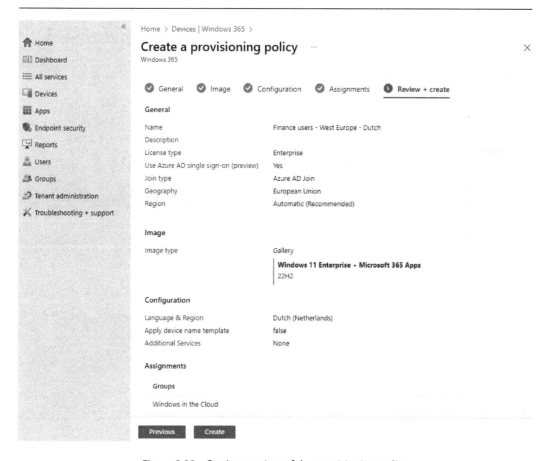

Figure 3.33 – Settings review of the provisioning policy

Setting up Windows 365 Frontline is very similar to provisioning regular Cloud PCs in Microsoft Intune. The only difference is that you need to select **Frontline** as the license type:

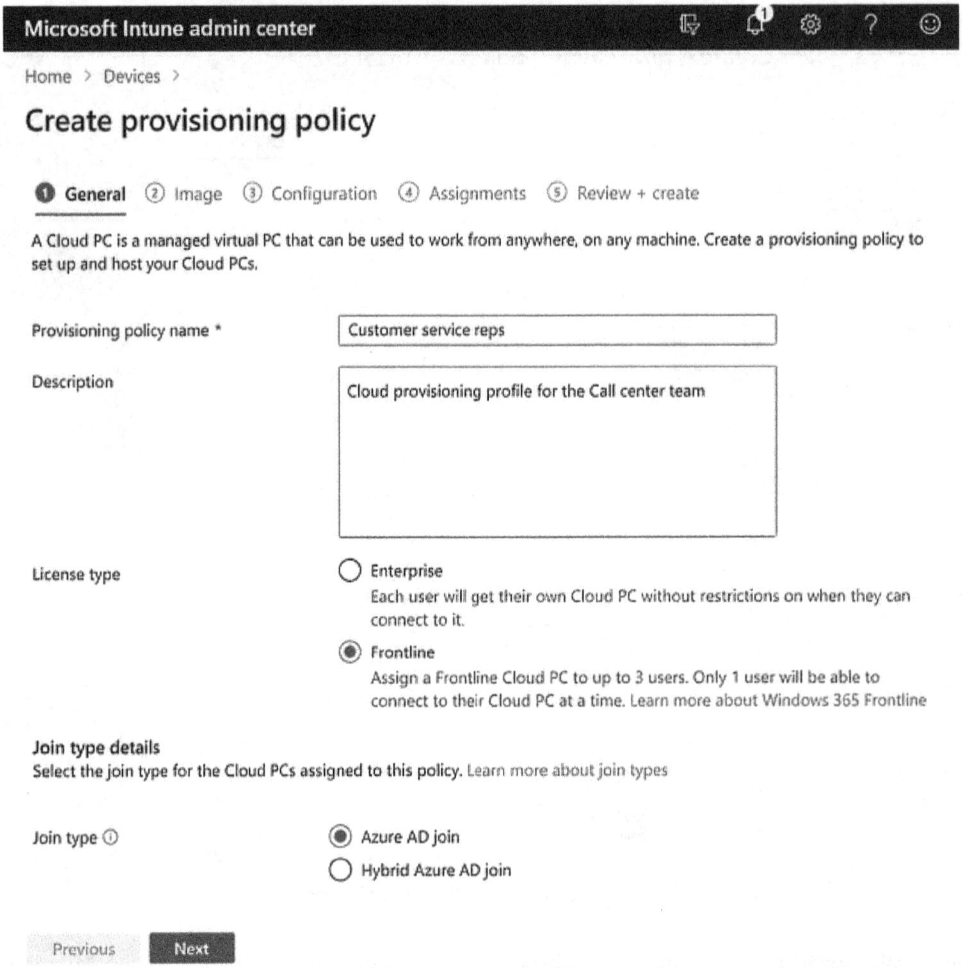

Figure 3.34 – Selecting the Frontline license type

Under **Assignments**, you can view the Windows 365 Frontline Cloud PCs that have been purchased by your organization and target them to a specific group of individuals. For example, you can see that you are entitled to provision 30 Cloud PCs because 10 licenses were purchased.

Select the **Customer service reps Manila** group you created earlier and assign the 2 vCPU/8-GB/128-GB Cloud PC configuration to this group:

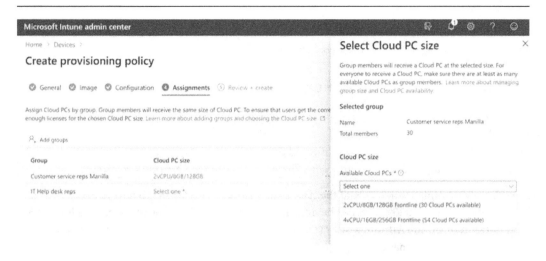

Figure 3.35 – Selecting the Cloud PC size

After assigning the right Frontline Cloud PC size per Azure AD group configuration, you are ready. The Cloud PC will start provisioning automatically if the user(s) you want to assign a Frontline Cloud PC with are in the Azure AD group assigned.

Make sure to review the set of configuration items in the **Review + create** menu. Once ready, hit the **Create** button.

This wraps up how to provision a Cloud PC. Let's continue with a look at custom images, the requirements, and how to create them.

Creating custom images

When configuring your provisioning policy, you will be able to choose between **gallery images** and **custom images.** This section will describe and show you how to create a custom image for your Windows 365 environment.

Even though a custom image sounds like a good idea at first, always remember to consider the management overhead you will create by using custom images. We recommend using the gallery images because that will simplify the overall management of the Windows 365 environment. The gallery images will be updated monthly after the security patch release schedule of Windows servicing and delivery. The components that will be updated are as follows:

- Windows 10/11 monthly image updates
- Microsoft 365 apps security and feature updates
- Microsoft Teams updates
- WebRTC Redirector Service updates

If the built-in gallery images do not meet your needs and you do need to deploy Cloud PCs with a custom image, don't worry, we have got you covered.

Custom image pre-requirements

Before you can get started creating an image, some components need to be in place. You are not able to just upload any image from your local computer. The image must come from **Microsoft Azure**. This means uploading a custom image requires an Azure subscription. The image you want to upload must be of the **Managed Image** resource type; Shared Gallery images are not supported.

Besides having administrator access to the Azure subscription, you'll need to have access to image management in Windows 365. This can be done by having a **Global Administrator**, **Windows 365 Administrator**, or **Intune Administrator** role within Azure AD or creating a custom Windows 365 role that grants access to image management.

The custom image you create must fulfill the following requirements:

- Windows 10 Enterprise 20H2 or later.
- Windows 11 Enterprise 21H2 or later.
- Generation 2 images only.
- Only images from generalized VMs are supported.
- Multi-session images are not supported.
- A recovery partition is not supported.
- The minimum OS disk size should be 64 GB. It will be resized to the specified size depending on the Windows 365 license SKU.

Now that we have covered all the pre-requirements, let's get started with creating the custom image. There are three main steps we must go through, creating a virtual machine, creating a managed image, and uploading a custom image to Windows 365.

Creating a virtual machine

To get started, we need a virtual machine in an Azure subscription in the same tenant as our Windows 365 environment. When creating the virtual machine, it's important to remember the previous requirements:

1. Go to **Microsoft Azure** and begin the creation of a virtual machine. Fill out the required information – remember not to choose a multi-session image and choose a generation 2 image. Under **Security type**, choose **Standard**:

Home > Resource groups > RG-W365CUSTOMIMAGE-PROD-001 > Marketplace >

Create a virtual machine   ···   ✕

Basics   Disks   Networking   Management   Monitoring   Advanced   Tags   Review + create

Create a virtual machine that runs Linux or Windows. Select an image from Azure marketplace or use your own customized image. Complete the Basics tab then Review + create to provision a virtual machine with default parameters or review each tab for full customization. Learn more ⍐

Project details

Select the subscription to manage deployed resources and costs. Use resource groups like folders to organize and manage all your resources.

Subscription * ⓘ	pedholtlab-VSE ⌄

Resource group * ⓘ	RG-W365CUSTOMIMAGE-PROD-001 ⌄
                                Create new

Instance details

Virtual machine name * ⓘ	w365customimage ✓

Region * ⓘ	(Europe) West Europe ⌄

Availability options ⓘ	No infrastructure redundancy required ⌄

Security type ⓘ	Standard ⌄

Image * ⓘ	•— Windows 11 Enterprise, version 22H2 - x64 Gen2 ⌄
See all images	Configure VM generation

VM architecture ⓘ   ◯ Arm64
                      ⦿ x64

                      ❶ Arm64 is not supported with the selected image.

Review + create		< Previous	Next : Disks >	⅀ Give feedback

Figure 3.36 – Virtual machine creation | basic information

2. You can select any size you want. Keep in mind the cost, even though this is a virtual machine that will have a short lifetime.

3. Next type in a username and password for the local administrator.

4. Choose whether you would like to have inbound ports open for connections. Finally, confirm you have an eligible Windows 10/11 license. Once this is done, click **Next**.

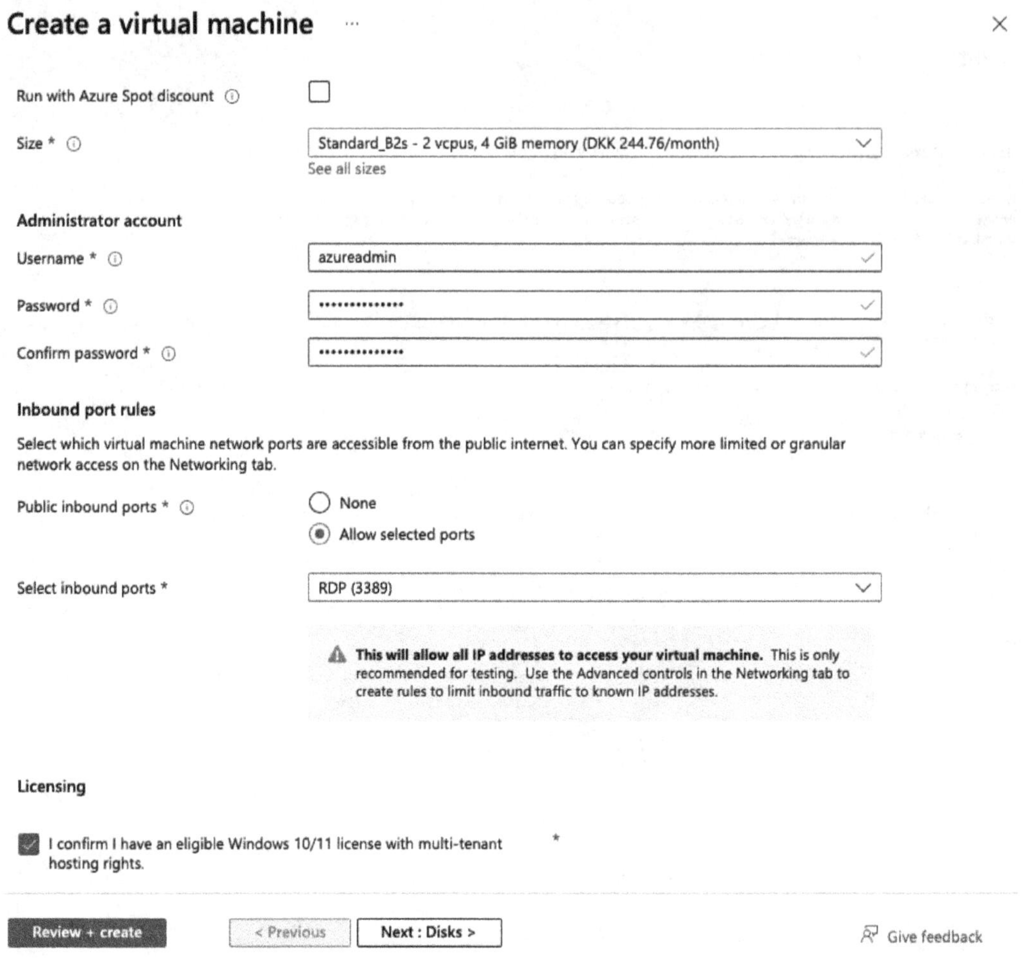

Create a virtual machine   ...   ✕

Run with Azure Spot discount ⓘ   ☐

Size * ⓘ   Standard_B2s - 2 vcpus, 4 GiB memory (DKK 244.76/month)   ˅
                                 See all sizes

Administrator account

Username * ⓘ   azureadmin   ✓

Password * ⓘ   ••••••••••••••   ✓

Confirm password * ⓘ   ••••••••••••••   ✓

Inbound port rules

Select which virtual machine network ports are accessible from the public internet. You can specify more limited or granular
network access on the Networking tab.

Public inbound ports * ⓘ   ◯ None
                                 ⦿ Allow selected ports

Select inbound ports *   RDP (3389)   ˅

                                 ⚠ **This will allow all IP addresses to access your virtual machine.** This is only
                                    recommended for testing. Use the Advanced controls in the Networking tab to
                                    create rules to limit inbound traffic to known IP addresses.

Licensing

☑ I confirm I have an eligible Windows 10/11 license with multi-tenant   *
  hosting rights.

[Review + create]   [< Previous]   [Next : Disks >]   ⨎ Give feedback

Figure 3.37 – Virtual machine creation | local administrator

5.   Now, choose which disk type you want to create the virtual machine with. You can leave
     everything with the default settings if you like. Once everything is chosen, click on **Next**.

Home > Virtual machines >

Create a virtual machine   ···   ✕

| Basics | **Disks** | Networking | Management | Monitoring | Advanced | Tags | Review + create |

Azure VMs have one operating system disk and a temporary disk for short-term storage. You can attach additional data disks. The size of the VM determines the type of storage you can use and the number of data disks allowed. Learn more ☐

VM disk encryption

Azure disk storage encryption automatically encrypts your data stored on Azure managed disks (OS and data disks) at rest by default when persisting it to the cloud.

Encryption at host ⓘ   ☐

        ⓘ Encryption at host is not registered for the selected subscription.
        Learn more about enabling this feature ☐

OS disk

OS disk type * ⓘ | Standard SSD (locally-redundant storage)   ∨ |

Choose Premium SSD disks for lower latency, higher IOPS and bandwidth, and bursting. Single instance virtual machines with Premium SSD disks qualify for the 99.9% connectivity SLA. Learn more

Delete with VM ⓘ   ☐

Key management ⓘ | Platform-managed key   ∨ |

Enable Ultra Disk compatibility ⓘ   ☐
        Ultra disk is not supported with selected security type.

Data disks for w365customimage

You can add and configure additional data disks for your virtual machine or attach existing disks. This VM also comes with a temporary disk.

LUN	Name	Size (GiB)	Disk type	Host caching	Delete with VM ⓘ

Create and attach a new disk   Attach an existing disk

| Review + create | | < Previous | Next : Networking > | ⅋ Give feedback |

Figure 3.38 – Virtual machine creation | disk overview

6.   Now it's time to specify the virtual network settings. You can create a new virtual network or choose an existing one. Click on **Next** when done configuring the **Networking** section.

> **Note**
>
> Remember that you will have to connect to this virtual machine once done creating, which can be done by a public IP or a private IP. If you want to connect with a private IP, you will need another device that has access to the virtual network.

Home > Virtual machines >

Create a virtual machine ···   ✕

Basics	Disks	**Networking**	Management	Monitoring	Advanced	Tags	Review + create

Define network connectivity for your virtual machine by configuring network interface card (NIC) settings. You can control ports, inbound and outbound connectivity with security group rules, or place behind an existing load balancing solution.
Learn more ⧉

Network interface

When creating a virtual machine, a network interface will be created for you.

Virtual network * ⓘ

    (new) w365customimage-vnet   ⌄
    Create new

Subnet * ⓘ

    (new) default (10.2.0.0/24)   ⌄

Public IP ⓘ

    (new) w365customimage-ip   ⌄
    Create new

NIC network security group ⓘ

    ○ None
    ○ Basic
    ◉ Advanced

Configure network security group *

    (new) w365customimage-nsg   ⌄
    Create new

Delete public IP and NIC when VM is
deleted ⓘ   ☐

Enable accelerated networking ⓘ   ☐
                                           The selected VM size does not support accelerated networking.

Load balancing

You can place this virtual machine in the backend pool of an existing Azure load balancing solution. Learn more ⧉

Place this virtual machine behind an   ☐
existing load balancing solution?

Review + create		< Previous	Next : Management >		℞ Give feedback

Figure 3.39 – Virtual machine creation | Networking overview

7. In the **Management** section, you can leave things as default or disable everything. As we said before, this virtual machine will have a limited lifetime. Click **Next** once you are done.

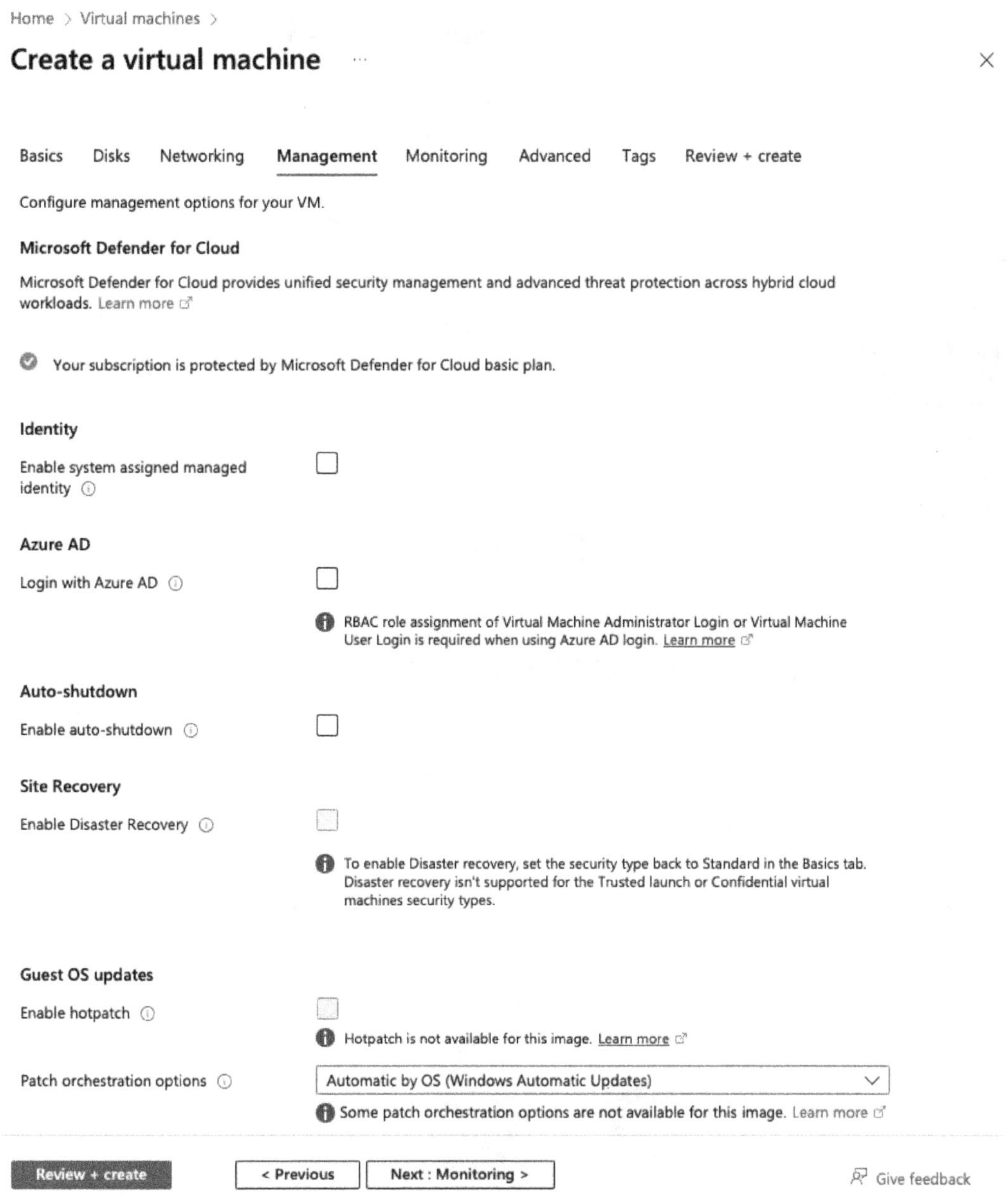

Home > Virtual machines >

Create a virtual machine   ...   ✕

Basics   Disks   Networking   **Management**   Monitoring   Advanced   Tags   Review + create

Configure management options for your VM.

Microsoft Defender for Cloud

Microsoft Defender for Cloud provides unified security management and advanced threat protection across hybrid cloud workloads. Learn more ⬚

✔ Your subscription is protected by Microsoft Defender for Cloud basic plan.

Identity

Enable system assigned managed identity ⓘ   ☐

Azure AD

Login with Azure AD ⓘ   ☐

ⓘ RBAC role assignment of Virtual Machine Administrator Login or Virtual Machine User Login is required when using Azure AD login. Learn more ⬚

Auto-shutdown

Enable auto-shutdown ⓘ   ☐

Site Recovery

Enable Disaster Recovery ⓘ   ☐

ⓘ To enable Disaster recovery, set the security type back to Standard in the Basics tab. Disaster recovery isn't supported for the Trusted launch or Confidential virtual machines security types.

Guest OS updates

Enable hotpatch ⓘ   ☐
ⓘ Hotpatch is not available for this image. Learn more ⬚

Patch orchestration options ⓘ | Automatic by OS (Windows Automatic Updates)   ⌄ |
ⓘ Some patch orchestration options are not available for this image. Learn more ⬚

| Review + create | | < Previous | Next : Monitoring > | ⏏ Give feedback

Figure 3.40 – Virtual machine creation | Management overview

8. In the **Monitoring** section, you can leave everything here as default and click on **Next**.

Home > Virtual machines >

Create a virtual machine   ...   ✕

Basics   Disks   Networking   Management   **Monitoring**   Advanced   Tags   Review + create

Configure monitoring options for your VM.

Alerts

Enable recommended alert rules ⓘ   ☐

Diagnostics

Boot diagnostics ⓘ   ⦿ Enable with managed storage account (recommended)
                                       ○ Enable with custom storage account
                                       ○ Disable

Enable OS guest diagnostics ⓘ   ☐

| Review + create | | < Previous | Next : Advanced > | | ℞ Give feedback |

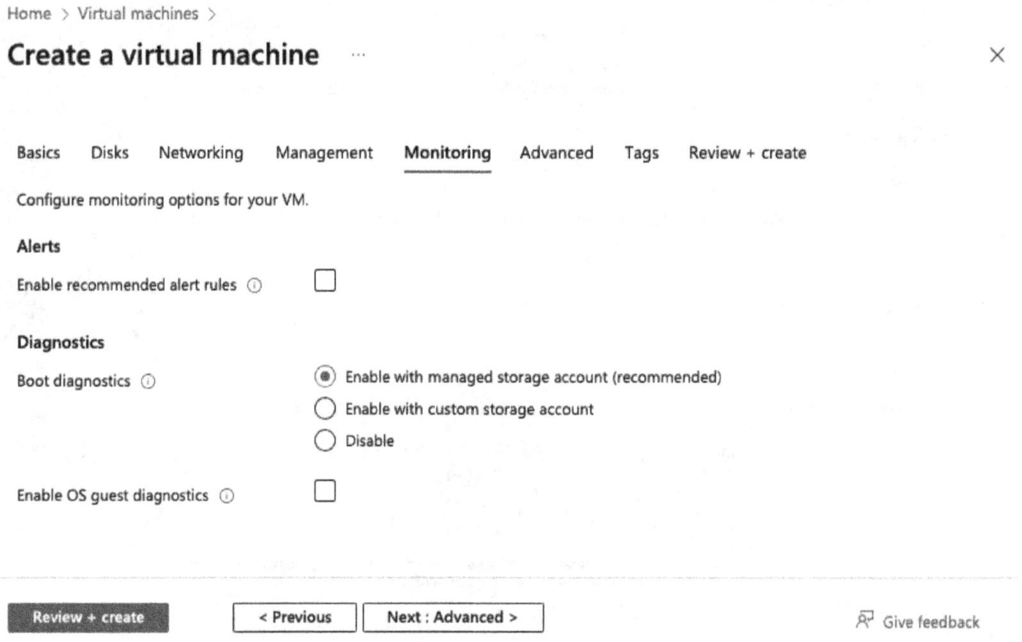

Figure 3.41 – Virtual machine creation | Monitoring overview

9. In the **Advanced** section, leave everything here as default and click on **Next**.

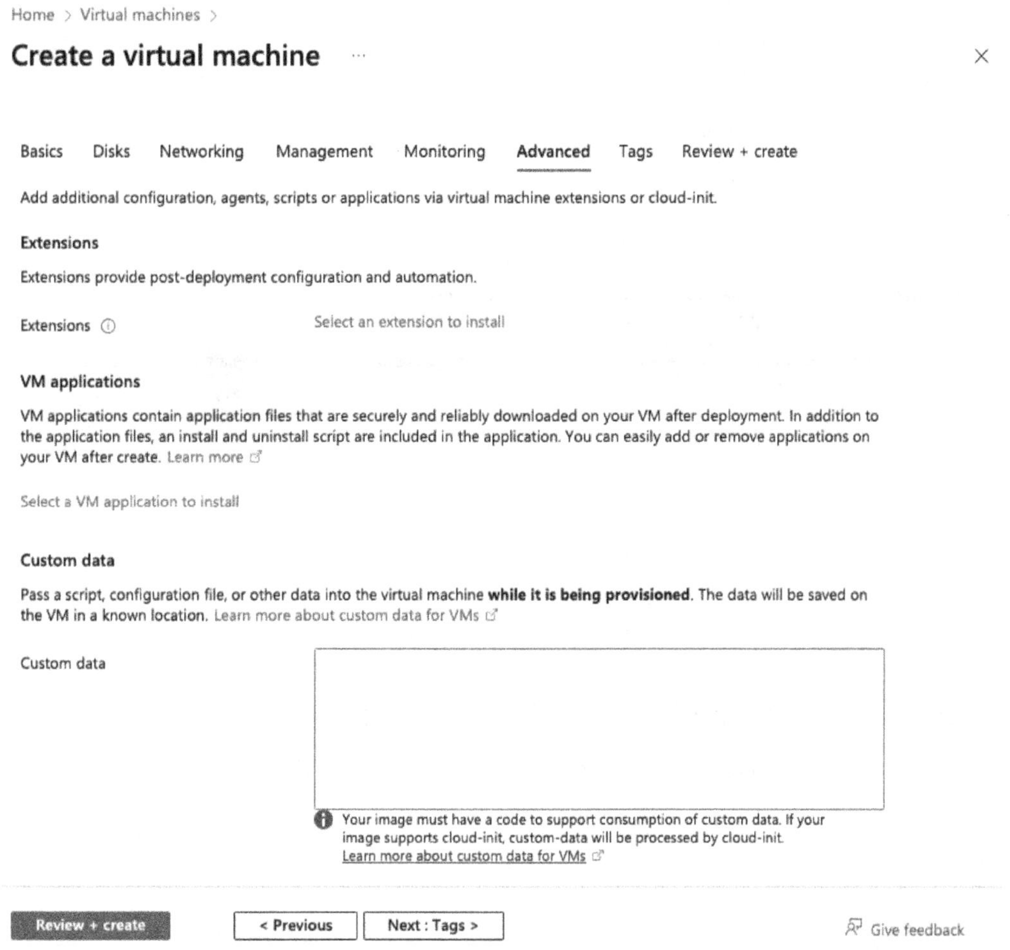

Home > Virtual machines >

Create a virtual machine   ...   ×

Basics   Disks   Networking   Management   Monitoring   **Advanced**   Tags   Review + create

Add additional configuration, agents, scripts or applications via virtual machine extensions or cloud-init.

Extensions

Extensions provide post-deployment configuration and automation.

Extensions ⓘ   Select an extension to install

VM applications

VM applications contain application files that are securely and reliably downloaded on your VM after deployment. In addition to the application files, an install and uninstall script are included in the application. You can easily add or remove applications on your VM after create. Learn more ⌕

Select a VM application to install

Custom data

Pass a script, configuration file, or other data into the virtual machine **while it is being provisioned**. The data will be saved on the VM in a known location. Learn more about custom data for VMs ⌕

Custom data

ⓘ Your image must have a code to support consumption of custom data. If your image supports cloud-init, custom-data will be processed by cloud-init.
Learn more about custom data for VMs ⌕

[Review + create]   [< Previous] [Next : Tags >]   ⯈ Give feedback

Figure 3.42 – Virtual machine creation | Advanced overview

10. In this section, you can fill in your Azure Tags if you have any. Once done, click on **Next**.

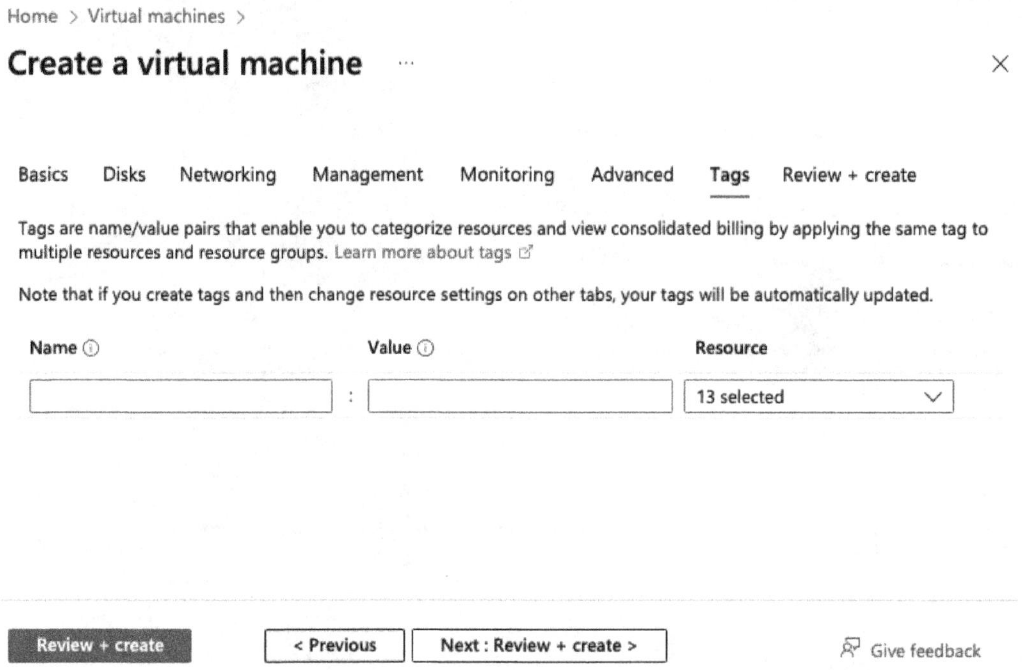

Home > Virtual machines >

Create a virtual machine   ...   ✕

Basics   Disks   Networking   Management   Monitoring   Advanced   **Tags**   Review + create

Tags are name/value pairs that enable you to categorize resources and view consolidated billing by applying the same tag to multiple resources and resource groups. Learn more about tags ☑

Note that if you create tags and then change resource settings on other tabs, your tags will be automatically updated.

Name ⓘ		Value ⓘ	Resource
	:		13 selected ⌄

[Review + create]   [< Previous]   [Next : Review + create >]   🗩 Give feedback

Figure 3.43 – Virtual machine creation | Tags overview

11. Review all the settings and click **Create**.

Home > Virtual machines >

Create a virtual machine   ...   ✕

✓ Validation passed

Basics   Disks   Networking   Management   Monitoring   Advanced   Tags   **Review + create**

> ⓘ Cost given below is an estimate and not the final price. Please use Pricing calculator for all your pricing needs.

Price

1 X Standard B2s	Subscription credits apply ⓘ
by Microsoft	**0.3353 DKK/hr**
Terms of use | Privacy policy	Pricing for other VM sizes

TERMS

By clicking "Create", I (a) agree to the legal terms and privacy statement(s) associated with the Marketplace offering(s) listed above; (b) authorize Microsoft to bill my current payment method for the fees associated with the offering(s), with the same billing frequency as my Azure subscription; and (c) agree that Microsoft may share my contact, usage and transactional information with the provider(s) of the offering(s) for support, billing and other transactional activities. Microsoft does not provide rights for third-party offerings. See the Azure Marketplace Terms for additional details.

Basics

Subscription	pedholtlab-VSE
Resource group	(new) rg-w365customimage-prod-001
Virtual machine name	w365customimage
Region	West Europe
Availability options	No infrastructure redundancy required

| Create | | < Previous | Next > | Download a template for automation | ⅋ Give feedback |

Figure 3.44 – VM creation | review settings

12. Now that we have a virtual machine in Azure, we can log in to the virtual machine and customize it. Once we are done with that, proceed to the next section where we will convert that virtual machine into a managed image.

Creating a managed image

Now that we have a virtual machine with all the custom configurations we want, it's time to convert that machine into a managed image.

1. To do this, we need to log in to the machine and start Sysprep. It's important to choose the following in the Sysprep process:

    - **System Cleanup Action: Enter System Out-of-Box Experience (OOBE)**

    - **Generalize:** Yes

    - **Shutdown Options: Shutdown**

2. Connect to the machine, go to `C:\Windows\System32\Sysprep`, and start `Sysprep.exe` as an administrator. Once you are ready, click **OK**. The process will now begin, and the virtual machine will now be shut down:

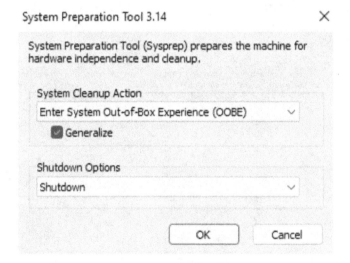

Figure 3.45 – Sysprep settings

3. Once Sysprep is done and the status of the virtual machine is shown as **Stopped** in the virtual machine overview in Azure, go ahead and select **Capture** in the top panel.

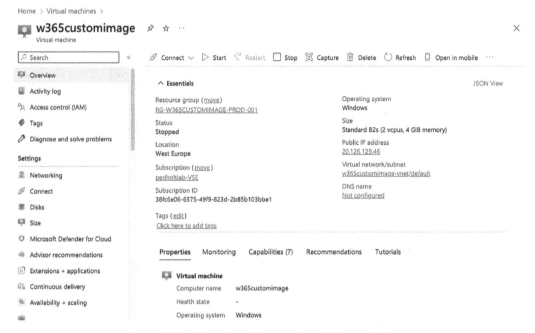

Figure 3.46 – Virtual machine overview in Microsoft Azure

4. Under the **Capture** section, select **No, capture only a managed image**. Custom images are not supported with Windows 365. Once that is defined, fill out the other information as you want to. Click on **Next**.

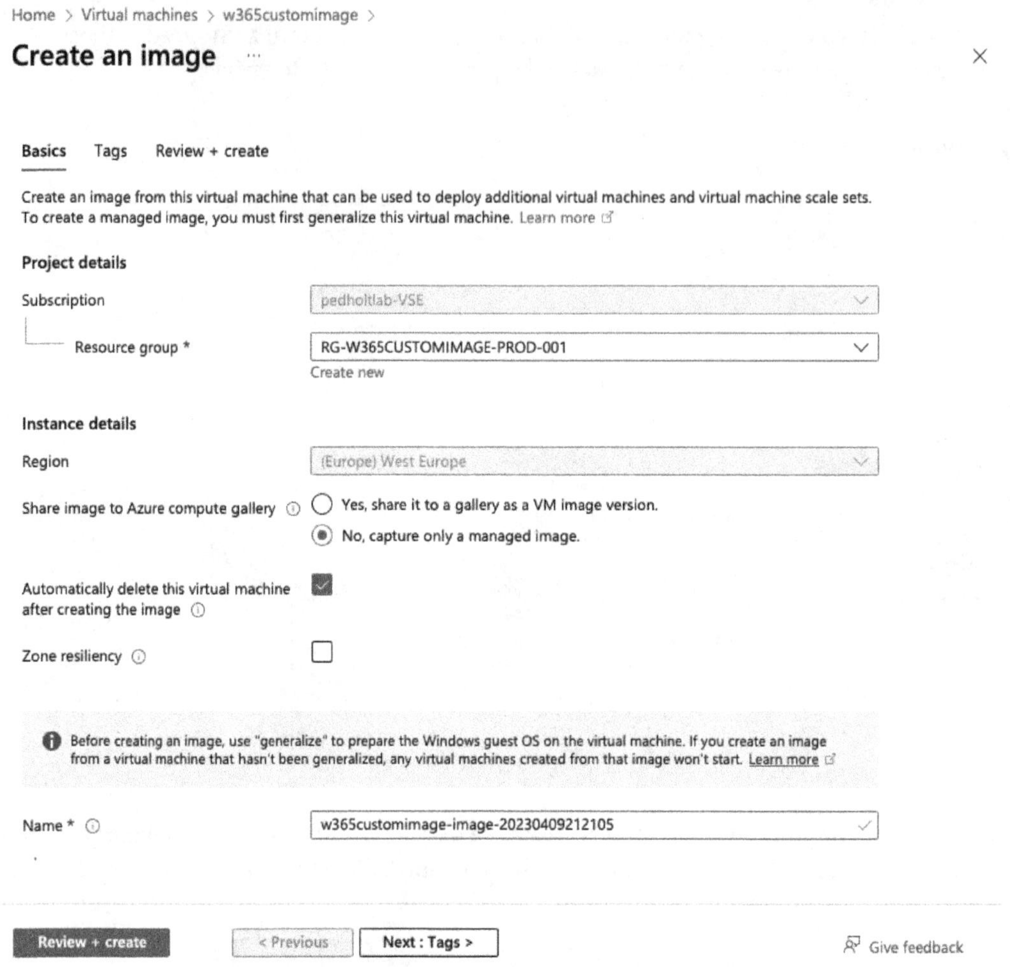

Home > Virtual machines > w365customimage >

Create an image   ...   ✕

Basics   Tags   Review + create

Create an image from this virtual machine that can be used to deploy additional virtual machines and virtual machine scale sets.
To create a managed image, you must first generalize this virtual machine. Learn more ⎘

Project details

Subscription | pedholtlab-VSE   ⌄ |

Resource group * | RG-W365CUSTOMIMAGE-PROD-001   ⌄ |
                                                  Create new

Instance details

Region | (Europe) West Europe   ⌄ |

Share image to Azure compute gallery ⓘ   ◯ Yes, share it to a gallery as a VM image version.
                                             ◉ No, capture only a managed image.

Automatically delete this virtual machine   ☑
after creating the image ⓘ

Zone resiliency ⓘ   ☐

> ⓘ Before creating an image, use "generalize" to prepare the Windows guest OS on the virtual machine. If you create an image
> from a virtual machine that hasn't been generalized, any virtual machines created from that image won't start. Learn more ⎘

Name * ⓘ | w365customimage-image-20230409212105   ✓ |

[Review + create]   [< Previous]   [Next : Tags >]   ⧎ Give feedback

Figure 3.47 – Create a managed image | Basics settings

5. Next, you can fill in your Azure Tags if you have any. Once done, click on **Review + create**:

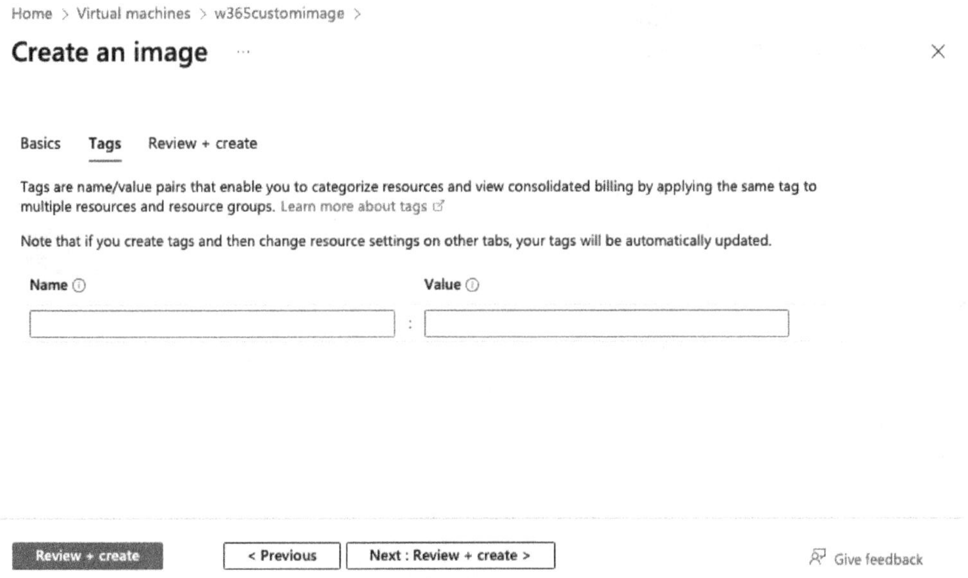

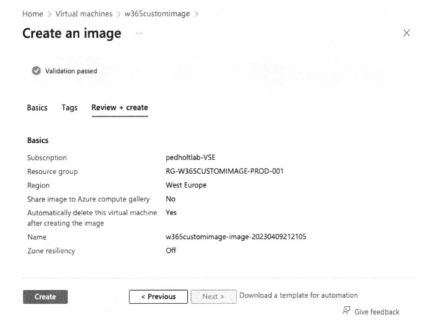

Figure 3.48 – Creating a managed image | Tags settings

6. Next review the settings you just specified in the previous steps and click on **Create**:

Figure 3.49 – Creating a managed image | review settings

After the creation is done, you should have a managed image inside the resource group you have chosen.

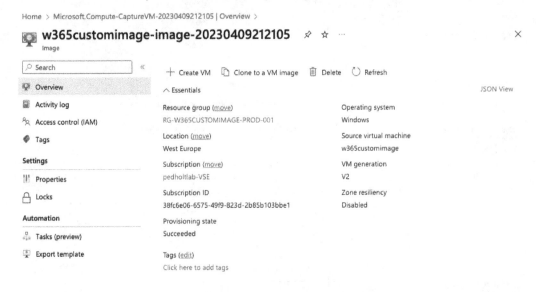

Figure 3.50 – Managed image overview

Uploading a custom image to Windows 365

Now we have the managed image, it is time to upload it to Windows 365:

1. Go to the **Custom Image** section under **Windows 365** in **Microsoft Intune**. From here, click on **Add**.

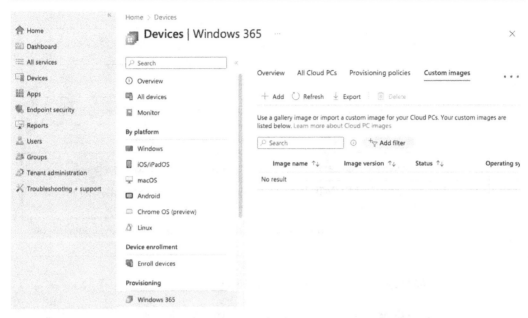

Figure 3.51 – Custom image upload section in Microsoft Intune

2. Give the image a name and version number. Select a **Subscription** option and under **Source image**, select the newly created custom image. Once that is done, click on **Add**:

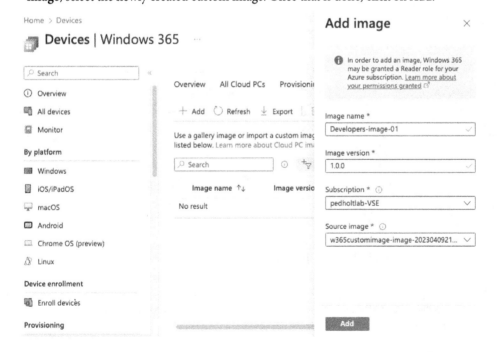

Figure 3.52 – Adding a custom image to Windows 365

3. When the upload begins, there are several steps that will be taken to ensure all the requirements are fulfilled and it will be supported in any region where you might have a network connection.

Step	Description
1	Copies the image to a temporary Azure subscription managed by Microsoft
2	Checks all custom image requirements are met
3	Creates a temporary virtual machine to verify the custom image
4	If you have a HAADJ ANC, Windows 365 replicates the image across all Azure regions where you have an Azure network connection
5	If you have an AADJ ANC, Windows 365 replicates the image to the provisioned region during provisioning

Table 3.8 – Upload flow of a managed image to Windows 365

Once the image is done uploading, you will see it in the overview with custom images, you will be able to see information about the image such as the image version, operating system, and OS support status:

Figure 3.53 – Uploaded custom image information overview

You are now all set to use the image with your Cloud PCs. When you create or edit a provisioning policy, you can select the custom image. You can go ahead and delete the custom image in your Azure subscription if you want to.

Configuring Windows 365 Boot

Windows 365 Boot is one of the newest Windows integrations released as part of Windows 365 and Windows 11. The feature allows users to boot directly to Cloud PCs from the initial Windows login screen, meaning that the friction of logging on to local Windows first, opening the Windows 365 app, and clicking **Connect** completely vanishes!

In this section, we will explain how you can push the Windows 365 Boot components to your Windows 11 endpoints via Microsoft Intune via a simplified guided flow scenario that is purposely built for this feature. Let us get started!

1. Go to **Devices** | **Provisioning** | **Overview** and open the **Windows 365 Boot** guide. You will be forwarded to the Boot to Cloud guided flow scenario:

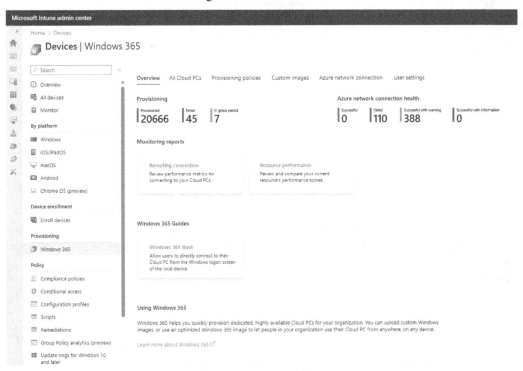

Figure 3.54 - Windows 365 section in Microsoft Intune

> **Note**
>
> To move forward, you need to have at least Group and Intune Administrator rights.

2. Click on **Next: Basics >** to start the configuration:

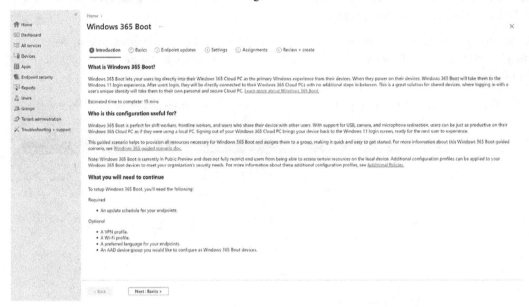

Figure 3.55 – Microsoft Intune Boot to Cloud PC guide

3. The following setting is optional but can be extremely useful to rename your endpoints to start with something such as BTC for Boot to Cloud PC to identify endpoints remotely.

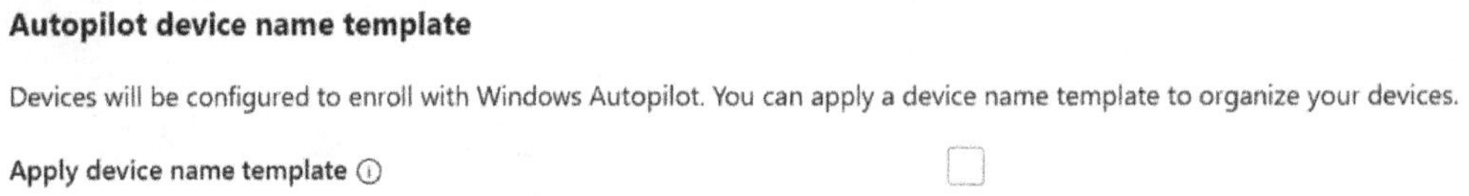

Autopilot device name template

Devices will be configured to enroll with Windows Autopilot. You can apply a device name template to organize your devices.

Apply device name template ⓘ

Figure 3.56 – Autopilot device name template

During this setup, the setup creates the following resources:

*   \<prefix\> Windows 365 app
*   \<prefix\> AVD host app
*   \<prefix\> ESP

- `<prefix>` Autopilot profile

- `<prefix>` Device Configuration

- `<prefix>` PREVIOUS AAD group

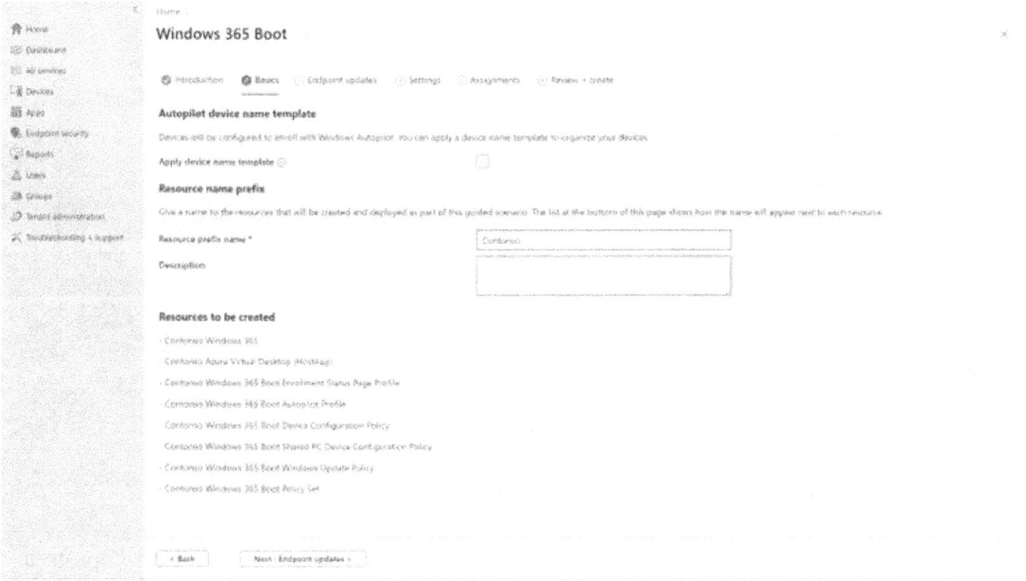

Figure 3.57 – Resource prefix name

The following list of settings is all related to Windows Updates. As there is no local Windows UI/shell available to the user, and it is a shared PC, it is important that you ensure that Windows remains secure proactively.

> **Note**
>
> Windows 365 Boot also supports Windows Autopatch to relieve you of doing patch management on the Boot to Cloud endpoint.

The first setting ensures that quality and feature updates are being applied after they are released, for example, on Patch Tuesday.

The second setting provides the option to add working hours during which a restart can be applied so as not to disturb the productivity of an end user.

The last setting is to ensure updates are being installed and applied in a certain amount of time to ensure your end users are always using Windows securely when connecting to their Cloud PC:

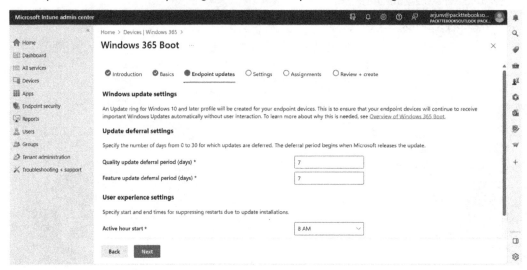

Figure 3.58 – Endpoint update settings

Once ready with your Windows Updates preferences, you can pre-configure VPN and Wi-Fi profiles to push to the endpoint. This setting is optional.

The **Language** setting is to provide the local language you prefer to use on the endpoint, for example, for the Windows login screen. All languages that Windows 11 supports are configurable.

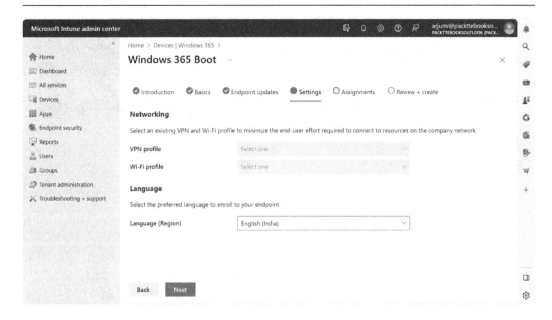

Figure 3.59 – Networking and Language settings

The last setting is simple – you must either create or assign an existing Azure AD group to the set of resources to assign to:

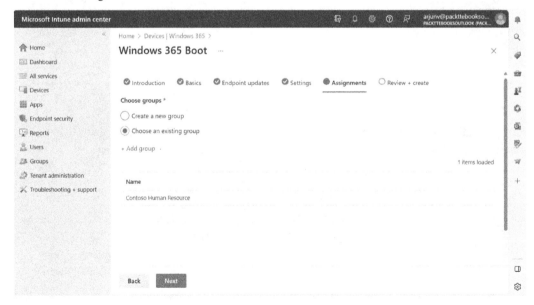

Figure 3.60 – User assignment

Check all your settings on the summary page and proceed. We recommend assigning the settings to Windows 11 endpoints that received a wipe or just came out of the box. If you deploy Windows 365 Boot to existing Windows 11 endpoints, we recommend you remotely wipe the endpoint after finishing this configuration:

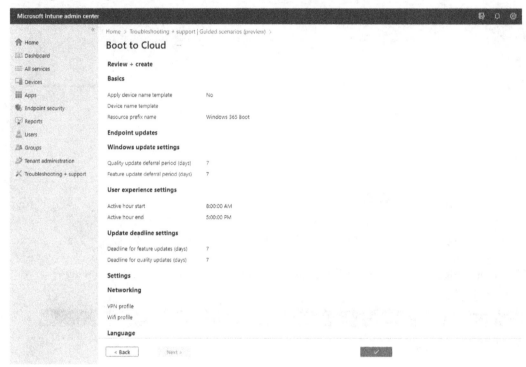

Figure 3.61 – Summary page

Once ready, all your endpoints in the AAD group you either attached or created new will get the resources assigned and be transformed into Boot to Cloud mode in a couple of hours.

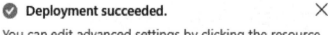

Figure 3.62 – Deployment succeeded notification

You have now learned how easy it is to configure Windows 365 Boot. Let's now talk about the migration part.

Migrating to Windows 365 – profiles and data

In this section, we will go through what to consider in terms of migrating existing solutions to Windows 365. The solutions we typically hear about are traditional **Virtual Desktop Infrastructure** (**VDI**) solutions such as Citrix, Amazon Workspaces, Remote Desktop Services, and others.

VDI environments have a lot of different components and policies that you wouldn't have to consider on a Windows 365 environment such as profile disk configuration, actions that prevent users from changing settings impacting all users on the VDI platform, the infrastructure behind the solution, and more.

What needs to be focused on are the user data, applications, settings configurations, and overall security around the existing environment. As Windows 365 is fully integrated into Microsoft Intune, we recommend configuring applications and security configurations there. It's of course also possible outside of Microsoft Intune – for example, using Configuration Manager (ConfigMgr). Because the Cloud PCs inside Windows 365 are personal computers, they should be configured as existing personal computers to simplify the management overhead of all devices. Let's focus on how to move these things to Microsoft Intune and where we can configure them.

Applications and configurations

For standard applications such as Microsoft 365 Apps and Microsoft Edge, it's quite easy to get started and deploy them. There is a built-in template you can use to deploy those apps, alongside Microsoft Store Apps. Other applications must be wrapped into a `.Intunewin` file to deploy it from Microsoft Intune. Windows settings can be configured within a Configuration Profile that can hold one or more settings just as you might know from Group Policy Management in Active Directory. The key thing here is to get an overview of all the applications and Windows settings that should be moved over to the new Windows 365 environment. It's a good time to walk through the different things and do a bit of cleanup from old applications and configurations from the past.

We will include more on how to deploy applications and configure Configuration Profiles in *Chapter 4*.

Security

There are different security tools available on the market to keep your devices secure. You are most likely already to have a security tool installed on your physical PCs, and you will most likely be able to use the same tool on Cloud PCs. We do, however, have good experience and recommend using Microsoft Defender for Endpoint, not only because it's fully integrated into Microsoft Intune, so the deployment process is very easy, but also because it contains a lot of features such as machine learning for detecting and responding to attacks, including malware, ransomware, and zero-day exploits. Besides that, it can work together across Microsoft services that you might already use to get a complete picture if something happens.

We have more on onboarding your Cloud PC devices into Microsoft Defender for Endpoint in *Chapter 6*. If you already are onboarding all your Intune devices into Microsoft Defender for Endpoint, your future Cloud PC devices will automatically be onboarded as well.

User data

User data such as saved documents, pictures, and browser favorites is most likely to be the most common things end users will start using when coming onto a new environment like a Cloud PC. We don't want to manually tell the users to copy their data out of the current environment and upload it to their new Cloud PC as this will be very frustrating for them and there are also some security concerns about that approach.

To make the process more seamless and secure, we can use Microsoft OneDrive to carry over the saved documents under the `Pictures`, `Desktop`, and `Documents` folders. Microsoft OneDrive allows users to store, sync, and share files, documents, and photos across devices.

To carry over browser favorites, a Microsoft Edge Configuration Profile can be made to automatically synchronize settings and favorites with a company identity across devices. Both the Microsoft OneDrive and Microsoft Edge configuration must be done on the current environment you are migrating from. This is required to capture the data and Edge configuration and synchronize it with the new environment. We do recommend enabling and configuring it before the migration takes place to make sure every user has their files synchronized. This configuration can of course be made in Microsoft Intune, but you might not have your current environment enrolled in Microsoft Intune, in which case you are able to configure the same settings in Group Policy Management in Active Directory to enable and configure it.

When deploying new Cloud PCs from the available gallery images, OneDrive will already be preinstalled into those images and ready to use. If you have any intention of using custom images, you will have to install and configure OneDrive yourself. This can be done through the Microsoft 365 Apps and Configuration Profile section in Microsoft Intune.

A Microsoft Edge policy must always be created as a Configuration Profile for it to work.

That wraps up the migration part. Overall, it's important to gain visibility of all the configurations and settings you want to move to the Cloud PCs. Once you have that knowledge, you can start to plan what applications that need to be configured in Microsoft Intune and so on.

Let's jump into the last section of this chapter on how to enable Windows Autopatch.

Enabling Windows Autopatch

We explained Windows Autopatch in the first chapter of this book. In this section, we will explain how you can enable this service inside your Microsoft Intune tenant settings. Windows Autopatch works fully cloud with Microsoft Intune and co-management:

> **Note**
>
> Before you continue, ensure that you have the required licenses of Windows Autopatch enabled inside your tenant.

1. To enable Windows Autopatch, you must go to **Tenant admin | Tenant enrollment**. Run checks can help to see whether you need to perform steps before you can enable the service inside your tenant:

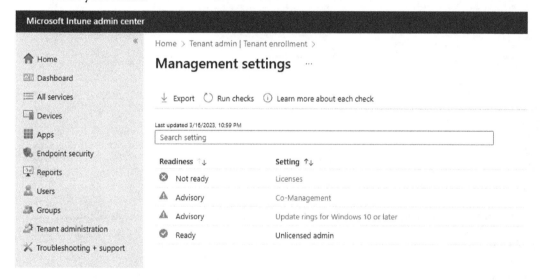

Figure 3.63 – Management settings

2. Enabling Windows Autopatch is simple. If you have the proper licenses, you only have to agree to the terms and conditions:

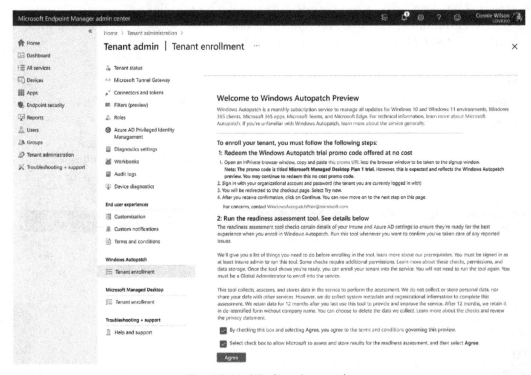

Figure 3.64 – Windows Autopatch

3. Once everything runs successfully, you can start the enrollment via the **Enroll** button.

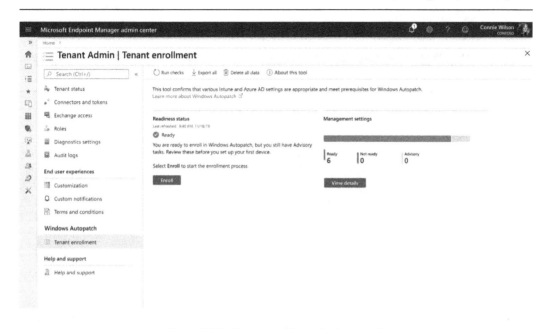

Figure 3.65 – Tenant enrolment in Autopatch

4.   As Autopatch is a service managed by Microsoft, you must provide certain delegated permissions to Microsoft. Once you agree, click on **Agree**.

Figure 3.66 – Enabling Autopatch in your tenant

5.   Provide your IT admin contact details to Microsoft. Once ready, hit **Complete**.

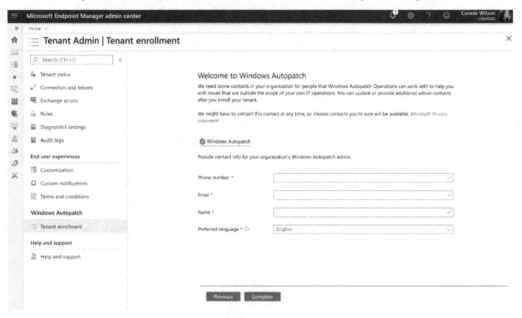

Figure 3.67 – Setting up Autopatch contact info

6.   Windows Autopatch will be set up; this takes only a few minutes:

Figure 3.68 – Setting up Autopatch

7.   Once the setup is complete, you will see the following confirmation screen.

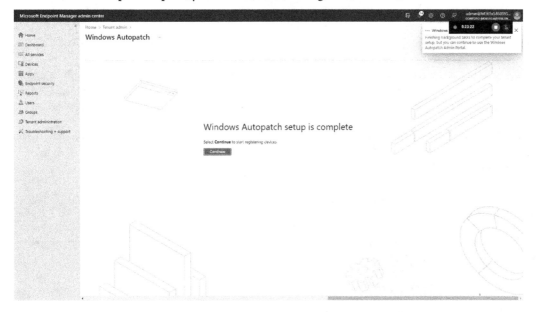

Figure 3.69 – Autopatch setup complete

8.   Once we are ready with the steps, you can flip the switch inside your Cloud PC provisioning policies to **Windows Autopatch** – under **Microsoft managed services**.

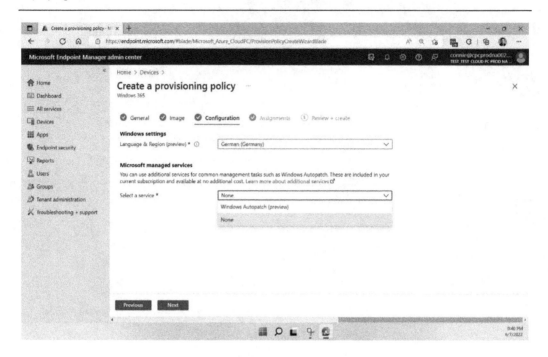

Figure 3.70 – Enabling Autopatch per provisioning policy

Summary

In the chapter, you learned everything about deploying Windows 365 Cloud PCs via Microsoft Intune, configuring networking, custom images, Windows 365 Boot, and how to approach a migration to Windows 365.

In the next chapter, we will cover how to manage different things such as resizing Cloud PCs, Windows settings, application deployment, and more – all the things that are essential to managing your Windows 365.

Questions

At the end of each chapter, we ask three questions to evaluate your learning and challenge you as well. Here are the next three questions:

1. How do you manually trigger a health check for an ANC?

2. What is the easiest way to set up Windows 365 Boot?

3. What generation images are supported for custom images in Windows 365?

Further reading

Please continue your learning journey while going through the other chapters. If you want to learn more about the subjects covered in this chapter, please visit any of these online resources:

- *To learn more about Azure networking and how you can create network architectures that best suit your needs, visit* `https://learn.microsoft.com/azure/networking`

- *To learn more about Microsoft Intune and how it can help manage your other company devices and even applications, visit* `https://learn.microsoft.com/intune`

- *To learn more about Microsoft's data protection and privacy principles, visit* `https://www.microsoft.com/trust-center/privacy`

4

Managing Cloud PCs

In this chapter, you will learn all the necessary steps to manage your Cloud PCs via the Microsoft Intune admin center. We will also review the features that help make your life as an IT admin much easier! Who doesn't want to learn about leaving more time free to drink beers and enjoy time with family due to the easiness of management?

In this chapter, we will cover the following subjects:

- Configuring an **Enrollment Status Page** (**ESP**) for a Cloud PC
- Moving Cloud PCs to another region
- Allowing users to reset their Cloud PCs
- Resizing Cloud PCs
- Bulk device actions
- Configuring configuration profiles
- Deploying applications to Cloud PCs
- Backing up and restoring Cloud PCs

Configuring an ESP for a Cloud PC

An ESP is commonly used to display the provisioning status when enrolling with Intune. It's a detailed progress indicator. An ESP is designed to be displayed while a user waits for their device to be ready. When using Windows Autopilot to provision new physical Windows devices, the ESP runs in two phases – the device ESP and the user ESP. The device ESP runs only during the default **out-of-the-box experience** (**OOBE**). When provisioning Cloud PCs, the device ESP is not used, as there's no OOBE phase – only the user ESP. An ESP helps to give the user the best first-time impression by ensuring the settings and applications are installed on their Cloud PC before they use the desktop for the first time.

Important ESP settings

Almost all the settings that are available within the ESP are basically down to how you want the experience to be for a user. There is, however, one thing that is important when configuring an ESP for Cloud PCs. The **Allow users to reset device if installation error occurs** setting must be set to **No**. If this setting is enabled, the user will be able to reset the device from the ESP screen if it fails during the installation. Even though this sounds like a good feature, if the reset is initiated from the ESP, the Cloud PC will not work because Cloud PCs are deployed with agents in a specific flow that allows users to connect. This is all handled when the Windows 365 service deploys the Cloud PC device.

If the ESP fails for a user, you as administrator should reprovision the devices within Microsoft Intune. You can give the user the ability to access their desktop if the ESP fails; that way, the user might still be able to be productive, and issues can be fixed along the way. To enable this feature, set **Allows users to use device if installation errors occurs** to **Yes**.

Assignment of the ESP

The ESP profile is applied in the early stages of the new deployment of a PC. The deployment flow for a Cloud PC works slightly differently from a physical device. The big difference is that Cloud PC deployment is a user-less enrollment. This means that the assignment must be targeted toward the devices and not user assignments.

Dynamic groups in Azure AD have been commonly used when targeting Intune policies to different device types. Because of the latency that dynamic groups have and the deployment flow of Cloud PCs, an ESP will not work with a dynamic group as the assignment. Instead, you need to use the **Filter** feature. The filter you create must be created with the enrollmentProfileName property.

We will cover how to configure a filter for Cloud PCs in the *Configuring configuration profiles* section later in this chapter.

To be clear – when assigning an ESP for Windows 365 devices, always use **All Devices** with a filter you have defined for your Cloud PCs.

Configuring an ESP

Now we know what's important when creating an ESP for Cloud PCs, let's have a look at how to configure it:

1. To get started, go to **Microsoft Intune | Devices | Windows | Windows enrollment**. To start configuring an ESP, select **Enrollment Status Page**.

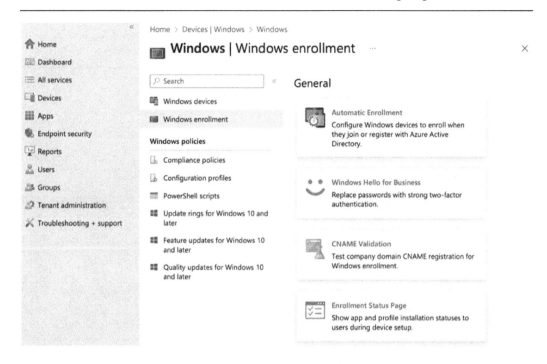

Figure 4.1 – A Windows enrollment overview

2.   Click on + **Create** at the top of the page:

Figure 4.2 – An ESP policy overview

3. Provide a name for the ESP policy. A description is optional.

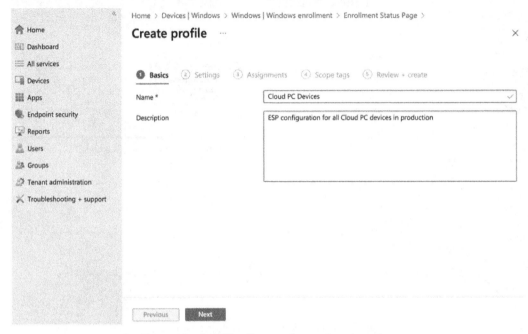

Figure 4.3 – An ESP policy creation settings overview

4. Select the setting you want; remember to set **Allow users to reset device if installation error occurs** to **No**. Once you are happy with the settings, select **Next**.

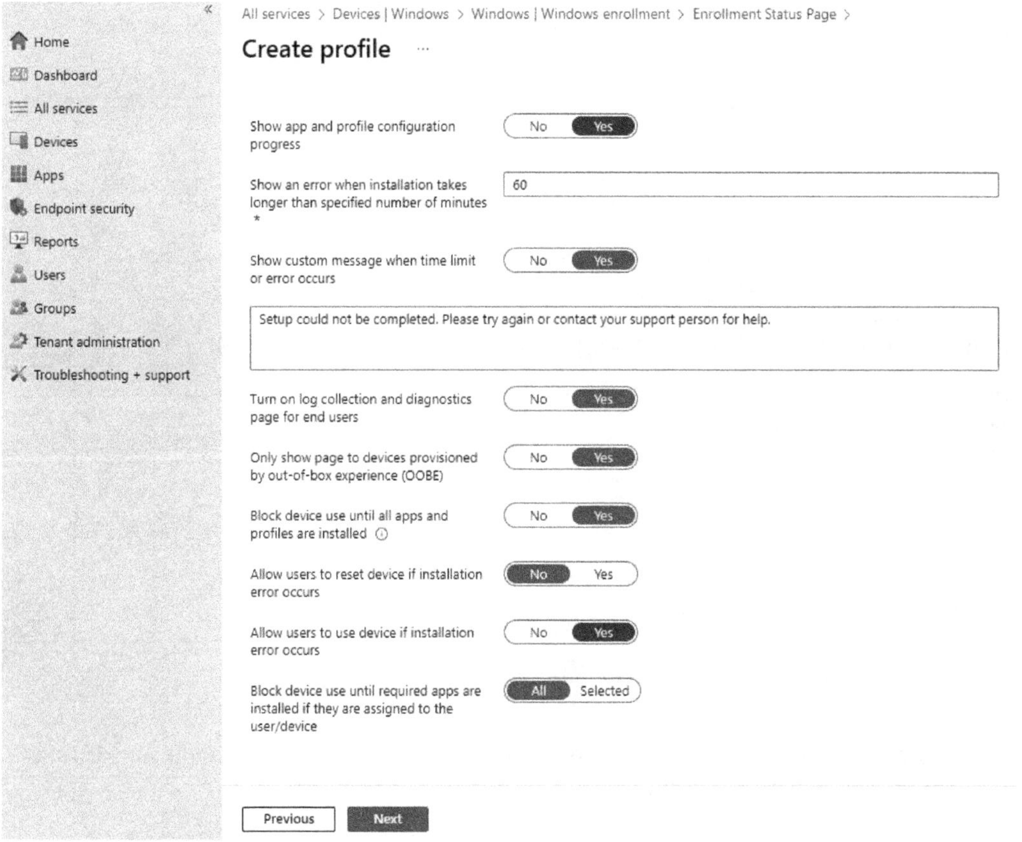

All services > Devices | Windows > Windows | Windows enrollment > Enrollment Status Page >

Create profile   ...

Show app and profile configuration progress — No **Yes**

Show an error when installation takes longer than specified number of minutes *

`60`

Show custom message when time limit or error occurs — No **Yes**

`Setup could not be completed. Please try again or contact your support person for help.`

Turn on log collection and diagnostics page for end users — No **Yes**

Only show page to devices provisioned by out-of-box experience (OOBE) — No **Yes**

Block device use until all apps and profiles are installed ⓘ — No **Yes**

Allow users to reset device if installation error occurs — **No** Yes

Allow users to use device if installation error occurs — No **Yes**

Block device use until required apps are installed if they are assigned to the user/device — **All** Selected

[Previous]   [Next]

Figure 4.4 – ESP policy creation settings definition

5.   Assign the ESP to **All devices** with a filter you have defined for Cloud PCs. Select **Next**.

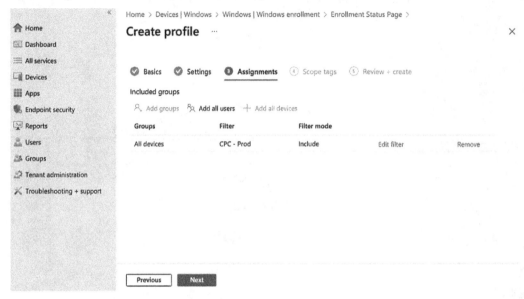

Figure 4.5 – ESP policy creation assignments

6.   Choose the scope tags you will use and select **Next**. Now, review all the configured settings; when you are happy, select **Create**.

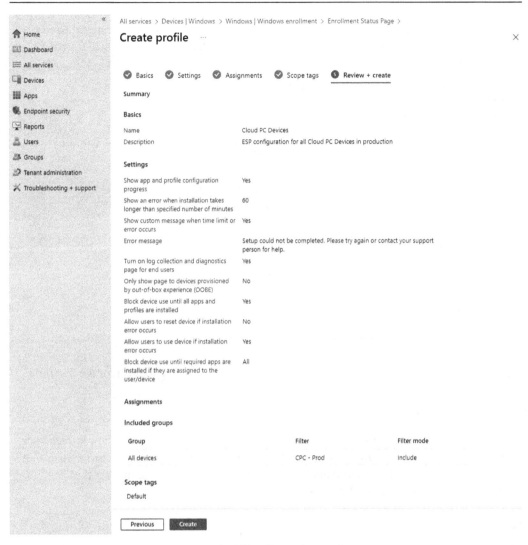

Figure 4.6 – ESP policy review settings

7. Once the ESP is created, you should see it in the ESP overview. You can rearrange the priority if you have multiple ESPs assigned to the same devices. The highest priority will start at **1**.

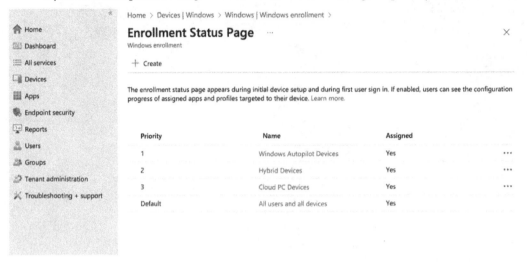

Figure 4.7 – An ESP policy overview after creation

Now that the ESP is configured, let's see how it looks to a user when they connect for the first time.

An end user experience

In *Figure 4.8*, you can see, the user will be presented with an ESP as you might know it from your enrollment on physical devices. Even though it's the same screen, some information isn't available for the ESP on the Cloud PC. The user will only see the account setup because of the way the Cloud PC is provisioned compared to physical devices.

> **Note**
>
> Seeing that a Cloud PC has been provisioned successfully doesn't mean the user has been through the ESP experience. An ESP will start the first time the user accesses their Cloud PC.

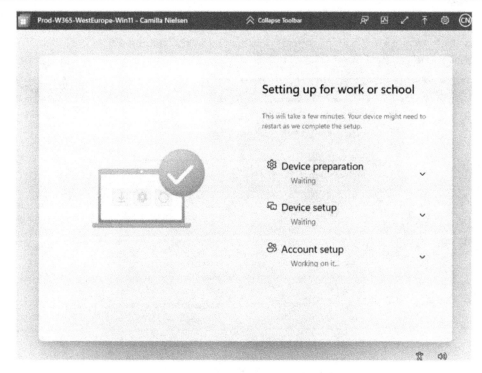

Figure 4.8 – An ESP as seen by a Cloud PC user

As you can see, we are able to deliver the same first-time experience to end users' Cloud PCs as their physical devices. Let's now move on to one of the newer features, where we can move a Cloud PC to another region.

Moving Cloud PCs to another region

Customers can now change the region in their Windows 365 provisioning policy and, with a click of a button, move all their Cloud PCs (including their user data) to a different region.

It works very simply – once you change the region inside an existing provisioning policy, you should now be able to click on a new button called **Apply region change to existing Cloud PCs**.

When you press this button, all the Cloud PCs in the Azure AD group attached to that provisioning policy will move to the new region. To ensure VM integrity and coherency, and to have the ability to restore to a last-known good point in case of accidental corruption, these Cloud PCs are backed up and shut down before being moved to the new region.

During the move, you can view the status in the **All Cloud PCs** list. The move is complete when the status says **Provisioned**.

We will use this feature for more purposes in the future. Imagine your Cloud PC will move with you automatically to ensure a low-latency **round trip time** (**RTT**) connection? Pretty cool, right? Well, who knows? You might see it soon!

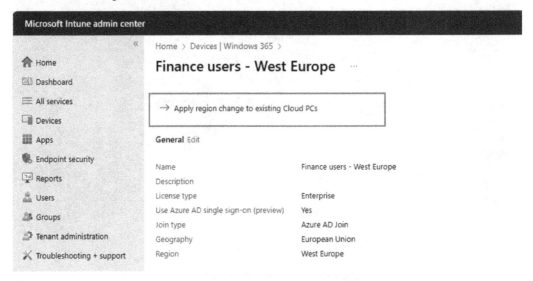

Figure 4.9 – Moving Cloud PCs

Enabling users to reset their Cloud PCs

Enabling this setting will allow targeted users to reprovision their Cloud PC from within the Windows 365 app and web app.

If enabled, a reset option is shown in the Windows 365 app and portal for users in the assigned groups. Resetting wipes and reprovisions the Cloud PC, deleting all user data and apps.

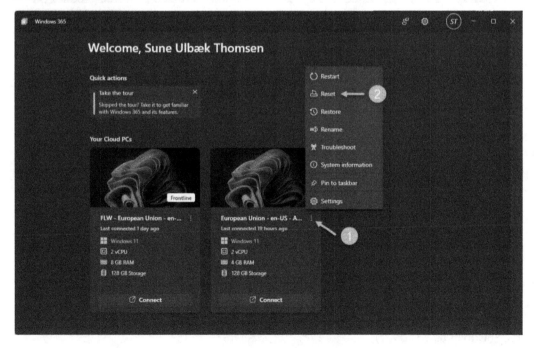

Figure 4.10 – Allow users to reset their Cloud PCs

In the following screenshot, you can see the result of this setting for the end user. The end user is now able to find a new **Reset** option in the Windows 365 app menu – under the three vertical dots next to the Cloud PC menu.

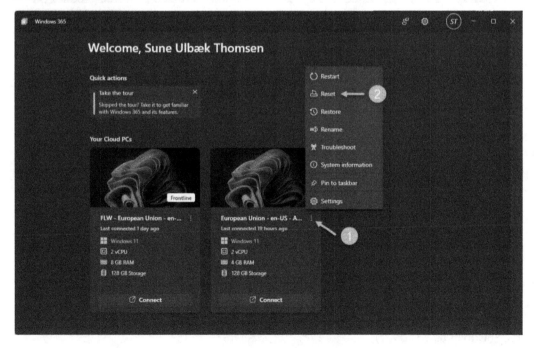

Figure 4.11 – Users can reset a Cloud PC in the Windows 365 app

A user always must confirm the reset, as most of the data and applications installed will be lost. If you configured Intune and OneDrive, they will return in just a snap!

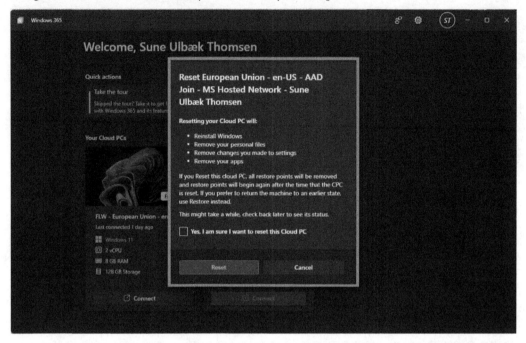

Figure 4.12 – Users can reset a Cloud PC in the Windows 365 app

In the next section, we will cover how you can resize a Cloud PC.

Resizing Cloud PCs

As an IT admin, you will be able to upgrade or downgrade Cloud PCs. This means that the user will go, for example, from 2vCPU/4 GB of RAM to 2vCPU/8 GB of RAM so that more resources are available for their workload.

> **Note**
> You can resize your Cloud PC to a license type (SKU) with more disk space. It's not possible to downsize the disk size – for example, from 256 GB to 128 GB.

Resizing Cloud PCs will retain user data. The Cloud PC will only be rebooted once with the higher or lower SKU, and you are good to go. Resizing a Cloud PC can be done in different ways depending on how the Windows 365 license is assigned. A user can have a license assigned directly or as part of a group (a group-based license).

The following diagram shows what the resize flow looks like:

Figure 4.13 – The IT admin resize process

Let's continue by resizing a Cloud PC that has been provisioned with a license directly assigned to a user.

Resizing a Cloud PC provisioned by a direct assigned license

1. To get started, log in to **Microsoft Intune** and find the Cloud PC device under **Devices**. In this case, we will resize a Cloud PC named CPC-mp-H9HDRBH0 to a smaller SKU. Once you have found the device, select **Resize**:

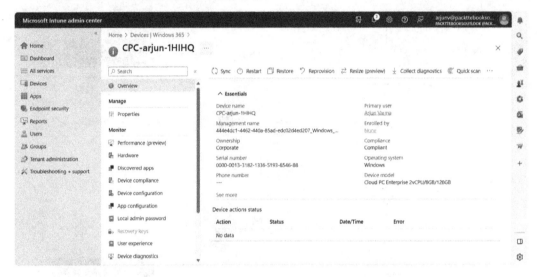

Figure 4.14 – Resizing a Cloud PC

2. Select the hardware configuration. Click on **Resize**.

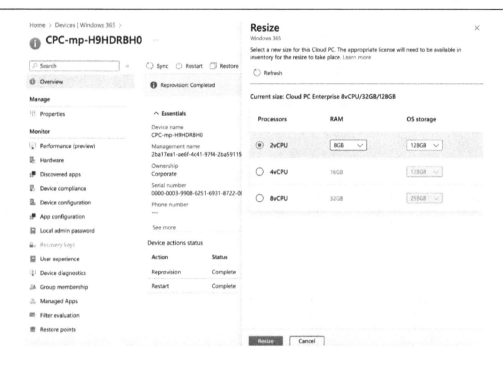

Figure 4.15 – Selecting a new Cloud PC configuration

3. Returning to the overview of the device in Microsoft Intune, we can see that the resize has been initiated and is currently pending.

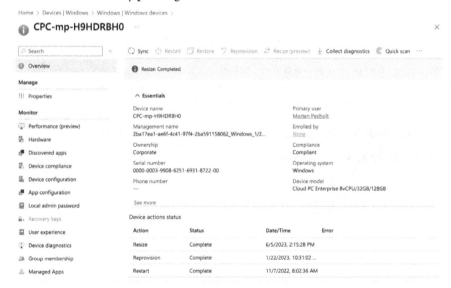

Figure 4.16 – The Cloud PC device action status – Pending

4. After the Cloud PC is resized, the user can log in to the device again.

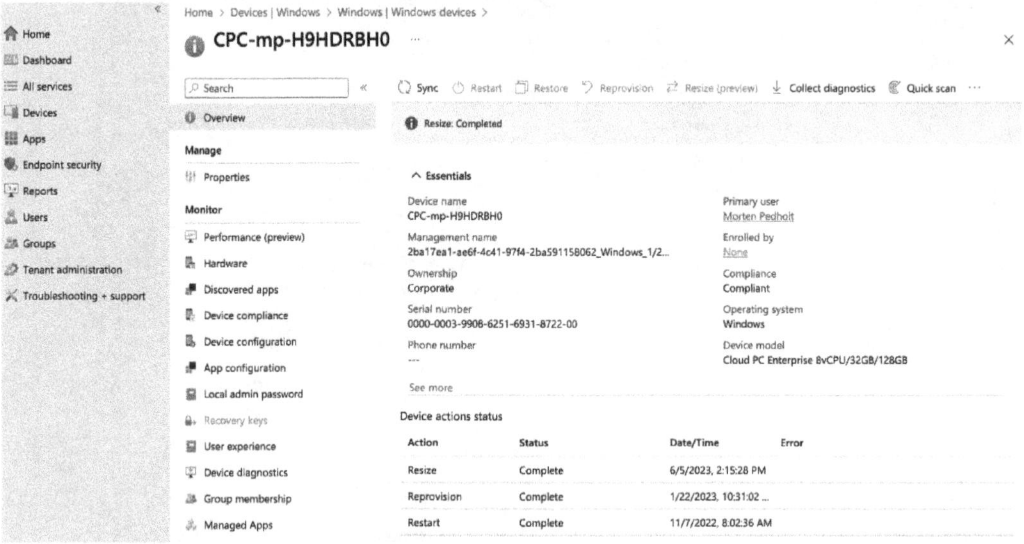

Figure 4.17 – The Cloud PC device action status – Complete

With a few simple steps, we can resize users' Cloud PCs with a directly assigned Windows 365 license. Larger organizations typically want to manage their licenses in groups instead of assigning them individually to users. This is defined as group-based licensing. Let's try to resize a Cloud PC from a user who has a license from a group.

Resizing a Cloud PC provisioned by a group-based license

Let's start by getting an overview of the configuration and what we want to achieve. As an example, we want to resize a Cloud PC named CPC-mp-H9HDRBH0 from 2vCPU/8 GB RAM to 8vCPU/32 GB RAM. In the environment, we have our Windows 365 licenses added to two Azure AD groups:

- 2vCPU/8 GB RAM > LicensGroup-Windows365Enterprise-2vCPU-8GB-128GB

- 4vCPU/32 GB RAM > LicensGroup-Windows365Enterprise-8vCPU-32GB-128GB

We can start resizing now that we have an overview of the environment:

1. Log in to **Microsoft Intune** and go to **Devices** | **Windows**.

2. Select **Bulk device actions**.

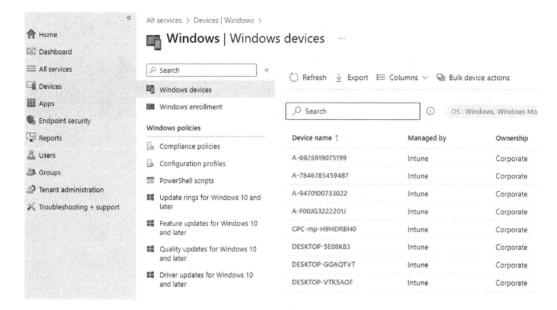

Figure 4.18 – An overview of all Windows devices

3. Select **Windows** as the OS, **Cloud PCs** as the device type, and **Resize** as the device action. Select the source and target size; in our example, the source is **2vCPU/8GB/128GB** and our target is **8vCPU/32GB/128GB**. Once you are done, click **Next**.

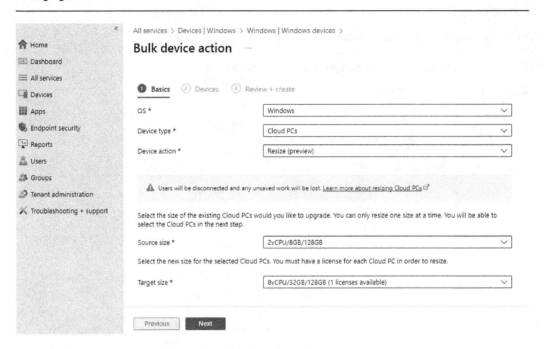

Figure 4.19 – Selecting the bulk device action

4. Choose **Select individual devices across your environment** as the selection type. Next, click on **Add devices** and select the Cloud PC you want to resize. Once done, click on **Next**.

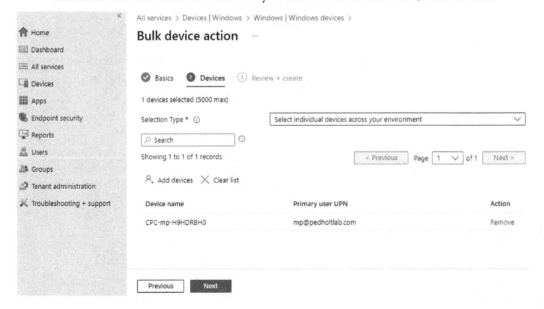

Figure 4.20 – Selecting the Cloud PC to be resized

5. Review the selected setting and click **Create**.

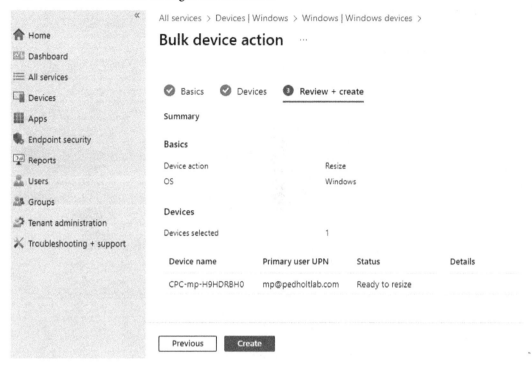

Figure 4.21 – The review settings of the bulk device action

6. The Cloud PC will now have the **Resize pending license** status.

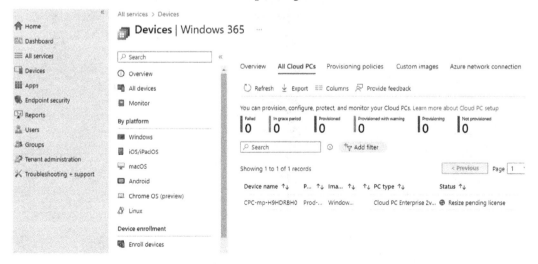

Figure 4.22 – The Cloud PC resize pending status

7. Find and remove the user from the source group. In our scenario, it's **LicensGroup-Windows365Enterprise-2vCPU-8GB-128GB**.

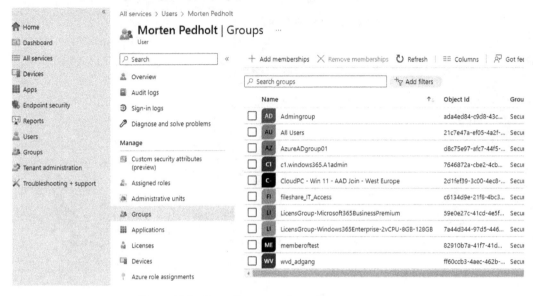

Figure 4.23 – Removing a user from the source group

8. Add the user to the target group; in our scenario, it's **LicensGroup-Windows365Enterprise-8vCPU-32GB-128GB**

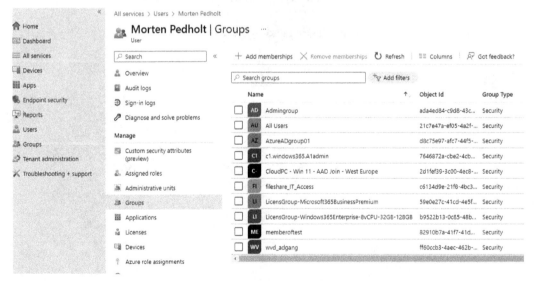

Figure 4.24 – Adding a user to the target group

Once that is done, the Cloud PC will begin to resize:

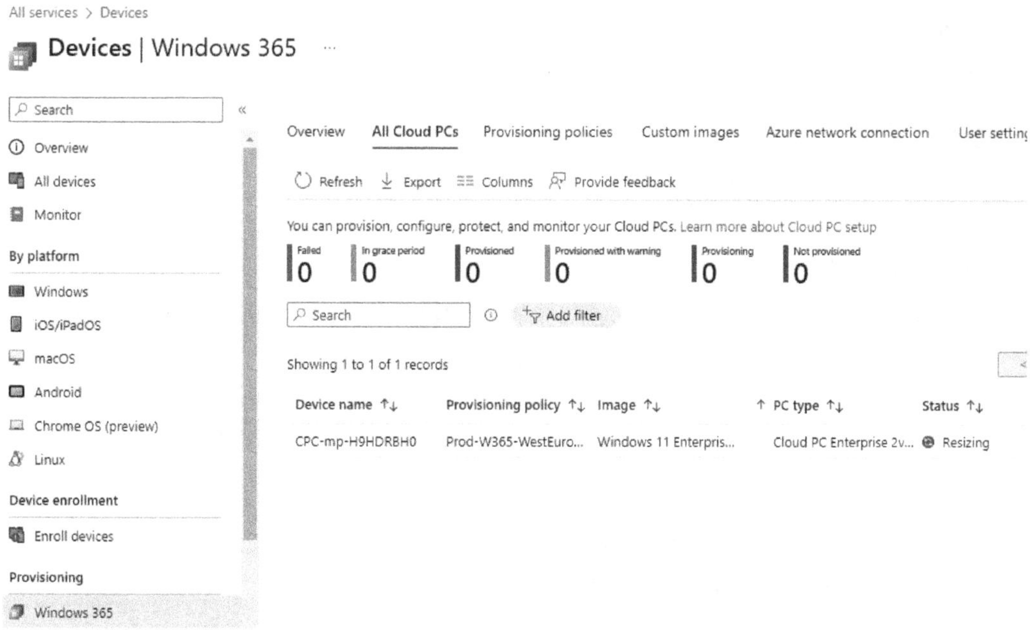

Figure 4.25 – Resizing the Cloud PC

This concludes the resizing experience; you are now able to resize multiple Cloud PCs simultaneously under **Bulk device actions**, with a maximum of 5,000 Cloud PCs at a time.

In the next section, we will explore bulk actions.

Bulk device actions

To manage your Windows 365 Cloud PC environment, you sometimes need to push configuration settings to the endpoint.

Under **Devices | Windows,** you can find your endpoint objects to perform individual device actions on, such as the following:

- Sync settings

- Power on/off (frontline Cloud PCs only)

- Restarting the Cloud PC

- Restoring to a previous point in time

- Reprovisioning the Cloud PC

- Resizing

- Collecting diagnostics

- Windows Defender settings (scanning, updating an agent, etc.)

- Rotating a local admin password

- Configuring remote assistance

- Placing the Cloud PC under review (eDiscovery)

Luckily, you are able to enable most of these settings in bulk. The following screenshot provides a view of the individual actions.

Figure 4.26 – A device actions overview

If you go back to **Devices** | **All devices**, you can see the **Bulk Device Actions** option on the menu:

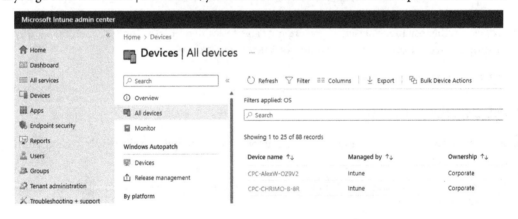

Figure 4.27 – An All devices overview

Select the OS type, which is always **Windows** for Windows 365. Select the device type, which is always **Cloud PCs**, and then select the device action you want to push to multiple Cloud PCs/endpoints:

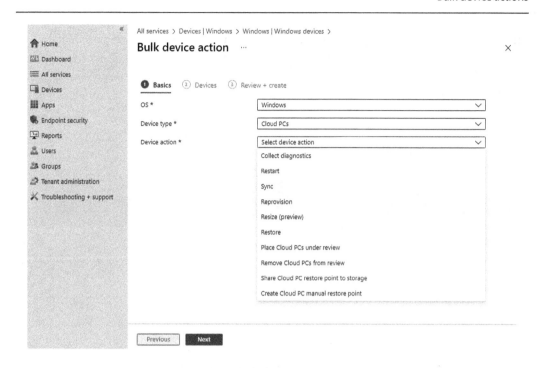

Figure 4.28 – Selecting the bulk device action

In this example, we will use the **Restart** option for maintenance. Remember that users will not automatically be notified by the remote action you take. Make sure that the user has saved their work before initiating a restart action. After the selection, select the devices you want to perform the bulk action for.

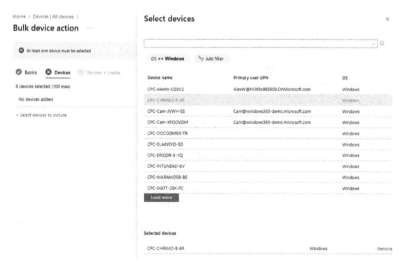

Figure 4.29 – Bulk device action – Select devices

Once ready, make sure to confirm the setting, and click on **Create** to perform the bulk action(s).

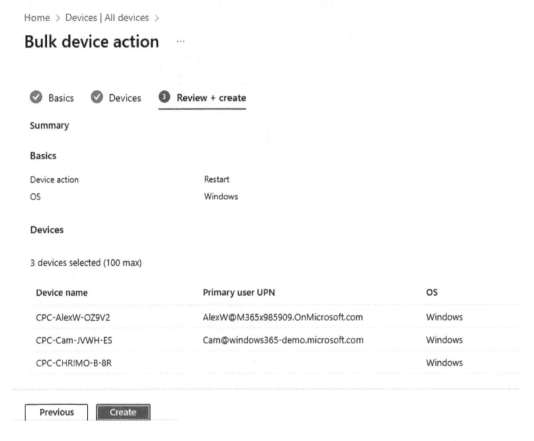

Figure 4.30 – Bulk device action – Review + create

In the next section, we will explain everything about configuration profiles and other management aspects of a Cloud PC via Microsoft Intune.

Configuring configuration profiles

For many years, IT administrators have used Group Policy Management to configure and control the end user devices in their environment. There is no question that Microsoft Intune has come to rule the management aspect of end user devices. With Microsoft Intune, you can configure and control your end user devices as you used to, but this is now handled with **Configuration Profiles (Configuration service providers** or **CSPs)**, which is a more modern and simplified way to manage your devices.

The good thing about Windows 365 is its integration with **Microsoft Intune** (`https://intune.microsoft.com/`); this means all the effort and time that is put into a Microsoft Intune environment can be reused for Windows 365 Cloud PCs.

You might already work with Intune and have experience with CSPs. If so, that is great. We hope you are still able to find some valuable information in this section about CSPs and learn how to manage the assignment. We will look at a more specific Cloud PC setting that might be useful in a Windows 365 environment. Besides that, we will cover how to ensure your assignment of CSPs targets a Cloud PC only.

> **Note**
>
> If you already have CSPs configured for your physical devices, you can reuse them for your Cloud PC devices. Remember to include your Cloud PC devices under the assignments of those CSPs.

Structuring assignments with filters

Targeting a specific device or user type in Intune has, most of the time, been done with static and dynamic Azure AD groups. Not too long ago, Microsoft released a new feature called **filters**. This is a great feature that lets you assign policies to a specific device or user type with fast evaluation. The best part is how easy it is to structure assignments in Intune.

When it comes to structuring your assignment for Windows 365, we recommend having a filter for production and test environments. Being able to spin up a Cloud PC in a test environment might be handy if a new application or configuration should be tested, or if you are looking into enabling new security features and want to get an overview of how it affects the environment.

Filters have many properties available that we can use. To define production and test environments, we will need to use a property called `enrollmentProfileName`.

When a Cloud PC is created, it will have a property on a device called `enrollmentProfileName`; the value is the provisioning policy name we have specified for that Cloud PC.

To be more precise, let us see an example:

Environment	Name of Provisioning Policy	EnrollmentProfileName value on a Cloud PC device
Production	`Prod-W365-WestEurope-Win11`	`Prod-W365-WestEurope-Win11`
Test	`Test-W365-WestEurope-Win11`	`Test-W365-WestEurope-Win11`

Table 4.1 – An EnrollmentProfileName value example

As you can see, things are all tied together. Let us look at how to create a filter that we can use for the CSP we will create later.

Creating a filter for Windows 365

Now that we know what property we can use with filters, let's make a filter that only targets our Cloud PCs in production:

1.   Find **Filters** under **Devices** in **Microsoft Intune**. Click on **Create** and choose **Managed devices**:

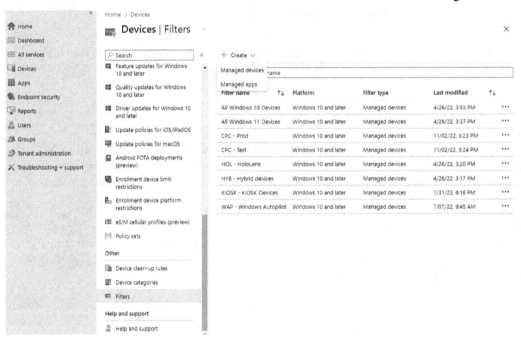

Figure 4.31 – Creating filters in Microsoft Intune

2.   Type in a name for the filter, and choose **Windows 10 and later** as a platform:

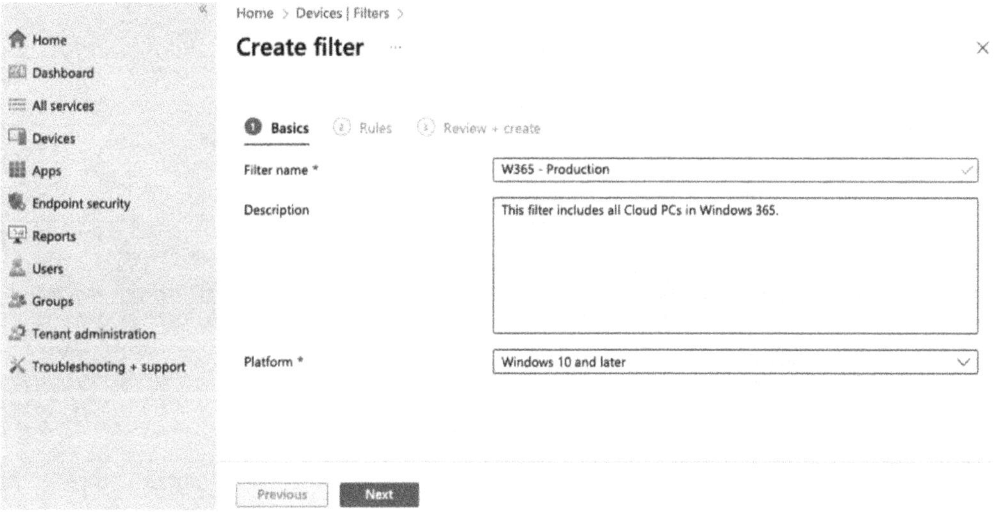

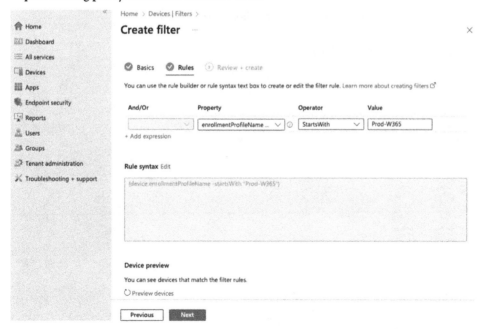

Figure 4.32 – Creating the filter's basic information

3.   Make sure to select **enrollmentProfileName** under **Property**, and **StartsWith** under **Operator** allows you to target multiple provisioning policies in the same filter; just make sure that the provisioning policy starts with the same value:

Figure 4.33 – Creating a filter rule syntax

4. You can click on **Preview devices** to check which devices will be included in your filter. Once you are ready, go to the next page:

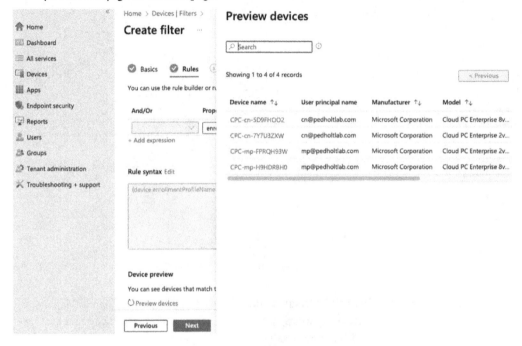

Figure 4.34 – Creating filter preview devices

5. Review the settings and click **Create**.

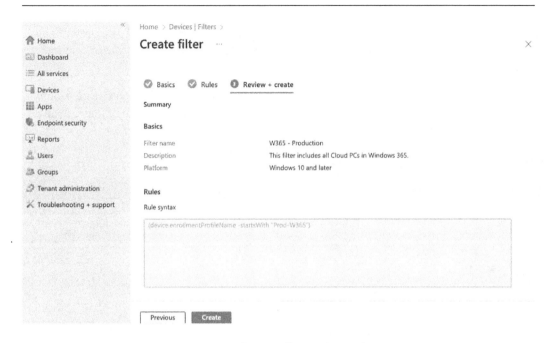

Figure 4.35 – Creating filter review settings

Now that the configuration of filters is done, let's have a look at how we can use filters to assign CSPs alongside how to create them.

Creating a CSP

Now that we have the structure for the assignment ready, it's almost time to create a CSP. Before we do that, it's important to understand what a CSP contains. A CSP has two sets of profile types:

- **Templates**: These have a logical group of settings that you can configure for your devices, such as email, kiosk devices, and certificates. These settings are limited in their number of options.

- **Settings catalog**: Here, you will have a list of all the settings you could imagine, similar to Group Policy Management in Active Directory. You are able to search for specific settings within categories and the names of the categories – for example, if you search for Home Page, it will return all the categories that have any settings related to that, such as Microsoft Edge and Google Chrome. From here, you can select each category and see the setting related to your search.

The settings catalog is the preferred way to configure settings for your devices from Microsoft Intune. Let's configure a CSP to control **Remote Desktop Protocol** (**RDP**) redirections from an end user's physical device to their Cloud PC:

1. Find **Configuration profiles** under **Devices** in **Microsoft Intune**. Click on **Create profile**, choose **Windows 10 and later** under **Platform**, followed by **Settings catalog** under **Profile type**, and click on **Create**.

Figure 4.36 – A CSP creation overview

2. Give the CSP a name and click **Next**.

Figure 4.37 – Configuration profiles – the Basics settings

3. Click on **Add settings**. You can browse or search for the settings. Select the checkbox for each setting, or click **Select all these settings** to add all the settings from the settings catalog to the CSP. Once added, you can configure each setting as necessary.

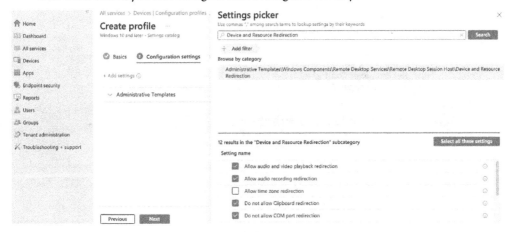

Figure 4.38 – CSP – choosing the settings

4. You are now able to enable or disable the settings as you require. Any new settings from the settings catalog that are added to the CSP are marked as **Disabled?**.

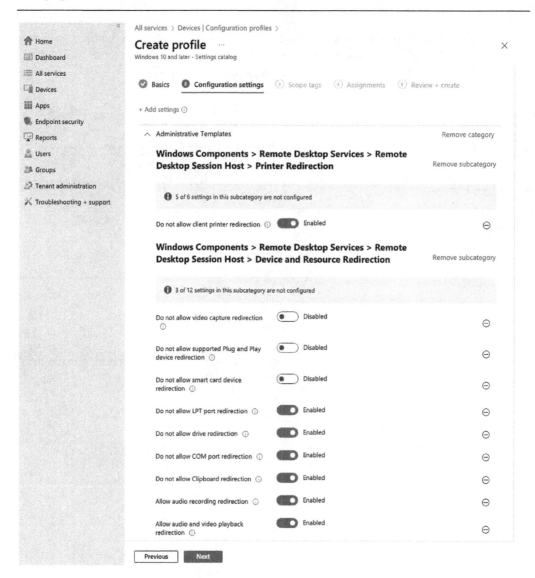

Figure 4.39 – CSP – enabling settings

5.   Select the scope tags if there are any configured for your environment.

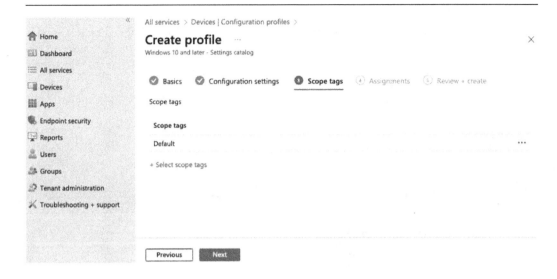

Figure 4.40 – CSP – Scope tags

6. It is now time to assign the filter we created earlier. Assign either **All devices** or **All users**, choose **Edit filter**, set the filter mode to **Include**, and select the **W365 - Production** filter or any other filter you have configured:

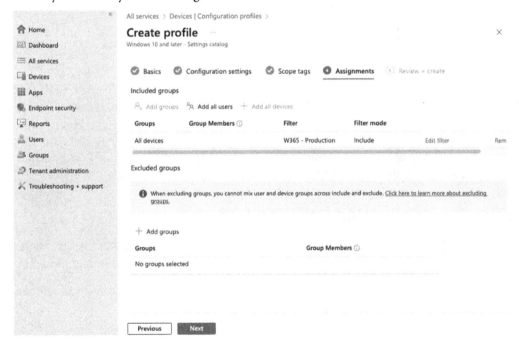

Figure 4.41 – CSP – applying a filter to the assignment

7. Review the settings and click on **Create**. The policy is now created and assigned to the Cloud PCs in production.

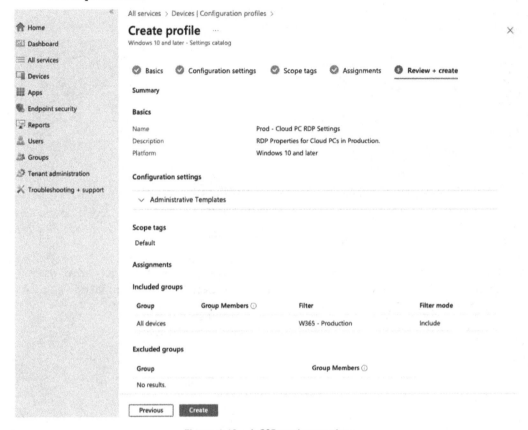

Figure 4.42 – A CSP settings review

This wraps up the flow of how to configure settings targeted specifically to Cloud PCs. Let's now proceed with how to install and manage applications on Cloud PCs through Microsoft Intune.

Deploying applications to Cloud PCs

Applications are incredibly important as without them, users cannot be productive. Microsoft Intune supports application delivery as a core component of the unified management services it offers.

In the following steps, you will learn how to deploy applications to your Cloud PCs. Microsoft Intune supports the following application types:

- The Microsoft Store app (new):

  - Store-based applications (e.g., the Windows 365 app).

- A line-of-business app:

  - Windows apps (`.msi`, `.appx`, `.appxbundle`, `.msix`, and `.msixbundle`).

- A Windows app (Win32):

  - A custom or in-house Win32-based app. Upload the app's installation file in the `.intunewin` format.

- A Windows web link:

  - With this option, you can add web apps (SaaS) to a user's start menu – the **All apps** list.

1. Go to **Apps** | **All apps** to start the application deployment process.
2. Click on + **Add**.

> **Note**
>
> The process of targeting apps to physical PCs is almost identical in Microsoft Intune.

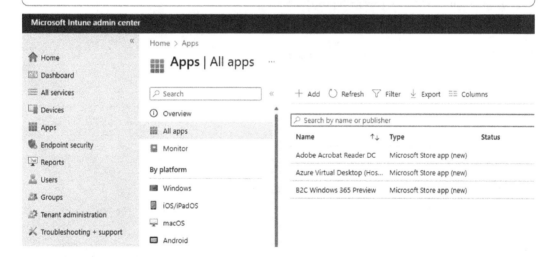

Figure 4.43 – An overview of all apps

3. Select the app type you prefer to configure – use the previous list of apps as guidance.

   For this first example, let's use **Microsoft Store app (new)**:

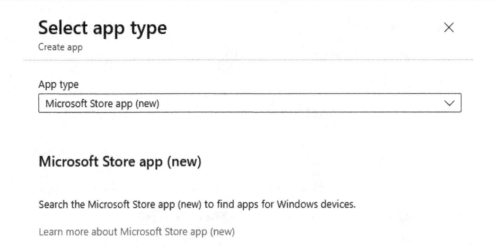

Figure 4.44 – Selecting the app type

This new feature works via **WinGet**, which makes it easy to deploy apps via the store and offers the possibility of adding private repositories.

4.   Search for the app that you want to deploy via the search engine:

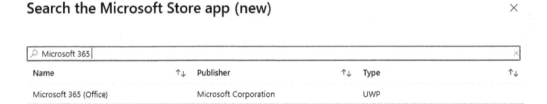

Figure 4.45 – Selecting the Microsoft Store app

> **Note**
> If you are a business that does not want users to have access to the Microsoft Store, the following settings catalog setting allows you to deploy Store-based apps via Intune while disabling the use of the Store for the end user.

Figure 4.46 – Allowing Store-based apps via Intune while disabling the use of the Store for the end user

5. In the next blade, you can customize the name, logo, and other settings that automatically come from the Microsoft Store. You can leave them as default and click on **Next**.

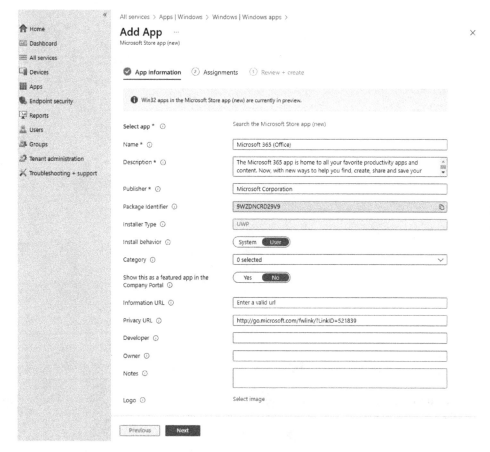

Figure 4.47 – Deploying Microsoft 365 – App information

Most likely, you will want to assign apps to users in a specific (e.g., department-based) Azure AD group.

You can target apps to devices and users. Targeting apps to users means that the users first must log on before the apps enroll.

Target apps to the Cloud PC device object if you want to install the app before the user logs on:

- **Required**: This setting means the app will install be forced to install

- **Available for enrolled devices**: This setting means users will optionally install the application – for example, via the company portal app

- **Uninstall**: This setting means the app will be forced to uninstall

As an example, we will push the application as a required app to **All devices** with a Cloud PC filter.

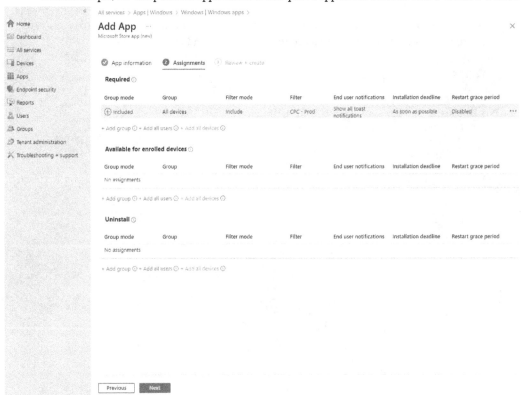

Figure 4.48 – Deploying Microsoft 365 – Assignments

5. Once ready, confirm the settings in the **Review + create** blade. You can follow the same step for all your other apps:

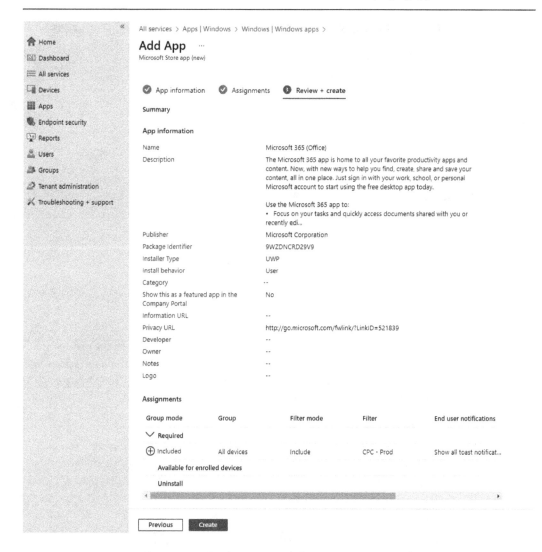

All services > Apps | Windows > Windows | Windows apps >

Add App ...
Microsoft Store app (new)

✓ App information   ✓ Assignments   3 Review + create

Summary

App information

Name	Microsoft 365 (Office)
Description	The Microsoft 365 app is home to all your favorite productivity apps and content. Now, with new ways to help you find, create, share and save your content, all in one place. Just sign in with your work, school, or personal Microsoft account to start using the free desktop app today.
	Use the Microsoft 365 app to:
	• Focus on your tasks and quickly access documents shared with you or recently edi...
Publisher	Microsoft Corporation
Package Identifier	9WZDNCRD29V9
Installer Type	UWP
Install behavior	User
Category	--
Show this as a featured app in the Company Portal	No
Information URL	--
Privacy URL	http://go.microsoft.com/fwlink/?LinkID=521839
Developer	--
Owner	--
Notes	--
Logo	--

Assignments

Group mode	Group	Filter mode	Filter	End user notifications
∨ Required				
⊕ Included	All devices	Include	CPC - Prod	Show all toast notificat...
Available for enrolled devices				
Uninstall				

Previous   **Create**

Figure 4.49 – Deploying Microsoft 365 – Review + create

Tip – deploying Store-based apps via Autopilot as part of the ESP

The new Microsoft Store with ESP is now available to Intune tenants. As the Store grows and expands its app capabilities, Windows Autopilot will continue to evaluate the relevance of these new experiences and incorporate them into the device provisioning flow when possible. This is a setting that is very convenient for Windows endpoints connecting to a Windows 365 Cloud PC – for example, via the Windows 365 app.

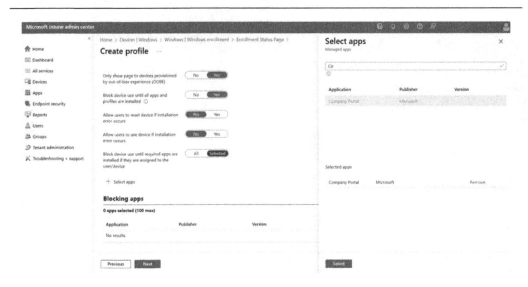

Figure 4.50 – ESP – Select apps

If you need to add a custom Windows application (e.g., `.msi` or `.exe` files), the process is a little more advanced. You need to use the **Win32** option during the application type selection process. Be sure to use the latest version of the Microsoft Win32 Content Prep Tool: `https://learn.microsoft.com/mem/intune/apps/apps-win32-add`.

6. Unzip the tool on the `C:\` drive.

7. Save your application `.exe` or `.msi` file in – for example – the same folder as the Prep Tool. Of course, you can save it somewhere else too. We will use Notepad++ for this example because it's free.

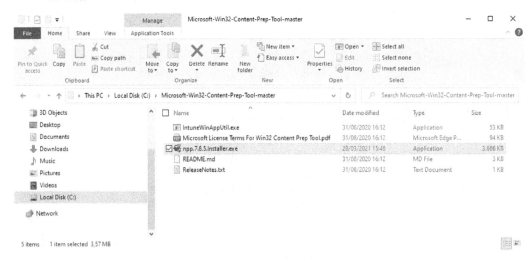

Figure 4.51 – File Explorer with the application and the IntuneWinAppUtil tool

8. Now, we start to create the `Win32.Intunewin` package.

9. Open **PowerShell** and change the CMD directory location to the Intune Prep Tool location – for example, `C:\Microsoft-Win32-Content-Prep-Tool-master`:

```
cd "C:\Microsoft-Win32-Content-Prep-Tool-master"
```

Figure 4.52 – Powershell – application packaging process

10. Run `.\IntuneWinAppUtil.exe` and fill in the following requirements:

> **Note**
>
> It's not unusual to add multiple applications to one package and reuse the package for other application installations; especially when plugins are related to the application, it might be convenient to put them in the same package.

- Please specify the source folder: `C:\Microsoft-Win32-Content-Prep-Tool-master`
- Please specify the setup file: `npp.7.8.5.Installer.exe`
- Please specify the output folder: `C:\Microsoft-Win32-Content-Prep-Tool-master`
- Do you want to specify catalog folder (Y/N)?: Enter N

You can customize the folders as you like. This is just an example.

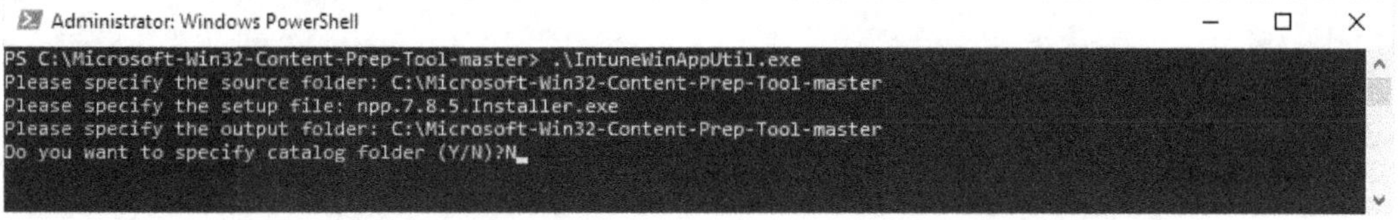

Figure 4.53 – Running the IntuneWinAppUtil.exe tool

If everything ran successfully, you should be able to see the `.intunewin` file listed in the folder:

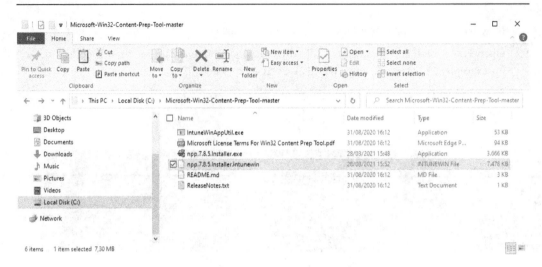

Figure 4.54 – The .intunewin file in File Explorer

We can now switch to the Microsoft Intune admin center. From here, go into **Apps**, select **All Apps** in the menu on the left, and click on **Add**. Select **Windows app (Win32)** from the app type drop-down list.

On the **App Information** pane, select **App package file** and choose the previously created .intunewin file:

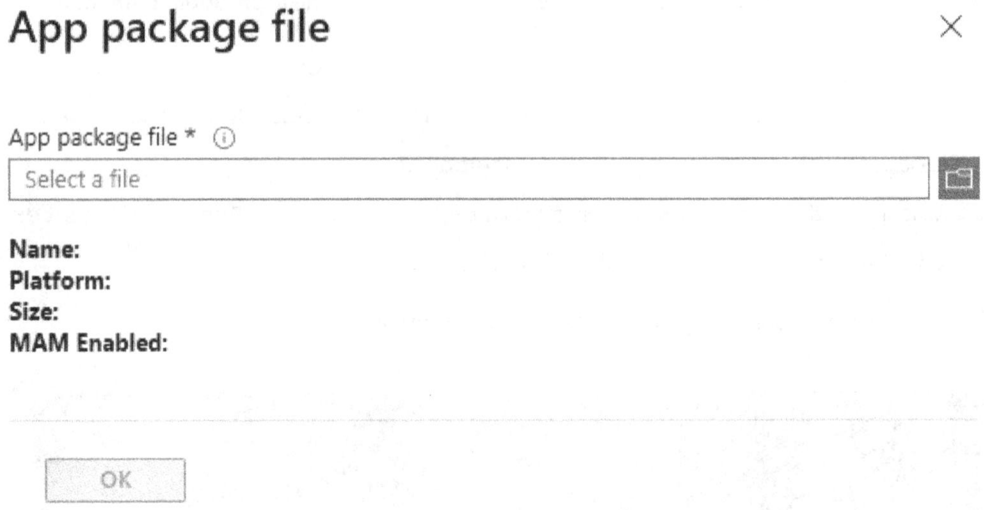

App package file   ✕

App package file * ⓘ

```
Select a file
```

Name:
Platform:
Size:
MAM Enabled:

```
OK
```

Figure 4.55 – Uploading the .intunewin package

Once the `.intunewin` file has been uploaded, you will be able to customize a lot of things in your application. The required things you must configure are the name, publisher, installation behavior, device requirements, and detection rules. We will go through each step as follows:

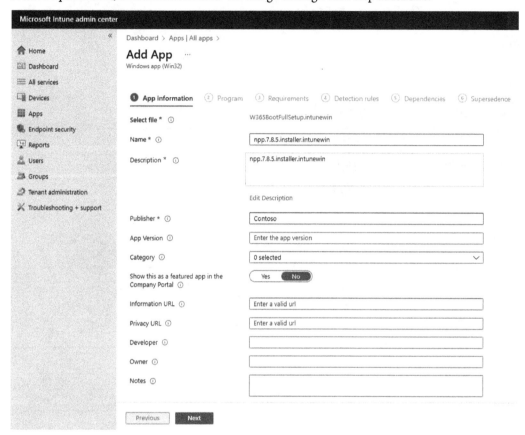

Figure 4.56 – The App information overview under the creation of the Win32 app

Ensure that you add the right installation and uninstallation commands and the information to install the app in either the **System** or **User** context:

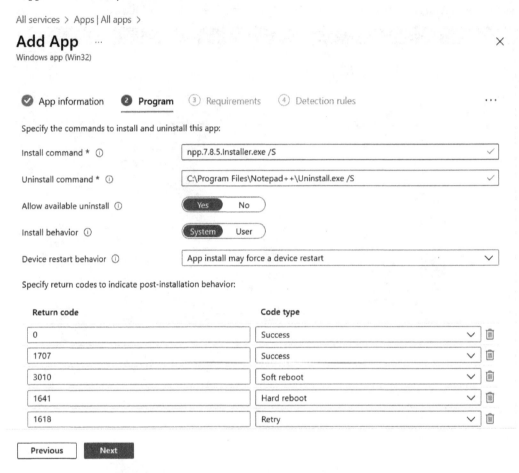

Figure 4.57 – The Program overview under the creation of the Win32 app

Provide the right level of OS requirements for your application:

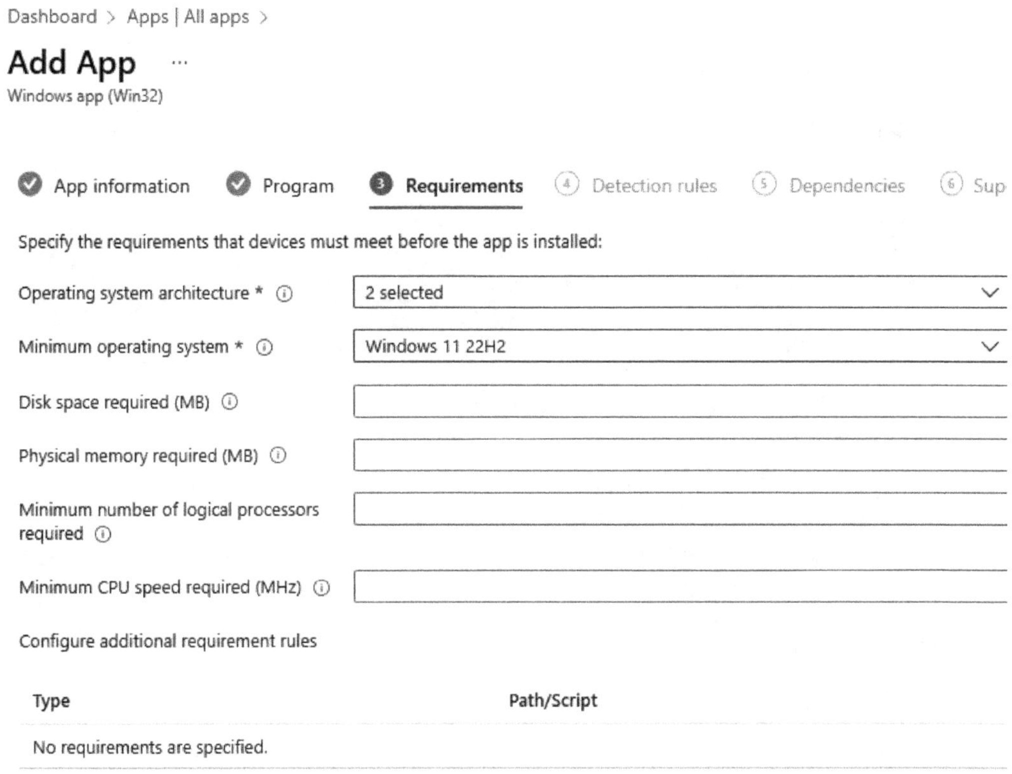

Dashboard > Apps | All apps >

Add App ···
Windows app (Win32)

✓ App information   ✓ Program   ❸ **Requirements**   ④ Detection rules   ⑤ Dependencies   ⑥ Sup

Specify the requirements that devices must meet before the app is installed:

Operating system architecture * ⓘ | 2 selected   ⌄ |

Minimum operating system * ⓘ | Windows 11 22H2   ⌄ |

Disk space required (MB) ⓘ | |

Physical memory required (MB) ⓘ | |

Minimum number of logical processors | |
required ⓘ

Minimum CPU speed required (MHz) ⓘ | |

Configure additional requirement rules

Type   **Path/Script**

No requirements are specified.

Figure 4.58 – The Requirements overview under the creation of the Win32 app

You can generate different types of detection rules to ensure that Intune knows when the app has been installed successfully. I will choose the Program Files location.

Detection rule   ✕

Create a rule that indicates the presence of the app.

Rule type * ⓘ

| File | ⌄ |

Path * ⓘ

| C:\Program Files\Notepad++\ | ✓ |

File or folder * ⓘ

| notepad++.exe | ✓ |

Detection method * ⓘ

| File or folder exists | ⌄ |

Associated with a 32-bit app
on 64-bit clients ⓘ   (Yes   **No**)

Figure 4.59 – The Detection rule overview under the creation of the Win32 app

If you have dependency apps that need to be installed in a specific order, you can add more apps before this app installs.

Add dependency   ✕

| | ✓ | ⓘ |

Name	Publisher	Dependency Count
Printers cloud PC	Contoso	0
Remote Desktop Per-User	Microsoft	0

Figure 4.60 – The Add dependency overview under the creation of the Win32 app

When you supersede an application, you can specify which apps will be directly updated or replaced. To update an app, disable the **Uninstall previous version** option. To replace an app, enable the **Uninstall previous version** option.

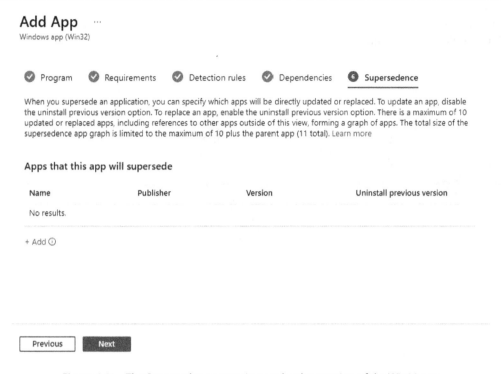

Figure 4.61 – The Supersedence overview under the creation of the Win32 app

> **Note**
>
> There is a maximum of 10 updated or replaced apps, including references to other apps outside of this dashboard view showed in the preceding figure, forming a graph of apps.

The rest of the setup is identical to the earlier process explained for Microsoft Store apps. Make sure to assign the app to the right group once again, and you are all set!

There are partner solutions available to migrate and convert applications from Configuration Manager into Intune to avoid performing the preceding steps for every application. Example solutions are Rimo3 and Patch My PC.

There are also free community solutions for this, such as the tool from Microsoft MVP Ben (https://github.com/byteben/Win32App-Migration-Tool) and community group MSEndpointMgr (https://msendpointmgr.com/intune-app-factory).

> **Note**
>
> Repeat the preceding steps for all your other Windows applications that are not available via the Microsoft Store.

Finally, add the assignments as required, and the targeted users will get the application installed on their Cloud PC within no time.

Figure 4.62 – Adding assignments to an application in Intune

We have now discovered how to deploy applications to our devices in Intune with `.intunewin` files. Now, let's have a look at how to configure backup and restore Cloud PCs if needed.

Backing up and restoring Cloud PCs

Windows 365 Enterprise allows you to configure point-in-time restore settings, giving you the option to set the frequency of restore points and determine whether end users are allowed to initiate a restore action.

How do restore points work?

Restore points are a point-in-time snapshot of a Cloud PC. These allow administrators and users to recover to a last known good state or a state at a particular time if a Cloud PC enters an undesirable state. There are three types of restore points:

- Short-term
- Long-term
- On-demand

A short-term restore point interval can be set in a user setting under the **User Settings** section in **Microsoft Intune**. There is a maximum limit of 10 restore points for each Cloud PC. You can choose between 4, 6, 12, 16, or 24 hours when configuring the policy. The longer the intervals you set between each restore point, the longer the period you can go back. If you don't configure a user setting with a point-in-time restore, the default configuration for all Cloud PCs is set to 12 hours. If you decide to change the configuration, you can always edit your settings, and they will be applied to all existing and new devices created for users associated with that user setting.

Besides the short-term restore points, there are automatically created long-term restore points. These long-term restore points are not configurable and are saved every week as a total of four. This gives you the option to go as far back as four weeks. This is useful in scenarios where a user back from a long vacation finds an issue, malware, ransomware, or something else of that nature and needs to restore to a last known good point.

On-demand manual restore points can be created by administrators for either a single Cloud PC or multiple Cloud PCs through bulk actions. These restore points serve different purposes, such as creating a backup before performing management actions or during employee offboarding, with the sharing of a restore point. Please note that manual restore points can only be created by administrators, and each Cloud PC can only have one manual restore point at any given time.

One last note before we start configuring restore points – a user can only have one user setting configuration applied at any time. If the user is included in multiple user settings, the latest modified setting will take effect.

Configuring restore points

1. Let's get started by going to **Microsoft Intune** and finding the **User settings** section under **Windows 365**. From here, click **+ Add** to start configuring the policy.

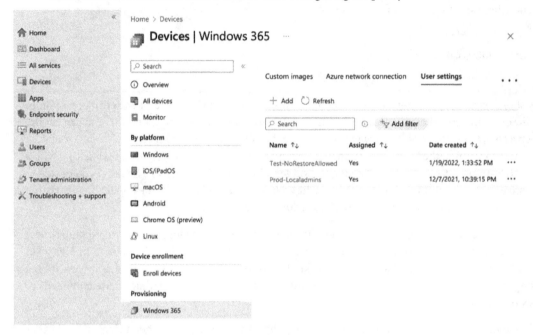

Figure 4.63 – A User settings overview

2. Define the interval of the restore points you want, and choose whether the user is allowed to initiate a restore themselves. Once done, click **Next**.

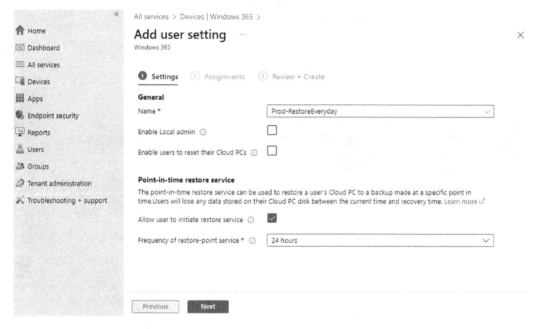

Figure 4.64 – A restore settings configuration overview

3. When all the settings have been configured, choose a group to assign a policy to. You might want to create dedicated groups for managing your user settings. When you are done, click **Next**.

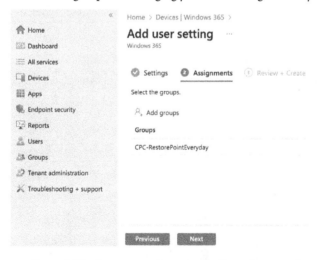

Figure 4.65 – A restore assignment configuration overview

4.   Finally, review the settings and assignments and click **Create**.

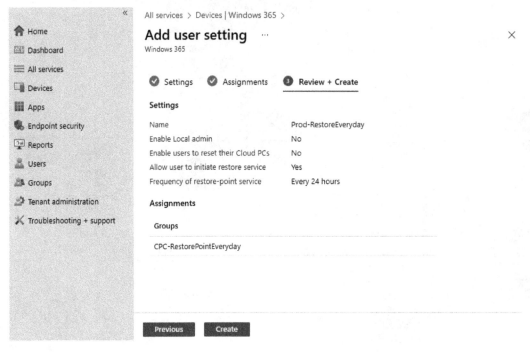

Figure 4.66 – A restore settings configuration review

The restore point service is now configured and applied. Let's have a look at how you as an administrator can restore a Cloud PC.

How to restore a Cloud PC as an admin

A restore action can be initiated for a device at `https://intune.microsoft.com/:`

1. Find the Cloud PC under **Devices** and select **Restore** in the action bar at the top.

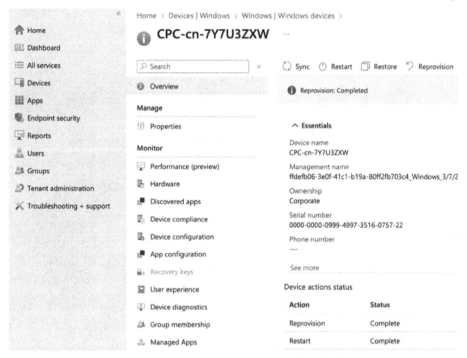

Figure 4.67 – The Restore option under a Cloud PC device

2. Choose the restore point you want to go back to, click on **Select**, and then confirm your selection.

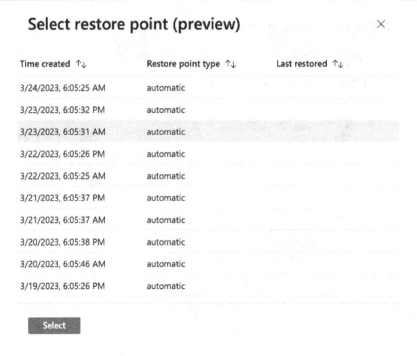

Figure 4.68 – The restore points of a device

3. You will be able to keep track of the restore job in the **Device actions status** section under the device overview in Microsoft Intune.

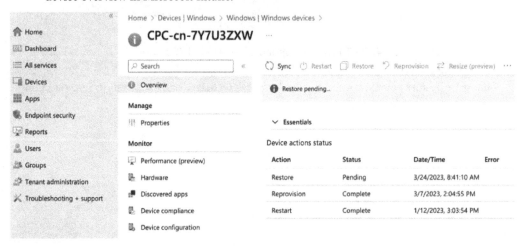

Figure 4.69 – The pending restore status in Microsoft Intune

4. Once the restore is completed, the user will be able to log in again.

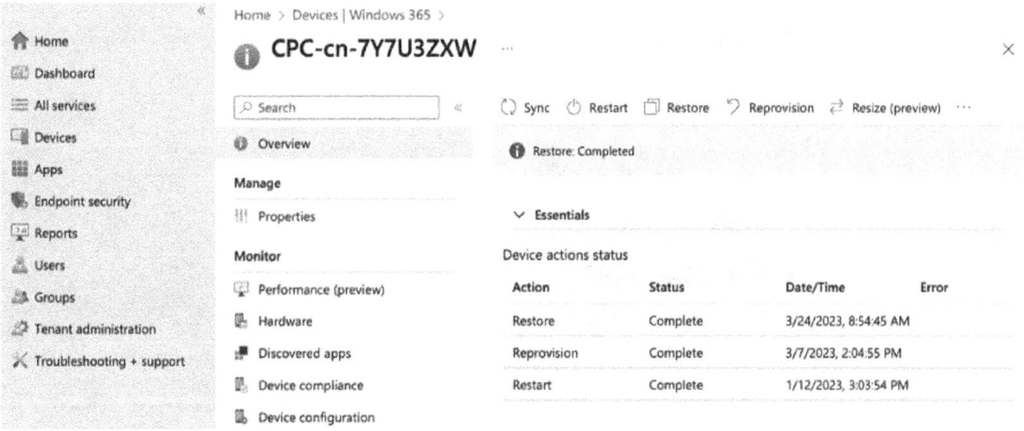

Figure 4.70 – The completed restore status in Microsoft Intune

Let's jump into the next section and look at how a user can initiate a restore of their own Cloud PC if allowed.

How can a user restore their Cloud PC?

If you have checkmarked the **Allow user to initiate Restore service setting**, a user will be able to restore their Cloud PC to a previous point by using the Windows 365 app or from the Windows 365 web client, using the following steps:

1. From the Windows 365 app or Windows 365 web client, select the three vertical dots on the Cloud PC and choose **Restore**.

Figure 4.71 – The Windows 365 app user action options

2.   Select the desired restore point and click on **Restore**.

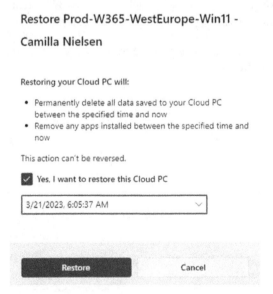

Figure 4.72 – The Windows 365 app – starting a restore

3. While the Cloud PC is restored, the user will be able to see its status.

Figure 4.73 – The Windows 365 app Cloud PC being restored

4.   When the Cloud PC has finished restoring, the user can connect to it again.

Figure 4.74 – The Windows 365 app restored

Now we have looked at how to restore a single Cloud PC, let's jump into how to restore multiple Cloud PCs at once.

How to bulk-restore multiple Cloud PCs

You will be able to restore multiple Cloud PCs simultaneously under **Bulk Device Actions**. Initiating a bulk restore can be done from the **Devices** overview at `https://intune.microsoft.com/`:

1. Click on **Bulk Device Actions** to get started.

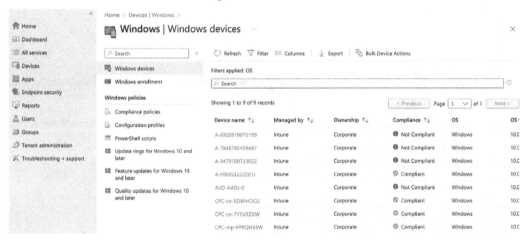

Figure 4.75 – An overview of devices in Microsoft Intune

2. Select **Windows** in the **OS** section, and choose **Cloud PC** as the device type and **Restore** as the device action.

3. Next, specify a date and time; this will help the service determine what restore point to use, depending on what is defined in the **Restore Point Time Range** option.

   You have three options to choose in the final option:

   - **Before specified date and time**: The restore point that is closest to the date and time will be used.

   - **After specified date and time**: The restore point that is closest after the date and time will be used.

   - **Whichever is closest**: The restore point that is closest to the date and time will be used. This can be a restore point before or after the date and time.

Once you have filled out all options, click **Next** to select the devices.

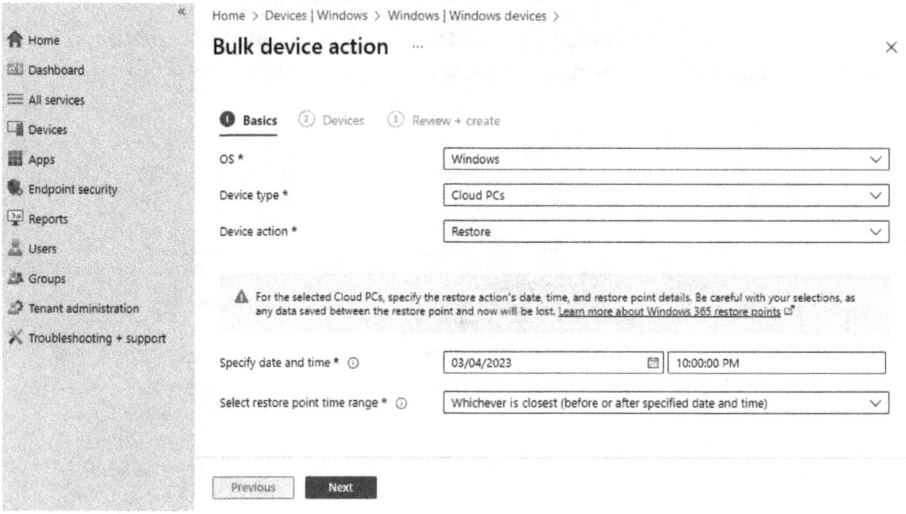

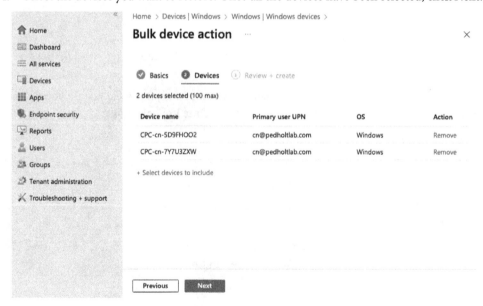

Figure 4.76 – The bulk restore basic information

4.   Select the devices you want to restore. Once all the devices have been selected, click **Next**.

Figure 4.77 – The bulk restore selected devices

5. Review the specified settings and click on **Create** once you are ready. This will initiate a restore of all the selected Cloud PCs.

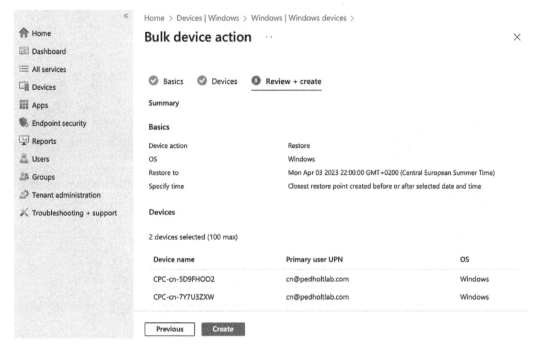

Figure 4.78 – A bulk restore settings overview

Automatically scheduled restore points are great, but what if you need to manually create one yourself? Let's have a look at how to do that.

Manually creating a restore point

Manually creating a restore point outside of the configured schedule in a user setting might be useful in some scenarios. You, as an IT administrator, might plan a substantial change to a specific Cloud PC and want to ensure that there is a restore point from a specific time you have chosen yourself.

To initiate the creation of a restore point, go to **Microsoft Intune** and find the Cloud PC device you want to create a restore point for. Then, go to **Restore points** and select **+Create Restore** Points. Now, you just need to confirm the creation of it; making the restore point can take up to one hour. You can create restore points for multiple Cloud PCs by using **Bulk device actions**.

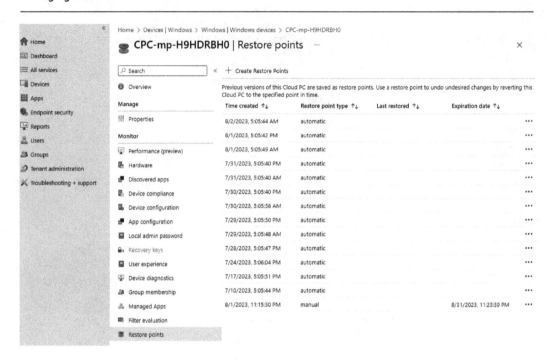

Figure 4.79 – Manually creating a restore point for a Cloud PC

Let's take a look at how to share restore points to an Azure storage account.

Sharing restore points with an Azure storage account

Sharing a restore point with a storage account in Azure can be useful if you want to store a Cloud PC for a period during the offboarding of an employee, or if you want to mount the **Virtual Hard Disk** (**VHD**) of the Cloud PC to another PC.

You'll need to have a storage account in Microsoft Azure in the same tenant as your Windows 365 environment. If you don't have a storage account, go ahead and create one. The only important thing is to leave the **Performance** setting as **Standard**. Fill out the required fields, and leave anything else as the default unless you have some other preferences.

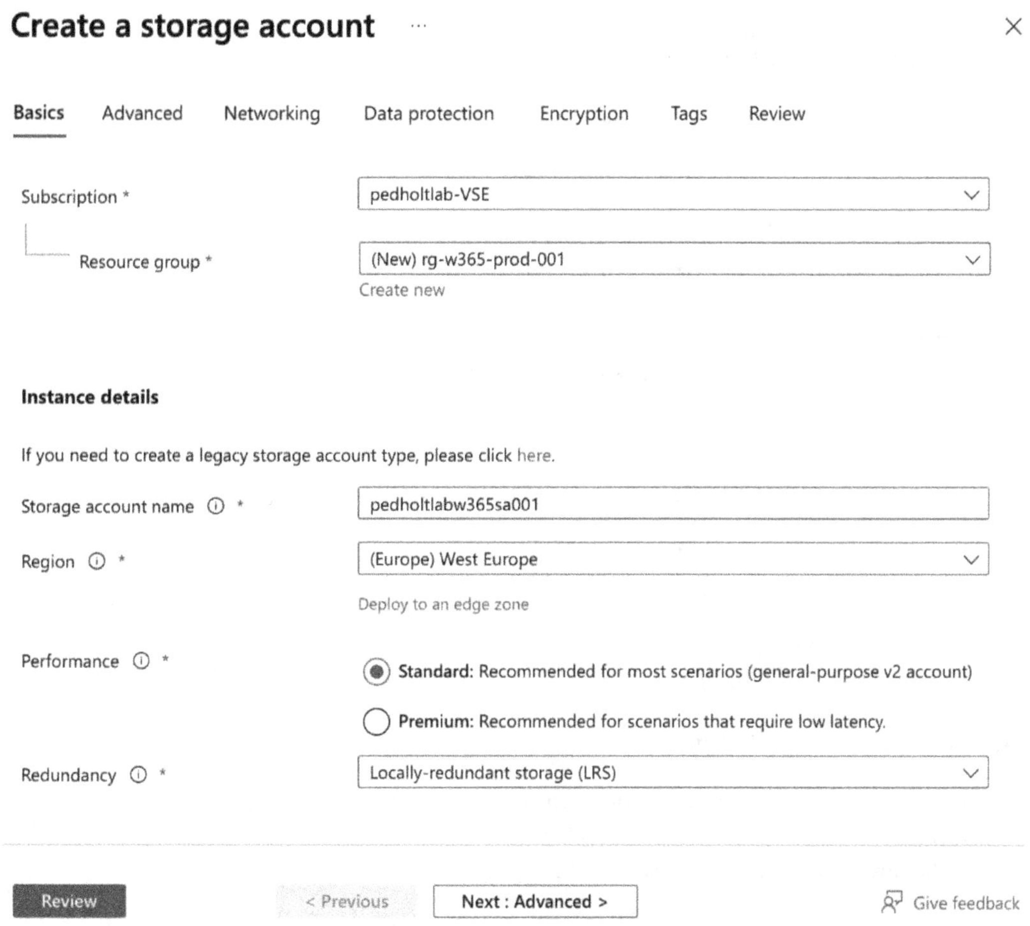

Create a storage account   ···   ✕

Basics   Advanced   Networking   Data protection   Encryption   Tags   Review

Subscription * | pedholtlab-VSE   ⌄ |

⌐
└──── Resource group * | (New) rg-w365-prod-001   ⌄ |
                                  Create new

Instance details

If you need to create a legacy storage account type, please click here.

Storage account name ⓘ * | pedholtlabw365sa001 |

Region ⓘ * | (Europe) West Europe   ⌄ |
                                  Deploy to an edge zone

Performance ⓘ *   (●) **Standard:** Recommended for most scenarios (general-purpose v2 account)

                                (○) **Premium:** Recommended for scenarios that require low latency.

Redundancy ⓘ * | Locally-redundant storage (LRS)   ⌄ |

──

[Review]   < Previous   [Next : Advanced >]   ⤵ Give feedback

Figure 4.80 – Creation of an Azure storage account

When the creation is done, the Windows 365 service needs to have access to the storage account. This can be done by giving it a role named **Storage Account Contributor**.

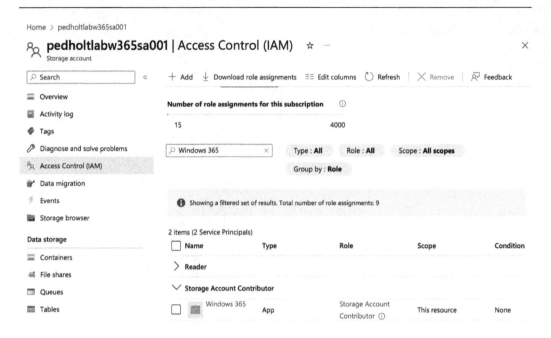

Figure 4.81 – A role assignments overview of an Azure storage account

Now, we will explain how to initiate a restore:

1. To initiate a restore to a storage account, go to **Microsoft Intune | Devices | All devices | Select your Cloud PC Device**. From here, navigate to **Restore Points** in the panel on the left, click on the three dots (**...**) on the restore point you want to share, and select **Share**.

Note

Bulk device actions are also available to share multiple restore points with a storage account in Microsoft Azure.

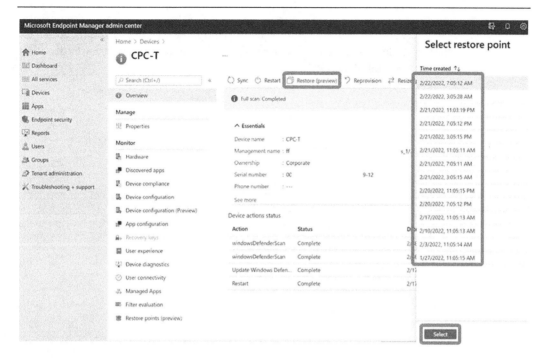

Figure 4.82 – The restore points section under a Cloud PC

2. Now, it's time to select the Azure subscription and storage account you want to store the restore point in. Once you have done that, click **Share**.

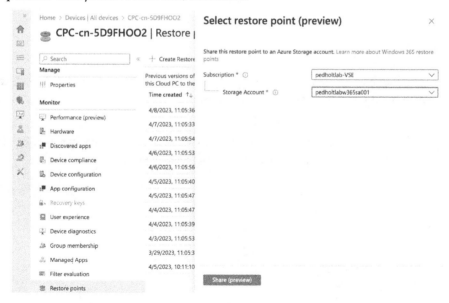

Figure 4.83 – Selecting the Azure subscription and storage account

3. Once the share is complete, you can find the VHD of the Cloud PC inside the storage account you have selected. A blob container will be named after the Cloud PC so that you easily can locate it if there are multiple Cloud PCs.

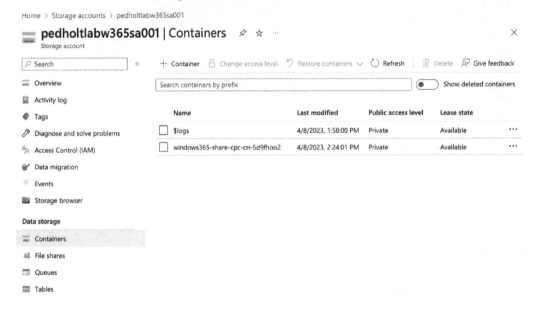

Figure 4.84 – A blob container overview inside the Azure storage account

This concludes the last section of this chapter; let's now summarize what we have learned.

Summary

In the chapter, you learned everything about managing Windows 365 Cloud PCs via Microsoft Intune, setting up configuration policies, deploying applications, resizing, and allowing users to reset their own Cloud PCs.

In the next chapter, we will go deeper into the world of end user experiences and show you how Windows and Windows 365 have come together to provide new integrated experiences with Windows 11.

Questions

At the end of each chapter, we ask three questions to evaluate your learning and challenge you. Here are the three questions:

1. What Azure Storage service does Windows 365 use to capture a copy of a user's Cloud PC for forensic analysis? Does Windows 365 support bulk restore point actions?

2. How do you set short-term restore points for Windows 365 Cloud PCs?

3. Can Cloud PC users become local administrators?

Further reading

Please continue your learning journey while exploring the other chapters. If you want to learn more about the subjects covered in this chapter, please visit any of the following online resources:

*   *To learn more about restore points, visit* `https://techcommunity.microsoft.com/t5/windows-it-pro-blog/windows-365-cloud-pc-point-in-time-restore/ba-p/3264287`

*   *To learn more about CSPs in Intune, visit* `https://learn.microsoft.com/mem/intune/configuration/device-profile-create`

*   *Learn more about how Windows 365 makes digital forensics for Cloud PCs easy here:* `https://learn.microsoft.com/windows-365/enterprise/digital-forensics`

Part 3:
Accessing, Securing, and Analyzing Cloud PCs

The third part of the book is centered around accessing, securing, and analyzing Cloud PCs. You will learn how to access Cloud PCs and take advantage of different features, as well as how to secure their connection. This part also covers securing the connection and content with digital rights management. Additionally, you will gain a comprehensive understanding of how to analyze and monitor Windows 365 Cloud PCs, including utilizing data and tools for troubleshooting and remote help. By the end of this part, you will have learned how to configure MFA, secure Cloud PCs, create Windows 365 alert rules, and utilize the available tools and data within Windows 365.

This part contains the following chapters:

- *Chapter 5, Accessing Cloud PCs*
- *Chapter 6, Securing Cloud PCs*
- *Chapter 7, Analyzing, Monitoring, and Troubleshooting Cloud PCs*

5
Accessing Cloud PCs

In this chapter, you will learn how to access your **Cloud PC** and how to take advantage of different features such as **Windows 365 Boot** and **Switch**. Furthermore, you'll learn how to utilize enhancements such as graphics.

By the end of this chapter, you will know how to access your Cloud PC from any device, anywhere, securely. You will also gain knowledge on specific features that can enhance the access experience.

In this chapter, we will cover the following topics:

- Accessing Cloud PCs from any device
- Introducing the Windows 365 app for Windows
- Exploring Windows 365 Boot
- Diving into Windows 365 Switch
- Using the Windows 365 web client
- Performing user actions on a Windows 365 Cloud PC
- Knowing about the alternate clients
- Meeting endpoint requirements
- Implementing protocol enhancements
- Utilizing graphics enhancements

Accessing Cloud PCs from any device

Windows 365 delivers on its promise of simplicity by providing easy access to Cloud PCs. The intuitive client experience eliminates the need for extensive training, making it effortless for most users to access their Cloud PCs.

Users can access Windows 365 Cloud PCs and control them using the **Windows 365 app**, **Windows 365 web client**, the **Microsoft Remote Desktop app**, and even their own website or line-of-business application.

There are client apps available for all popular platforms, including **Windows**, **macOS**, **iOS**, **Android**, **Linux**, and the **web**. The following table lists the platforms and how you are able to connect to your Cloud PC:

Windows	Windows 365 app Windows 365 Boot Windows 365 Switch
Web	Windows 365 web client (`windows365.microsoft.com`)
macOS, iOS	Microsoft Remote Desktop for macOS, iOS, and iPadOS
Android	Microsoft Remote Desktop for Android
Linux	Approved Windows 365 clients from partners (more details in the *Partners* section)

Table 5.1 – Supported endpoints

These clients can be used across different types of devices and form factors, such as desktops, tablets, smartphones, TVs (via a web browser), and even virtual reality headsets (such as the Meta Quest 2) and augmented reality headsets (such as Microsoft Hololens 2).

Now we have an overall idea of which devices we can connect, it's time to take a deeper look into the different products that allow us to initiate a connection.

Introducing the Windows 365 app for Windows

The Windows 365 app allows you to access your Cloud PC directly from your desktop. You can get a personalized experience suited to your settings and work style. The Windows 365 app utilizes single sign-on to automatically sign you in with your Windows login identity, eliminating the need for you to manually sign in to the app.

The app is supported by all Windows 10 and 11 devices and can be accessed from the taskbar or start menu. You can use your Cloud PC in fullscreen mode and get the full Windows 10 and 11 experiences while moving between your Cloud PC and local device, or you can have your Cloud PC in window mode.

The app is delivered from the Microsoft Store directly to the end user's devices with an easy centralized installation option in Microsoft Intune. With high performance, regular automatic app updates, and self-service actions delivered directly to the user, as shown in the following screenshot, the Windows 365 app enhances the Windows 365 experience.

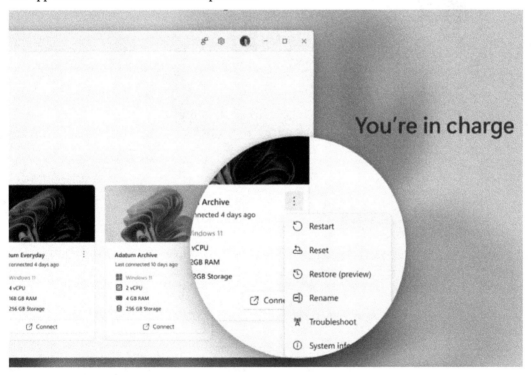

Figure 5.1 – Some of the available actions users can perform from the Windows 365 app

One of the great features of the Windows 365 app is the option to pin your Cloud PC to your taskbar. It just makes good sense to be able to initiate the connection directly from the user's taskbar. Let's have a deeper look at how it works.

Pinning your favorite Cloud PC to the Windows taskbar

End users can now pin their Cloud PC to the taskbar in the Windows 365 app. This lets them launch the Cloud PC from the taskbar icon without going into the connection center. Once you click on the three dots (…) on your Cloud PC, you will be able to choose the **Pin to taskbar** action, as shown in the following screenshot:

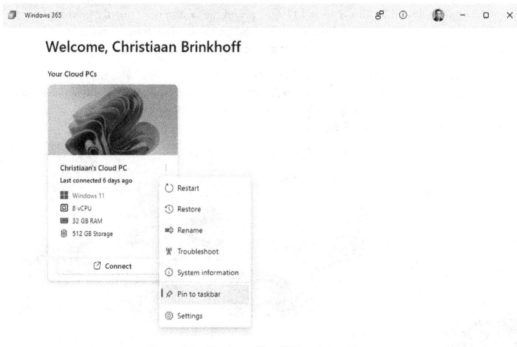

Figure 5.2 – Pinning a Cloud PC to the taskbar

After you click on **Pin to taskbar**, a notification in the Windows 365 app will show you that the Cloud PC has been pinned to the Windows taskbar, as shown in the following screenshot:

Your Cloud PCs

Figure 5.3 – Cloud PC pinned to taskbar notification

A new icon will be added to the taskbar that looks like squares with a cloud in the middle. It makes your Cloud PCs very easy to use and available at your fingertips so that when you start your workday, you only need to click on the new Cloud PC icon on the taskbar and you're ready to go. You can see the pinned Cloud PC icon all the way to the right in the following screenshot.

Figure 5.4 – Pinned Cloud PC icon

Next, let's explore how to control display settings in the Windows 365 app.

Connection settings

Users can also configure their display configuration via the **Settings** menu, which you can find by selecting the three dots (**…**) on the Cloud PC card. From here, you can change the display configuration, as shown in the following screenshot:

Figure 5.5 – Setting the display in the Windows 365 app

Now to something that is important for many people and is crucial when working into the late evening hours – dark mode capability.

Dark mode support

The Windows 365 app supports dark mode. End users have the option to set the Windows 365 app to light or dark mode or to match system settings. This can be done from the app settings in the top-right corner, as shown in the following screenshot.

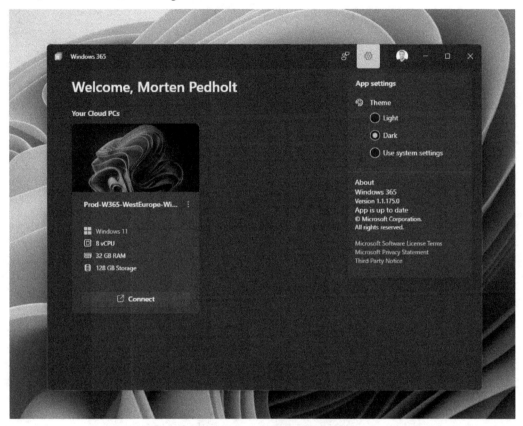

Figure 5.6 – Dark mode support

Now that we have looked at some of the features the Windows 365 app provides, it will be ideal to look at how to install it.

Installing from the Microsoft Store

Users can download the Windows 365 app from the **Microsoft Store**. The Microsoft Store will keep the Windows 365 app up to date. This eliminates the need for IT admin to maintain the application. Follow these steps to get the Windows 365 app:

> **Note**
> Microsoft Store access is required. You can prevent users from installing Microsoft Store apps by enabling the private store access-only policy. This is explained in the next section.

1. Go to **Microsoft Store**. Search for **Windows 365**.

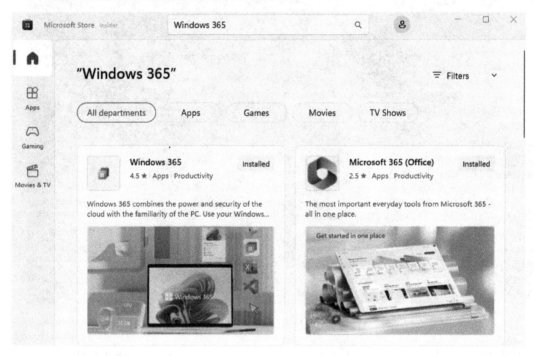

Figure 5.7 – Searching for the Windows 365 app in the Microsoft Store

2. Select **Get** to install the Windows 365 app.

3. Select **Open**.

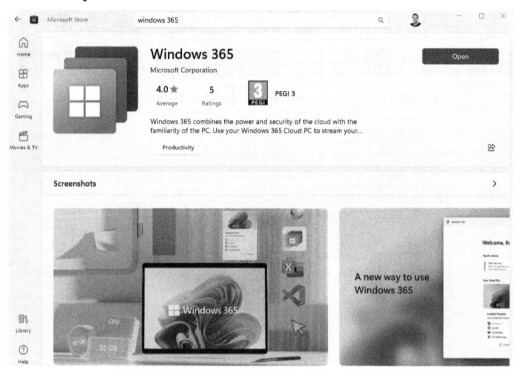

Figure 5.8 – Windows 365 app in the Microsoft Store

4. You can also download the Windows 365 app directly from `windows365.microsoft.com`.

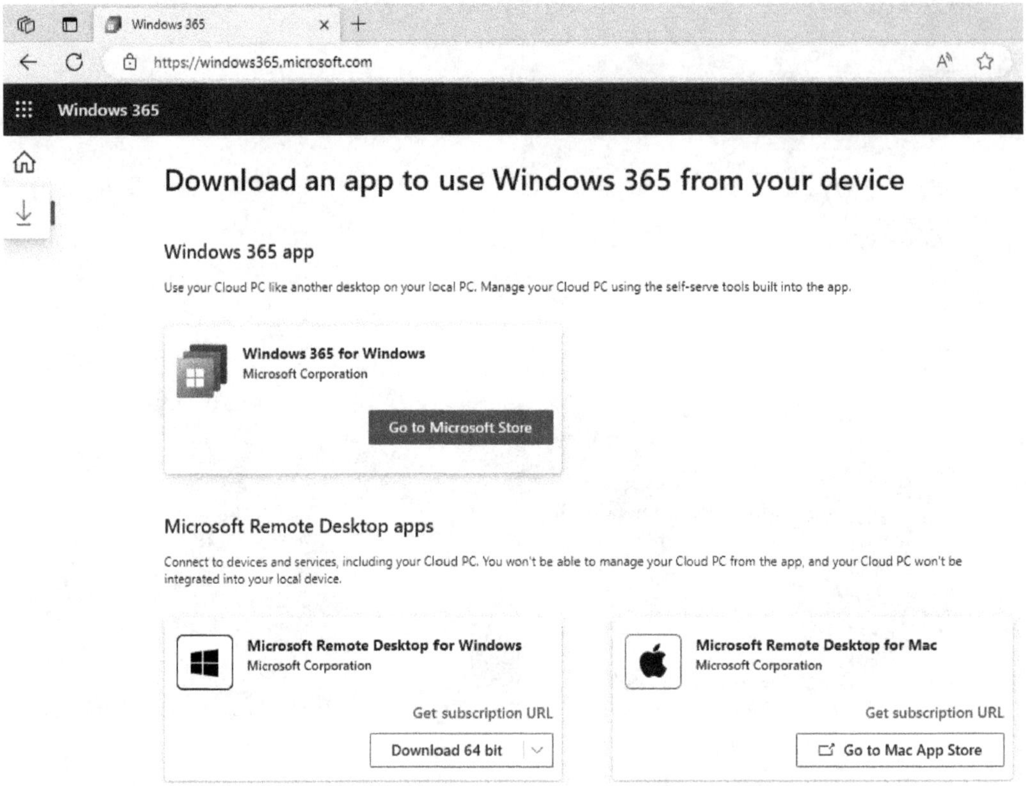

Figure 5.9 – Download the Windows 365 app from the web portal

Even though users can download the Windows 365 app themselves, it is a good idea to manage the installation of the Windows 365 app from an endpoint management solution. Let's have a look at how to do it from Microsoft Intune.

Deploying the Windows 365 app using Microsoft Intune

Deploying the Windows 365 app from Microsoft Intune can be done in a few steps. Before we look at how we can do that, it's important that the Microsoft store is allowed to install apps on the user's physical device. If you are a business that doesn't want to allow Microsoft Store access to users, a configuration profile with the setting displayed in the following screenshot allows you to deploy store-based apps via Intune while disabling the use of the store for the end user.

> **Note**
>
> The Windows 365 app requires the AVD host app to run. It is not required to also add the AVD host app as part of this process as the AVD host app will install within 5–10 seconds of the first launch. If you want to avoid waiting during the initial launch, you can also deploy the AVD host app via Microsoft Intune.

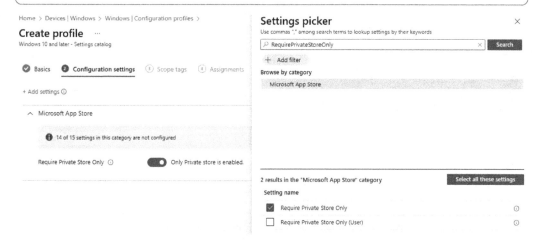

Figure 5.10 – Allow private Microsoft Store only

Now we have got that covered, let's deploy the Windows 365 app from Microsoft Intune. Start by going to the Microsoft Intune admin portal (`https://intune.microsoft.com`). Once you have logged in with an administrative account, follow these steps:

1. Go to **Apps | All apps** to start the application deployment process. Click on **+ Add**.

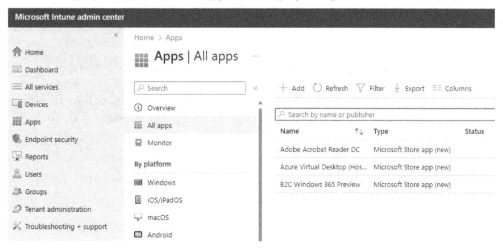

Figure 5.11 – Application overview in Microsoft Intune

2.   Select the **Microsoft Store app (new)** app type:

Figure 5.12 – App type selection under the deployment section of store app in Intune

3.   Search for and select **Windows 365**.

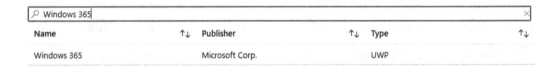

Figure 5.13 – Searching for the Windows 365 app in the Microsoft Store in Intune

4.   On the next blade, you can customize **Name**, **Logo**, and other settings. You can leave the settings as the default unless you have something you want to change. Once done, click on **Next**.

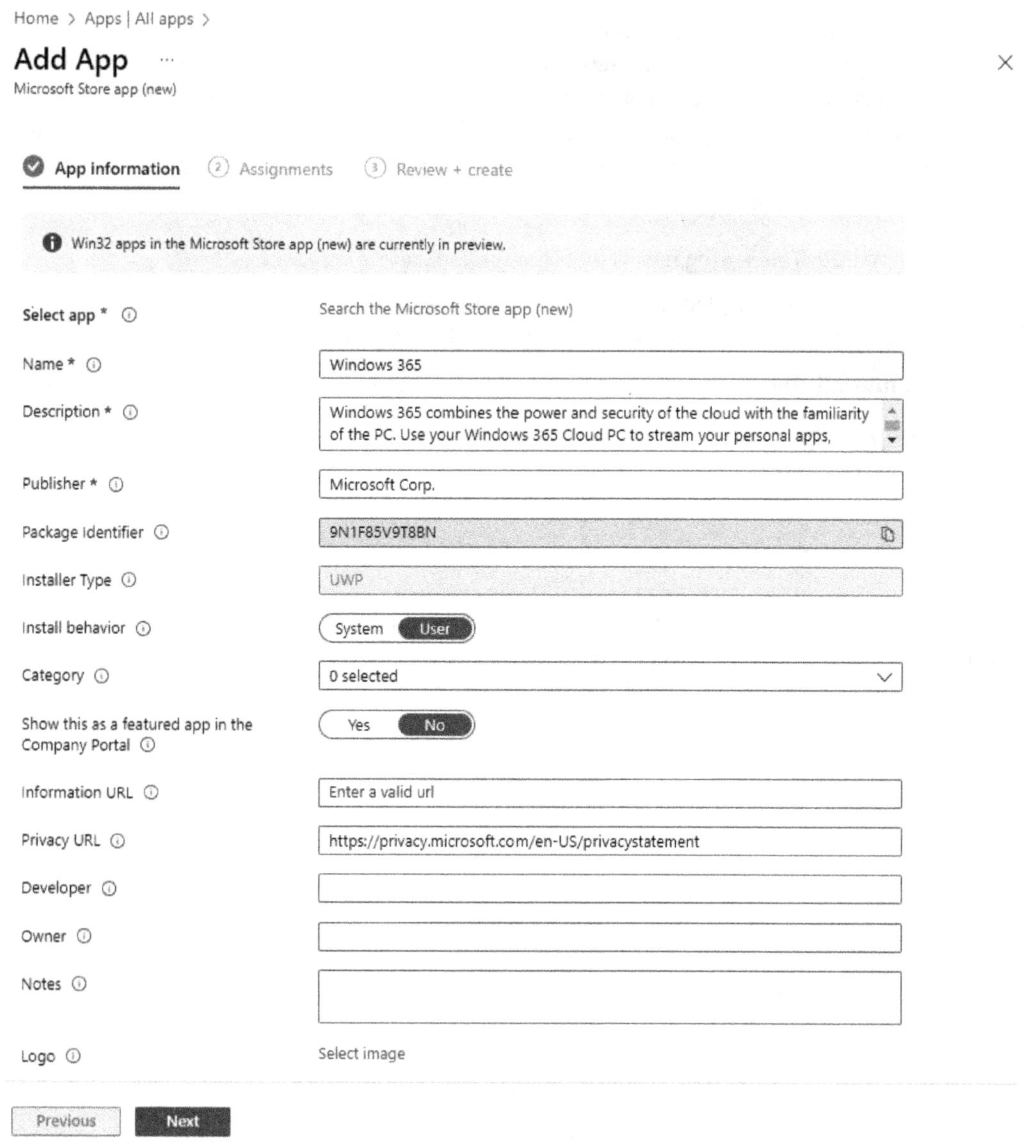

Home > Apps | All apps >

Add App   ...
Microsoft Store app (new)   ✕

✅ **App information**   ② Assignments   ③ Review + create

ℹ️ Win32 apps in the Microsoft Store app (new) are currently in preview.

Select app * ⓘ   Search the Microsoft Store app (new)

Name * ⓘ | Windows 365 |

Description * ⓘ | Windows 365 combines the power and security of the cloud with the familiarity ▲
of the PC. Use your Windows 365 Cloud PC to stream your personal apps, ▼ |

Publisher * ⓘ | Microsoft Corp. |

Package Identifier ⓘ | 9N1F85V9T8BN   ⧉ |

Installer Type ⓘ | UWP |

Install behavior ⓘ   (System **User**)

Category ⓘ | 0 selected   ⌄ |

Show this as a featured app in the (Yes **No**)
Company Portal ⓘ

Information URL ⓘ | Enter a valid url |

Privacy URL ⓘ | https://privacy.microsoft.com/en-US/privacystatement |

Developer ⓘ | |

Owner ⓘ | |

Notes ⓘ | |

Logo ⓘ   Select image

[Previous]   [**Next**]

Figure 5.14 – App information for Windows 365 app deployment from Intune

5. You might want to assign apps to users in a specific **Azure AD** group (e.g., department-based). You can target apps to devices and users. Targeting apps to users means that the users first have to log on before the apps are installed. Target apps to the physical device if you want to install the apps before the user logs on. We can either enforce the installation of an app or allow the user to install it from the company portal themselves. If we want to remove it later on, there is also an option for that:

I.   **Required**: This setting means that installing the app is enforced.

II.   **Available for enrolled devices**: This setting means the users have the option to install the application (e.g., via the **Company Portal** app).

III. **Uninstall**: This setting means the app will be uninstalled.

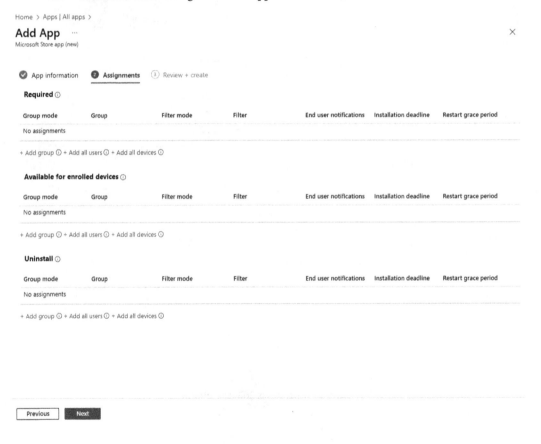

Figure 5.15 – Assignment of Windows 365 app deployment from Intune

6.   As an example, we are going to *push* the application as a *required* app to the **Engineers** group.

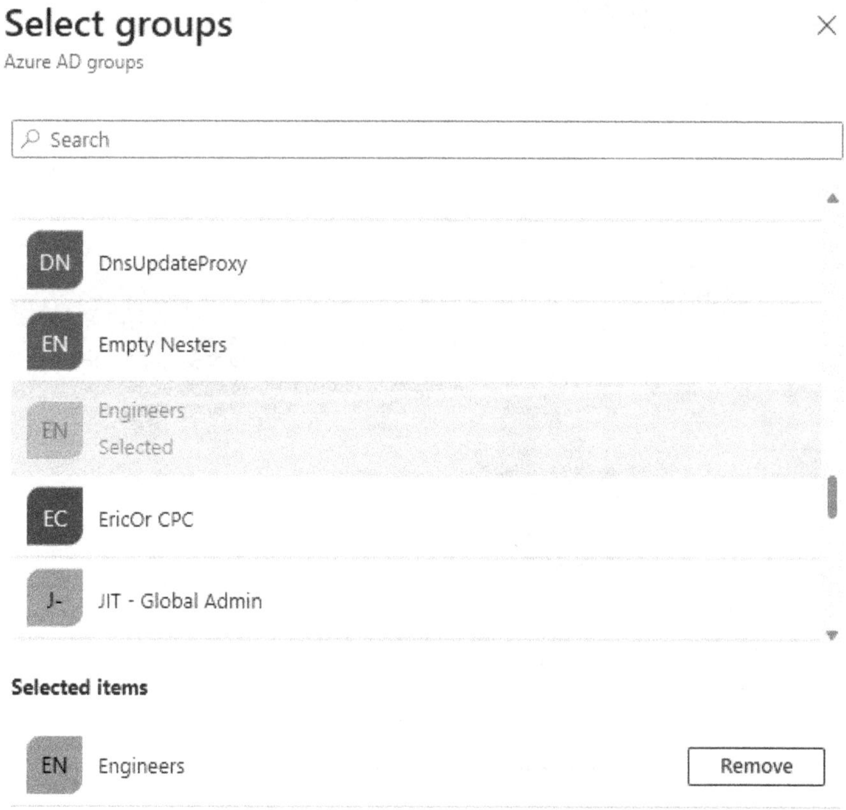

Select groups ✕
Azure AD groups

🔍 Search

▲

DN   DnsUpdateProxy

EN   Empty Nesters

EN   Engineers
         Selected

EC   EricOr CPC

J-   JIT - Global Admin

▼

Selected items

EN   Engineers | Remove |

Figure 5.16 – Selecting a target group to install the Windows 365 app

7.   Once you're ready, confirm the settings in the **Review + create** blade by clicking on **Create**.

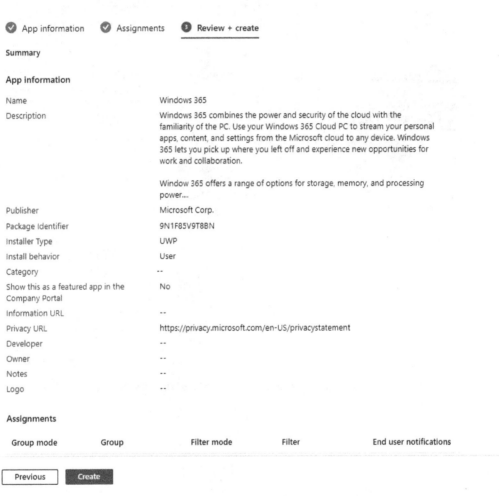

Figure 5.17 – Review the installation settings of the Windows 365 app

The Windows 365 app setup is now complete and will enroll to the Cloud PCs automatically per Intune. This way, users can start using their Cloud PC right away.

Let's jump into what Windows 365 Boot is and how to configure it.

Exploring Windows 365 Boot

Windows 365 Boot enables a user to log directly into their Cloud PC and designate it as the primary Windows experience on the device. This is a great solution for shared devices where different users can log in directly to their own personal, secure Windows 365 Cloud PC with their credentials.

In *Chapter 3*, we explained how you can enroll the Windows 365 Boot feature to your managed Windows 11 endpoints. In this section, we showcase the end user experience from the moment the user is on the login screen after turning on their physical PC. Then we will look at how they access their Cloud PC.

Once the user turns on their physical PC that's set up for Windows 365 Boot, they will be presented with a lock screen like the one shown in the following screenshot.

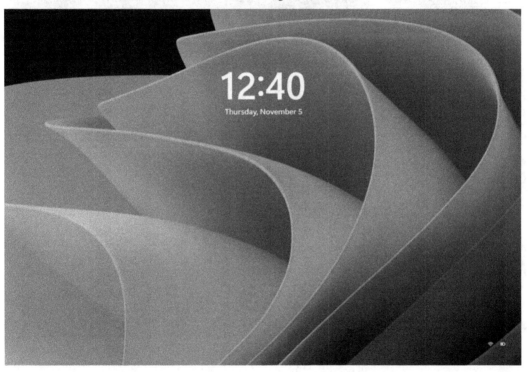

Figure 5.18 – Windows 11 lock screen

From here, the user will need to log in to their Cloud PC, performing these actions in sequence:

1.   Unlock the screen by clicking on the image or press *Enter*. Next, type in the credentials.

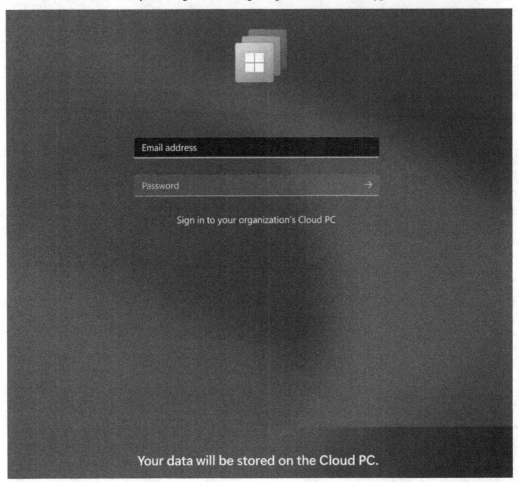

Figure 5.19 – Provide credentials to log in

2. Once the credentials are validated, the user will see the connecting screen shown here.

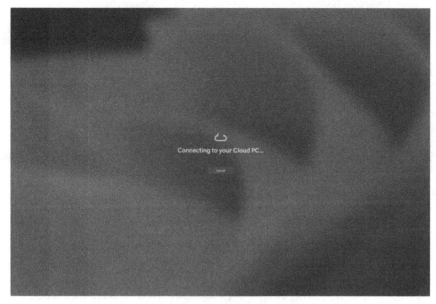

Figure 5.20 – Establishing a connection between a physical PC and a Cloud PC

3. When the user sees the desktop as a physical device, they are logged in to their Cloud PC. They can also confirm that by looking at the connection bar at the top.

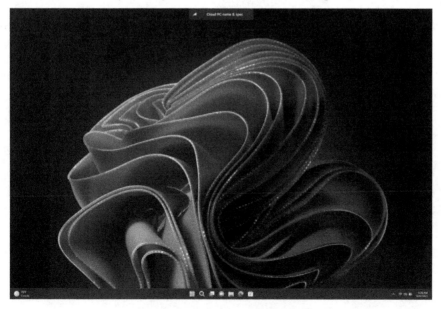

Figure 5.21 – Cloud PC desktop

4. If the user has no license assigned, the following error will be shown:

Figure 5.22 – Connection error for Cloud PC

If your users need to connect to another Wi-Fi connection, they will be able to do this from the Windows lock screen. In the lower-right corner, they will find the Wi-Fi icon to set up the connection. Another great thing is that when the user logs off from within the Cloud PC, they are presented with the local Windows logon screen, hence making the experience like a local experience.

This concludes the Windows 365 Boot experience for end users. Let's take a look at another feature of Windows 365 that helps end users connect and interact with their Cloud PC.

Diving into Windows 365 Switch

With Windows 365 **Switch**, you can seamlessly switch between your Cloud PC and your local desktop using the same keyboard shortcuts, mouse clicks, or swipe gestures. You don't need to leave Windows 11, as everything is integrated with the **Task View** feature. All you need is the Windows 365 app on your physical PC. Once you have it, you can access your Cloud PC from the **Task View** feature (see *Figure 5.24*):

Figure 5.23 – Using Windows 365 Switch

The hidden gem here is that users can do the same in their Cloud PC – go to **Task View** and switch back to the local PC. To use this feature, you need to meet the following requirements:

- Windows 11-based endpoints (Windows 11 Pro and Enterprise 23H2 or higher)
- Windows 365 Cloud PC license

This new round-tripping feature is extremely valuable for **Bring-Your-Own-Device (BYOD)** scenarios when the user connects from their own Windows device to a secure company-owned Cloud PC. Especially in times when businesses want to do more with less, this is a great experience.

> **Important note**
> **Task View** can be found on the Windows taskbar, next to the **Search** button, after installing the Windows 365 app.

First, make sure to get the Windows 365 app. Here's how to do so:

1. Go to the Microsoft Store for Windows.

2. Search for **Windows 365**.

3. Select **Get** to install Windows 365.

4. Select **Open**.

5. You can also download the Windows 365 app directly from `windows365.microsoft.com`.

6. Wait a few hours before Switch is fully enabled on your device.

7. Now, you are ready to start the Windows 365 app and use the new Windows 365 Switch experience

8. Switch first-run experience For new Windows 365 customers, the first-run experience will walk through the new way to connect to Windows 365.

9. Run through the first-run experience wizard.

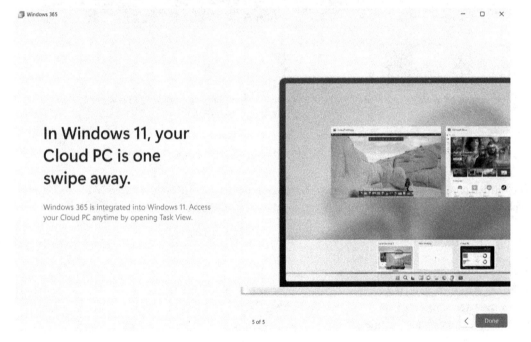

Figure 5.24 – Task View first-run experience

10. After you run through the first-run experience for Switch, you will be notified about the Switch feature by a tooltip on top of the **Task View** icon in the Windows 11 taskbar:

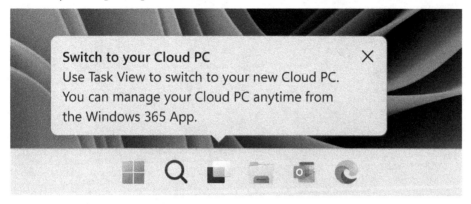

Figure 5.25 – Task View first-run experience

11. For existing Windows 365 customers, the first-run experience teaches them how to connect using Windows 365 Switch:

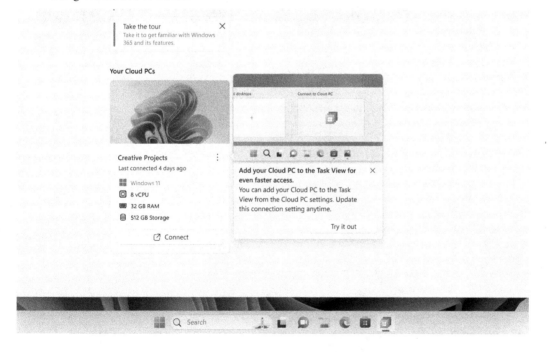

Figure 5.26 – Task View first-run experience

12. The following tooltip explains where to find all the right features inside the Windows 365 app and how to access Switch via the Windows **Task View** feature.

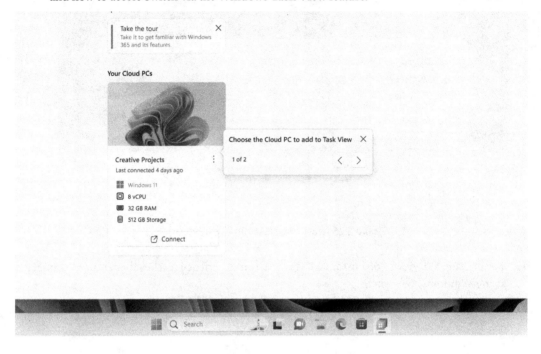

Figure 5.27 – Task View first-run experience

13. Click on **Add to Task View** in the user actions menu to enable Switch.

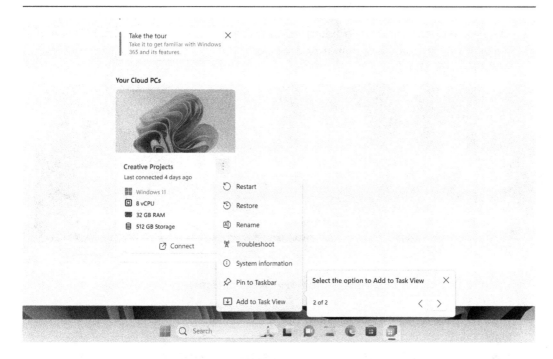

Figure 5.28 – Task View first-run experience

14. You can now open the **Task View** feature with Switch enabled, via the Windows 11 taskbar!

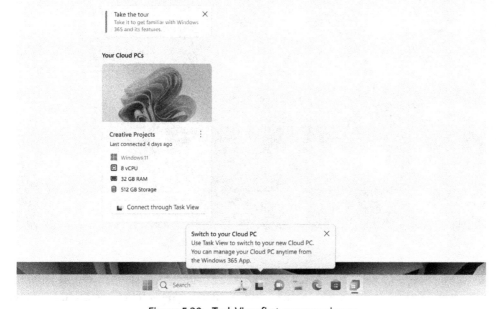

Figure 5.29 – Task View first-run experience

15. Once you click on Connect to Windows 365 in Task View, an experience similar to Windows 365 Boot will start. However, now, from a Windows 11 device that has Windows 365 Switch available on the local PC.

Figure 5.30 – Task view – list of desktops

16. Once you are connected to the Cloud PC, an onscreen indication will confirm this, as shown in the following screenshot:

Figure 5.31 – Switch connection experience

17. Once you have a Cloud PC session running, you can open the **Task View** feature from the Windows 11 taskbar once more. In there, on the left side, you will find the **Local Desktops** option. Once you click on this, you will switch back to the local PC.

> **Important note**
>
> Once you establish the connection to the Cloud PC, switching to and from the Cloud PC will happen within less than a second!

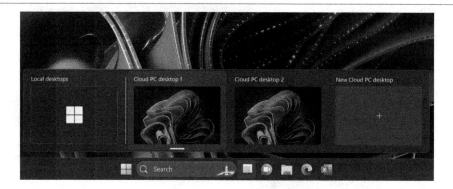

Figure 5.32 – Task View desktops from within Cloud PC

This wraps up the Windows 365 Switch feature. It brings the ability for users to get a good experience switching between their physical PC and a Cloud PC quickly and easily utilizing the capabilities of the Windows 365 app.

The Windows 365 app is not the only way to connect to a Cloud PC. Let's explore how a user can connect from anywhere by using the Windows 365 web client in any supported browser.

Using the Windows 365 web client

It's not only from the Windows 365 app that users can connect to their Cloud PCs. They will also be able to connect from any device, anywhere using a web browser. The connections can be launched from the Windows 365 user portal available at `windows365.microsoft.com`.

> **Software requirements**
>
> The Windows 365 web client is supported only on Microsoft Edge, Google Chrome, Apple Safari, or Mozilla Firefox running on Windows, macOS, ChromeOS, or Linux. For the latest information on the minimum supported version for each of the preceding browsers, please refer to the Microsoft documentation. Also, note that the richest end user experience is available when connecting using the Windows 365 app.

The Windows 365 user portal lists all Cloud PCs assigned to the user. Users have two options to connect to their Cloud PC – using the browser or desktop app. Selecting **Open in browser** launches the Windows 365 web client in a new browser tab. Choosing **Desktop app** will give the user the option to choose between the Windows 365 app or the Remote Desktop client for Windows.

In the following screenshot, you can see a user is logged in to the Windows 365 user portal, showing the available Cloud PC.

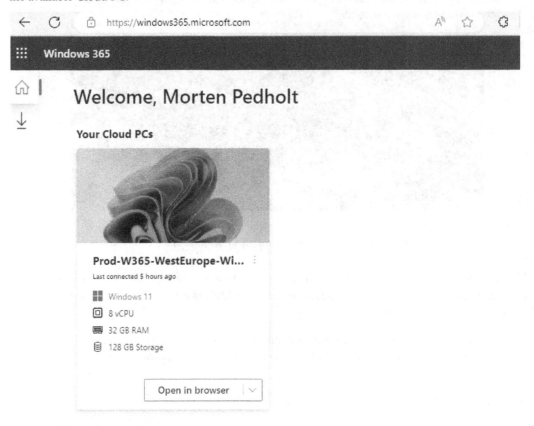

Figure 5.33 – Home page of the Windows 365 user portal

When selecting the **Open in browser** option, the user is then presented with a dialog box named **In Session Settings**, where users can configure which of their local devices can be used in their Cloud PC, such as a printer, clipboard, camera, and more, as shown in the following screenshot:

In Session Settings

Select the devices or features your Cloud PC can use.

☑ Printer

☑ Microphone

☑ Clipboard

☑ Camera (Preview)

☑ Location (Preview)

☑ Keyboard shortcuts (Preview)
Learn about keyboard shortcuts on Cloud PCs

Show Advanced Settings ∧

Alternative Keyboard Layout   ⬤ On

Use an alternative keyboard layout to enter complex characters. Select remote keyboard layout that you want to use in your remote session. This keyboard must be installed in the remote session.

| None   ∨ |

☐ Don't show again   Connect

Figure 5.34 – In Session Settings supported devices

Location

Location redirection lets Cloud PCs access the user's approximate location safely without privacy concerns. For the location to be redirected correctly, the user will need to allow location access to the web browser at the OS level. With this, most apps in the Cloud PC can use the location of the user's physical device apps (please note that the Weather widget isn't currently supported). At the time of publication of this book, this feature is in preview – `https://support.microsoft.com/windows/windows-location-service-and-privacy-3a8eee0a-5b0b-dc07-eede-2a5ca1c49088`. Organizational settings might override the location settings set by the user. For example, your organization might disable location redirection for all Cloud PCs it manages.

Keyboard shortcuts

Users can also use special keyboard shortcuts (combination keys with the Windows key, *Esc*, and so on) when in a Cloud PC session. When the keyboard shortcuts feature is turned on, the Cloud PC session opens in fullscreen as this feature only works in fullscreen mode. The browser shortcut for full screen using *F11* isn't supported when this feature is enabled. Users must use the fullscreen mode from the toolbar.

For a full list of shortcuts, see the Windows documentation at `https://aka.ms/ WindowsKeyboardShortcuts`. At the time of publication of this book, this feature is in preview.

Additionally, in the same **In Session Settings** window, users can choose alternate keyboard layouts. At the time of the publication of this book, the following alternate keyboard layouts are supported:

Figure 5.35 – Supported alternative keyboard layouts

Once connected to the Cloud PC, users can change the in-session settings if they, for example, forgot to select the correct alternative keyboard layout. This prevents the user from needing to start a new connection – they can do it on the fly instead. They can simply go to **Settings** in the top-right corner and select the **In session** menu:

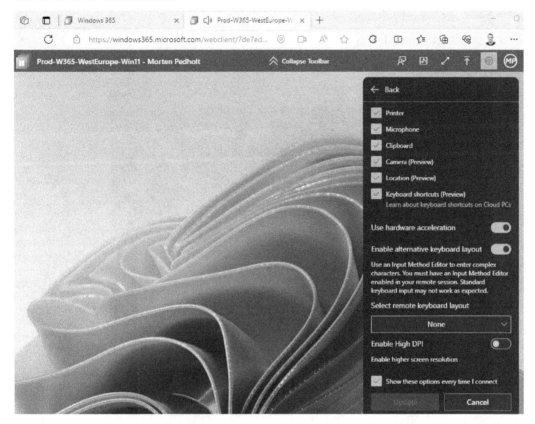

Figure 5.36 – In session menu options while connected to the Cloud PC

Additionally, users can enable features such as **Hardware Acceleration** and **High Dots per Inch (High-DPI)** mode, for enhanced experiences when using the Windows 365 web client. Hardware acceleration uses a local endpoint hardware decoder to accelerate the decoding of the **Remote Desktop Protocol (RDP)**, stream. The high-DPI feature ensures the user content is crisp and clear when using a high-DPI monitor.

Now that we have covered the basics of how a user can use the Windows 365 user portal to connect to their Cloud PC, we will go through the actions and features the user is able to use when they are connected to their Cloud PC from a web browser.

Connection details

If a user has an issue with their connection or thinks their Cloud PC feels slow and laggy, the user can view and download connection details:

1. Select the **Connection details** icon.
2. Click on **Show details**:

Figure 5.37 – Details of connection

3. To download a text file containing the connection details, select **Download report**:

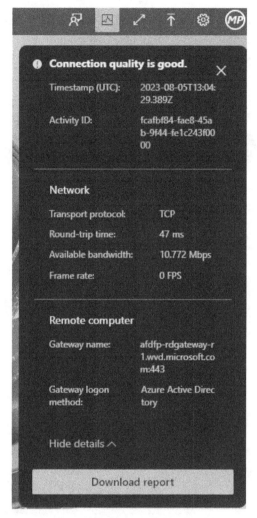

Figure 5.38 – Details of connection

Being able to view network details for a troubleshooting scenario is essential to understand what the issue might be. With that covered, let's jump into how users are able to transfer files between their physical PC and a Cloud PC connected via a web browser.

Transferring files to and from a Cloud PC

Being able to transfer local files to and from a Cloud PC can be useful in certain situations when the files aren't located on OneDrive. It's important to note that if Windows 365 Security Baselines are configured with all the default settings, transferring files like this will not be possible. With that said, let's start with transferring files from local devices to a Cloud PC:

1. Start by selecting the upload icon to launch **File Explorer** on the local device. The upload icon can be found next to the **Settings** icon in the remote session. Select the file and click on **Open**.

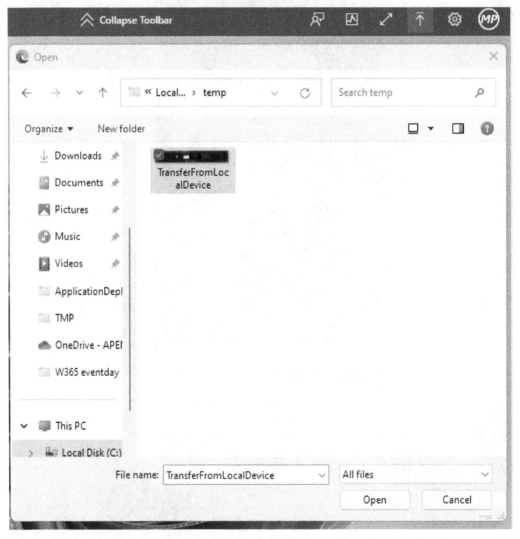

Figure 5.39 – File Explorer opened on the local device after selecting upload

2. Start File Explorer on the Cloud PC and open the `Uploads` folder by either typing in the `\\tsclient\Windows365 virtual drive\Uploads` path or browsing, starting from **This PC | Windows365 virtual drive on RDWebClient | Uploads**. From here, you can move the files locally to the Cloud PC.

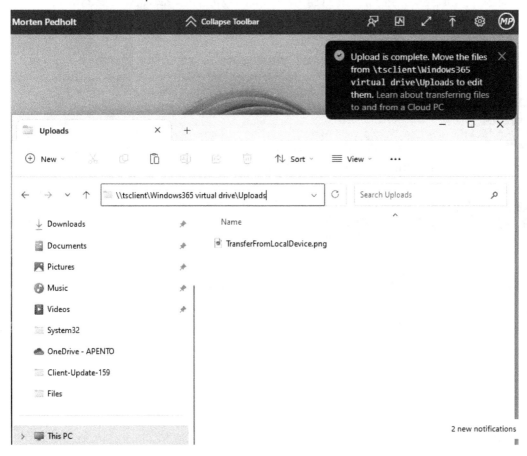

Figure 5.40 – Accessing file uploaded from a local device to a Cloud PC

Transferring files from a Cloud PC to a local device is not that different. Follow these steps to get started:

> **Note**
>
> A prompt will show up the first time you are transferring files to a local device. You will need to select **Yes** to start transferring files.

1. Start File Explorer on the Cloud PC and open the Downloads folder by either typing in the `\\tsclient\Windows365 virtual drive\Downloads` path or browsing, starting from **This PC | Windows365 virtual drive on RDWebClient | Downloads**. Copy the files to the folder.

2. Once the files have been copied to the Downloads folder, the web client will automatically start to download the files in the browser on the local device. Once the download is completed, the files will be removed from the Downloads folder.

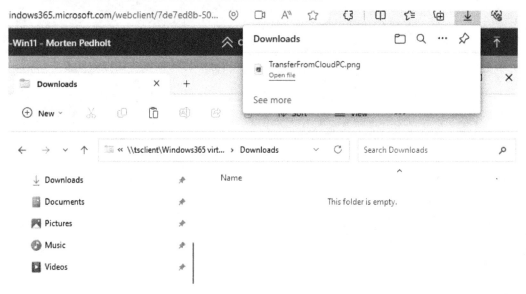

Figure 5.41 – Download file from Cloud PC to local device

Another useful thing to know is how to collect logs when using a Cloud PC from the browser.

Collecting user logs

Users can collect logs of their Cloud PC sessions. The logs are collected from the browser and the user can choose the save location.

To turn on log collection, on the connection bar in the client, select the gear icon and then **Capture logs**.

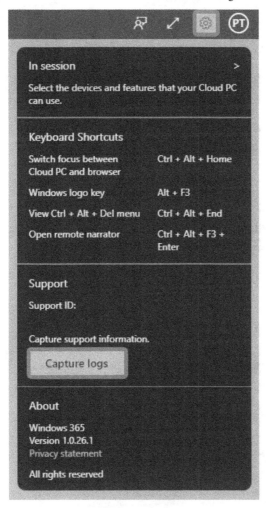

Figure 5.42 – Capture logs

We have now walked you through all the great Windows 365 web app client features. Let's continue the journey in the next section.

Dark mode

To switch the Windows 365 web portal (`windows365.microsoft.com`) to dark mode, take the following steps:

1. Go to `windows365.microsoft.com`.
2. Select the settings icon and turn on the **Dark Mode** setting:

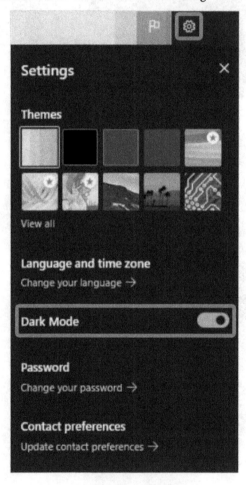

Figure 5.43 – Enable Dark Mode

Now that we have learned how users can manage their connection settings when using a web client, let's look at how users can perform actions on their Cloud PCs when using the Windows 365 web portal.

Performing user actions on Windows 365 Cloud PC

Users being able to perform actions on their Cloud PC is one of the core elements in giving users an optimal experience compared to traditional VDI environments where they are very limited. Windows 365 makes it easy for users to take action on their Cloud PCs without having to depend on IT. Users are able to perform actions from the Windows 365 user portal and the Windows 365 app.

User actions are available under the three dots (…) on a Cloud PC card:

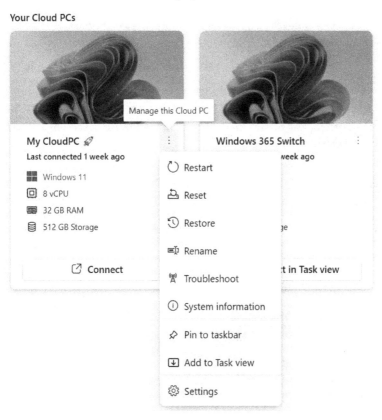

Figure 5.44 – Cloud PC user actions

- **Restart** restarts the Cloud PC.
- **Reset** does the following:

  - Reinstalls Windows (with the option to choose between Windows 11 and Windows 10).
  - Removes personal files.

- Removes any changes to settings.

- Removes apps installed by the user.

> **Important note**
>
> Before resetting your Cloud PC, make sure to back up any important files you need to keep in a cloud storage service or external storage. Resetting your Cloud PC will delete these files.

- **Restore** recovers the Cloud PC from a snapshot. We covered the backup and restore of Cloud PCs in detail in *Chapter 4*.

- **Rename** changes the name of the Cloud PC shown to the user that's logged in to the website.

> **Important note**
>
> This action doesn't affect any names in **Microsoft Intune**, **Azure AD**, on the device, or in **Microsoft Remote Desktop** apps.

- **Troubleshoot** troubleshoots connection issues and attempts to resolve any issues that may be preventing a user from connecting to their Cloud PC. The checks include the following:

  - The installation state and availability of all software required by Windows 365

  - Ensuring that the Azure resources are available

Here are the results of running the troubleshooter:

Return state	Description
No issues detected	None of the checks discovered an issue with the Cloud PC.
Issues resolved	An issue was detected and fixed.
Can't connect to Cloud PC. We're working to fix it, try again later.	A Microsoft service required for connectivity is unavailable. Try connecting again later.
We couldn't fix issues with your Cloud PC. Contact your administrator.	An issue was detected but it couldn't be fixed. This issue exists because of an ongoing Windows update or another issue. If this error persists for an extended period, the Cloud PC may need to be reset.

Table 5.2 – Troubleshooter return state and description

System information displays information about the Cloud PC specification. **Pin to taskbar/Unpin from taskbar** adds or removes, respectively, a shortcut to the Windows taskbar so that users can launch a connection to their Cloud PCs without needing to open the Windows 365 app.

Add to Task view/Remove from Task view adds or removes, respectively, a shortcut to Windows **Task View** so that users can utilize the new Windows 365 Switch feature to connect to their Cloud PCs.

Settings allows users to customize connection properties to their Cloud PC.

Getting to know the different available user actions is crucial to get the full experience that Windows 365 offers. Once end users understand the use and capabilities of these actions, it can benefit them greatly.

Next, we'll look at some different clients that can be used to establish a connection to Windows 365 Cloud PCs.

Knowing about alternate clients

In addition to Windows 365 clients, users can also use alternate clients to connect to Windows 365. In this section, we will look at alternate clients from Microsoft as well as approved partners.

Microsoft Remote Desktop client

Users can also use the Microsoft Remote Desktop app on Windows, macOS, iOS/iPadOS, and Android to access their Cloud PCs. Here are the instructions to set up the Remote Desktop client:

1. Download and install the Remote Desktop client from the platform-specific store.

   - Windows: `https://aka.ms/AVDWin`

   - macOS: `https://aka.ms/RDMac`

   - iOS/iPadOS: `https://aka.ms/RDiOS`

   - Android: `https://aka.ms/RDAnd`

2. Open the Remote Desktop client.

3. Select **Subscribe** or **Add Workspace**, depending on the client. If you're asked for a workspace URL, enter the following: `https://rdweb.wvd.microsoft.com/api/arm/feeddiscovery`.

4. Enter the Azure AD credentials.

5. The Cloud PC appears in the list, and it can be double-clicked to launch it.

> **Note**
> There is an option to remove step 3 for Windows clients. This can be done by creating a configuration profile with the **Auto-subscription** catalog setting configured to `https://rdweb.wvd.microsoft.com/api/arm/feeddiscovery`.

Now let's see how users can use non-Microsoft clients to connect to Windows 365.

Approved Linux thin clients

Linux-based thin clients from various renowned manufacturers such as **10ZiG**, **Dell**, **HP**, **IGEL**, **NComputing**, **Stratodesk**, and others offer seamless connectivity to your Windows 365 Cloud PCs. These approved partners offer advanced management tools specific to their offerings, which you can explore further in *Chapter 8* on **Windows 365 Partner Solutions**.

Alternatively, you can utilize the Windows 365 web client on **Linux thin clients**.

> **Important note**
>
> If you face problems while connecting to Windows 365 using an approved partner's thin client, check whether the issue is specific to that client. To do this, try reproducing the issue on any Windows 365 app or Remote Desktop client. If the issue is unique to the thin client, contact the respective thin client provider for assistance.

Connecting from a company website or application

Windows 365 has simplified the process for customers to showcase Cloud PCs on their company website and line-of-business applications, allowing seamless launching of connections in either the Windows 365 web client or the Windows client. This functionality is achieved through the use of **Microsoft Graph APIs** specifically designed for Cloud PCs.

> **Important note**
>
> The Azure AD administrator must grant the **CloudPC.Read.All** permission to the website or line-of-business application so that it can read the Cloud PC properties on behalf of the user.

The following steps illustrate how you can use Cloud PC Graph APIs within your own web and native applications.

Step 1 – getting the user's Cloud PCs

Run the following request for the user with the sandeep@masteringw365.com **User Principal Name (UPN)** and make a note of the Cloud PC ID:

```
Request
Example Request if running in the context of the user:
GET https://graph.microsoft.com/beta/me/cloudPCs
Example request if running with elevated privileges:
GET https://graph.microsoft.com/beta/users/{userID or UPN}/cloudPCs
GET https://graph.microsoft.com/beta/users/sandeep@masteringw365.com/
cloudPCsResponse (Example)
HTTP/1.1 200 OK
```

```
Content-Type: application/json
{
  "value": [
    {
      "@odata.type": "#microsoft.graph.cloudPC",
      "aadDeviceId": "f5ff445f-7488-40f8-8ab9-ee784a9c1f33",
      "id": "2c6d9f4c-16f4-4f32-a868-f5e5d7f5a5f1",
      "displayName": "Demo-1",
      "imageDisplayName": "Windows-10 19h1-evd",
      "servicePlanId": "dbb9148c-ff83-4a4c-8d7f-28752e93ffff",
      "servicePlanName": "lite",
      "servicePlanType": "enterprise",
      "status": "provisioned",
      "lastModifiedDateTime": "2020-11-03T10:29:57Z",
      "statusDetails": null,
      "gracePeriodEndDateTime": "2020-11-010T20:00:34Z",
      "provisioningType": "dedicated",
      "diskEncryptionState": "encryptedUsingPlatformManagedKey"
    }
  ]
}
```

Now that we have retrieved the Cloud PCs assigned to the user, let's look at how to launch the connection.

Step 2 – launching the connection

In this step, we will look at how to launch connections to loud PCs using the Windows 365 web client as well as the Windows 365 app.

The web client

To launch the connection in the Windows 365 web client, append the Cloud PC ID from the preceding response, as illustrated:

```
https://windows365.microsoft.com/webclient/{cloudPCId}
```

```
https://windows365.microsoft.com/webclient/2c6d9f4c-16f4-4f32-a868-
f5e5d7f5a5f1
```

The Windows client

To launch the connection in the Windows 365 app, run the following request with the Cloud PC ID:

```
Request
GET https://graph.microsoft.com/beta/me/cloudPCs/{cloudPCId}/
getCloudPcLaunchInfo
GET https://graph.microsoft.com/beta/me/cloudPCs/2c6d9f4c-16f4-4f32-
a868-f5e5d7f5a5f1/getCloudPcLaunchInfo
```

Response (example)

If successful, this method returns a 200 OK response code and a cloudPC object in the response body.

```
HTTP/1.1 200 OK
Content-Type: application/json
{
   "@odata.context": "https://graph.microsoft.com/
beta/$metadata#microsoft.graph.cloudPcLaunchInfo",
   "cloudPcId": "2c6d9f4c-16f4-4f32-a868-f5e5d7f5a5f1",
   "cloudPcLaunchUrl": "https://rdweb-r0.wvd.microsoft.com/api/
arm/weblaunch/tenants/9e662874-97f5-4b01-b7c2-3d08e816eaaa/
resources/50c9bb56-0c09-4f3a-a771-2fcb1ce07e8e",
}
```

From the preceding response, make a note of the workspace ID and resources ID from cloudPcLaunchUrl. These are as follows in the preceding example:

- Workspace ID = 9e662874-97f5-4b01-b7c2-3d08e816eaaa

- Resources ID = 50c9bb56-0c09-4f3a-a771-2fcb1ce07e8e

Now launch the connection using this URL: ms-avd:connect?env=avdarm&workspaceid={workspaceid}&resourceid={resourceid}&username={UPN}&version=0.

Here is an example output:

```
ms-avd:connect?env=avdarm&workspaceid=9e662874-97f5-4b01-b7c2-
3d08e816eaaa&resourceid=50c9bb56-0c09-4f3a-a771-2fcb1ce07e8e&
username=sandeep@masteringw365.com&version=0
```

With the preceding two steps, you can now provide your users with a completely tailored connection center experience.

Meeting endpoint requirements

In this section, we will explore the hardware requirements for accessing a Cloud PC. These requirements differ based on the client, platform, and peripherals. Additionally, we will delve into additional hardware options that can enhance the overall experience, taking it from satisfactory to extraordinary!

One of the major advantages of Cloud PCs is their ability to leverage cloud resources for seamless performance. However, it's important to note that there are minimal resource requirements on the endpoint side. As your endpoint setup expands, such as with multiple monitors or higher resolutions such as 4K, and the inclusion of specific offloaded workloads such as Teams, the minimum hardware requirements will increase. The Cloud PC experience can be impacted by other applications running on the endpoint. To ensure a smooth experience, it's always recommended to consult the hardware manufacturer or software developer for any additional hardware needs. The following subsections cover the software and hardware requirements of each of the popular endpoint operating systems.

Windows

The Windows 365 app for Windows can be run on any Windows device that meets the requirements of Windows 11 or Windows 10 and the following:

CPU	2vCPU with 1 GHz
RAM	4 GB
Hard drive	200 MB
.NET Framework	4.6.1
Video	DirectX 9 or later with WDDM 1.0 driver

Table 5.3 – Minimum requirements for running the Windows 365 app on Windows

These are the additional requirements for Microsoft Teams and Multimedia offload:

CPU	2vCPU with 1.6 GHz and support for AVX2 instruction set

Table 5.4 – Additional requirements for running Microsoft Teams and MMR offload

Web browsers

The Windows 365 web client is compatible with web browsers that support **WebAssembly** and **WebGL** technologies. The endpoint device must satisfy the specific requirements of the chosen browser for optimal performance.

macOS and iOS

Connections to Windows 365 using the Microsoft Remote Desktop client are supported on any Apple endpoint that supports the following:

macOS	10.14 or later
iOS/iPadOS	15.0 or later

Table 5.5 – Minimum requirements for running the Microsoft Remote Desktop app on Apple platforms

Android

Connections to Windows 365 using the Microsoft Remote Desktop client are supported on any Android endpoint that supports the following:

Android	9 or later

Table 5.6 – Minimum requirements for running the Microsoft Remote Desktop app on Android

Linux

Linux-based thin clients from various manufacturers such as Dell, HP, IGEL, and others are available for connecting to your Windows 365 Cloud PCs. To ensure compatibility, we advise visiting their official websites to obtain the minimum configuration requirements.

Now that we understand how users can connect from different endpoints, let's look at how we can deliver premium end user experiences.

Delivering a premium experience

In this part of the chapter, we will take the liberty of sharing some technical information at a level that is different from the rest of the chapter. Hopefully, you'll enjoy geeking out in this section. The Windows 365 experience can be greatly enhanced with the appropriate hardware configuration. Windows 365 connections use RDP. RDP uses the following codecs:

- **Wavelet/Calista Progressive Codec**: Primarily used for image encoding.

- **Clear Codec Run-Length Encoding** (based on **NSCodec**): Specifically designed for text encoding.

- **AVC444/H.264**: A fullscreen codec that takes advantage of hardware decoding and encoding when available. Commonly utilized with thin clients.

- **AVC420/H.264**: A variant of the preceding codec optimized for video playback regions with reduced color space. Used in conjunction with Wavelet and Clear Codec.

- **RDP**: Used for the rest of the encoding tasks.

Furthermore, RDP incorporates different profiles, which can be summarized as follows:

- A combination of software codecs and H.264 for video encoding (default profile)
- Fullscreen H.264 encoding (forced profile)

To leverage hardware acceleration for H.264 decoding on the client side, RDP utilizes **DirectX Video Acceleration** (**DXVA**) and **Media Foundation** (**MF**). Additionally, for color conversion, RDP employs DXVA shader-based conversion or Streaming Single Instruction, Multiple Data Extension 2 (**SSE2**) optimized code for software-based conversion. These techniques ensure efficient processing and improved performance during encoding and decoding operations. Here are the decoding profiles the hardware should support:

Decode Profile Name	Decode Profile ID
DXVA_ModeH264_E	`{1b81be68-a0c7-11d3-b984-00c04f2e73c5}`
DXVA_ModeH264_F	{1b81be69-a0c7-11d3-b984-00c04f2e73c5}
DXVA_ModeH264_VLD_WithFMOASO_NoFGT	{d5f04ff9-3418-45d8-9561-32a76aae2ddd}
TS_DXVA2_Intel_ModeH264_VLD_NoFGT	{604f8e68-4951-4c54-88fe-abd25c15b3d6}
TS_DXVA2_Intel_ModeH264_VLD_FGT	{604f8e69-4951-4c54-88fe-abd25c15b3d6}

Table 5.7 – Remote Desktop Protocol decoding profiles

Additionally, the availability of the above hardware (e.g., a GPU) significantly improves Microsoft Teams and multimedia offload performance.

Web client performance can be improved when connecting from a browser that supports **WebCodecs**. The Windows 365 web client uses a hardware decoder instead of a software decoder when connecting from such a browser.

In this section, we looked at enhancements from an endpoint point of view. In the next section, we will look at them from a protocol and networking point of view.

Implementing protocol enhancements

Another critical element for providing enhanced end user experiences is the protocol used to deliver content. In this section, we will delve into new RDP enhancements, end user network enhancements, and improvements to Microsoft Teams workloads that are bandwidth-heavy.

RDP Shortpath

Cloud PCs can use **RDP Shortpath** to establish connections over the **User Datagram Protocol** (**UDP**). We covered RDP Shortpath in detail in *Chapter 2*, so please hop on over there for a refresher on what it is and why is it important. If your network's firewall blocks UDP traffic, RDP Shortpath will not be able to establish a data flow and will instead use **TCP-based reverse connect transport**. Let's have a look at the raw data differences. Start by looking at the following screenshot to see what a connection to a Cloud PC with TCP looks like.

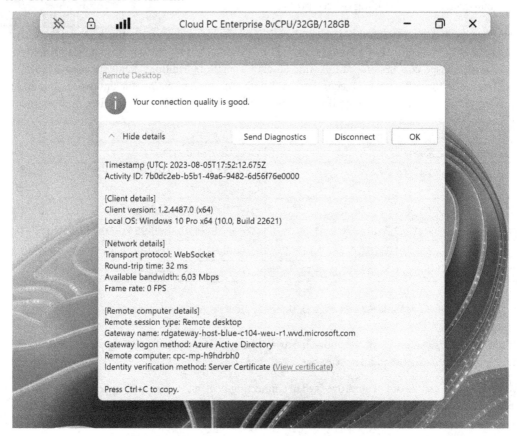

Figure 5.45 – Cloud PC utilizing a TCP-based connection

Now look at when the connection takes advantage of the UDP connection. It will boost the available bandwidth a lot, and everything will feel much faster as there are no handshake validations anymore.

Figure 5.46 – Cloud PC utilizing a UDP-based connection

While you don't usually need to do any special configurations to support RDP Shortpath in public networks, the direct connection may be negatively affected in some network configurations.

There may be different reasons why a Cloud PC isn't able to utilize RDP Shortpath. Enabling Teredo increases the likelihood of a successful RDP Shortpath connection in IPv4-only networks by adding additional NAT traversal candidates.

To enable Teredo, run the following command from an elevated PowerShell prompt:

```
Set-NetTeredoConfiguration -Type Enterpriseclient
```

If the user is connecting from their home network, having **Universal Plug and Play** (**UPnP**) enabled will improve the chances of a direct connection to Windows 365 Cloud PCs. UPnP is a standard technology used by various applications, such as online gaming, delivery optimization, and Teredo, among others. UPnP is generally available on modern home routers and is enabled by default. It is essential for users to verify that UPnP remains enabled and has not been disabled for any purpose.

We covered the network requirements to utilize RDP Shortpath in the *Networking dataflow* section in *Chapter 2*. There, you will find all the information associated with RDP Shortpath.

Now let's look at how to enhance the network on the end user side.

Enhancing the end user network

Windows 365 offers a highly efficient and flexible Cloud PC solution, empowering users to be productive from anywhere, anytime. However, to fully harness the potential of Cloud PC and ensure a seamless and extraordinary experience, it is crucial to set up your network correctly.

Windows 365 connections utilize intelligent algorithms that strike the right balance between performance and throughput, striving to deliver experiences that closely resemble local environments. This implies that the end user's network, in conjunction with the endpoint configuration, significantly influences the quality of experience they receive. Furthermore, keeping Windows 365 clients up to date contributes to improving connection reliability.

In this section, we will explore invaluable insights and best practices for enhancing network performance and minimizing latency, ultimately providing you with a seamless and immersive Cloud PC experience. We will delve into the key components of a Cloud PC network, offering comprehensive guidance and step-by-step instructions for optimal network configuration.

To optimize your network for an exceptional Cloud PC experience, there are several key considerations to keep in mind. First and foremost, your network hardware plays a critical role in providing stable connectivity. It is recommended to use a high-quality router capable of handling high bandwidth demands. Consider utilizing a wired Ethernet connection instead of relying solely on wireless connections to minimize latency and improve stability.

To maximize network performance, it is important to assess your internet connection speed and ensure it meets the minimum requirements for Cloud PC. Prioritizing Cloud PC traffic over other network activities can be achieved by implementing **Quality of Service** (**QoS**) settings on your router. This allows you to allocate sufficient bandwidth to Cloud PC and limit the consumption of other devices or applications running concurrently on the network. Additionally, closing unnecessary background applications or processes that consume bandwidth can significantly improve Cloud PC performance.

Reducing network latency is crucial for an immersive Cloud PC experience. Enabling QoS to prioritize Cloud PC traffic and minimizing latency caused by other network activities is recommended. When possible, utilizing a wired connection instead of wireless can help minimize latency introduced by signal interference or distance. Modern routers often offer QoS settings that allow you to prioritize Cloud PC traffic, ensuring it takes precedence over other types of traffic on your network.

Network security is paramount when utilizing Cloud PC. It is essential to keep your network and Cloud PC endpoints protected with up-to-date antivirus software and firewalls to prevent security threats. Enabling port forwarding or utilizing UPnP to ensure the necessary ports for Cloud PC are open is advised. Implementing a secure Wi-Fi password also helps prevent unauthorized access and potential disruptions to your Cloud PC experience.

To maintain network stability, it is recommended to reduce network disruptions by avoiding bandwidth-intensive activities on other devices during Cloud PC sessions. Ensuring that your Cloud PC endpoints are within range of the router and avoiding physical obstructions that can interfere with the wireless signal is important. Regularly updating firmware for network devices allows you to benefit from performance enhancements and bug fixes.

By following these best practices, such as optimizing network settings, managing bandwidth effectively, minimizing latency, ensuring network security, and maintaining network stability, you can create an exceptional Cloud PC environment. These efforts will enable you to enjoy an immersive and seamless Cloud PC experience, empowering you to be productive from any location and on any device.

In summary, to achieve an exceptional Cloud PC experience, end users can optimize their network for Cloud PC, which will reduce latency, improve stability, and enhance performance. Key factors in creating an immersive and seamless Cloud PC environment include prioritizing Cloud PC traffic, managing bandwidth effectively, minimizing latency, ensuring network security, and maintaining network stability. By following these best practices, users can be productive no matter where or which device they connect from.

Microsoft Teams

Microsoft Teams serves as a fundamental component of the Microsoft 365 services integrated into Cloud PC. With Windows 365, audio and video traffic are efficiently offloaded to your endpoint, ensuring a seamless Teams video experience comparable to that of a physical PC. In the *Networking dataflow* section in *Chapter 2*, we covered all the network requirements to get the optimal Microsoft Teams experience on a Cloud PC. To ensure the correctness of the setup, we recommend customers use the gallery images in Windows 365 that contain Microsoft 365 apps, Microsoft Teams optimizations, multimedia redirection, and other pre-installed settings.

Improving Microsoft Teams calls

To enhance calling and meeting experiences in Microsoft Teams, it is crucial to prioritize important network traffic using **Quality of Service (QoS)**. Network congestion can result in video freezes or call drops when voice and video traffic, represented by IP packets, arrive out of sequence or encounter delays. Implementing QoS can address this issue.

QoS allows for the prioritization of time-sensitive network traffic, such as voice and video streams, granting them precedence over less sensitive traffic such as downloading applications. By leveraging **Windows Group Policy Objects** and **Port-based Access Control Lists**, QoS identifies and marks packets in real-time streams, ensuring voice, video, and screen-sharing traffic receives dedicated network bandwidth.

For a comprehensive understanding of implementing QoS for Teams, please refer to the article on Teams QoS mentioned in the *Further reading* section.

In this section, we learned about protocol and network enhancements and how to implement them. Now, let's look at graphics enhancements for improved content fidelity, and therefore a better end user experience.

Utilizing graphics enhancements

In this section, we will explore various graphics enhancements, delving into the diverse defaults across protocols and vendors. By understanding these differences, you will gain insights into optimizing graphics quality while considering resource utilization on Cloud PC endpoints.

RDP profiles

When it comes to graphics enhancements for improved end user experiences, it is important to consider the impact of default settings on both quality and resource utilization. Each protocol has its own set of defaults that influence these factors. Notably, default graphics quality settings vary among different vendors, leading to variations in performance and visual output.

For instance, RDP, used by Windows 365, prioritizes image quality and maintains 100% fidelity without compromising color accuracy (a.k.a. 4:4:4 chroma subsampling). On the other hand, many video codecs utilize 4 : 2 : 2 chroma subsampling (instead of 4 : 4 : 4) to optimize content, but this approach can result in a reduction in color fidelity.

The following table details the different RDP profiles and how to enable them using **Group Policy Objects (GPOs)** on Cloud PCs under **Windows Components | Remote Desktop Services | Remote Desktop Session Host | Remote Session Environment**.

Profile	Value	How to set up using Group Policy Editor
Balanced	2	This is the default profile when the GPO **Configure RemoteFX Adaptive Graphics** setting is **Not Configured** or set to **Enabled** with **Let the system choose the experience for the network condition** selected in the drop-down list.
Maximum Compression	4	Select the GPO **Configure compression for RemoteFX data** setting and set it to **Enabled** with **Optimized to use less network bandwidth** selected in the drop-down list.
Lossless Profile	8	Select the GPO **Configure image quality for RemoteFX Adaptive Graphics** setting and set it to **Enabled** with **Lossless** selected in the drop-down list.
Thin client profile	128	This is turned on automatically when connecting from low-powered **ARM-based endpoints**.
Fullscreen AVC 444 profile	2048	Select the GPO **Prioritize H.264/AVC 444 graphics mode for Remote Desktop Connections** setting and set it to **Enabled**.

Table 5.8 – Remote Desktop Protocol profiles

These RDP profiles can also be set using Microsoft Intune using the following steps:

1. Go to **Microsoft Intune admin center | Devices | Configuration Profiles**.

2. Create a configuration profile by setting **Platform** as **Windows 10 and later** and **Profile type** as **Templates** and select **Administrative templates**.

3. Once on the **Configuration settings** tab, navigate to **Computer Configuration | Windows Components | Remote Desktop Services | Remote Desktop Session Host | Remote Session Environment**.

4. Click on the setting you want to configure and make the changes as described in the preceding table.

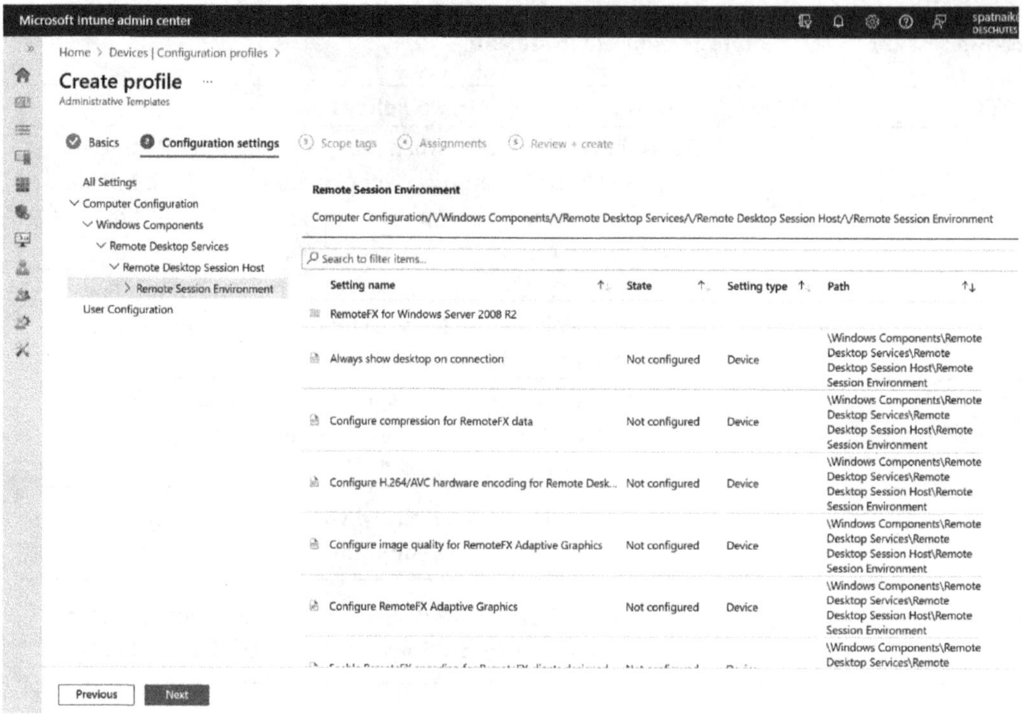

Figure 5.47 – RDP profile settings in Microsoft Intune admin center

5. Next, set **Scope tags**, **Assignments**, and finally, **Review** and select **Create**. For detailed instructions, please refer to the *Creating a CSP* section in *Chapter 4*.

Setting frame rates

The RDP is smart enough to only update frames if there are any changes on the screen. However, in cases where the screen is frequently changing, the frame rate is capped at 30 **frames per second (fps)**, by default. The maximum frame rate can be updated by setting the **DWMFRAMEINTERVAL** entry in the Windows Registry to change the maximum frame rate limit on the remote session host. Here are the steps:

1. Open Registry Editor and navigate to `HKEY_LOCAL_MACHINE\SYSTEM\CurrentControlSet\Control\Terminal Server\WinStations`.

2. In the **Edit** menu, select **New**, and then select **DWORD(32-bit) Value**.

3. Type `DWMFRAMEINTERVAL` and then press *Enter*.

4. Right-click **DWMFRAMEINTERVAL** and select **Modify**.

5. Select **Decimal** and type in the **Value data** box the appropriate number from the following list:

   - 15 decimal = 60 frames

   - 10 decimal = 40 frames

   - 5 decimal = 20 frames

   - 1 decimal = 4 frames

6. Select **OK** and exit Registry Editor, and then restart the computer for the changes to take effect.

Setting frame rates from Microsoft Intune

Even though we can set the frame rates manually, it's not a user-friendly way to do it, and the user might not have the knowledge and permission to do it. There is no setting for this in Microsoft Intune, but we can use the PowerShell script functionality that allows us to run a PowerShell script on devices.

Before we go into Intune, we need to have the script ready:

1. On a Windows device, open the PowerShell ISE.

2. Paste the following code in and replace the value data if needed:

```
New-ItemProperty -Path "HKLM:\SYSTEM\CurrentControlSet\Control\
Terminal Server\WinStations" -Name "DWMFRAMEINTERVAL" -Value 15
-PropertyType DWord
```

3. Save the file as `.ps1` on the Windows device.

4. Log in to Microsoft Intune.

5. Go to **Devices** | **Windows** | **PowerShell Scripts** and click on **+ Add**.

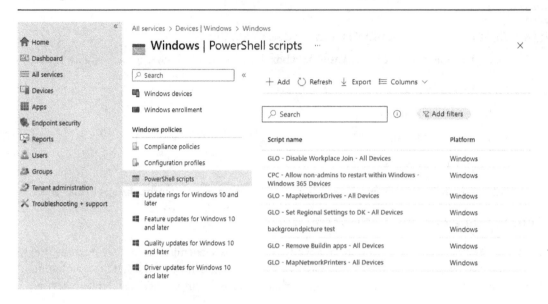

Figure 5.48 – Deploy a PowerShell script from Intune

6. Provide a name for the PowerShell script deployment and click on **Next**.

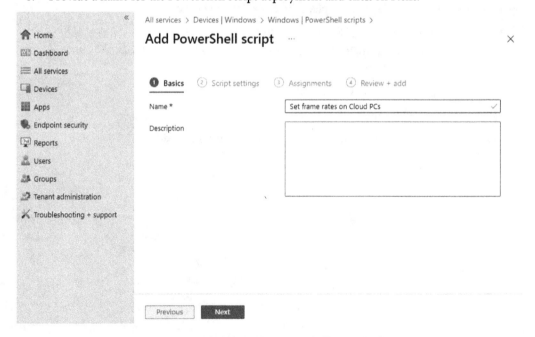

Figure 5.49 – Provide a name for PowerShell script deployment

7. In **Script location**, browse to the file you saved earlier. Make sure **Run this script using the logged on credentials** is set to **No**. This will ensure the script will run in a system context that is allowed to change Registry settings. Set **Run script in 64 bit PowerShell Host** to **Yes**. Click on **Next**.

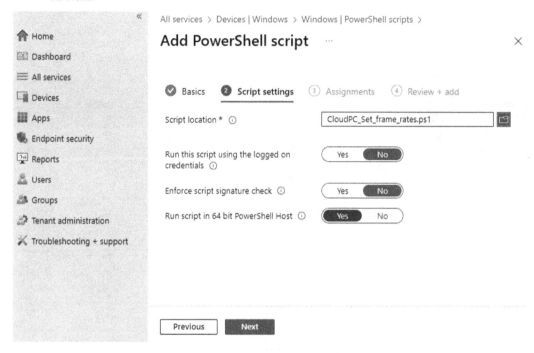

Figure 5.50 – Upload PowerShell script

8.   Select a group with the Cloud PCs you want to apply this setting in. Click **Next**.

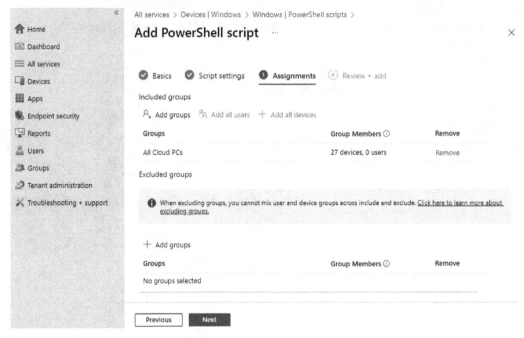

Figure 5.51 – Choose an assignment group

9.   Review the settings and click **Add** to finalize the PowerShell script deployment of frame rates to Cloud PCs.

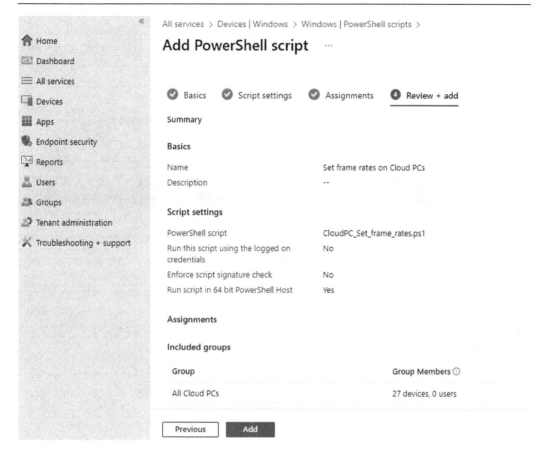

Figure 5.52 – Review PowerShell deployment settings

Now that we have seen how to enhance the user experience of high frame rate content on the Cloud PC side, let's look into improving it on the endpoint side with protocol improvements such as multimedia redirection.

Multimedia redirection

In Windows 365 Cloud PCs, **Multimedia Redirection** (**MMR**) ensures seamless video playback when watching videos in Microsoft Edge or Google Chrome. By redirecting media content from the Cloud PC to the endpoint, MMR accelerates processing and rendering, resulting in enhanced performance and a like-local experience.

We recommend customers use the gallery images with Microsoft 365 apps, Microsoft Teams optimizations, MMR, and other settings pre-installed. We also recommend these images as the starting point for creating custom images.

> **Important note**
>
> Multimedia redirection is only available for the *Windows 365 app* and *Remote Desktop Client for Windows* (at the time of writing this book).

Even though all MMR components get installed automatically when using gallery images, the MMR extension itself is not enabled by default. This means users need to go in and enable the extension when they first get their Cloud PC. To help with that experience, we can configure a configuration profile that helps enable Microsoft Edge and Google Chrome extensions.

We will not show the whole configuration profile creation as it's the same process as in previous chapters in this book (e.g., *Chapter 3*). Let's, however, look at the required catalog settings that need to be configured. For Microsoft Edge, find the setting called **Control which extensions are installed silently**. After enabling that setting, specify the following extension ID: `lfmemoeeciijgkjkgbgikoonlkabmlno`. For Google Chrome, find **Configure the list of force-installed apps and extensions**. Provide the following extension ID after enabling the setting: **joeclbldhdmoijbaagobkhlpfjglcihd**.

Once all the settings are configured, it should look like the following screenshot. We do recommend managing Microsoft Edge and Google Chrome in separate configuration profiles.

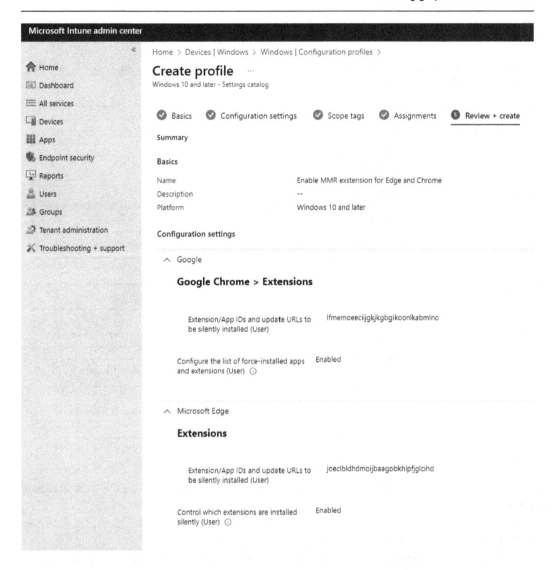

Figure 5.53 – Enable MMR extensions for Edge and Chrome

Supported websites

At the time of the publication of this book, the media content from the following websites can be redirected using the MMR feature:

AnyClip	Fox Weather	Twitch
AWS Training	IMDB	Twitter
BBC	Infosec Institute	Udemy
Big Think	LinkedIn Learning	UMU
Bleacher Report	Microsoft Learn	U.S. News
Brightcove	Microsoft Stream	Vidazoo
CNBC	NBC Sports	Vimeo
Coursera	The New York Times	The Wall Street Journal
Daily Mail	Pluralsight	Yahoo
Facebook	Politico	Yammer
Fidelity	Reuters	YouTube (including embedded videos)
Flashtalking	Skillshare	
Fox Sports	The Guardian	

MMR status

The following table illustrates the different states of the MMR feature based on the icon state in the browser:

Icon State	Definition
	A grayed-out icon means that multimedia content on the website can't be redirected or the extension isn't loading.
	The red square with an X inside of it means that the client can't connect to multimedia redirection. You may need to uninstall and reinstall the extension, then try again.
	The default icon appears with no status applied. This icon state means that multimedia content on the website can be redirected and is ready to use.

	The green square with a play button icon inside of it means that the extension is currently redirecting video playback.
	The green square with a phone icon inside of it means that the extension is currently redirecting a WebRTC call.

Table 5.9 – Multimedia redirection status

When you click on the icon, a pop-up menu will appear, presenting a list of supported features on the current page. From there, you have the option to enable or disable multimedia redirection for all websites and gather logs. Additionally, the menu provides version numbers for each component of the service, enabling you to verify the correct installation of versioned components crucial for the proper functioning of multimedia redirection.

Multimedia redirection components

Multimedia redirection has some required components that must be installed on the Cloud PC and the physical device. It's a good practice to know about these components for a potential troubleshooting scenario.

> **Important note**
>
> All the required components will automatically be installed on the Cloud PC when using gallery images. It's the same as required components on physical devices when installing the *Windows 365 app* or the *Remote Desktop Client for Windows* – you will be fine without having to do any configuration.

The Cloud PC must have the following components installed:

- Microsoft Visual C++ Redistributable 2015-2022, Version 14.32.31332.0 or later (`https://learn.microsoft.com/cpp/windows/latest-supported-vc-redist`)

- MSMmrHostMsi (`https://aka.ms/avdmmr/msi`)

- Microsoft multimedia redirection browser extension (`https://microsoftedge.microsoft.com/addons/detail/wvd-multimedia-redirectio/joeclbldhdmoijbaagobkhlpfjglcihd`) (`https://chrome.google.com/webstore/detail/wvd-multimedia-redirectio/lfmemoeeciijgkjkgbgikoonlkabmlno`)

The physical PC does require a **Dynamic Link Library (DLL)** file called `MsMmrDVCPlugin.dll`, located in the `C:\Program Files\Remote Desktop` folder.

Having the newest Windows 365 app or Remote Desktop client helps stabilize and improve multimedia redirection, so remember to keep the clients up to date.

This wraps up the multimedia redirection section. It gives end users the same experience with video and audio when using a web browser on their Cloud PC. This closes the circle of this chapter, giving Cloud PC users the best possible experience on a virtual device in the cloud.

Summary

In the chapter, you've learned everything about enabling users to access their Cloud PCs from any device in a secure way, as well as about optimizations available to deliver premium experiences. We went deep into the new, modern user experiences that you get when choosing Windows 365 that are different from any other virtualization solutions on the market. We hope you liked it!

In the next chapter, you will learn how to secure Cloud PCs.

Questions

1. What hardware do you need for Windows 365 Boot?
2. What are the hardware requirements for Microsoft Teams as part of Cloud PCs?
3. How can you optimize an endpoint to deliver an outstanding end user experience?

Further reading

Please take advantage of the following resources to learn more:

-   *Uniform Resource Identifier schemes with the Remote Desktop client for Azure Virtual Desktop* – (https://learn.microsoft.com/azure/virtual-desktop/uri-scheme)

-   *Understanding multimedia redirection on Azure Virtual Desktop - Azure* – (https://learn.microsoft.com/azure/virtual-desktop/multimedia-redirection-intro)

-   *Monitor and improve call quality for Microsoft Teams - Microsoft Teams* – (https://learn.microsoft.com/microsoftteams/monitor-call-quality-qos)

-   *Implement Quality of Service in Microsoft Teams - Microsoft Teams* – (https://learn.microsoft.com/microsoftteams/qos-in-teams)

-   *For more information about multimedia redirection and how it works, see* https://learn.microsoft.com/azure/virtual-desktop/multimedia-redirection-intro

6
Securing Cloud PCs

By now, you will have a good understanding of how to deploy and access a Cloud PC. In this chapter, we will learn how to secure the connection and content with **digital rights management** (**DRM**) such as lock-down features, security baselines, watermarking, and more to ensure your Cloud PC is secure!

By the end of this chapter, you will be able to configure Azure **multi-factor authentication** (**MFA**) and other security features' baseline settings to secure your Cloud PCs. The topics we will cover are as follows:

- Conditional Access and MFA
- Compliance policies
- eDiscovery mode
- How to become a local administrator of your Cloud PC
- Windows Local Administrator Password Solution
- Screen capture protection
- Watermarking
- RDP device redirection
- Microsoft Defender for Endpoint
- Security baselines

Configuring Conditional Access – MFA

Securing access to the Cloud PC devices in your Windows 365 environment is a must-do. **Conditional Access** (**CA**) can help with securing your environment based on different conditions and we do highly recommend enforcing MFA to your Windows 365 environment from unknown locations. As an extension to that, you might want to enforce authentication with security keys based on **Fast Identity Online** (**FIDO**).

If you want to secure your environment with security keys based on FIDO2 authentication, you'll need to allow users to use those in Azure AD; this can either be targeted to all users or a group of users. To access the security key settings, log in to **Azure AD | Security | Authentication Methods**; from here, you can enable the FIDO2 security key:

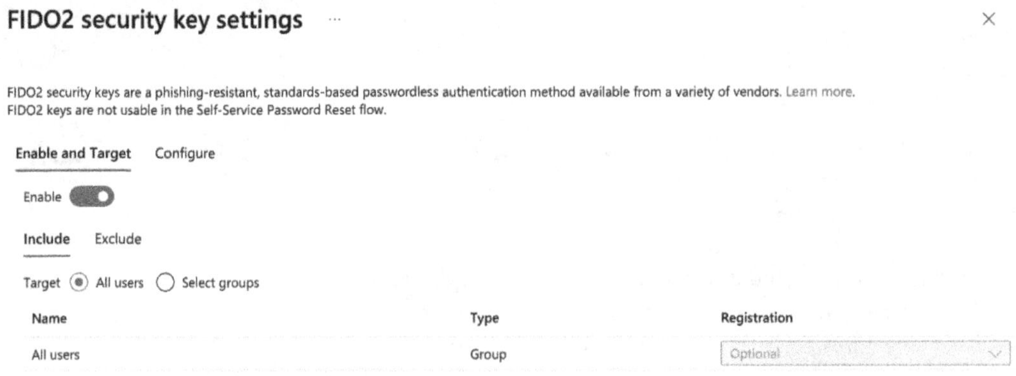

Figure 6.1 – FIDO2 security key settings

We need to include the cloud apps **Windows 365** and **Azure Virtual Desktop** in our CA policy to secure all the different ways the users can connect to their Cloud PC. The Windows 365 cloud app ensures we can secure users connecting from the Windows 365 app and Windows 365 user portal. We need to include Azure Virtual Desktop because users can use the Remote Desktop client to connect to their Cloud PC. The Remote Desktop client corresponds to Azure Virtual Desktop in CA.

> **Note**
> Azure Virtual Desktop might be called Windows Virtual Desktop in some Azure AD tenants.

Managing CA policies can be done in Azure AD or Microsoft Intune. In the following examples, we will do it through Microsoft Intune. The configuration is the same if you do it in Azure AD.

Configuring a CA policy to enforce MFA

Follow the next steps to get started securing your Windows 365 environment with MFA:

1. Log in to Microsoft Intune.

2. Go to **Endpoint security | Conditional Access | Policies**.

3. Click on + **New policy** at the top.

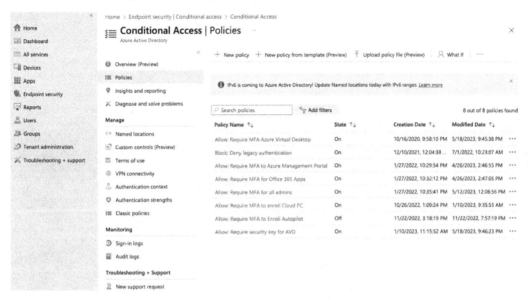

Figure 6.2 – Overview of CA policies in Microsoft Intune

4. Give the policy a name and go to the section called **Users**. Include the users or groups you want to use MFA when connecting to their Cloud PC. In this example, we are including **All users**, as shown in the following screenshot:

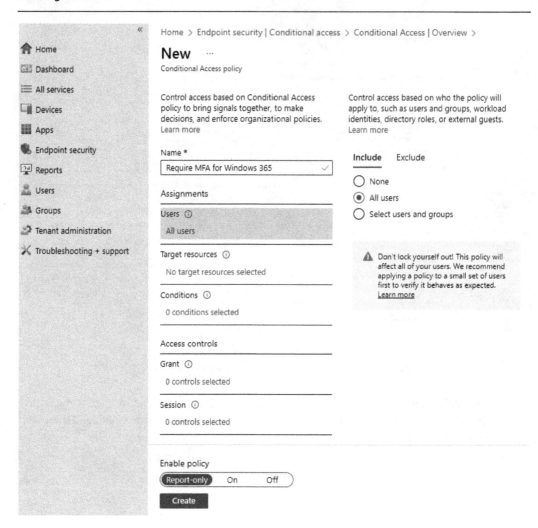

Figure 6.3 – User selection in CA policy for MFA

5. Under **Target resources**, select **Azure Virtual Desktop** and **Windows 365**:

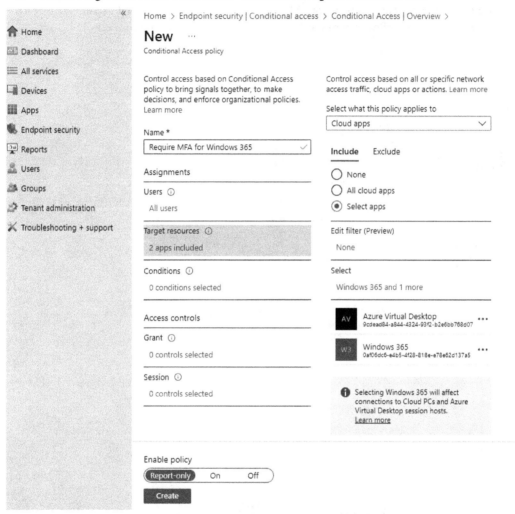

Figure 6.4 – Cloud apps selection in the CA policy for MFA

6. Select the conditions as you wish for your policy. We don't configure anything here as we want to secure our environment with MFA everywhere. You might find it useful to configure **Locations**, as it will allow you to specify where users will get an MFA prompt:

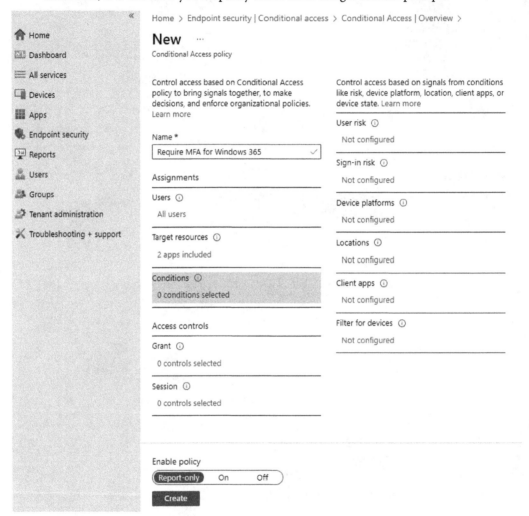

Figure 6.5 – Conditions selection in the CA policy for MFA

7. Select **Require multifactor authentication** under **Grant**:

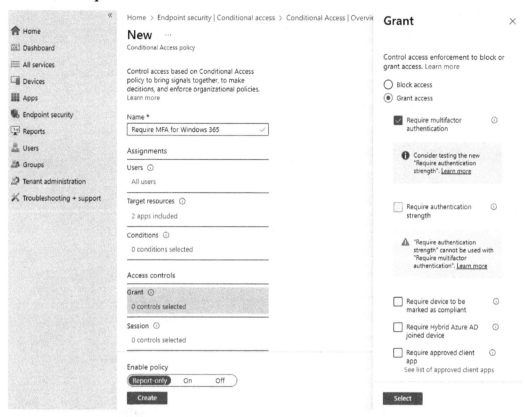

Figure 6.6 – Access control selection in the CA policy for MFA

8. In the **Session** section, we can control how often we want the users to reauthenticate with MFA. In this case, we want the users to do it every week.

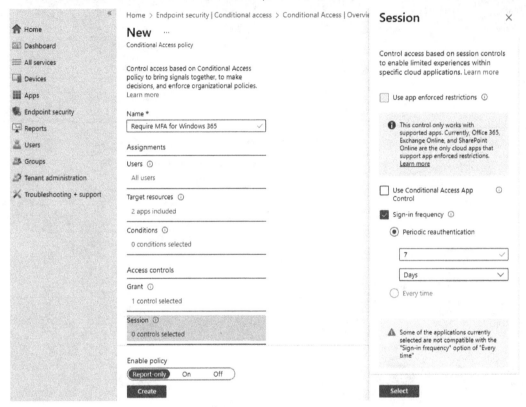

Figure 6.7 – Session control selection in the CA policy for MFA

9. Now, we just need to enable the policy, which is done at the bottom of the page. Set **Enable policy** to **On** and click on **Create**. Always remember to test your policies on a selected group of users before deploying them to production.

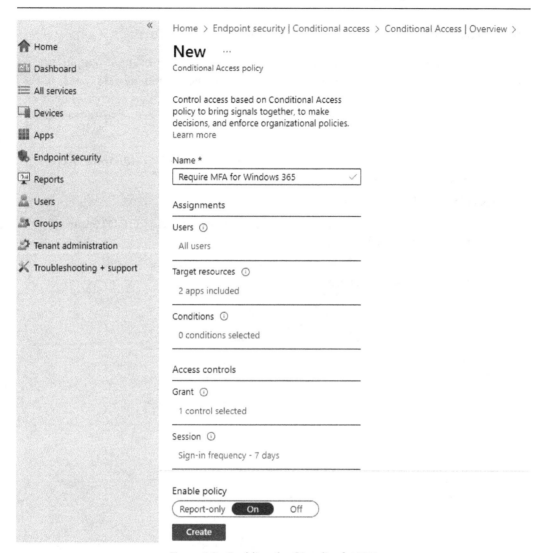

Figure 6.8 – Enabling the CA policy for MFA

Now we have the MFA configuration in place, let's configure secure access with FIDO2 security keys.

Configuring the CA policy with FIDO authentication

Before we start creating a CA policy, we need to configure a new authentication strength. With authentication strength, we can define which combination of authentication methods needs to be used to get access to a resource. This allows us to expand on how different user scenarios need to authenticate to get access. With that said, let's configure a new authentication method so we can require security key sign-in to Cloud PCs:

1. Start by going to **Microsoft Intune | Endpoint security | Conditional Access | Authentication strengths**.

2. Click on **New authentication strength**.

3. Choose a name for the authentication strength configuration and select **FIDO2 Security Key**. Click on **Next** at the bottom:

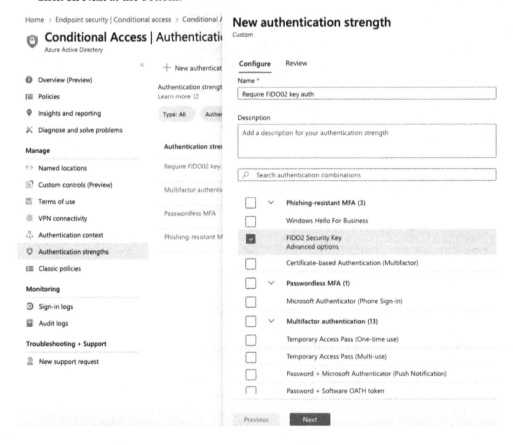

Figure 6.9 – Creating a new authentication strength

4. Review the settings specified and click on **Create**.

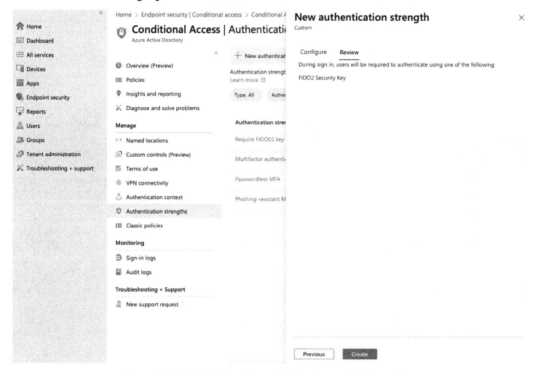

Figure 6.10 – Reviewing the authentication strength settings

Now we can start configuring the CA policy.

5. Go to **Microsoft Intune | Endpoint security | Conditional Access | Policies**. From here, create a new policy.

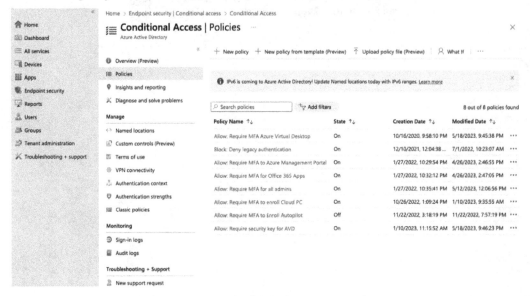

Figure 6.11 – Overview of CA policies in Microsoft Intune

6. Give the policy a name and go to the section called **Users**. Include the users or groups you want to authenticate with a security key when connecting to their Cloud PC:

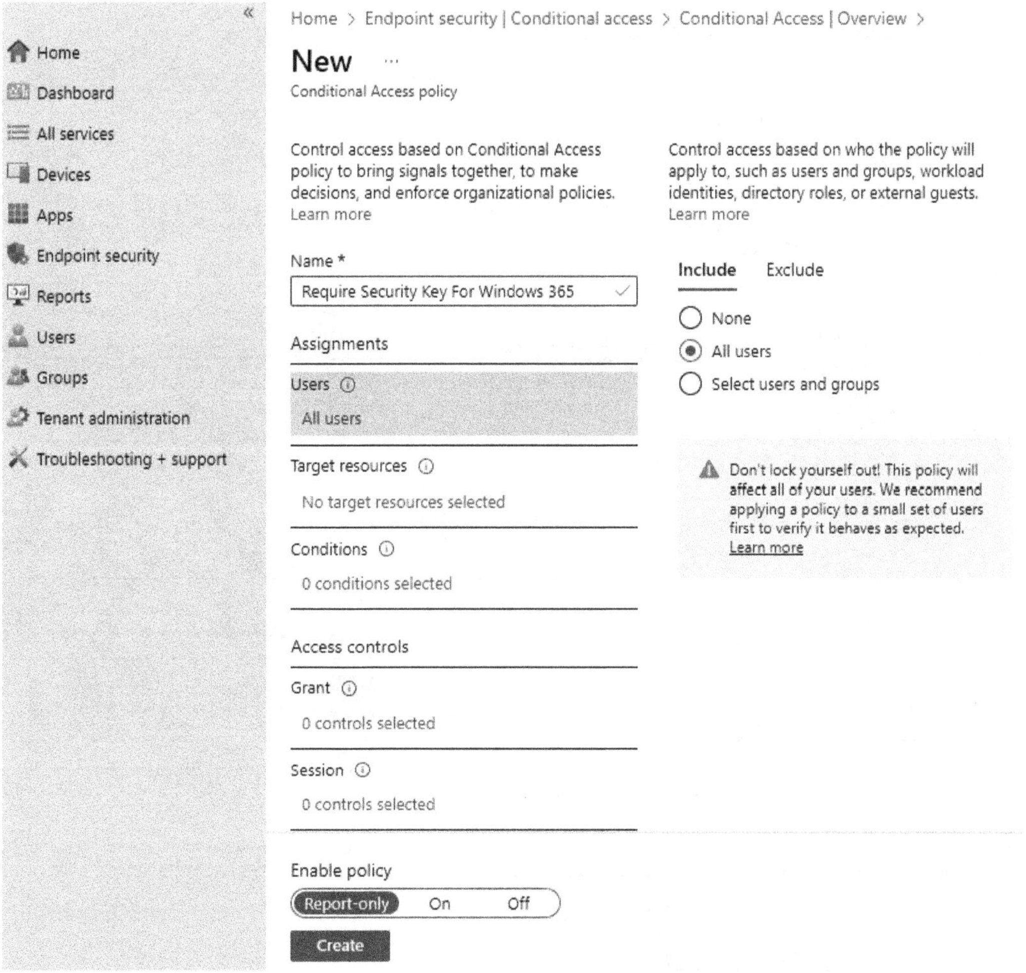

Home > Endpoint security | Conditional access > Conditional Access | Overview >

New ...

Conditional Access policy

Control access based on Conditional Access policy to bring signals together, to make decisions, and enforce organizational policies. Learn more

Control access based on who the policy will apply to, such as users and groups, workload identities, directory roles, or external guests. Learn more

Name *

Require Security Key For Windows 365 ✓

Include   Exclude

Assignments

○ None

Users ⓘ

◉ All users

All users

○ Select users and groups

Target resources ⓘ

No target resources selected

⚠ Don't lock yourself out! This policy will affect all of your users. We recommend applying a policy to a small set of users first to verify it behaves as expected.
Learn more

Conditions ⓘ

0 conditions selected

Access controls

Grant ⓘ

0 controls selected

Session ⓘ

0 controls selected

Enable policy

(Report-only   On   Off)

Create

Figure 6.12 – User selection in the CA policy for the security key

7.   Select **Azure Virtual Desktop** and **Windows 365** under **Target resources**.

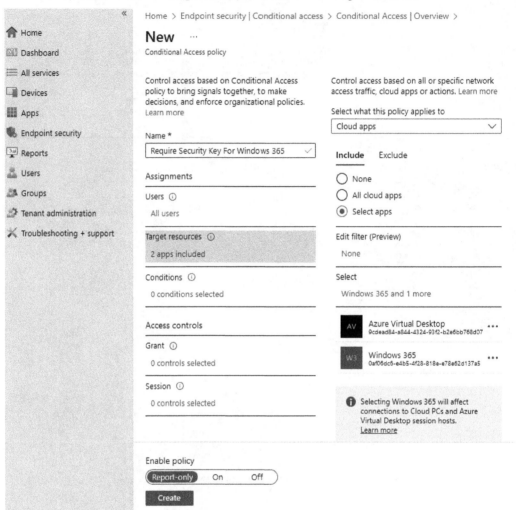

Figure 6.13 – Cloud apps selection in the CA policy for the security key

8.   Select the conditions as you wish for your policy. We don't configure anything here as we want to secure our environment from everywhere. You might find it useful to configure **Locations**, as it will allow you to specify where users will need to authenticate with a security key.

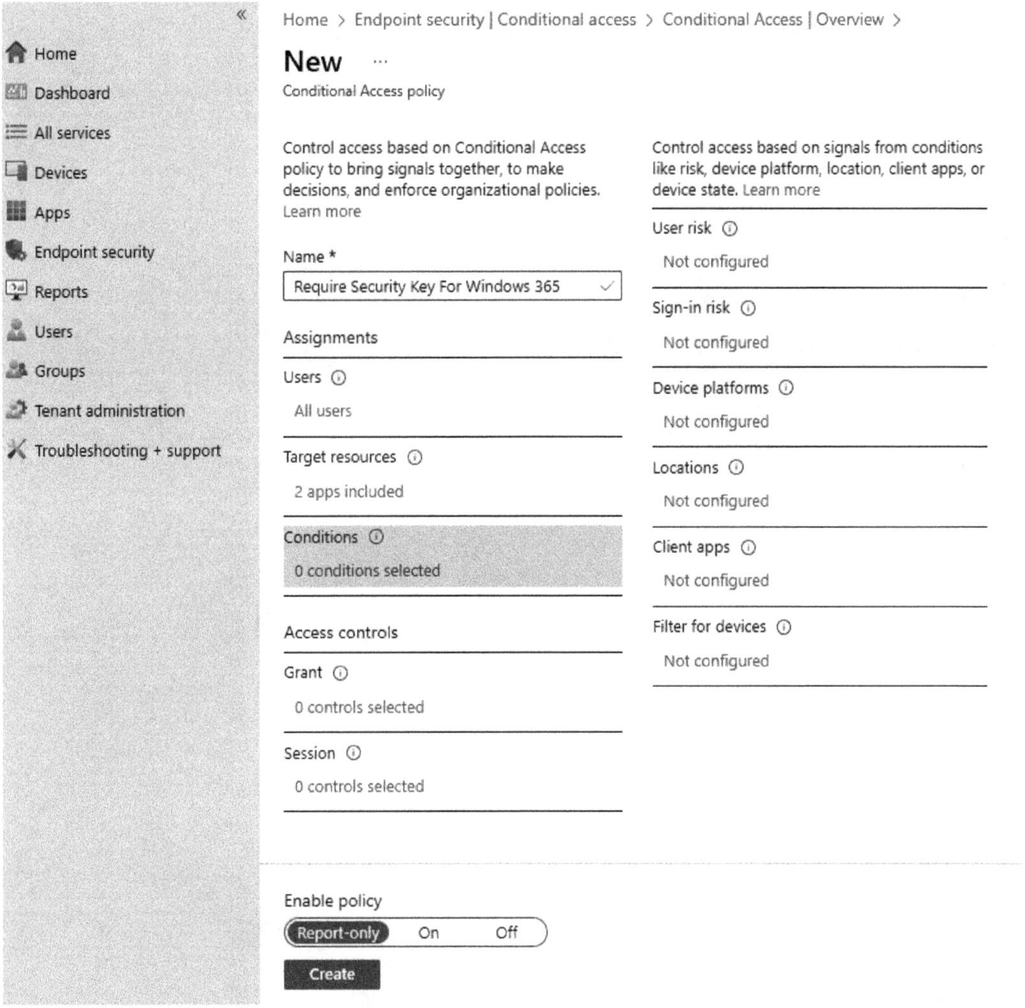

Home > Endpoint security | Conditional access > Conditional Access | Overview >

New ...

Conditional Access policy

Control access based on Conditional Access policy to bring signals together, to make decisions, and enforce organizational policies. Learn more

Name *

Require Security Key For Windows 365

Assignments

Users ⓘ

All users

Target resources ⓘ

2 apps included

Conditions ⓘ

0 conditions selected

Access controls

Grant ⓘ

0 controls selected

Session ⓘ

0 controls selected

Control access based on signals from conditions like risk, device platform, location, client apps, or device state. Learn more

User risk ⓘ

Not configured

Sign-in risk ⓘ

Not configured

Device platforms ⓘ

Not configured

Locations ⓘ

Not configured

Client apps ⓘ

Not configured

Filter for devices ⓘ

Not configured

Enable policy

Report-only | On | Off

Create

Figure 6.14 – Conditions selection in the CA policy for the security key

9. In the **Grant** section, select **Require authentication strength**, and then select the authentication strength you configured earlier:

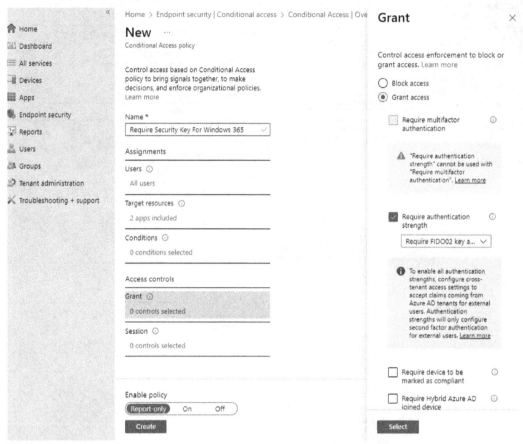

Figure 6.15 – Grant selection in the CA policy for the security key

10. In the **Session** section, you can configure how often users will need to reauthenticate with their security key. In this example, we set it to every 48 hours.

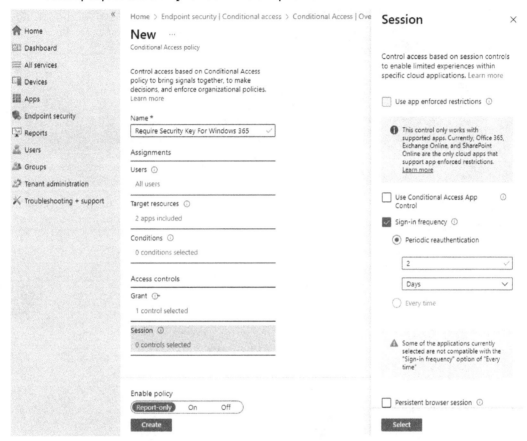

Figure 6.16 – Session selection in the CA policy for the security key

11. Now, we just need to enable the policy; this is done at the bottom of the page. Set **Enable policy** to **On** and click on **Create**. Always remember to test your policies on a selected group of users before deploying them to production:

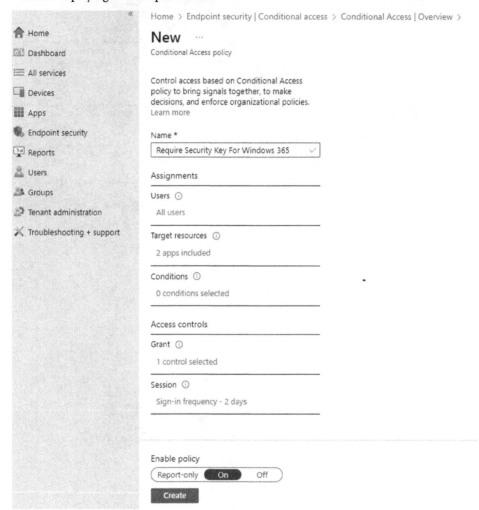

Figure 6.17 – Enabling the CA policy for the security key

This concludes the setup of the CA policy with MFA and the security key. Remember, enforcing MFA alone will help secure your environment in roughly 98% of all attacks. It's quite straightforward to do for all services in Microsoft 365. Let's look at how we can get an overview of which security features are enabled on devices.

Compliance policies

Compliance policies in Microsoft Intune are widely used to help keep track of device compliance with certain requirements such as whether the device has a firewall or real-time protection activated.

> **Note**
>
> A compliance policy does not configure any setting we choose such as Windows Firewall; it will only monitor whether the security feature is enabled and report it back to us.

Not only can we get an overview of which devices do or do not meet our security requirements but we can tie it in with a CA policy, such as the one we just configured in the previous section.

As an example, the following CA policy requires devices to be compliant with the policies we have assigned to them. If they are non-compliant, they will not get access to the selected target resources – in this case, Microsoft 365 apps.

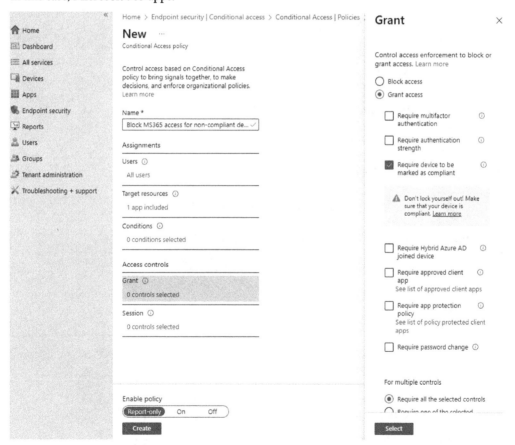

Figure 6.18 – CA policy requiring compliant devices

Next, we will look at how to create a compliance policy and assign it to Cloud PCs.

Creating a compliance policy

Follow these steps to create a compliance policy:

1. Start by logging in to the Microsoft Intune admin center.
2. Next, go to **Devices** | **Windows** | **Compliance policies**.
3. Click on **+ Create policy**.

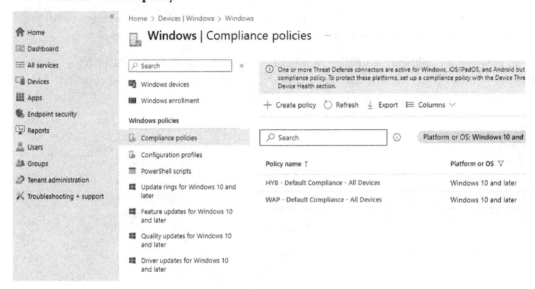

Figure 6.19 – Adding a new compliance policy

4. For **Platform**, select **Windows 10 and later** and then click on **Create**.

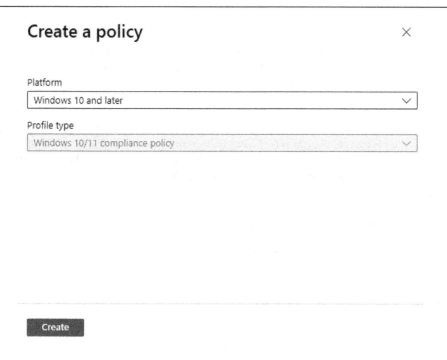

Figure 6.20 – Selecting a platform for the compliance policy

5.   Give the compliance policy a name and select **Next**.

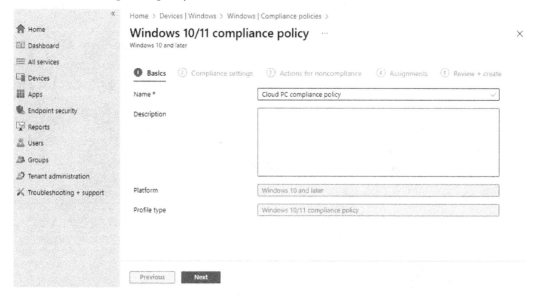

Figure 6.21 – Specifying the compliance policy name

6. From here, we can select our requirements to make a device compliant. There are a bunch of options, including the option to upload a custom compliance script. As an example, we will require Windows Firewall to be activated, as shown in the following figure. Once done, select **Next**.

> **Note**
>
> BitLocker is one of the most common compliance settings to select because it has an important security purpose for physical hardware. Cloud PCs do not support BitLocker configuration; therefore, this always returns non-compliant, if selected. Cloud PCs are, however, always automatically encrypted at rest with 256-bit **Advanced Encryption Standard (AES)** encryption

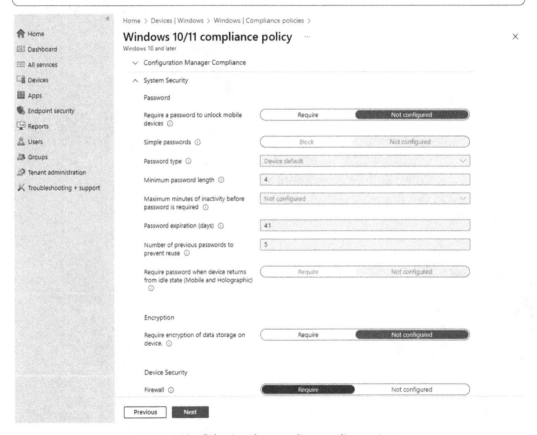

Figure 6.22 – Selecting the compliance policy settings

7. Specify what action should be taken if a Cloud PC reaches a state of non-compliance. Once done, select **Next**.

Figure 6.23 – Configuring Actions for noncompliance

8. Select an assignment for the new compliance policy. To narrow the assignment down to only Cloud PCs, you can use a filter, as we also covered in *Chapter 4*. Click on **Next**.

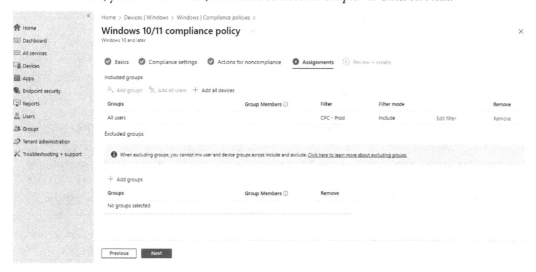

Figure 6.24 – Compliance policy assignments

9. Review the settings specified for the compliance policy. When you're ready, click on **Create**.

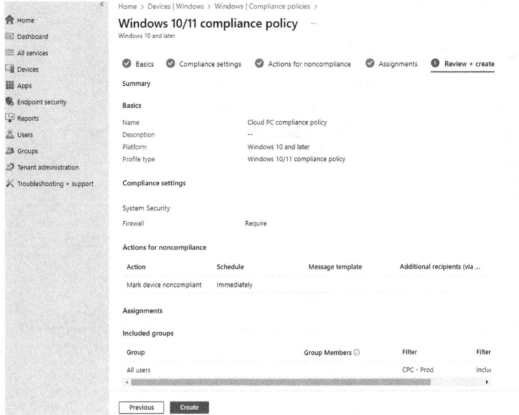

Figure 6.25 – Reviewing the settings of the compliance policy

We have now created a compliance policy to keep track of security settings that should be enabled on our Cloud PCs. Alternatively, you can incorporate Cloud PCs into your physical device policy, which means you don't need a separate policy for Cloud PCs as long as you assign them accordingly. Remember, compliance policies do not configure anything; configured settings will only be monitored, we can then wrap security action around that with CA. Next, let's look at how we can capture the current state of a Cloud PC if needed for any forensics investigation.

eDiscovery mode

Being able to secure files or the current state of a Cloud PC for forensics investigation can be very handy. Windows 365 has a feature called **Place Cloud PC under review**. With this feature, you can take snapshots of a Cloud PC to secure data and safely hand it over for investigation.

Besides taking snapshots, you will also be able to block access to the current Cloud PC while it's being investigated.

Before we can put a Cloud PC under review, we need to create a storage account and give the Windows 365 **Storage Account Contributor** access to that storage account.

Creating an Azure storage account and assigning permissions

Follow these steps to create a new Azure storage account:

1. Log in to **Microsoft Azure** and go to **Storage accounts**:

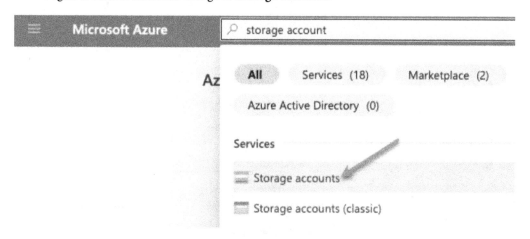

Figure 6.26 – Storage accounts in Azure

2. Once you are in **Storage accounts**, click on **Create**. Start by specifying the name and resource group. Next, choose the **Performance** tier; both **Premium** and **Standard** will work so select the one that suits your needs. Premium storage will give you the best performance but it's also more expensive than Standard storage. Usually, Standard storage is fine for this kind of use case. Once you are done configuring the storage account, select **Review**.

> **Note**
> If you select **Premium** as the **Performance** tier, make sure to select **Page Blobs**.

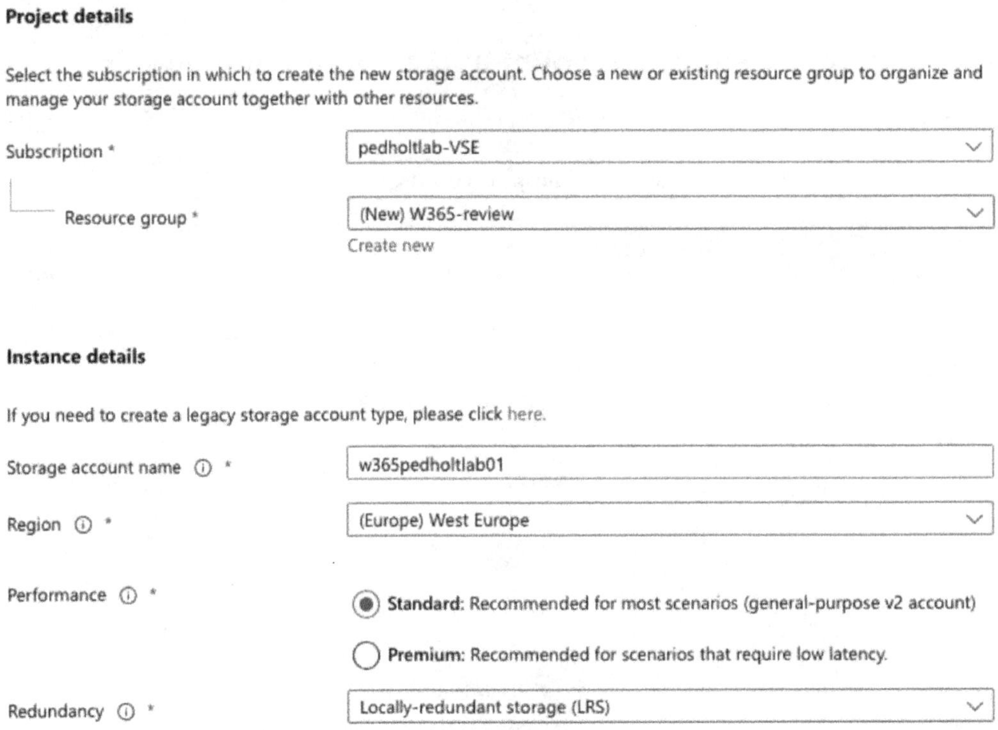

Project details

Select the subscription in which to create the new storage account. Choose a new or existing resource group to organize and manage your storage account together with other resources.

Subscription *   pedholtlab-VSE   ⌄

  └── Resource group *   (New) W365-review   ⌄
                          Create new

Instance details

If you need to create a legacy storage account type, please click here.

Storage account name ⓘ *   w365pedholtlab01

Region ⓘ *   (Europe) West Europe   ⌄

Performance ⓘ *   ● **Standard**: Recommended for most scenarios (general-purpose v2 account)

                            ○ **Premium**: Recommended for scenarios that require low latency.

Redundancy ⓘ *   Locally-redundant storage (LRS)   ⌄

Figure 6.27 – Creation of a new storage account

3. Review the settings of the storage account and select **Create** to complete the creation.

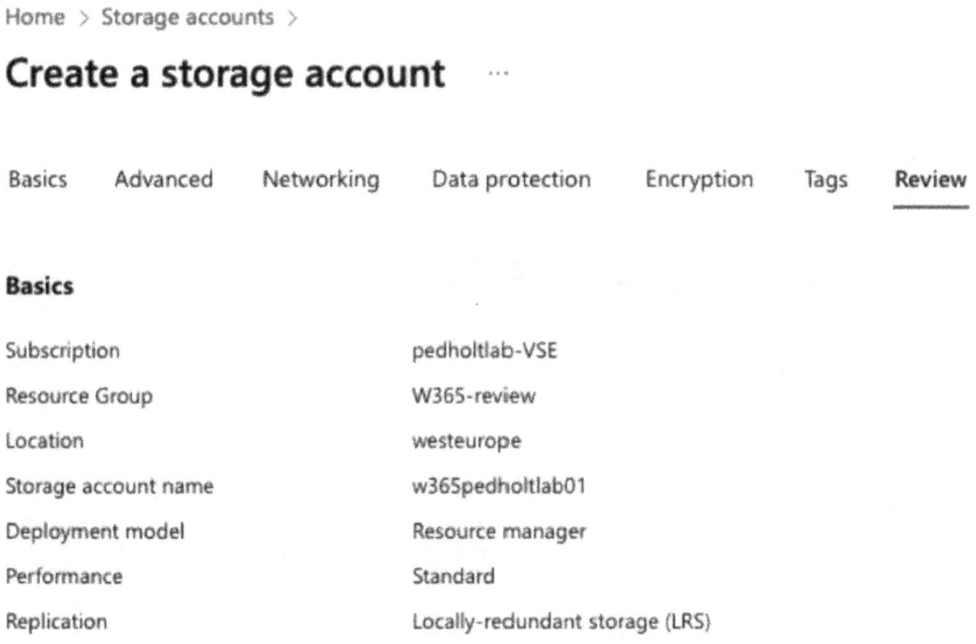

Home > Storage accounts >

Create a storage account   ...

Basics   Advanced   Networking   Data protection   Encryption   Tags   **Review**

Basics

Subscription	pedholtlab-VSE
Resource Group	W365-review
Location	westeurope
Storage account name	w365pedholtlab01
Deployment model	Resource manager
Performance	Standard
Replication	Locally-redundant storage (LRS)

Figure 6.28 – Reviewing the settings of the storage account

Now the storage account has been created, we need to give the Windows 365 service access.

4. Inside the newly created storage account, go to **Access Control**, click on + **Add**, and then select **Add role assignment**.

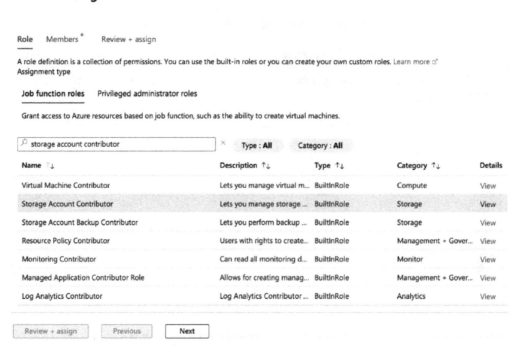

Figure 6.29 – Storage account overview

5.   Find and select the **Storage Account Contributor** role and select **Next**.

Home > Storage accounts > w365pedholtlab01 | Access Control (IAM) >

Add role assignment ...

Role   Members*   Review + assign

A role definition is a collection of permissions. You can use the built-in roles or you can create your own custom roles. Learn more ☐
Assignment type

Job function roles   Privileged administrator roles

Grant access to Azure resources based on job function, such as the ability to create virtual machines.

Name ↑↓	Description ↑↓	Type ↑↓	Category ↑↓	Details
Virtual Machine Contributor	Lets you manage virtual m...	BuiltInRole	Compute	View
Storage Account Contributor	Lets you manage storage ...	BuiltInRole	Storage	View
Storage Account Backup Contributor	Lets you perform backup ...	BuiltInRole	Storage	View
Resource Policy Contributor	Users with rights to create...	BuiltInRole	Management + Gover...	View
Monitoring Contributor	Can read all monitoring d...	BuiltInRole	Monitor	View
Managed Application Contributor Role	Allows for creating manag...	BuiltInRole	Management + Gover...	View
Log Analytics Contributor	Log Analytics Contributor ...	BuiltInRole	Analytics	View

Review + assign   Previous   Next

Figure 6.30 – Selecting the role for the storage account

6. Select **Windows 365** and click on **Review + assign**.

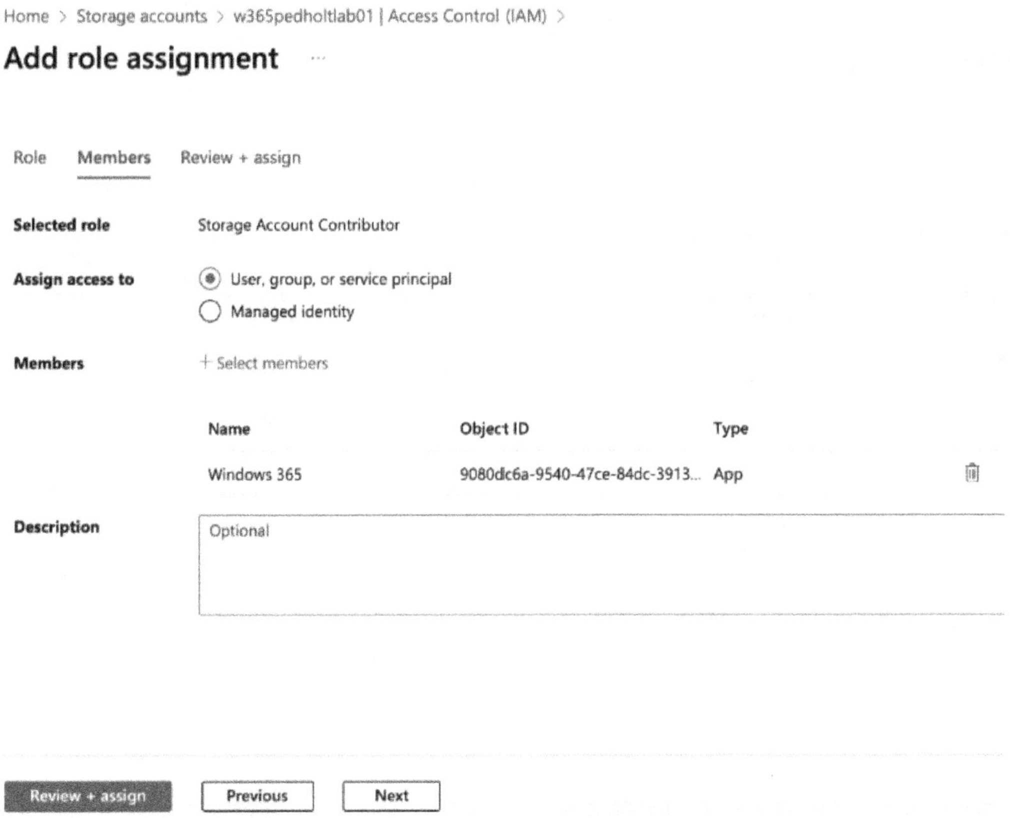

Home > Storage accounts > w365pedholtlab01 | Access Control (IAM) >

Add role assignment   ...

Role   Members   Review + assign

Selected role   Storage Account Contributor

Assign access to   ⦿ User, group, or service principal
                         ◯ Managed identity

Members   + Select members

Name	Object ID	Type	
Windows 365	9080dc6a-9540-47ce-84dc-3913...	App	🗑

Description   Optional

Review + assign   Previous   Next

Figure 6.31 – Selecting the members for the storage account

7.   Review the assignment and click on **Review + assign**.

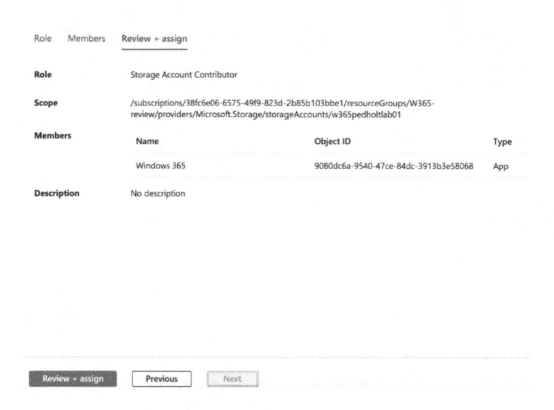

Figure 6.32 – Reviewing the settings for the storage account assignment

Now that we have created the storage account, we can place a Cloud PC under review.

Placing a Cloud PC under review

To place a Cloud PC under review, follow these steps:

1.   Log in to **Microsoft Intune | Devices | Windows 365 | All Cloud PCs**. Select the Cloud PC device.

> **Note**
> The Windows 365 administrator account you are using to place a Cloud PC under review does not need to have permissions to the storage account you have created.

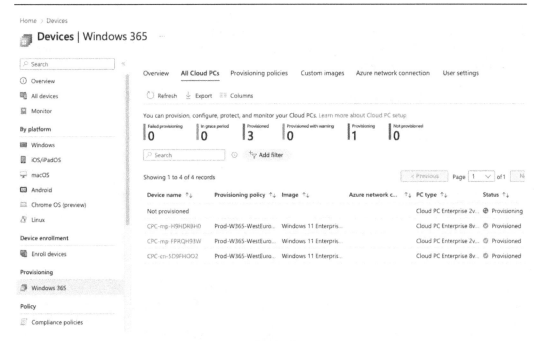

Figure 6.33 – All Cloud PCs overview

2.   From the overview of the selected device, choose **Place Cloud PC under review**.

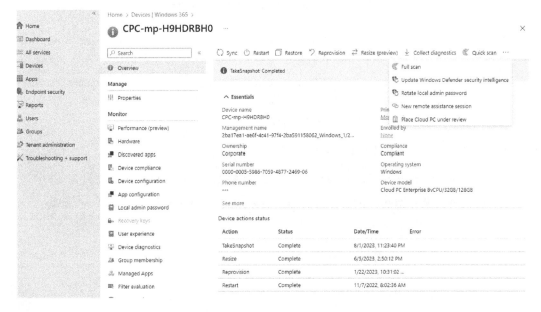

Figure 6.34 – Overview of a Cloud PC device

3. In the panel to the right, select the storage account under the subscription you have configured. Choose whether the user can access the Cloud PC while it's under review. Once you're done, click on **Place under review**.

Figure 6.35 – Place Cloud PC under review options

There will now be a new restore point created that will be placed in the selected storage account. An administrator with access to that storage account will be able to access the restore point.

Now that we know how to place a Cloud PC under review, let's remove it from review again.

Removing a Cloud PC under review

To remove a Cloud PC from review, follow these steps:

1. Log in to **Microsoft Intune | Devices | Windows 365 | All Cloud PCs**. Select the Cloud PC device.

2. Click on the **View details and configure settings** link in the **Overview** panel of the device:

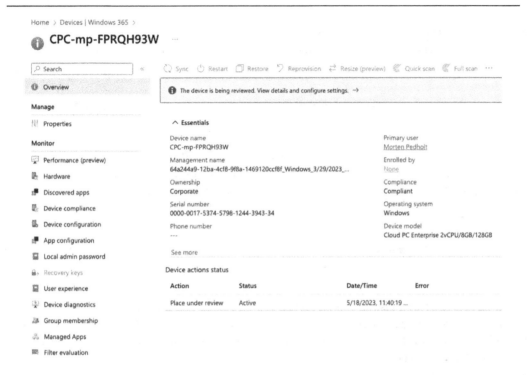

Figure 6.36 – Overview of the Cloud PC device that is under review

3. Click on **Remove from review** and confirm by selecting **Remove**:

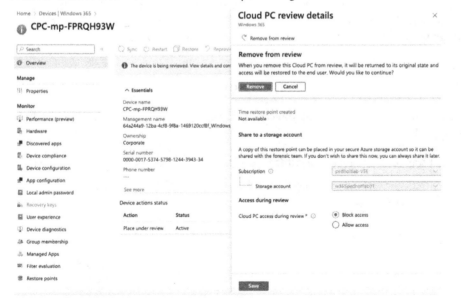

Figure 6.37 – Remove from review

We have now covered the creation of the storage account, and how to place and remove a Cloud PC from review. Let's jump into something that is usually a big topic at many companies: local administrator rights.

How to become a local administrator of your Cloud PC

Generally, being a local administrator on a PC is not recommended; however, there might be cases where it's necessary for a user to be a local administrator on their PC. If there is a need for a user to be a local administrator on their Cloud PC, Windows 365 Enterprise has a built-in setting that is easy to enable and manage.

> **Note**
> Intune Suite V2 **Endpoint Privilege Management** (EPM) is being worked on. Most likely when you read this book, it's officially supported!

Giving the user local administrator rights on their Cloud PC is configured within the **User settings** section in Microsoft Intune. This is also where you can configure restore point intervals, as we covered in *Chapter 4*. This setting can be set before or after the user has started using their Cloud PC. The settings will be evaluated on logon.

> **Note**
> It's important to remember a user can only have one user setting configuration applied at any time. If the user is included in multiple user settings, the latest modified setting will take effect. If there already is a user setting assigned to a user group, you might want to edit that or unassign the specific user from the user setting and create a new one.

Configuring the local admin setting

When you create or edit a user setting, you can check the checkbox called **Enable Local admin**. Let's see how to do this:

1. To get started, log in to **Microsoft Intune** | **Devices** | **Windows 365** | **User settings**.
2. From the **User settings** pane, click on **+ Add** to start configuring a user setting:

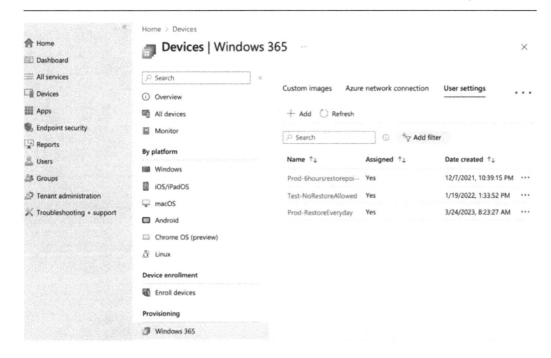

Figure 6.38 – Adding a local admin setting

3. Provide a name for the user setting, check the **Enable Local admin** checkbox, and click **Next**.

> **Note**
>
> We strongly advise configuring a point-in-time restore to align with the policies you established earlier to prevent any configuration conflicts.

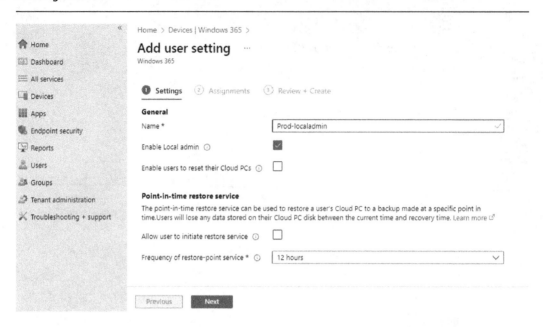

Figure 6.39 – Configuring the local admin setting

4.   Assign a group where the users you want to make local administrators are. Once that is selected, click on **Next**.

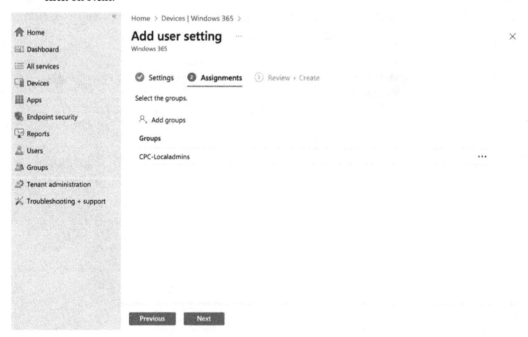

Figure 6.40 – Assigning the local admin setting

5. Review the settings you have specified and select **Create**.

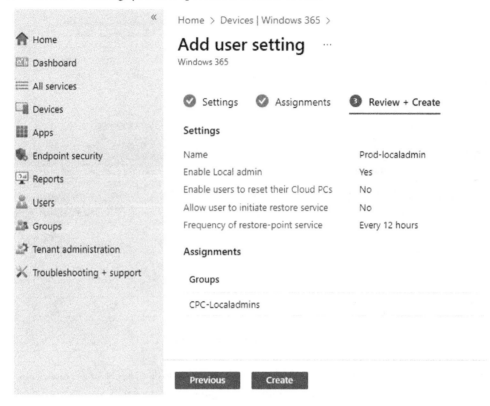

Figure 6.41 – Reviewing and creating the local admin setting

6.   You should now be able to see the new user setting in the overview of **User settings**:

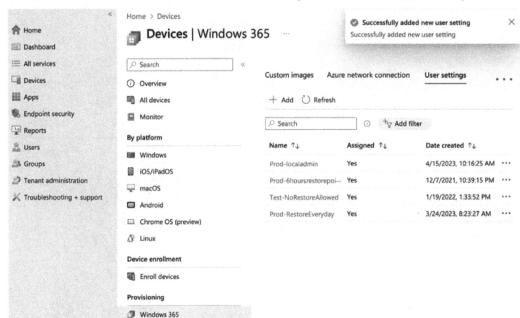

Figure 6.42 – User settings overview

Remember the user has to log out and log in again for the new user setting to apply. In the next section, we will explain how you can configure local administrator password rotation.

Windows Local Administrator Password Solution

A local administrator account is a great tool to have on a physical device in case you need to log in/ elevate with admin rights when no other domain/Azure AD account works on that device. On Cloud PCs, only the primary user can connect to the Cloud PC, but a local administrator can still be a great tool to have if admin rights are needed and other domain/Azure AD accounts aren't able to elevate. Even though the local administrator is a handy tool for both physical and Cloud PCs, it has certain security concerns. The major one is that it is difficult to ensure that every device has a different local administrator password.

This is where **Windows Local Administrator Password Solutions (Windows LAPS)** saves the day.

Windows LAPS ensures that the password is frequently rotated and the password on each device will be randomly generated based on settings you can choose.

When configuring Windows LAPS, you will be able to define the following settings:

- **Backup Directory**: Choose where to save the password. It can be saved in Azure AD and Active Directory.

- **Password Age**: Choose how frequently the password should change. For AADJ devices, the minimum is 7 days, while for HAADJ devices, it can be set to 1 day.

- **Administrator Account Name**: Specify the name of the local administrator user you want Windows LAPS to target. This will not create the user itself.

- **Password Complexity**: Choose how strong and complex the password should be. It can include uppercase and lowercase alphabets, numbers, and special characters.

- **Password Length**: Choose between 8 and 64 characters.

- **Post Authentication Actions**: Choose what will happen upon expiration of the configured password age.

To view a password for a device, you must have one of the following administrator roles:

- Cloud Device Administrator

- Intune Administrator

- Global Administrator

Windows LAPS works with both AADJ and HAADJ devices. This feature has no license required but the device must meet one of the following operating system requirements:

- Windows 11 22H2 – April 11 2023 update

- Windows 11 21H2 – April 11 2023 update

- Windows 10 – April 11 2023 update

- Windows Server 2022 – April 11 2023 update

- Windows Server 2019 – April 11 2023 update

To back up the password to Azure AD, we need to enable it in the Azure AD portal. Follow these steps to do so:

1. Go to **Azure AD**.
2. Find **Device settings** under **Devices**.

3. Select **Yes** for **Enable Azure AD Local Administrator Password Solution (LAPS)**:

Home > Devices

⚙ **Devices** | Device settings   ···
Pedholt Consulting - Azure Active Directory

«   🖫 Save   ✕ Discard | ⟨⟩ Got feedback?

ⓘ Overview

🖳 All devices

⚙ Device settings

⚙ Enterprise State Roaming

🔑 BitLocker keys (Preview)

🔑 Local administrator password
recovery (Preview)

✕ Diagnose and solve problems

Activity

🗒 Audit logs

👥 Bulk operation results (Preview)

Troubleshooting + Support

👤 New support request

Users may register their devices with Azure AD ⓘ
(**All**   None)

ⓘ Learn more on how this setting works

Require Multi-Factor Authentication to register or join devices with Azure AD ⓘ
(Yes   **No**)

⚠ We recommend that you require Multi-Factor Authentication to register or join devices with Azure AD using
Conditional Access. Set this device setting to No if you require Multi-Factor Authentication using Conditional Access.

Maximum number of devices per user ⓘ
| 20 (Recommended)   ⌄ |

Local administrator settings

Manage Additional local administrators on all Azure AD joined devices

Enable Azure AD Local Administrator Password Solution (LAPS) (Preview) ⓘ
(**Yes**   No)

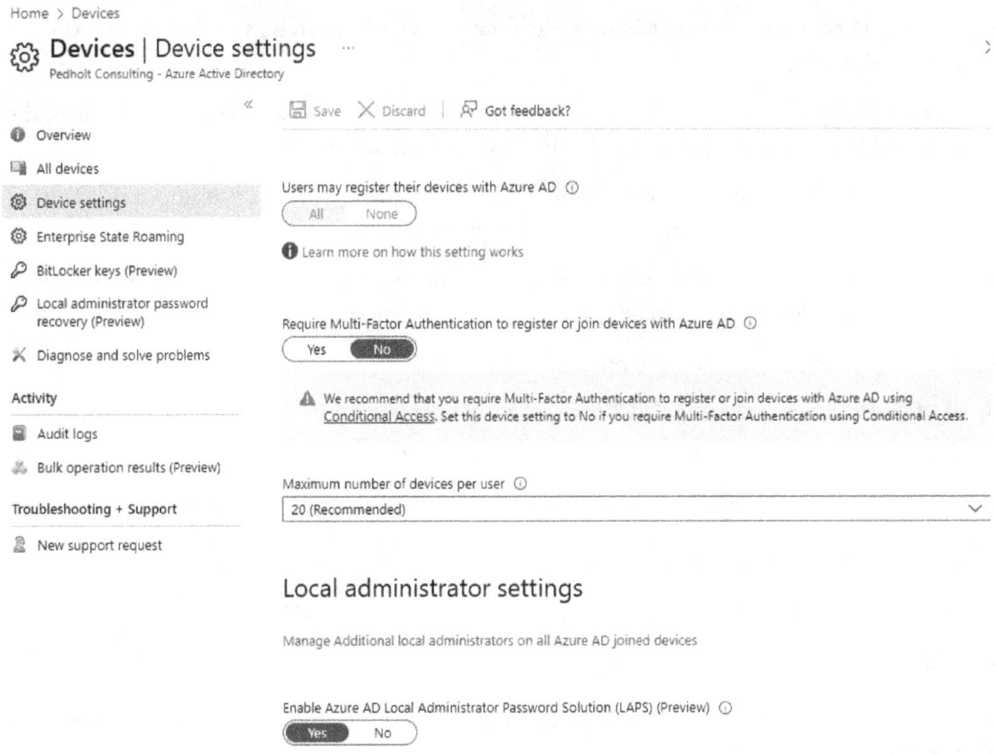

Figure 6.43 – Enabling Windows LAPS backup to Azure AD

Now that we have covered what Windows LAPS is and we have enabled the backup of the password to Azure AD, let's look at how we can enable the built-in administrator.

Enabling the built-in administrator

If you want to configure Windows LAPS toward the built-in Administrator account on an AADJ device, you must enable the user as it is disabled when enrolling a new device.

> **Note**
>
> We do, in general, recommend having the built-in administrator account disabled and using another custom-created local account instead. This can be done with a PowerShell script deployed from Microsoft Intune. Windows LAPS won't be able to create a local administrator account for you.

Follow these steps:

1. Go to **Devices** in **Microsoft Intune** and select **Create profile** under **Configuration profiles**:

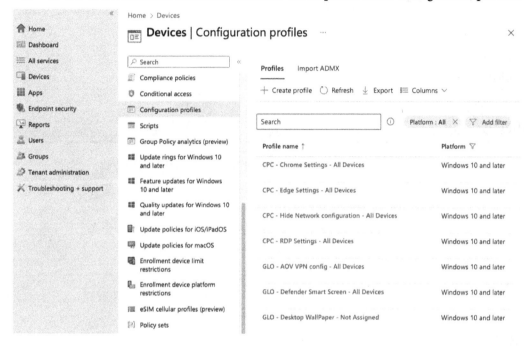

Figure 6.44 – Configuration profiles overview

2.   Select **Windows 10 and later** in **Platform** and **Settings catalog** in **Profile type** and click **Create**:

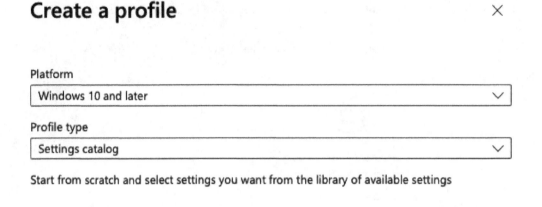

Create a profile   ✕

Platform

| Windows 10 and later   ∨ |

Profile type

| Settings catalog   ∨ |

Start from scratch and select settings you want from the library of available settings

Create

Figure 6.45 – Profile configuration

3.   Give the configuration profile a proper name and select **Next**.

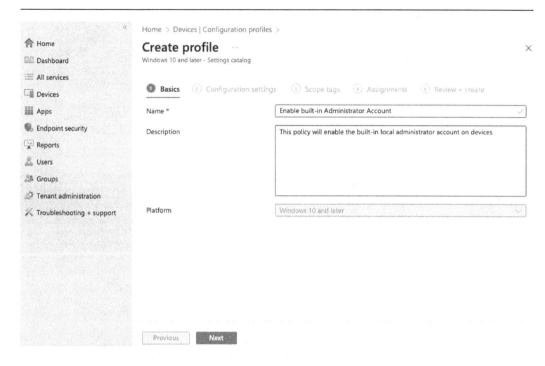

Figure 6.46 – Configuration profile Basics information

4. Click on **+ Add settings**, type Enable administrator account into the search box, and check the checkbox called **Accounts Enable Administrator Account Status** in the **Local Policies Security Options** category.

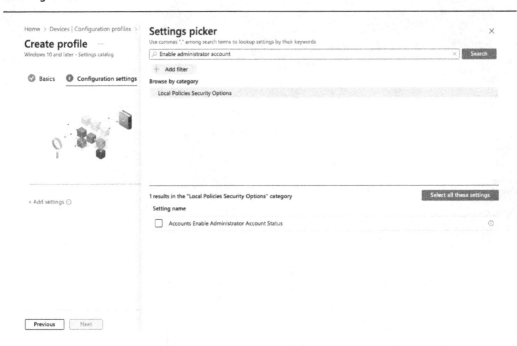

Figure 6.47 – Configuration profile Settings picker overview

5. Make sure to enable the setting and click on **Next**:

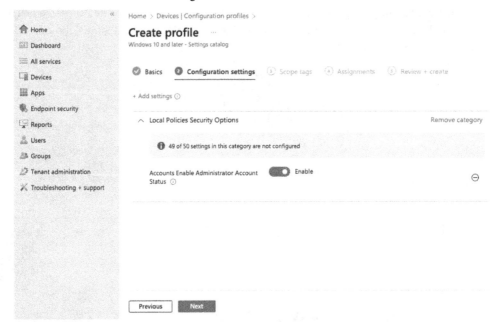

Figure 6.48 – Enable setting in the configuration profile

6. Select **Scope tags** if you are using any. Then, click **Next**.

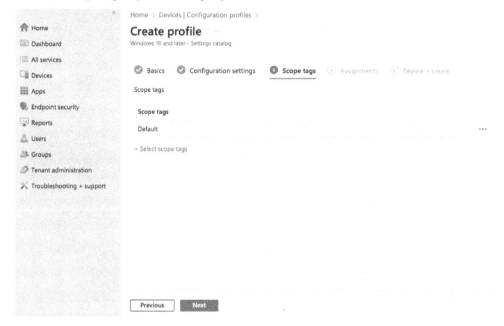

Figure 6.49 – Configuration profile Scope tags overview

7. Assign the configuration profile to either users or devices. Once you're done, click on **Next**.

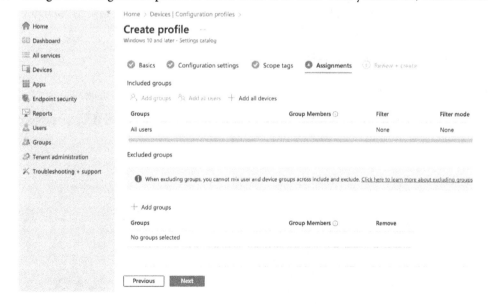

Figure 6.50 – Configuration profile Assignments overview

8.   Review the settings and click on **Create**.

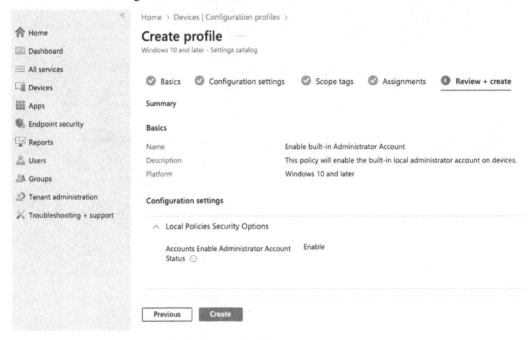

Figure 6.51 – Configuration profile settings review

Now that we know the local administrator account is created and enabled, it's time to configure the Windows LAPS policy.

Configuring Windows LAPS policy

To configure the Windows LAPS policy, follow these steps:

1.   Go to **Endpoint security** in **Microsoft Intune** and select **+ Create Policy** under **Account protection**.

Figure 6.52 – Endpoint security overview

2. For **Platform**, select **Windows 10 and later**, and select **Local admin password solution (Windows LAPS)** for **Profile**:

Figure 6.53 – Creating a profile in Endpoint security

3. Give the profile a proper name and click **Next**.

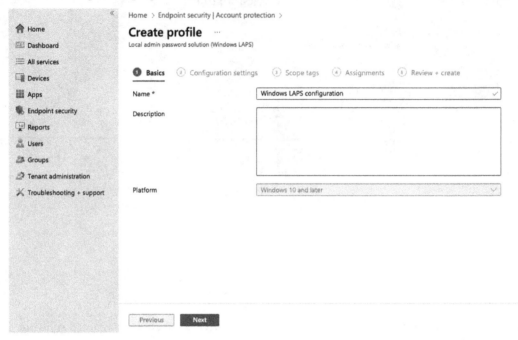

Figure 6.54 – Endpoint security profile Basics information

4. Set the settings as you want them to be for your Windows LAPS configuration. Once you're done, select **Next**.

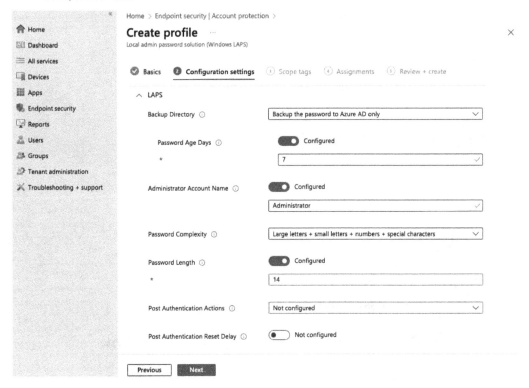

Figure 6.55 – Endpoint security profile configuration settings

5.   Select **Scope tags** if you are using any. Then, click **Next**:

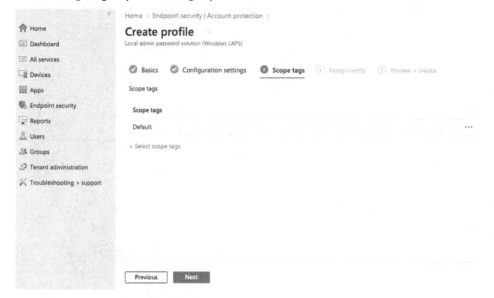

Figure 6.56 – Endpoint security profile Scope tags settings

6.   Assign the profile to either users or devices. Once you're done, click on **Next**.

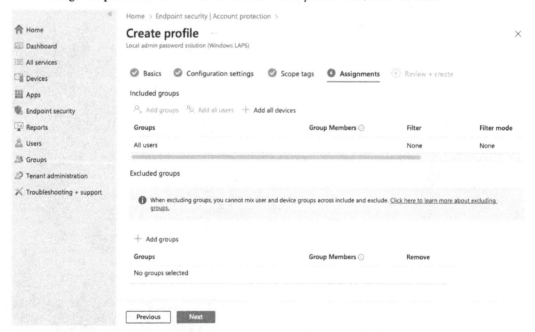

Figure 6.57 – Endpoint security profile Assignments overview

7. Review the settings and select **Create**.

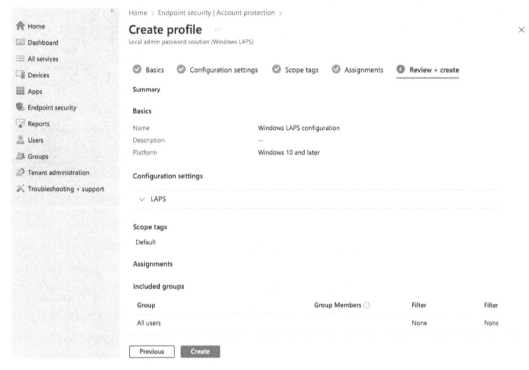

Figure 6.58 – Endpoint security profile review settings

Next, we'll go and find the password backed up into Azure AD for a device.

How to find the password for a device

The local administrator password for a device can be found in **Microsoft Intune** under the Intune device itself. Find the device you want to get the password for and select **Local admin password** in the **Monitor** panel to the left.

Figure 6.59 – Local admin password overview

To view the password, click on **Show local administrator password**.

Figure 6.60 – Viewing the local administrator password

This ends the section about Windows LAPS and how to ensure a different password for all your devices. Next, we'll be covering how to protect the Cloud PC connection screen from capture tools.

Screen capture protection

The screen capture protection feature prevents sensitive information from being captured on endpoints. When this feature is enabled, remote content is either blocked or hidden in screenshots and screen sharing. Additionally, the client apps mask content from any potentially malicious software that may attempt to capture the screen.

Figure 6.61 – Screenshot of a Cloud PC desktop when screen capture protection is enabled

To configure screen capture protection, follow these steps:

1. Go to **Microsoft Intune admin center** | **Devices** | **Configuration Profiles**.

2. Create a configuration profile by setting **Platform** as **Windows 10 and later** and **Profile type** as **Templates**, then select **Administrative templates**.

3. Once on the **Configuration settings** tab, navigate to **Computer Configuration** | **Windows Components** | **Remote Desktop Services** | **Remote Desktop Session Host** | **Azure Virtual Desktop**.

4.   Click on the **Enable screen capture protection** setting.

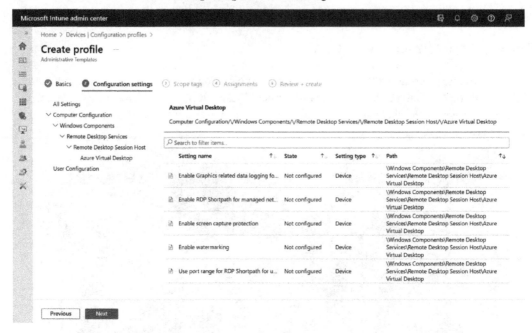

Figure 6.62 – Screen capture protection setting in the Microsoft Intune admin center

5.   Select **Enabled** and then select **Block screen capture on client and server** or **Block screen capture on client** based on your need to block on both the client and server or just the client, respectively. Then, select **OK**.

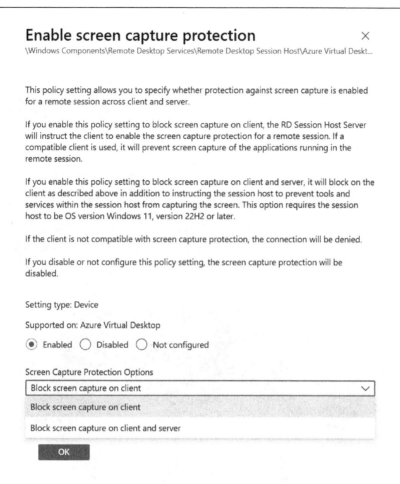

Figure 6.63 – Screen capture protection enablement in the Microsoft Intune admin center

6. Next, set **Scope tags** and **Assignments**, and finally, **Review** and select **Create**. For detailed instructions, please refer to the *Creating configuration profile* section in *Chapter 4*.

> **Note**
>
> When screen capture protection is enabled, connections are allowed only from clients that support this feature, such as the Windows 365 app, and Microsoft Remote Desktop client on Windows and macOS. Also, to enable this feature, Cloud PCs must be running Windows 11, 22H2, or later.

Watermarking

In this section, we will explore the concept of watermarking as a means to safeguard sensitive information from being captured on client endpoints. Similar to screen capture protection, watermarking involves the inclusion of QR code watermarks within the Cloud PC desktop. These QR codes contain unique **connection IDs**, allowing IT administrators to trace Cloud PC sessions. The process of enabling watermarking involves configuring it on the Cloud PC and ensuring compliance by the client endpoints.

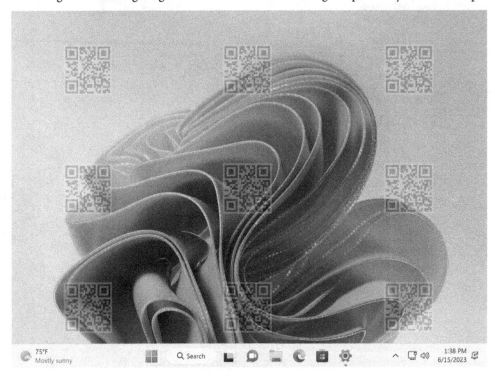

Figure 6.64 – Screenshot of the Cloud PC desktop when watermarking is enabled

To configure watermarking, follow these steps:

1. Go to **Microsoft Intune admin center | Devices | Configuration Profiles**.
2. Create a configuration profile by setting **Platform** as **Windows 10 and later** and **Profile type** as **Templates**, then select **Administrative templates**.
3. On the **Configuration settings** tab, navigate to **Computer Configuration | Windows Components | Remote Desktop Services | Remote Desktop Session Host | Azure Virtual Desktop**.

4. Click on the **Enable watermarking** setting and select **Enabled**. Then, select **OK**.

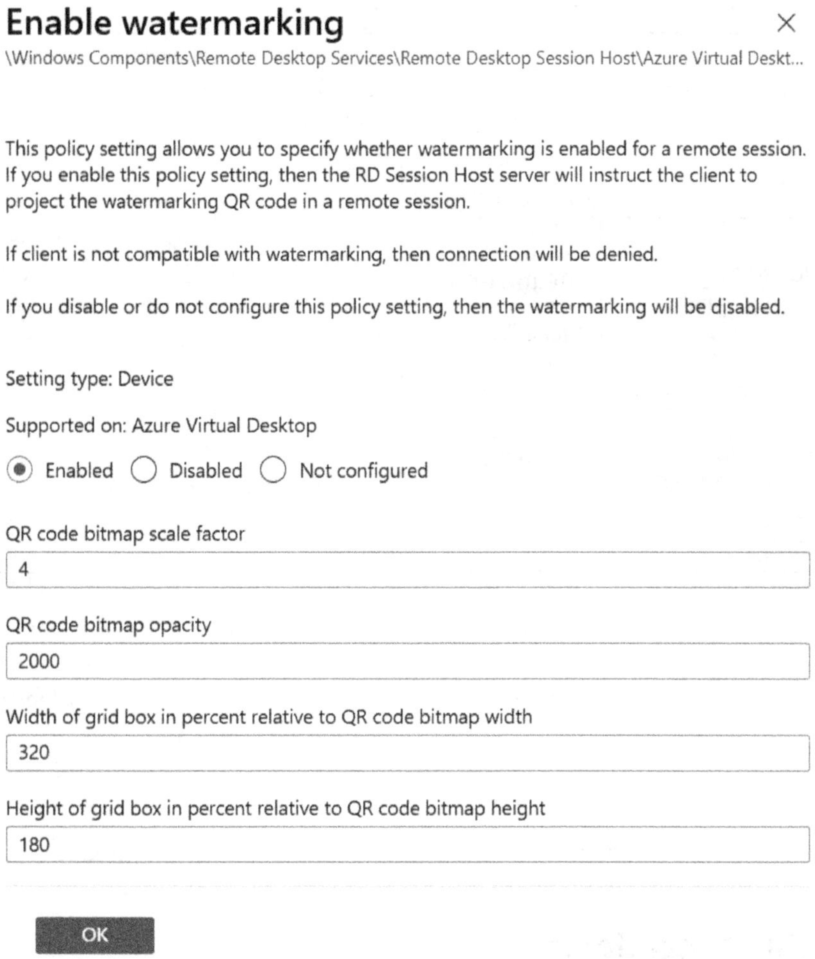

Enable watermarking   ✕

\Windows Components\Remote Desktop Services\Remote Desktop Session Host\Azure Virtual Deskt...

This policy setting allows you to specify whether watermarking is enabled for a remote session. If you enable this policy setting, then the RD Session Host server will instruct the client to project the watermarking QR code in a remote session.

If client is not compatible with watermarking, then connection will be denied.

If you disable or do not configure this policy setting, then the watermarking will be disabled.

Setting type: Device

Supported on: Azure Virtual Desktop

◉ Enabled   ○ Disabled   ○ Not configured

QR code bitmap scale factor

4

QR code bitmap opacity

2000

Width of grid box in percent relative to QR code bitmap width

320

Height of grid box in percent relative to QR code bitmap height

180

OK

Figure 6.65 – Watermarking enablement in the Microsoft Intune admin center

Additional options available for configuration are shown here:

Option	Values	Description
QR code bitmap scale factor	1 to 10 (default = 4)	The size in pixels of each QR code dot. This value determines the number of squares per dot in the QR code.
QR code bitmap opacity	100 to 9999 (default = 2000)	How transparent the watermark is, with 100 being fully transparent.
Width of grid box in percent relevant to QR code bitmap width	100 to 1000 (default = 320)	Determines the distance between the QR codes in percent. When combined with the height, a value of 100 would make the QR codes appear side-by-side and fill the entire screen.
Height of grid box in percent relevant to QR code bitmap width	100 to 1000 (default = 180)	Determines the distance between the QR codes in percent. When combined with the width, a value of 100 would make the QR codes appear side-by-side and fill the entire screen.

Table 6.1 – Additional configuration option5

5. Next, set **Scope tags** and **Assignments**, and finally, **Review + create**. For detailed instructions, please refer to the *Creating configuration profile* section in *Chapter 4*.

> **Note**
>
> When watermarking is enabled, connections are allowed only from clients that support this feature.

Redirecting local devices

Redirecting things such as local drives from the physical device to the Cloud PC can help the end user to easily transfer local files between the devices. Generally, there is nothing wrong with allowing the redirection of local drives or other local resources such as the clipboard. The important thing is to be aware of it and understand the impact it can have. If you want to use Windows 365 to create a secure and closed platform for users and potential external partners, you might want the documents and files to stay within the environment and not allow users to move files between the two devices.

> **Note**
>
> You will find a full list of all supported RDP redirection settings here: `https://learn.microsoft.com/windows-365/enterprise/manage-rdp-device-redirections`.

All the settings that can be redirected to a Cloud PC can be managed with a configuration profile within Microsoft Intune. We covered how to create a configuration profile in *Chapter 4*. When creating the configuration profile, you will be able to find the **Redirection** settings in the following categories in **Settings catalog**:

- `Administrative Templates\Windows Components\Remote Desktop Services\Remote Desktop Session Host\Printer Redirection`
- `Administrative Templates\Windows Components\Remote Desktop Services\Remote Desktop Session Host\Device and Resource Redirection`

> **Note**
>
> Be careful not to block all redirections unintentionally. Other local hardware devices such as cameras and microphones are transferred through RDP redirection, allowing users to participate actively in Microsoft Teams meetings.

Allowing the redirection of different settings is not dangerous in itself; it's when there is no awareness or any decision behind it that it becomes dangerous. Now, let's continue into the next chapter after first looking at Microsoft Defender for Endpoint.

Microsoft Defender for Endpoint

Securing Cloud PC devices is as important as physical devices. Defender for Endpoint helps to detect, prevent, investigate, and respond to threats against your organization's endpoints. The built-in intelligence can help stop an attack before it gets out of control. If your organization is using other security products from Microsoft 365, all solutions can collaborate and help create a complete picture of a potential incident.

Enabling Defender for Endpoint in Intune

Getting your Cloud PC devices onboarded into Microsoft Defender for Endpoint is quite simple. The first step is to ensure the service connection to Microsoft Intune is enabled:

1. Start by going to `https://security.microsoft.com` and then to **Settings | Endpoints | Advanced features**. From here, set **Microsoft Intune connection** as **On**.

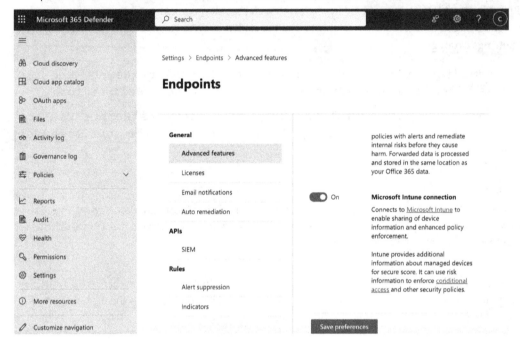

Figure 6.66 – Screen capture protection setting in Microsoft Intune admin center

2. After the connection is enabled, an **Endpoint Detection and Response** (EDR) policy will automatically be created and target all your devices.

> **Note**
>
> It is possible to create your EDR rule to only target specific devices and not all devices as the default rule will do. Alternatively, you can incorporate Cloud PCs into your physical device policy, which means you don't need a separate policy for Cloud PCs as long as you assign them accordingly.

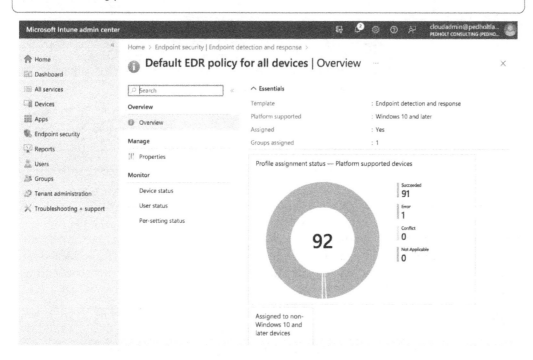

Figure 6.67 – Overview of EDR profile assignment status

3. You will now be able to see and manage your Cloud PC devices in the Microsoft 365 Defender portal, just like any other physical device.

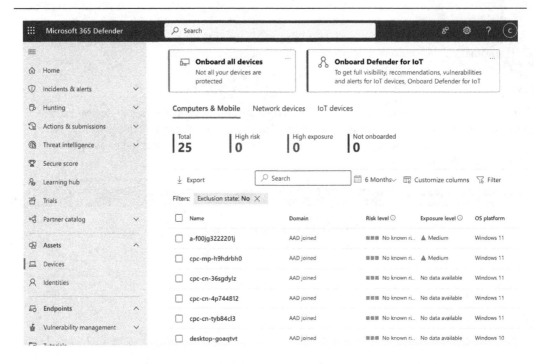

Figure 6.68 – Overview of devices in the Microsoft 365 Defender portal

It is crucial to have a product such as Microsoft Defender for Endpoint not only to help your organization get a security overview of a potential incident but also, more importantly, to prevent the incident from happening to start with. Now, we will jump into how security baselines can help with configuring security settings inside the Cloud PCs.

Security recommendations

Microsoft Defender also recommends activating different features in order to increase the security level of your desktops in the **Security Recommendations** tab. In there, you can find multiple settings that you can directly enable and push into Intune when you set up the connection correctly to your Intune tenant environment.

Security baselines

Security baselines are preconfigured groups of Windows settings that help you apply the security settings that are recommended by the relevant security teams. The baselines you deploy can be customized to enforce only the settings and values required by you. There are multiple security-related settings in Windows, as well as for Microsoft Edge for your endpoints. Another great asset is the option to do versioning and filtering based on different operating systems or scenarios that have to be stricter.

You no longer have to use GPOs to ensure the security settings on your endpoints – just create a security baseline profile and you're all set.

Windows 365 delivers its own branded set of security baselines that include different best practices that are optimized for Cloud PC virtualized scenarios. We highly recommend customers use these as they come from experience from real-world implementations. You can use these policies to lower the risk while increasing the security boundaries of your Cloud PCs. You can use security baselines to get security recommendations that can help lower risk.

The Windows 365 baselines enable security configurations for Windows 10, Windows 11, Edge, and Microsoft Defender for Endpoint. They include versioning features and help customers choose when to update user policies to the latest release:

Figure 6.69 – Security baselines in Microsoft Intune

Summary

In the chapter, you've learned everything about enabling users to access their Cloud PCs from any device in a secure way as well as optimizations available to deliver premium experiences. We went deep into the new modern user experiences that you get when choosing Windows 365 that are different than any other virtualization solution on the market. We hope you enjoyed it!

In the next chapter, you will learn how to analyze, monitor, and troubleshoot Cloud PCs.

Questions

Answer the following questions to test your knowledge from this chapter:

1. How can you enable Conditional Access for users when connecting to Cloud PCs?

2. What is the easiest way to secure your Cloud PCs?

3. How can you enable screen capture protection and watermarking for Cloud PCs?

Further reading

Please take advantage of the following resources to learn more about the topics covered in this chapter:

- *Conditional Access in Azure AD*: `https://learn.microsoft.com/azure/active-directory/conditional-access/overview`

- *Windows security baselines guide*: `https://learn.microsoft.com/windows/security/operating-system-security/device-management/windows-security-configuration-framework/windows-security-baselines`

- *Windows LAPS overview*: `https://learn.microsoft.com/windows-server/identity/laps/laps-overview`

7
Analyzing, Monitoring, and Troubleshooting Cloud PCs

In this chapter, we will go over what is most likely the most important part of your Windows 365 implementation – how you can proactively ensure that the performance of your Cloud PC remains unchanged and get the right insights into your environment to solve issues before users notice!

In this chapter, we will cover the following topics:

- Endpoint analytics
- The Cloud PC performance dashboard
- System alerts and email notifications
- The Cloud PC utilization dashboard
- Troubleshooting and tips and tricks

Endpoint analytics

Endpoint analytics provides insights for measuring how your organization's Cloud PCs are working and the quality of the experience you're delivering to your users.

Endpoint analytics can help identify policies or hardware issues that may be slowing down devices, high-latency connections, or other issues and help you proactively make improvements before end users generate a help desk ticket.

You can find **Endpoint analytics** under the **Reports** section in the Microsoft Intune admin center portal. When accessing **Endpoint analytics** for the first time, you will have to select a deployment method. You can choose between **All cloud-managed devices** or **Selected devices**. We recommend selecting **All cloud-managed devices**.

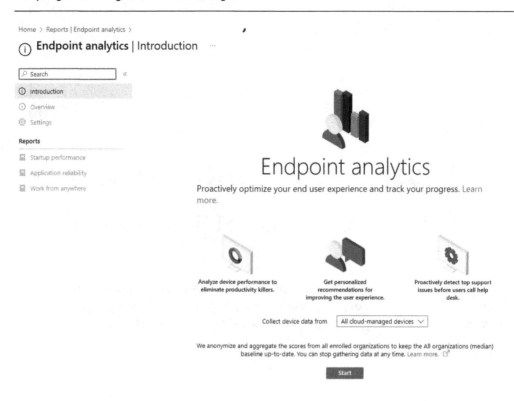

Figure 7.1 – Enable Endpoint analytics

Going forward, the overview page will open, which has the Endpoint analytics score for your total environment, collecting metrics from both physical and Cloud PCs in one view.

Endpoint analytics sets a score in different categories in the range of 0 to 100. A lower score indicates there is room for improvement. You can gain insights into the different scores in the report sections. As an example, on reviewing your startup score, you may see the score is 61, which is higher than the baseline of 50 for all organizations. When you start to break down the startup score, you find your environment excels during the core boot phase with a score of 77. However, the average time to get to the desktop is slower than expected and you suspect long-running startup processes are the cause of this. The core sign-in score is 46. Reviewing the collected data from Endpoint analytics, you can see that long-running processes are responsible for the impact on the score.

If you would prefer different baseline settings to conform to your own standards, you can add your own profiles under the **Settings** menu:

Figure 7.2 – Endpoint analytics baseline

In the following screenshot, you can see the **Overview** page of Endpoint Analytics.

Figure 7.3 – Endpoint analytics overview

In the **Reports** menu option, you can find the different dashboards that are available to monitor and analyze the performance of your Cloud PCs and other Windows devices:

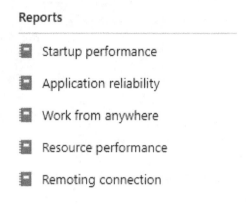

Figure 7.4 – Report categories in Endpoint analytics

Now let us dig deeper into each of these reports.

Startup performance

The **Startup performance** report dashboard helps you to improve the startup performance to optimize the time from power-on to productivity. Review your current score and see how it compares to the selected baseline.

The **Startup performance** score is a feature that helps IT administrators get users from power-on to productivity quickly, without lengthy boot and sign-in delays. The startup score is a number between 0 and 100. This score is a weighted average of the boot score and sign-in score:

- The **boot score** calculates the average time from power-on to the user sign-in page. It stores the last boot time for each device and scores it from 0 (poor) to 100 (good). It excludes update phases in the boot time score.

- The **sign-in score** calculates the average time from the user entering their credentials to having access to a responsive desktop. The last sign-in time for each device is scored from 0 (poor) to 100 (good). It excludes first sign-ins and sign-ins after a feature update.

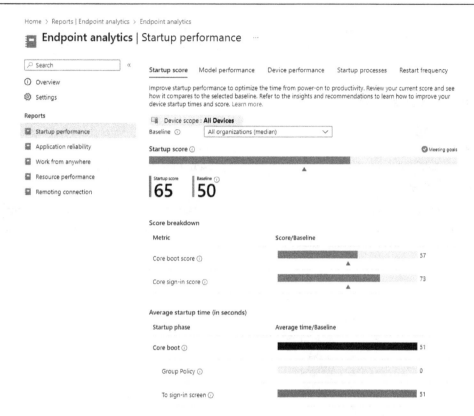

Figure 7.5 – Endpoint analytics overview of startup score dashboard

- **Device performance** – The **Startup performance** score can help IT optimize the sign-in process so users can get on their Cloud PCs and start working quickly:

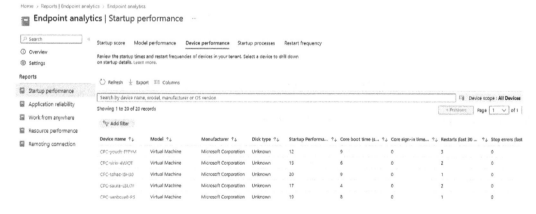

Figure 7.6 – Endpoint analytics – Device performance overview

Ensuring users can log in and be productive fast is important. This is where the **Startup performance** report is useful in giving an overview of where to improve. Next, let's check out the **Application reliability** report.

Application reliability

Application reliability reports help identify applications that have potential issues that might impact the user's experience with applications. It's easy to get an overview of which applications have the most failures and are potentially preventing users from working. From the report, you can go into specific device data and get an overview of app reliability events.

Healthy, performant applications enable people in your organization to be productive. Review your current app reliability score and see how it compares to the selected baseline. Refer to the insights and recommendations to learn how to improve the score.

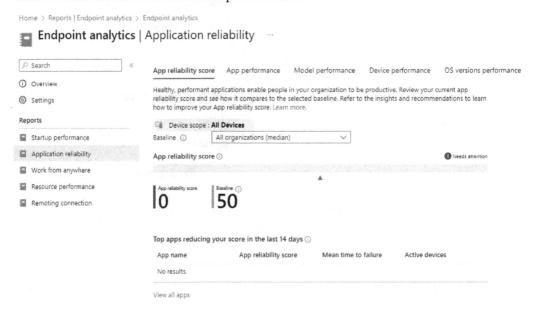

Figure 7.7 – Endpoint analytics – Application reliability report

Next, let's check how we can gain some insights while upgrading our Windows devices.

Work from anywhere

This report provides you with insights while you are upgrading to newer versions of Windows, for example, from Windows 10 to Windows 11. The Windows metric measures the percentage of devices on supported versions of Windows. The recommended remediation actions vary depending on how the devices are managed:

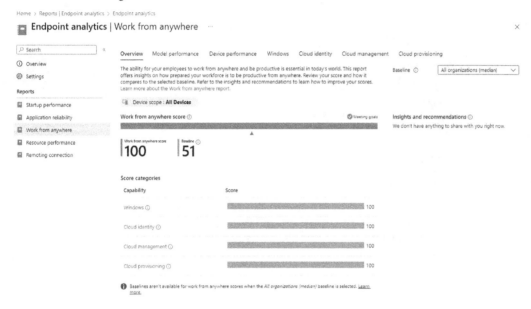

Figure 7.8 – Endpoint analytics – Work from anywhere report

For example, in the Windows view, you can find how many of your devices support Windows 11 in terms of the hardware floor requirements. Windows 365 Cloud PCs provided after October 2021 have support for TPM and Secure Boot. These features are pre-enabled on all new provisioned Cloud PCs from June 2023 onward. Microsoft is working on providing Secure Boot to previously provisioned Cloud PCs as well. If you want to enable Secure Boot faster and your existing Cloud PC was provisioned before June 2023, you must reprovision your Cloud PC.

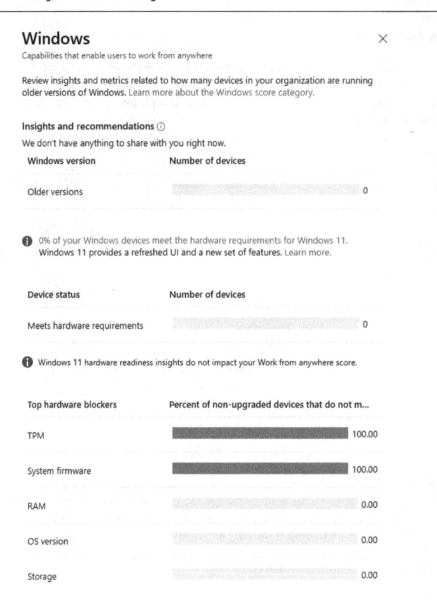

Figure 7.9 – Overview of Windows capabilities report

Let's delve into the **Resource performance** dashboard. This can help to identify performance issues. It also helps to determine whether the size of the Cloud PC is correct for the needs of the user. The Cloud PC size can be changed with the resize feature covered in *Chapter 4*.

Resource performance

The Windows 365 Resource performance report helps optimize vCPU and RAM resources on the devices in your organization. You can review your current resource performance score and see how it compares to the selected baseline.

This report helps you optimize vCPU and RAM resources on the Cloud PC devices in your organization.

The report includes three tabs of information – all include device history:

- **Resource performance score**
- **Model performance**
- **Device performance**

Figure 7.10 – Endpoint analytics – Resource performance report

Resource performance score gives an overall performance rating for all the Cloud PCs you have in the environment. The overall score is the average of the CPU spike time score and RAM spike time score:

- **CPU spike time %**: The **CPU spike time %** data shows the average CPU spike over a 14-day period. A spike is considered when usage is over 50%. The metric graph plots the ratio of CPU spike times to total usage time.

- **RAM spike time %**: The **RAM spike time** % data shows the average RAM spike over a 14-day period. A spike is considered when usage is over 50%. The metric graph plots the ratio of RAM spike times to total usage time.

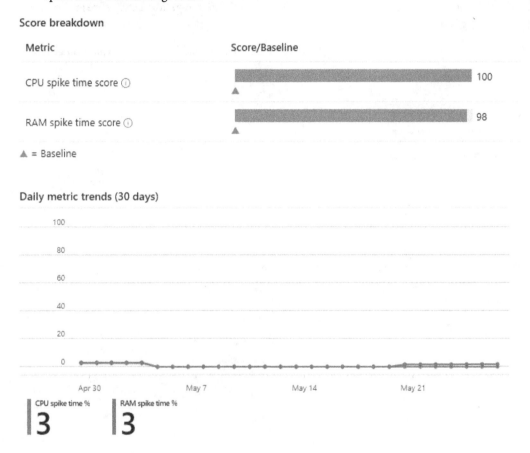

Figure 7.11 – Resource performance score metric

In the following section, we will look at the various reports related to connectivity.

Remoting connection

On the **Remoting connection** dashboard, you can find key performance metrics for connecting to your Cloud PCs and how what's impacting user connectivity. With sign-in time, we provide the time taken to connect to the Cloud PC. The **round trip time** (**RTT**) provides insights into the speed and reliability of network connections from the user location.

You can also monitor the connectivity history over time to see whether there's a correlation between an event that happened across other regions and users.

Figure 7.12 – Remoting connection report

If there's a latency issue, **Endpoint Analytics** will provide insights and recommendations to you:

Figure 7.13 – Example of insights and recommendations

When you click on **Device performance**, you can zoom into the individual latency/RTT information per user session to the Cloud PC.

You can see the device name, model, RTT latency, and sign-in time in seconds:

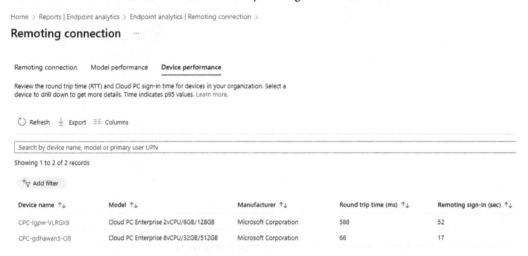

Figure 7.14 – Device performance in the Remoting connection report

Here you can see an example of the breakdown of a Cloud PC, including the following graphs:

- **Cloud PC sign-in time history (sec)**

- **Cloud PC round trip time history (ms)**

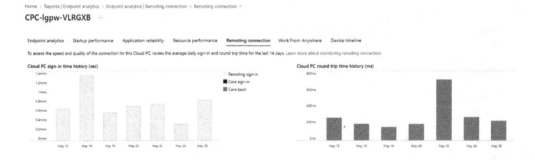

Figure 7.15 – Sign-in time and round trip history overview of a Cloud PC

In this section, we learned about the various reports available in the Microsoft Intune portal. In the next section, let's delve into Windows performance counters and how they can supplement the preceding reports.

Windows performance counters

Using performance counters is crucial to effectively diagnose performance issues in Cloud PCs. When applications run slowly or become unresponsive, identifying the underlying problem can be difficult. Typically, metrics such as CPU, memory, and disk input/output are collected and tools such as Windows Performance Analyzer are used to begin the diagnosis process. Windows Performance Monitor can be used to monitor the performance of a remote computer without logging on to it (see the *Further reading* section for a reference to the Microsoft documentation).

These metrics may not always reveal the root cause due to their frequent and significant variations. To address this challenge, the **User Input Delay** counter is an invaluable tool. This counter measures the amount of time that user input spends in the queue before being processed by a program (see *Figure 7.16*), allowing for quick identification of the cause of poor end user experiences. It is worth noting that this counter works in both local and remote sessions, ensuring a comprehensive analysis and effective troubleshooting.

The **User Input Delay** counter measures the longest time the user's input stays in the Windows kernel input queue, on the Cloud PC, before reaching the application. This delay can affect the speed of crucial and noticeable activities, such as typing.

To monitor this counter, follow these steps:

1. Open **Performance Monitor** (use the `perfmon` command).

2. In the **Performance Monitor** dialog box, expand **Monitoring Tools**, select **Performance Monitor**, and then select **Add**.

3. In the **Add Counters** dialog box, from the **Available counters** list, expand the **RemoteFX Graphics** section.

4. Add the **User Input Delay per Process** and **User Input Delay per Session** counters, as shown in the following screenshot.

5.   After adding the counters, select **OK**.

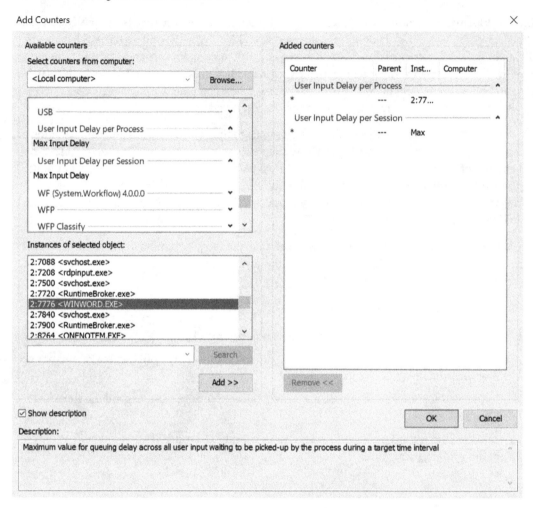

Figure 7.16 – Add performance counters

To illustrate user input delay, let's select the <WINWORD.EXE> process under **User Input Delay per Session** and **Max** under **User Input Delay per Session**.

The selected counters will start reporting user input delays as soon as you add them.

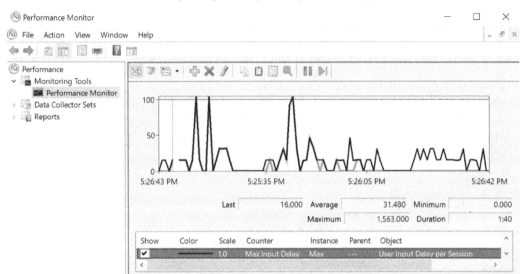

Figure 7.17 – Performance Monitor graph

It is worth noting that there is a correlation between CPU spikes and user input delay – as CPU usage increases, so does user input delay. While this performance counter is particularly helpful in cases where the Cloud PC is running low on resources, it can also be used to monitor user input delay related to a specific application.

Please note that the default interval for reporting user input delay with this performance counter is one second. If you need to adjust the performance counter sample interval property, simply right-click on the graph and select **Properties…**.

> **Note**
>
> You can use these counters via Microsoft tools such as Performance Monitor (`perfmon.exe`), Resource Monitor (`resmon.exe`), Log Manager (`logman.exe`), and `typeperf.exe`. Using third-party software components may also allow you to collect performance data via performance collection APIs or WMI performance counter classes.

Cloud PC device performance dashboard

Under the **Devices** menu in the Microsoft Intune admin center, you can find the recently released **Cloud PC Performance** dashboard, which shows a summary of all the collected metrics per Cloud PC via Endpoint Analytics. You can also access the performance dashboard upon selecting a Cloud PC object in Microsoft Intune.

This allows you to review performance (device performance, connectivity latency, and so on) and connection metrics and trends for a Cloud PC in one unified view, which makes it very convenient for troubleshooting purposes!

Figure 7.18 – Cloud PC performance overview

Now, we will explore how to configure system alerts and notifications for the Windows 365 environment.

System alerts and email notifications

Manually going into **Microsoft Intune** to check for failures is not an ideal workflow. When failures or anything unintended happens, they should be reported automatically to you through an external channel for a better response time. This is possible with the integrated alerts in Microsoft Intune, which enable an IT administrator to get a system notification inside the Intune portal and send an email to one or more addresses.

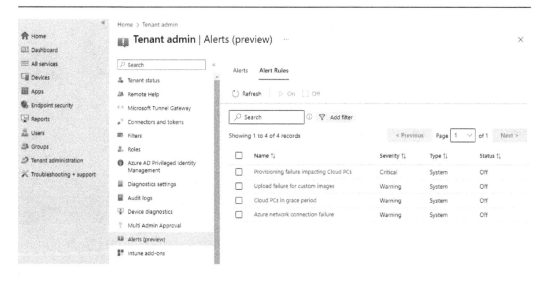

Figure 7.19 – Overview of Alerts in Microsoft Intune

Configuring notifications for the failed provisioning of Cloud PCs

Configuring an alert in Microsoft Intune is straightforward. We will show how to set up an alert notification if a Cloud PC fails under the provisioning state. The process is similar if you want to activate other alerts as well:

> **Note**
> You will only be able to use the predefined alerts. Custom alerts are not supported.

1. Start by going to Microsoft Intune | **Tenant admin** | **Alerts (preview)**.

2. From here, select **Alert Rules** and choose **Provisioning failure impacting Cloud PCs**.

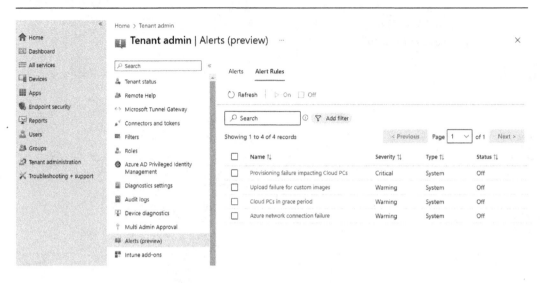

Figure 7.20 – Overview of possible alert rules

3. We need to define when an alert should be triggered. In this case, we want to get a notification whenever any Cloud PC fails during provisioning. So, we set **Threshold** to greater than or equal to 1. Next, we can define what severity the alerts should have. Make sure to set **Status** to **On**:

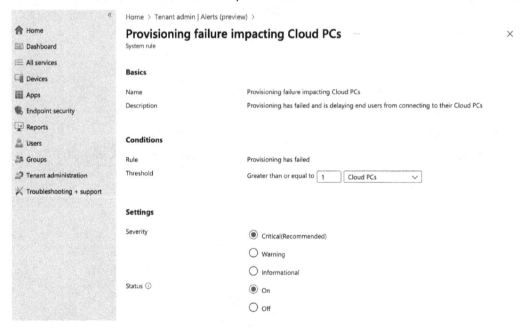

Figure 7.21 – Configure provisioning failure alert settings

4. Now it's time to choose how we would like to get the notification. Setting **Portal pop-up** will display a message in the Intune portal when you are logged in. Setting **Email** will send an email to the addresses you specify in the language of your choice. Once done configuring the settings, select **Apply** and the alert rules will now be active.

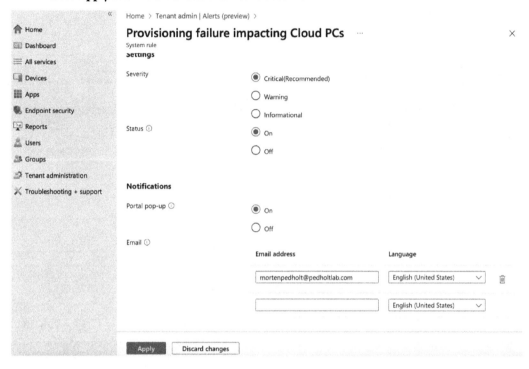

Figure 7.22 – Configure notifications for provisioning failure alert

You can get an overview of all the triggered alerts by going to Microsoft Intune | **Tenant admin** | **Alerts**:

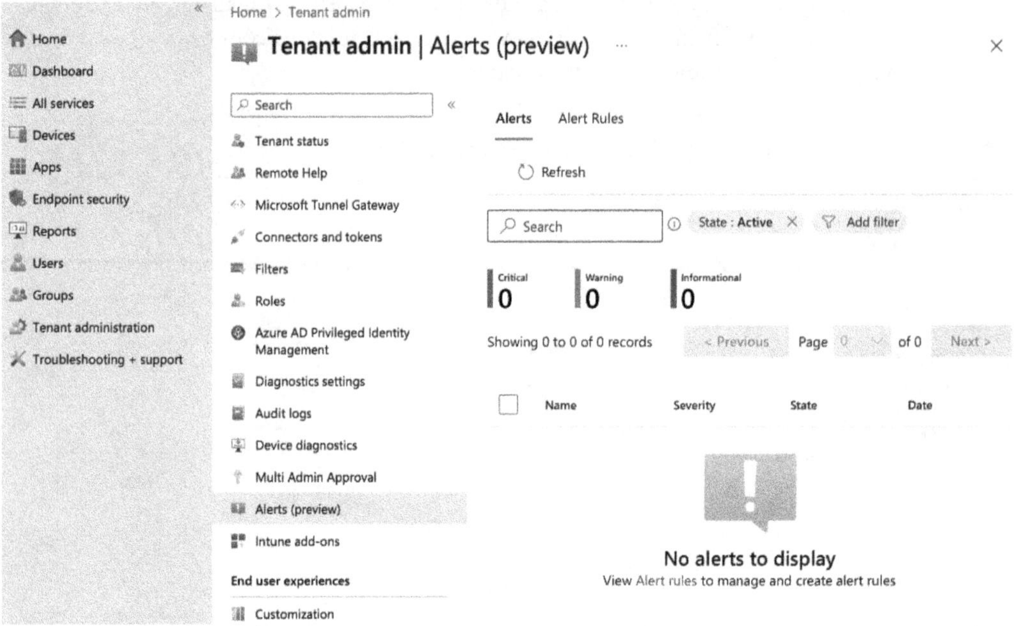

Figure 7.23 – Overview of triggered alerts

Configuring alerts can be a great help to get notice of failures sent directly to the IT department so they can act quickly. The next section will be about visualizing the utilization of Cloud PCs in a Windows 365 environment.

Cloud PC utilization dashboard

It can be very helpful to know a user's Cloud PC usage over time. For example, if a user doesn't use their Cloud PC, your organization might want to review their license usage or reallocate the license to another user who might benefit more from it. It could also be that the environment doesn't fulfill the user's needs anymore and from here, you can start investigating what has changed.

Microsoft Intune provides a built-in utilization report. There are currently two types of utilization reports, one for Cloud PCs and one for Frontline Cloud PCs.

Cloud PC utilization

When looking at the utilization of Cloud PCs, you will be able to see the following information about each Cloud PC: **Device Name**, **Primary UPN**, **Total time connected**, and **Days since last sign in**.

The utilization of a Cloud PC will be separated into three utilization categories based on the number of hours connected in the past 28 days. If **Days since last sign in** equals **0**, that means the user has signed in today.

The categories are as follows:

- **High time connected**: User has been connected for more than 80 hours

- **Average time connected**: User has been connected between 40 and 80 hours

- **Low time connected**: User has been connected for less than 40 hours

To view the utilization report, log in to Microsoft Intune and go to **Devices | Overview**. From here, click on **Cloud PC performance (preview)** and choose **View report** under **Cloud PC with low or no utilization**.

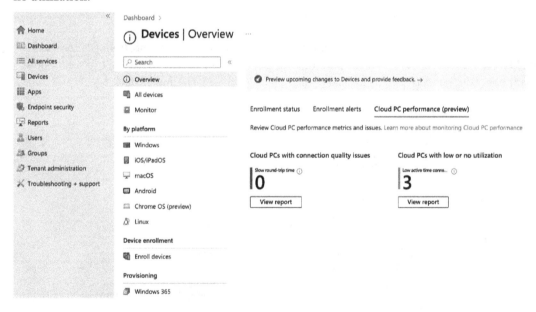

Figure 7.24 – Overview of access to Cloud PC utilization report

From utilizing Cloud PCs, we'll now move on to performance dashboards in Endpoint Analytics:

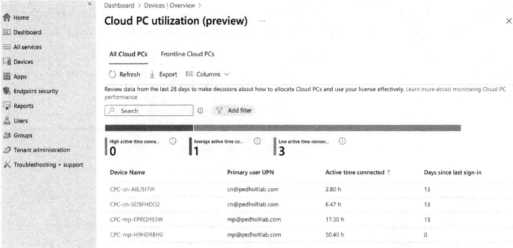

Figure 7.25 – Cloud PC utilization report

Clicking on a specific Cloud PC device name will take you to the **Overview** tab, from where you can find **Performance**. Besides seeing the performance metrics of the device, you are able to see for how many hours the user has been connected to the Cloud PC in the last 7 and 28 days:

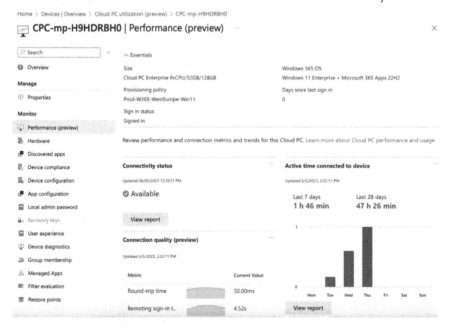

Figure 7.26 – Cloud PC utilization report on a specific device

Clicking on **View report** will show for how long the user was signed in to their Cloud PC device during each session:

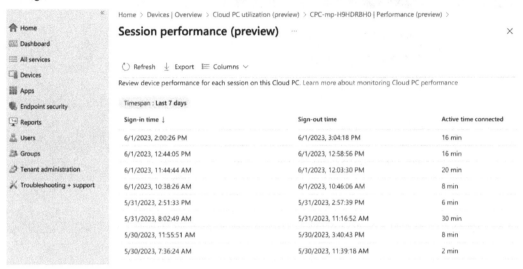

Figure 7.27 – Cloud PC utilization report time connected

In the next section, we will be taking a deeper dive into Windows 365 Frontline analysis and other options to determine the adequate licenses required for your organization.

Frontline Cloud PC utilization

The Frontline Cloud PC utilization report, available in the Microsoft Intune admin center, helps ensure that your organization has purchased an adequate number of licenses to meet the needs of your workforce.

To find this report, go to **Devices | Cloud PC performance (preview) | View report** (under **Cloud PCs with low utilization**).

For each Cloud PC size, you can view the following:

- The number of currently connected Cloud PCs
- The maximum number of connected Cloud PCs for a given day in the past 7 or 28 days
- The maximum concurrency limit

- Warnings if you're approaching and reaching the maximum concurrency limit

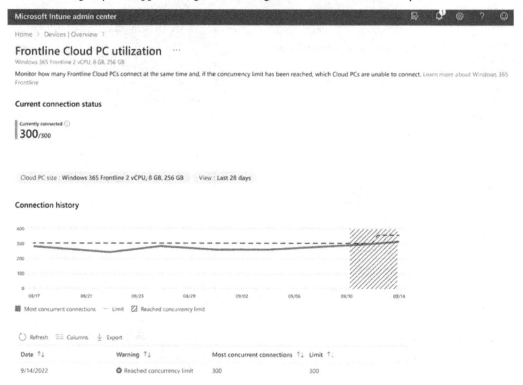

Figure 7.28 – Frontline Cloud PC utilization report

Having the utilization reports for both Frontline and regular Cloud PCs is a great help in understanding the usage of your environment. Having the data helps you make the right decisions for your Windows 365 environment going forward.

Troubleshooting

We've seen numerous problems with customers implementing Windows 365. Even though the process isn't very complex, there are still factors involved that could influence the connectivity or other elements that can disrupt a good performance or onboarding experience.

Here, you will discover valuable insights and solutions to address many of the challenges you may face while offering Windows 365 to your users. The troubleshooting guidance offered here aims to assist you in overcoming these hurdles and ensuring a smooth and secure Windows 365 experience.

Common implementation errors

Here's a list of issues we see most while implementing Windows 365. Network and DNS are the most reoccurring types of issues we see:

- Connectivity issues:

  - Frequent disconnects from Cloud PC sessions (a big driver here is VPN/network security software in the Cloud PC that is not configured to ignore RDP traffic, but could also be any sort of client network configuration issues)

  - Issues in configuring Remote Desktop clients to connect to the Cloud PC (the customer may not know how to set up these clients to connect to the Cloud PC)

  - "Generic" issues with connecting to Cloud PCs (the customer may not realize that their network setup or policies might be causing these issues. You might want to consider checking connectivity, using the troubleshoot option, making sure they don't have local/GPO/Intune policies blocking remote desktop connections, how to make sure the Cloud PC is healthy, etc.)

- Provisioning issues:

  - "Generic" provisioning failures related to issues with HAADJ configuration, Intune/GPO blocking script execution, and so on

  - Issues with license reassignment and the grace period (customers don't understand how grace periods affect the ability to provision new Cloud PCs after license reassignment, so we get a lot of cases around provisioning stuck in a "pending" state because a license is still in use during the grace period on another CPC, the customer losing their CPC and data because it went into the grace period, etc.)

  - Issues with CPCs deployed in the "wrong" region (for Windows 365 Business customers only – don't realize that their Cloud PCs are deployed in a region Microsoft determines)

- **Azure Network Connection** (**ANC**) check failures (usually related to connectivity, ANC setup issues, or configuration issues with AADJ/HAADJ)

- General errors – application update/install issues because users are not local admins in the Cloud PC (maybe related to user settings and troubleshooting)

In the following sections, we will delve into top problem areas.

Connectivity

In the Windows 365 world, connectivity is king. With such variation in endpoint devices and means of connecting to Cloud PCs, it's no wonder that connectivity issues are one of the top support call generators. In this section, we'll explore some common connectivity issues and how to troubleshoot them.

DNS settings – hybrid Azure AD-joined network connection

Confirm your virtual network's DNS settings and that it routes to your Active Directory domain if you are configuring Windows 365 with hybrid Azure AD as the domain configuration.

Always make sure to change your **Domain Name System** (**DNS**) server to **Custom** and enter the **Internet Protocol** (**IP**) address of the DNS service environment that can resolve your **Active Directory Domain Services** (**AD DS**) domain!

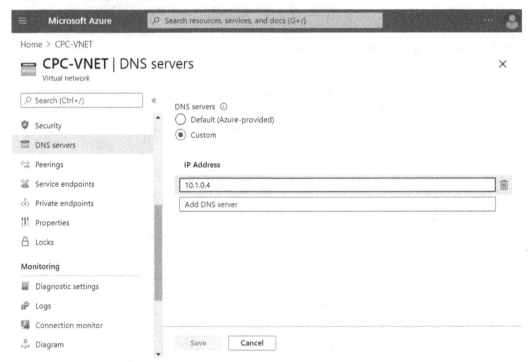

Figure 7.29 – Azure virtual network DNS settings

Incorrect username and password or permissions (hybrid Azure AD)

An enterprise requires a domain environment to join Cloud PCs to your AD domain. For resolution, the AD service account created for this and configured in the ANC needs to have permission to do the following:

- Create computer objects in the OU (join the computer to the domain)
- Delete computer objects in the OU (needed to de-provision the Cloud PC to remove the computer account from AD)
- Enumerate user objects so that they can be found, to be added to the local **Remote Desktop Users** group when provisioning

The other problem could be that you just entered the wrong credentials!

Service URL firewall traffic

Some customers prefer to block all outbound traffic unless it's verified. If that's the case in your organization, you must ensure that all the following URLs and ports are allowed to be used. If that's not the case, the deployment will return an error. Traffic to both MEM services – Intune and **Azure Virtual Desktop** (**AVD**) – should be allowed in your firewall. You can find all the URLs in the *Architecture* section in *Chapter 2*.

Web Proxy Auto-Discovery (WPAD)

The Cloud PC service uses the AVD agent to connect to the broker services of the virtualization control plane. When you use a proxy via WPAD via DNS, you could run into problems such as the machine account not being allowed to connect to the service URLs of both AVD and Intune. To resolve this, allow the machine account or IP addresses in your network to connect over the internet to the list of service URLs. As an alternative, you can remove the proxy settings so they are no longer applied to Cloud PCs and use a direct route to the internet (this is the preferred method).

Troubleshooting connection quality

The quality of the graphics during a remote desktop connection is influenced by various factors, such as the network configuration, network load, and load within the Cloud PC. These factors can affect the clarity, responsiveness, and overall visual experience. To maintain optimal graphical quality, it is essential to optimize network settings, manage the network load effectively, and allocate sufficient resources within the Cloud PC. By addressing these factors, users can improve their visual experience and enjoy a more seamless and immersive remote desktop connection.

While in a carefully curated network setup it is possible to get less than 10 **milliseconds** (**ms**) RTT, in practice, users will start noticing performance degradation above 200 ms and, in the cases of fast refreshing content (e.g., videos or PowerPoint animation), at 150 ms. Additionally, the quality of the remote desktop connection also relies on the internet connection of the user's machine. Users may encounter connection issues or input delay if the connection is unstable, the latency exceeds 200 ms, or the network is congested or rate-limited.

The overall connection experience and reduced RTT can be improved by taking the following steps:

- Admins should make sure the end users' Cloud PCs are deployed in the Azure region closest to their location. This minimizes latency and enhances connection responsiveness.

- Evaluate your network setup, including firewalls, ExpressRoute, and other network features that may impact the RTT. Optimize these configurations to reduce potential bottlenecks.

- Check for any interference or limitations in your network's available bandwidth. If necessary, adjust the network settings to improve connection quality and ensure optimal bandwidth allocation. Following the recommended network guidelines provided in previous chapters can help achieve better results.

- Monitor resource utilization by tracking relevant Windows performance counters. For example, monitor the % **Processor Time** counter under **Processor Information(_Total)** to gauge CPU utilization and the **Available Mbytes** counter under **Memory(*)** to assess available memory. If high CPU usage or insufficient available memory is consistently observed, consider upgrading the Cloud PC size or storage to adequately support user workloads.

- Check your network configuration. Firewalls, ExpressRoute, and other network configuration features can affect the RTT.

Validating your RTT

If you are experiencing user performance issues within your Cloud PC session, you could use the **Experience monitor** tool within the Windows 365 app or Remote Desktop client. The tool shows valuable information about the connection RTT, latency, protocol usage, and bandwidth usage.

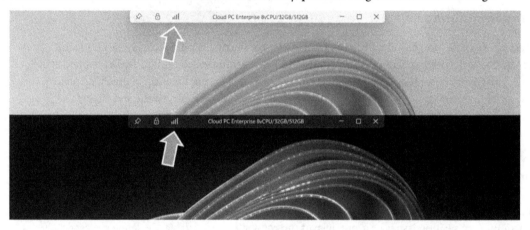

Figure 7.30 – Connection information icon

The following screenshot shows all the relevant information about the active connection. It also shows the gateway being used for the service as well as the quality of connection, RTT, and TCP or UDP (RDP Shortpath) usage:

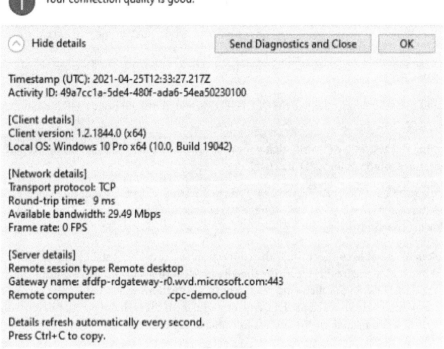

Figure 7.31 – Connection information

Troubleshooting UDP connections using RDP Shortpath

To confirm that your network connectivity is working correctly and that basic UDP functionality is enabled, you can perform the following steps to verify the STUN/TURN server connectivity and NAT type:

1. Download the `avdnettest.exe` executable file from the following link: `https://raw.githubusercontent.com/Azure/RDS-Templates/master/AVD-TestShortpath/avdnettest.exe`.

2. Execute `avdnettest.exe` by double-clicking the file or running it from the command line.

3. If the test is successful, the output of `avdnettest.exe` will resemble the following.

   You can run `avdnettest.exe` by double-clicking on the file or running it from the command line. The output will look like this if connectivity is successful:

   ```
   AVD Network Test Version 1.2303.10002.e62c947
   Checking DNS service ... OK
   ```

```
Checking TURN support ... OK
Checking ACS server 20.202.20.6:3478 ... OK
Checking ACS server 20.202.21.66:3478 ... OK

You have access to TURN servers and your NAT type appears to be
'cone shaped'.
Shortpath for public networks is very likely to work on this
host.
```

This indicates that your connectivity to the STUN/TURN endpoints and basic UDP functionality are both working correctly.

By performing this test, you can verify that your network connectivity is functioning properly and that the necessary protocols for AVD are enabled.

The `ShortpathTransportReliabilityThresholdFailure` error occurs when a specific packet fails to reach its destination, even though the connection remains active. This error can arise in the following situations:

- **Broken or instable connection**: If the connection was previously stable and suddenly stops working, it may trigger this error. The timeout for declaring a packet as lost varies depending on the RTT between the client and session host. In situations where the RTT is very low, one side may attempt to resend a packet frequently, causing it to reach the maximum retry limit of 50 tries in less time than the usual timeout value of 17 seconds.

- **Large packet size**: The maximum size of a transmitted packet is limited. While the packet size is validated, it can fluctuate and occasionally shrink. If the packet being sent becomes too large due to these fluctuations, it may consistently fail to be transmitted successfully.

It's important to be aware of these scenarios and consider them when troubleshooting connectivity issues to ensure a smooth and reliable connection.

Next, let's see how we can gather logs and help users remotely.

Collecting logs and helping users remotely

Being able to gather logs and help users remotely is important to resolve potential issues users might have with applications and Windows OS on their Cloud PCs just like on their local PCs.

Helping users remotely

If a user needs help with an application or Windows-related issue inside their Cloud PC, you must have a remote tool implemented so you can quickly help. A great remote tool to use is Remote Help. Remote Help is integrated directly into Microsoft Intune and comes with usage insights. There are some alternatives to Remote Help, such as TeamViewer.

Collecting logs

It might not always be possible to get remote access to a user's Cloud PC to help them right away. A great tool Microsoft Intune has is being able to gather diagnostics logs. We can then start the troubleshooting even before we get onto the user's Cloud PC. A selection of log files and folders are gathered with this feature. Check the full list of data that's collected, here: `https://learn.microsoft.com/mem/intune/remote-actions/collect-diagnostics#data-ocollected`.

Follow these steps to start gathering logs from a device in Intune:

1. Go to the device and click on **Collect diagnostics**.
2. Click on **Yes** to confirm this action.

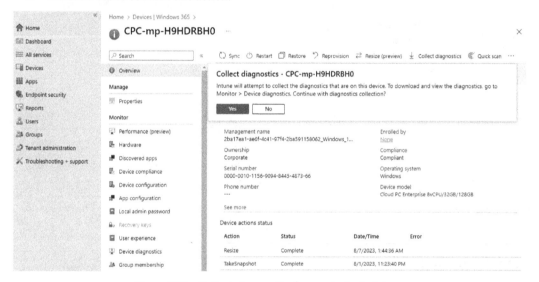

Figure 7.32 – Collect diagnostics from a device in Intune

3. Under the same device, select **Device diagnostics** in the menu to the left.

4. From here, you can select **Download**.

Figure 7.33 – Download diagnostics from a device in Intune

This will start a download of all the supported logs files on your local computer, and you are now able to start troubleshooting before getting access to the user's Cloud PC.

Helping users with issues in their Cloud PC is crucial for them to be productive and have a good experience. Next, let's check out some of the most common display issues.

Display and graphics

In this section, we will look at common display and graphics issues that users might face when connecting to a Windows 365 Cloud PC.

Diagnosing display issues

The most common display issues are blank screens and jitters in user input.

Blank screens can be caused by an application blocking Windows explorer (shell) from loading. A common culprit is VPN applications wanting to establish a connection before allowing the user's desktop to load. If you see a blank screen, please try disabling any VPN connections on the Cloud PC

If users experience a blank screen during sign-in, it may be due to synchronization issues with `AppReadiness`. To prevent a blank screen on a user's first sign-in, you can adjust the timeout window and set the following registry entries for the `AppReadiness` pre-shell task:

1. Open **Registry Editor**.

2. Navigate to the following registry key: HKEY_LOCAL_MACHINE\SOFTWARE\Microsoft\ Windows\CurrentVersion\AppReadiness.

3. Create the following DWORD values if they don't already exist:

   I.   `PreShelTimeout` – set its value to 30,000 (decimal)

   II.   `PreShelDelay` – set its value to 1 (decimal)

4. Restart your computer for the changes to take effect.

By making these changes, you can increase the timeout window for the `AppReadiness` pre-shell task and reduce the chances of encountering a blank screen during the user's first sign-in.

> **Note**
>
> Modifying the registry can be risky, so it's important to proceed with caution and create a backup before making any changes. If you're unsure about taking these steps, consider consulting with a knowledgeable IT professional or Microsoft support for further assistance.

If you encounter blank screens even after installing the latest updates, you can try performing a full memory dump and sharing it with Microsoft's support team. This will help them analyze the issue and provide further assistance in identifying and resolving the root cause of the problem. To enable and collect a dump file, please follow these steps:

1. Open **Registry Editor**.

2. Navigate to the following registry key: HKEY_LOCAL_MACHINE\SYSTEM\ CurrentControlSet\Control\CrashControl.

3. In the right pane, double-click on the `CrashDumpEnabled` value and change the value data to 1.

4. Close **Registry Editor** and restart your computer.

5. Reproduce the action that caused the blank screen.

6. After the blank screen occurs, press the Windows key + *Ctrl* + *Shift* + *B* to force the display driver reset.

7. Once the computer restarts, navigate to the %SystemRoot%\MEMORY.DMP folder.

8. Copy the MEMORY.DMP file to a USB drive or other external storage device.

9. Open a support case with Microsoft and provide the MEMORY.DMP file as an attachment.

Display issues on macOS

When using multiple monitors, you may encounter problems such as blank screens or cursor skipping. These issues can arise due to customized display configurations that create unusual scenarios for the client's graphics algorithm, for example, when retina optimizations are enabled.

If you experience display issues like those mentioned, there are several steps you can take to mitigate them. One option is to use a different display configuration that may be more compatible. Additionally, you can try disabling retina optimization, which may help alleviate the issues. To disable retina optimization, follow these steps:

1. Open the **Remote Desktop** macOS client.
2. Right-click on the Cloud PC for which you want to disable retina optimization.
3. Modify the display properties as needed.

Diagnosing graphics performance issues

In this section, we will look at how to diagnose and fix graphics performance issues.

There are four main categories of performance issues related to graphics, which include the following:

- **Low frame rate**: Low frame rate refers to slow-moving or updating graphics, which can result in a less smooth and fluid visual experience
- **Random stalls**: Random stalls are occasional interruptions or pauses in the graphics rendering that can disrupt the overall performance
- **High input latency**: High input latency refers to delays between user input and the corresponding visual response, which can make graphics feel sluggish or unresponsive
- **Poor frame quality**: Poor frame quality refers to visual artifacts or distortions that affect the overall clarity and fidelity of displayed graphics

Identifying the specific category of performance issue can help with troubleshooting and addressing the root causes to enhance graphics performance.

To determine what's causing graphics issues, we will need to investigate using the graphics performance counters available under the `RemoteFX Graphics` category by following these steps:

1. Identify your session ID. To get your session ID, run the `qwinsta` command in Command Prompt and note the `SESSIONNAME` value for the row that's in the `Active` state (e.g., `rdp-sxs230307500`).
2. Open **Performance Monitor** (use the `perfmon` command).
3. In the **Performance Monitor** dialog box, expand **Monitoring Tools**, select **Performance Monitor**, and then select **Add**.

4. In the **Add Counters** dialog box, in the **Available counters** list, expand the section for **RemoteFX Graphics**.

5. Select the counters you want to monitor.

6. In the **Instances** section, select the instances that match the SESSIONNAME value noted earlier.

7. After adding the counters, select **OK**.

The selected counters will start reporting performance data as soon as you add it.

Understanding the counters

The **Output Frames per Second** counter calculates the number of frames transferred to the client, and if this value falls below the **Input Frames per Second** counter, it implies that certain frames are being skipped. To identify the bottleneck, **Frames Skipped per Second** counters are available and come in three types:

- **Frames Skipped per Second (Insufficient Server Resources)**
- **Frames Skipped per Second (Insufficient Network Resources)**
- **Frames Skipped per Second (Insufficient Client Resources)**

A higher value observed in any of these counters implies that the bottleneck is related to the resource being tracked by that counter. For instance, when the client fails to render the frames at the same rate the server is providing them, then the **Frames Skipped per Second (Insufficient Client Resources)** counter value will be high.

If the count of the **Output Frames per Second** counter matches the **Input Frames per Second** counter, and you encounter unusual stalling or lag, it might be due to **Average Encoding Time** being too high. Encoding is a synchronous process executed either on the server in a single-session scenario or on the VM in a multi-session scenario. This process ought to be completed in less than 33 milliseconds. If **Average Encoding Time** is within this window, and you still face performance issues, then it could be due to the application or operating system being used.

> **Note**
>
> RDP, by default, supports an input frame rate of up to 30 **frames per second** (**fps**). The user might experience a lower frame rate in numerous instances as it is based on the frequency with which the source provides a frame to RDP. For example, when a user is watching a video at 30 fps, RDP will try to deliver content at 30 fps. However, when the user is editing or reading a document, RDP will deliver content only at a rate that matches the changes made to the screen/document without compromising the quality of the user's experience.

You can utilize the **Frame Quality** counter to identify any frame quality problems. This counter represents the quality of the output frame in comparison to the quality of the source frame, stated as a percentage. Any decrease in quality could be a result of either RemoteFX issues or an inherent issue in the graphics source. If the quality loss is due to RemoteFX, it might be because of insufficient resources on the network or server, leading to the transmission of low-fidelity content.

Mitigating graphics performance issues

Depending on the source of the issue, you can take the following mitigations:

- First and foremost, make sure that the latest updates to the operating system are installed on both the Cloud PC and endpoints. Also ensure that you are using the latest version of the client.

- Reduce the screen resolution if possible and acceptable. If that resolves the issue but you need a higher resolution, try one of the following mitigations.

- If the issue is on the Cloud PC side, size up your Cloud PC to make available more compute and memory resources.

- If the issue is on the endpoint side, increase the compute and memory resources on the endpoint.

- If the issue is on the network side, increase the available network bandwidth to the connection.

Logon performance

Logon performance can be impacted by several factors, including local endpoint performance, network performance, and Cloud PC logon performance. When you log on to your Cloud PC for the first time, it may take longer than subsequent logons because the Cloud PC needs to acquire Azure AD tokens for each service the client talks to.

Additionally, logging in to a new session on the Cloud PC side takes time due to the initiation of Windows components and startup apps. Therefore, it's important to optimize your Cloud PC to improve logon performance. Some of these optimizations are discussed later in this section.

Acquiring Azure AD tokens can take time, but once acquired, they are valid for 60 minutes, by default. You can adjust the lifetime of these tokens to align with your company's security posture. Connections initiated while the tokens are valid will be much faster than those initiated after the tokens have expired.

Enabling RDSAADAuth to reduce the connection time

RDSAADAuth is the new authentication protocol in the latest RDP stack, which is not only more secure but also much quicker than PKU2U. PKU2U was primarily built for USB-based communications instead of communications with cloud services – as a result, it passes a lot of the cert calls over the wire. However, the first connection using RDSAADAuth may take longer than subsequent connections due to the nature of how RSA key generation works. To generate the keys, the protocol uses entropy, which TPM can generate internally to pick two very large prime numbers, P and Q, that are very far apart.

Then, it multiplies P and Q to get the public key. Azure AD requires 2,048-bit keys, and checking a number for the primality of such large numbers involves a lot of division, which is not something that exists in RSA crypto accelerators. They are designed to accelerate encryption and decryption, not key generation. As a result, to create public keys, it might take up to 8 seconds on x64-based endpoints and up to 30 seconds on ARM64-based endpoints.

Optimizing Cloud PCs

Windows 365 Cloud PCs are optimized for peak performance for general workloads. Based on your users' needs, you can choose to optimize or customize them further. Optimizations typically include configuring operating system settings and configuring apps – sometimes even removing or disabling them. For more details, we recommend referring to the Microsoft documentation on recommended configuration for VDI desktops – `https://aka.ms/W365OSRecommendations`.

Authentication and identity

Here are some known issues and limitations when it comes to authentication and identity:

- **Login errors**: If you see one of the following errors, it could be the Conditional Access policies that are restricting access:

  - `We couldn't connect to the remote PC because of a security error`

  - `The sign-in method you're trying to use isn't allowed`

  To resolve the issue, please enforce Azure AD multi-factor authentication for your Azure AD-joined VMs.

- **Account switch detected on macOS**: If you see the **Account switch detected** error, you need to refresh the Azure AD token by following these steps:

  I.   Delete any workspaces from the Remote Desktop client.

  II. Open the **Keychain Access** app on your device.

  III. Under **Default Keychains**, select **login**, then select **All Items**.

  IV. In the search box, enter `https://www.wvd.microsoft.com`.

  V.   Double-click to open an entry with the name **accesstoken**.

  VI. Copy the first part of the value for **Account**, up to the first hyphen, for example, **70f0a61f**.

  VII. Enter the value you copied into the search box.

  VIII. Right-click and delete each entry containing this value.

IX.   If you have multiple entries when searching for `https://www.wvd.microsoft.com`, repeat these steps for each entry.

X.   Try to subscribe to Cloud PCs again.

- **Delete existing security tokens on iOS/iPadOS**: You will have issues connecting to the Cloud PC if the cached token has expired. Refresh the token using the following steps:

    I.   Open the **Settings** app for iOS or iPadOS.

    II.   From the list of apps, select **RD Client**.

    III.   Under **AVD Security Tokens**, toggle **Delete on App Launch** to **On**.

    IV.   Try to subscribe to a workspace again.

    V.   Toggle **Delete on App Launch** to **Off** once you can connect again.

- **WebAuthn redirection**: If you're experiencing issues with WebAuthn redirection in the Windows Hello for Business or security key authentication process, there are a few things you can check. First, ensure that the user is connecting from a supported operating system and that WebAuthn redirection is enabled as a device redirection. If both requirements are met but the option to use Windows Hello for Business or security keys is still not available when accessing Azure AD resources, you may need to enable the FIDO2 security key method for the user account in Azure AD. To do this, follow the instructions in the *Enable FIDO2 security key method* section of the Microsoft documentation – `https://learn.microsoft.com/azure/active-directory/authentication/howto-authentication-passwordless-security-key#enable-fido2-security-key-method`.

- If a user signs in to the Cloud PC with a single-factor credential, such as a username and password, they may not be able to use Windows Hello for Business to access Azure AD resources that require multi-factor authentication. In this case, the user should follow these steps to authenticate properly:

    I.   If the user isn't prompted for a user account, they should first sign out.

    II.   On the account selection page, select **Use another account**.

    III.   Next, choose **Sign-in options** at the bottom of the window.

    IV.   After that, select **Sign in with Windows Hello or a security key**. You should see an option to select Windows Hello or security authentication methods.

The Windows 365 app

Here are some limitations when it comes to using the Windows 365 app:

- The Windows 365 app is not supported on Windows 11 IoT
- The Windows 365 app does not support configuring device redirection properties

Here are some issues commonly encountered:

- **"Can't connect to Cloud PC" error when you click on the Connect button**: To resolve the issue, do the following:

    - Open **Windows Settings | Apps | Default apps**.
    - Find the AVD host app and update the default app for .avd files.
    - Run the following command to remove the old Remote Desktop client cache that could be causing this issue
    - `reg delete "HKEY_CLASSES_ROOT\progF3672D4C2FFE4422A53C78C345774E2D" /f`

- **Windows 365 app asks to select a new default app**: When the Microsoft Remote Desktop client is installed, you may receive a message asking you to choose a default app for a specific file type. To successfully launch the Cloud PC session, make sure to select **Azure Virtual Desktop (HostApp)** as the default app.

- **Windows 365 app doesn't show any Cloud PCs**: Please ensure you have signed in with an account that is enrolled with the Azure AD account that has Cloud PCs provisioned.

Remote Desktop clients

Monitoring the overall end user experience from the Windows 365 client side is just as important as doing it directly from Endpoint Analytics. In the next section, you will learn how to collect logs for the Remote Desktop client to transfer to Microsoft support or Tech Community for help.

Microsoft Remote Desktop client for Windows

If the mitigations discussed so far don't work, you will need to collect logs and share them with your support or Microsoft support. Here are the steps to collect logs:

1. Disconnect all sessions. You can do so by right-clicking on the **Remote Desktop** icon in the system tray and selecting **Disconnect all sessions**.
2. Navigate to the `%temp%\DiagOutputDir\RdClientAutoTrace` folder.

3. The latest logs are available in the latest versions of these ETL files:

    *   `msrdcw_<timestamp>.etl`

    *   `RdClientAutoTrace-WppAutoTrace-<timestamp>.etl`

You can convert .ETL logs into .CSV or .XML format for better readability by using the `tracerpt` command in a PowerShell prompt, as shown:

*   **CSV**: `tracerpt "<filename>.etl" -o "<filename>.csv" -of CSV`

*   **XML**: `tracerpt "<filename>.etl" -o "<filename>.xml" -of XML`

Microsoft Remote Desktop web client

Here are some of the known issues with the web client:

*   **Web client stops responding or disconnects**: If the Remote Desktop web client stops responding or keeps disconnecting, try closing and reopening the browser. If it continues, try connecting using another browser or one of the other clients. You can also try clearing your browsing data.

*   **Web client out of memory**: When the web browser has run out of memory, you will see the error message **Oops, we couldn't connect to Cloud PC**. To mitigate this issue, resize the browser window and try connecting to the Cloud PC.

Microsoft Teams

Here are some of the known issues and limitations:

*   Teams optimizations are only supported for the Windows 365 app and Remote Desktop client running on Windows 10 or later or macOS 10.14 or later.

*   The use of HTTP proxies isn't supported. Interestingly, they still work.

*   Zooming in/zooming out of chat windows isn't supported.

*   Incoming and outgoing video streams are limited to 720p resolution.

*   HID buttons or LED controls on devices are not supported.

*   If you need to take a screenshot of an incoming Teams video content, you must do so from the endpoint device.

*   Sharing redirected videos during screen or application sharing is not supported.

*   Minimized windows cannot be shared. Restore the application window before trying to share it.

*   When sharing an application, any occlusions – for example, another overlapping window – will result in the overlapped part of the shared application not updating or showing a black overlay.

- If you switch tenants while using Teams, you may experience call-related issues, such as screen sharing not rendering correctly. To mitigate these issues, restart your Teams client after switching tenants.

Collecting Microsoft Teams logs

If you're experiencing issues with the Teams desktop app in your AVD environment, you can collect client logs by navigating to `%appdata%\Microsoft\Teams\logs.txt` on the Cloud PC.

If you're encountering issues specifically with calls and meetings, you can start collecting Teams diagnostic logs by pressing the key combination *Ctrl + Alt + Shift + 1*. The logs will be written to `%userprofile%\Downloads\MSTeams Diagnostics Log DATE_TIME.txt` on the Cloud PC.

Multimedia redirection

Here are some of the known issues and limitations:

- For Windows endpoints, video playback redirection is functional exclusively with the Windows 365 app or the Microsoft Remote Desktop app for Windows.

- Protected content is not supported by video playback redirection, which means that videos with DRM from Netflix or Pluralsight will not be redirected. To mitigate the issue, turn off the extension to allow the video to play without optimizations.

- Sometimes, you may get a message that the extension is not loaded or that the redirection is not supported. To mitigate the issue, open a second tab. If the issue persists, please verify that all components and dependencies are installed correctly. If everything is in order but the extension still doesn't load, try to reinstall the extensions using Configuration Profile in Intune. Please refer to *Chapter 3, Deploying Cloud PCs,* for details.

- Sometimes, all videos are stuck in a loading state. To mitigate the issue, sign out of your Cloud PC and restart your session.

- On high-DPI monitors, you may see a gray pattern on the video screen.

- Sometimes, the video or video player controls may be obscured. To mitigate the issue, resize the video player window.

Collecting multimedia redirection logs

If you face any problems, you can gather logs from the extension and share them with the support team by following the instructions provided as follows:

1. Select the Multimedia Redirection Extension icon in your browser.

2. Select **Show Advanced Settings**.

3.   Select **Start**, next to **Collect logs**.

4.   Now, reproduce the scenario.

5.   Once done, select **Stop**.

6.   Save the host and extension logs when prompted by the browser.

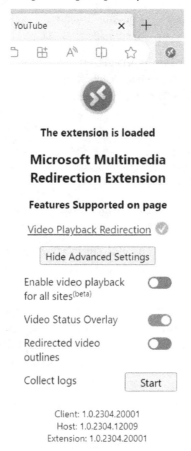

Figure 7.34 – Collect logs using the Multimedia Redirection Extension pane

Contacting Microsoft support

Under **Help and support**, select the **Windows 365** option to create help desk tickets. After that, enter a quick summary of the problem you have.

There is a chance that a resolution will be provided based on your input. If not, click on **Use search** to describe your issue and contact support, as illustrated in the following screenshot:

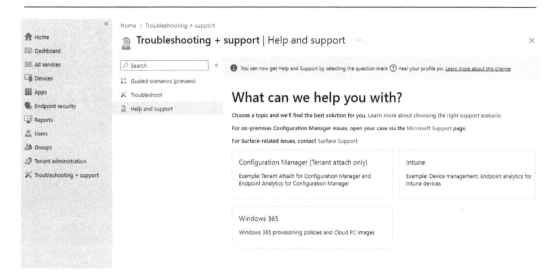

Figure 7.35 – Help and support selection

> **Note**
>
> To help a Microsoft help desk employee resolve your issue faster, please provide as much technical information as you can about the error in the **Contact support** form.

Screen capture protection

We learnt about the Screen capture protection feature in *Chapter 6, Securing Cloud PCs*. Here are some of the known issues and limitations of this feature:

- When **Screen capture protection** is turned on, connections from clients other than the Windows 365 app, and Microsoft Remote Desktop client on Windows and macOS, will be rejected. If a user tries to connect to a capture-protected session host with an unsupported client, the connection won't work and will instead show an error message with the code 0x11511.

- This feature protects the Remote Desktop window from being captured through a specific set of public operating system features and **application programming interfaces** (**APIs**). However, there's no guarantee that this feature will strictly protect content in scenarios where a user is to take a photo of their screen with a physical camera.

- For maximum security, customers should use this feature with watermarking while also disabling clipboard, drive, and printer redirection. Disabling redirection prevents users from copying any captured screen content from the remote session.

- Users can't share their Remote Desktop window using local collaboration software, such as Microsoft Teams, while this feature is enabled. When they use Microsoft Teams, neither the local Teams app nor Teams with media optimization can share protected content.

We hope this helps! Let us know if you have any questions through social media or other channels.

Summary

In the chapter, you learned how to analyze, monitor, and troubleshoot Windows 365 Cloud PCs. We looked at how the tools built into Microsoft Intune and the Windows operating system can help with doing these things.

In the next chapter, you will learn about Windows 365-approved partners and how they can extend Windows 365.

Questions

1. Where is the best place to analyze Cloud PC performance?
2. How can you add custom performance monitors to assess whether Cloud PCs meet your company's performance standards?
3. How can you troubleshoot connectivity issues?

Further reading

Please take advantage of the following resources to learn more:

- *Recommended configuration for VDI desktops | Microsoft Learn*: `https://aka.ms/ W365OSRecommendations`

- *Endpoint analytics via Microsoft Intune* | Microsoft Learn: (`https://learn.microsoft. com/mem/analytics/overview`)

- *Monitor performance of a remote computer without logging on to it | Microsoft Learn*: (`https:// learn.microsoft.com/troubleshoot/windows-server/performance/ monitor-remote-computer-performance`)

Part 4:
Extending Windows 365 with Partner Solutions

The final part of the book is dedicated to extending Windows 365 with partner solutions and emphasizes the significance of community experts. It offers valuable insights into the available partner solutions and explains how they can enhance Windows 365. Moreover, it introduces you to some of the most influential individuals in the Windows 365 community, providing opportunities for learning and networking.

This part contains the following chapters:

- *Chapter 8, Windows 365 Partner Solutions*
- *Chapter 9, Community Experts – Hall of Fame*

8

Windows 365 Partner Solutions

In this chapter, we will be going over the different partner solutions that can be integrated with Windows 365. In this chapter, you will become familiar with these partners, what value they add to the platform, and how to get access to their solutions.

We will cover the following topics in this chapter:

- Why are partners important?
- Protocol-enhanced partners – Citrix and VMware
- Client partners – IGEL Technology
- Package modernization partners – Rimo3
- Client modernization partners – LG and Motorola/Lenovo

Why are partners important?

Partners are extremely important to Microsoft and Windows 365, not because the solution isn't complete but to expand the service as a platform. In fact, Windows 365 was announced and released during Microsoft Inspire, Microsoft's largest annual partner conference.

Windows 365 provides opportunities for independent software vendors to reach a broader audience by delivering their value with Windows 365.

Protocol-enhanced partners – Citrix and Windows 365

Citrix and Microsoft have been partners for decades. With Windows 365 and Citrix used together, we get the benefits of Cloud PCs as a software-as-a-service platform together with Citrix HDX as a protocol. What does this mean?

With Windows 365 and Citrix, you can benefit from the value of Windows 365 as a service, as Intune is used to provision, manage, and analyze/monitor the Cloud PCs in the same way as in Windows 365 Enterprise. However, the Citrix HDX protocol extends the Windows 365 experience with Citrix HDX high-end graphics technology, support for a broader range of endpoint devices and peripherals, advanced security and policy controls, and third-party identity integrations.

| Provides a high-definition, interactive experience across a broad range of endpoint devices and peripherals | Applies granular policy controls to enhance security and protect corporate data | Allows employees to seamlessly switch to existing or new Citrix clients | Optimizes voice and video performance for multimedia applications | Integrates with third-party identity solutions |

Figure 8.1 – Citrix added value summary

Let's move on to a more technical explanation of Citrix's solution that enhances Windows 365.

What are the requirements?

In order to use Citrix and Windows 365 together, we have the following requirements:

- Citrix:

  - Citrix Cloud tenant with HDX Plus for Windows 365 entitlement

  - Citrix DaaS Premium

  - Citrix DaaS Premium Plus

  - Citrix DaaS Advanced Plus

  - Citrix DaaS Standard for Azure

  - Citrix administrator account with full administrator rights

- Microsoft:

  - Microsoft Intune entitlement

  - An Azure **Active Directory** (**AD**) domain in the same tenant as Microsoft Intune

  - Windows 365 Enterprise licenses in the same tenant as Microsoft Intune

  - Azure AD Global Administrator

  - Intune Global Administrator

In the next section, we will explain how you can install the Citrix connector agent via Microsoft Intune.

Enabling the Citrix connector in the Intune portal

1. Go to **Microsoft Intune** and log in with an account that has Global Administrator privileges in Intune.

2. Go to **Tenant Administration** | **Connectors and tokens** | **Windows 365 partner connectors**.

3. Click on **+ Add**.

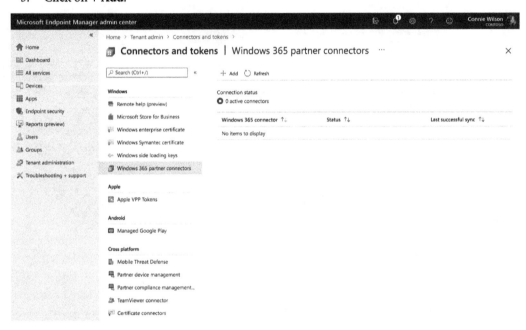

Figure 8.2 – Enable Windows 365 partner connection

4. From here, select the **Citrix** connector.

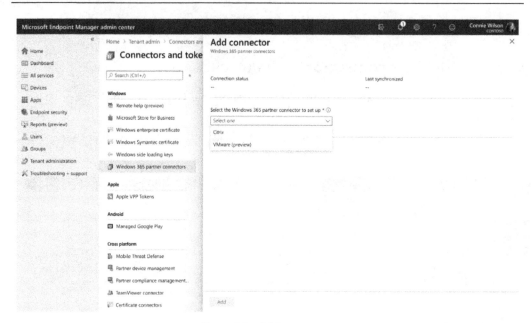

Figure 8.3 – Add connector

5.   Enable the **Allow people to use Citrix to connect to their Cloud PCs** setting.

6.   Click on **Add**.

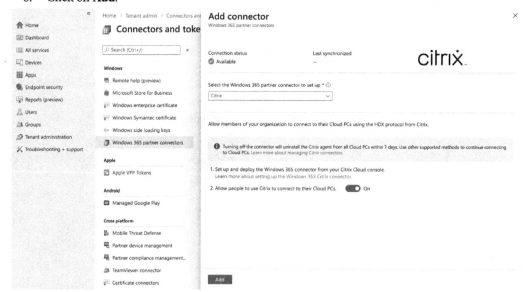

Figure 8.4 – Select Citrix as a connector

7.   The connector will automatically install itself in the background. Once ready, you will see it lighting up in the portal (as shown in *Figure 8.5*).

> **Note**
>
> Provisioning Cloud PCs is done in the same way as explained in *Chapter 3, Deploying Cloud PCs*. During provisioning, the Citrix agents will be added automatically. If you have existing Cloud PCs, they will also get the Citrix agents installed.

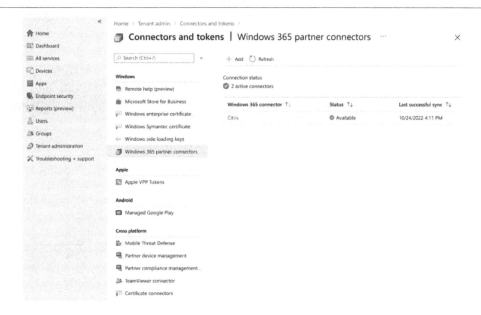

Figure 8.5 – Windows 365 partner connectors overview

Connecting Windows 365 to Citrix Cloud

The following steps are to be performed in the Citrix Cloud administrative console:

1. Click on the options menu in the upper-left corner, expand **My Services**, and select **DaaS**:

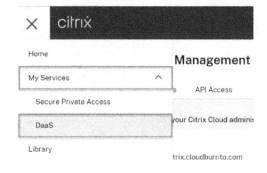

Figure 8.6 – My Services – Citrix Cloud

2. Place the cursor over the arrow in the **Manage** tab to expand the menu, and select **Full Configuration**.

3. Select **Quick Deploy** on the left side.

4. Select **Connect** under the **Connect to Windows 365** option:

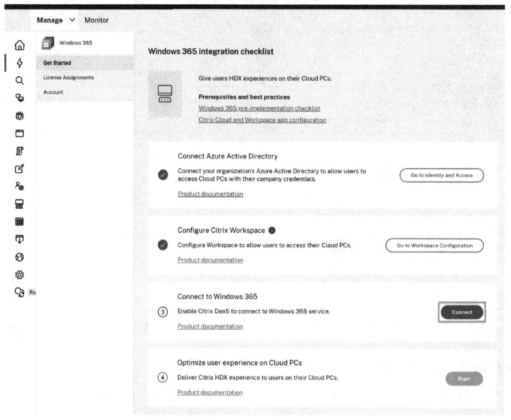

Figure 8.7 – Citrix Cloud onboarding checklist

5. Log in with the Global Administrator account and accept the requested permissions.

miguel.contreras@win365citrixdevint.onmicrosoft.com

Permissions requested
Review for your organization

Citrix Virtual Apps and Desktops - XAC
Citrix Systems, Inc. ✓

This app would like to:

∨   Read Cloud PCs

∨   Read all users' full profiles

∨   Read directory data

∨   Read all devices

∨   Sign in and read user profile

∨   Partner read and write Cloud PCs (Windows 365 3P)

∨   Partner read and write cloud pc

If you accept, this app will get access to the specified resources for all
users in your organization. No one else will be prompted to review these
permissions.

If you accept, Windows 365 3P will also have access to your user profile
information.

Accepting these permissions means that you allow this app to use your
data as specified in their terms of service and privacy statement. **The
publisher has not provided links to their terms for you to review.** You
can change these permissions at https://myapps.microsoft.com. Show
details

Does this app look suspicious? Report it here

Figure 8.8 – Tenant permissions request

Assigning Citrix licenses to users

Now we are going to assign the Citrix licenses:

1. Select **Start** under the **Optimize user experience on Cloud PCs** option. Alternatively, you may
    select **License Assignments** on the left.

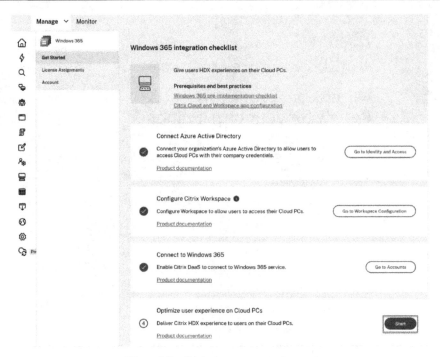

Figure 8.9 – Optimize user experiences

2.   Select **Manage Users**.

Figure 8.10 – Manage Users

3. Select **Add**.

Figure 8.11 – Add licenses to users

4. You now need to look for users that you want to assign a license for. You can use either part of the name or the **User Principal Name** (**UPN**) when searching.

5. Select the user to assign a license to and click **OK**.

Note

At present, you can select up to 10 users at a time.

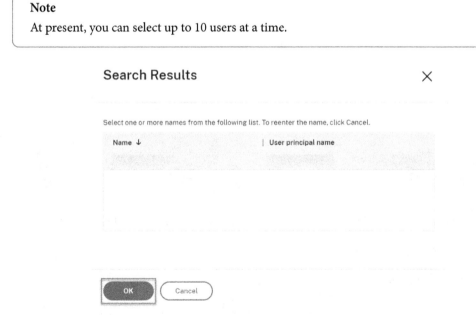

Figure 8.12 – Search for a user

6.   Select **Save**.

Figure 8.13 – Select Users

7.   Select **OK**.

8.   If the list of users does not reflect your selection, select the refresh button to update it.

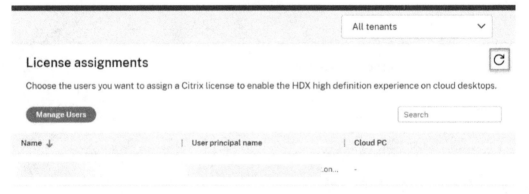

Figure 8.14 – Refresh

9.   Citrix communicates to the Windows 365 service that the selected users are entitled to use Citrix.

What about existing Cloud PCs?

If the selected users already have Cloud PCs provisioned, Windows 365 will automatically install the Citrix **Virtual Delivery Agent** (**VDA**) on those Cloud PCs and switch the user access to Citrix. If the selected users do not have Cloud PCs assigned yet, the VDA will be installed on them immediately after the Cloud PC is provisioned at the time of Cloud PC license assignment. The following screenshot shows how the end user will access their Cloud PC through Citrix Workspace.

Figure 8.15 – Citrix Workspace client experience

Now, you've learned how Citrix works together with Windows 365 and how you can enable this experience. In the next section, we will explain how VMware offers added value to Windows 365.

Protocol-enhanced partners – VMware and Windows 365

Microsoft and VMware have been working together to extend the Windows 365 experience to joint customers leveraging VMware's Blast protocol to deliver high-end display, robust remoting features, and hybrid deployment capabilities to Windows 365 Cloud PCs.

Desktop and application virtualization continues to be in high demand as organizations increasingly embrace hybrid and remote work for their employees. Leveraging the cloud is driving IT organizations to rethink desktop and app virtualization because using the cloud can help IT simplify desktop management while enabling new use cases, such as high availability, disaster recovery, and cloud bursting.

To help customers on their digital transformation journey, VMware has partnered with Microsoft to deliver desktop deployment solutions such as VMware Horizon Cloud on Microsoft Azure. Windows 365 delivers Cloud PCs with a complete and secure Windows experience hosted in the Microsoft cloud and accessible on any device. From temporary workers to software developers and remote employees, Windows 365 enables a variety of new scenarios for the new world of work:

| Provide a high-definition, consistent employee experience across all supported devices and peripherals | Enhance security and protect corporate data with robust policy controls | Allow employees to access key apps and switch seamlessly between existing or new VMware Intelligent Hub clients | Optimize media including voice and video for multimedia applications to enhance user experience | Integrate with third-party identity solutions to support just-in-time user provisioning or other custom configurations |

Figure 8.16 – VMware added value

Let's jump right into the specifics of the VMware Blast protocol in the next section.

Enhanced employee experience

The VMware Blast protocol can adapt to network settings such as low bandwidth or high latency to improve user experience through Intelligent Hub. Remote experience features such as printer and USB drive redirection further enhance the Cloud PC experience to match a user's native PC experience. VMware-validated peripherals, such as scanners, phones, and webcams, are supported on VMware services and can be used with Windows 365. Optimization packs for multimedia applications are also available to enhance the employee experience.

Hybrid cloud support

Customers can deploy Windows 365 Cloud PCs alongside their Horizon 8 on-premises, Horizon 8 on VMware Cloud, and Horizon Cloud on Azure desktop and published app deployments. Many Horizon customers have on-premises deployments and want to augment them with Windows 365 to take advantage of cloud capacity and scalability. The integration with Windows 365 makes it easy for users to access Cloud PCs and on-premises virtual desktops and apps.

Solution requirements

To get started with VMware and Windows 365, you will need the following:

- A Windows 365 tenant on Microsoft Azure

  - You will need to enable the VMware connector to allow users to broker using VMware's Blast protocol and Horizon Clients

- A VMware Horizon Cloud Service – next-gen tenant:

  - All Horizon Universal licenses support integration with Windows 365

  - You will need to create a VMware **Cloud Service Portal** (**CSP**) account

  - You will need to set up the same identity provider access being used by your Microsoft tenant

  - You will need to set up tenant-to-tenant connectivity

  - You will also need to enable the Microsoft connector to allow the VMware and Windows 365 tenants to communicate in order to facilitate the automated agent installation for entitled users

  - You will need to entitle users

Configuring Windows 365 with VMware in Intune

First, we must enable the Windows 365 partner connector for VMware. You can do this easily inside the tenant admin menu in the Microsoft Intune admin center:

1. Go to **Microsoft Intune** and log in with an account that has Global Administrator privileges in Intune.

2. Go to **Tenant Administration | Connectors and tokens | Windows 365 partner connectors**.

3. Click on **+ Add**.

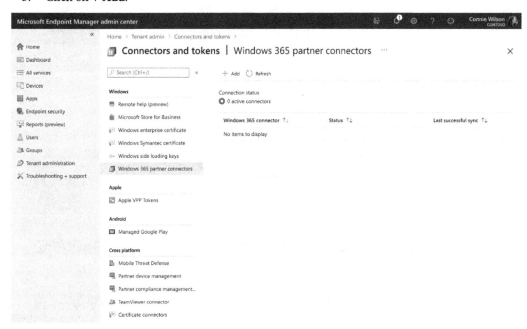

Figure 8.17 – Windows 365 partner connectors

4. From here, select the **VMware (preview)** connector.

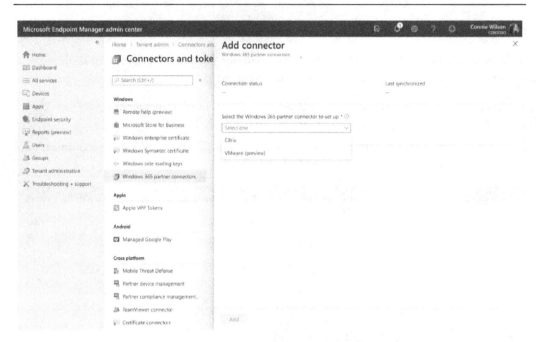

Figure 8.18 – Select VMware

5.   Enable the **Allow people to use VMware to connect to their Cloud PCs** setting. Then, click on **Add**.

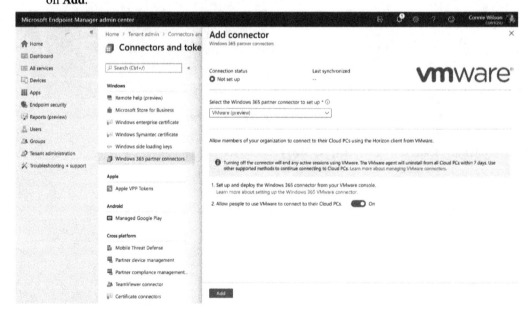

Figure 8.19 – Activate the connector

The connector will automatically install itself in the background. Once ready, you will see the connector status change in the portal (as shown in *Figure 8.20*).

> **Note**
> Provisioning Cloud PCs is done in the same way as explained in the *Provisioning Cloud PCs* section in *Chapter 3*. During provisioning, the VMware agents will be added automatically. If you have existing Cloud PCs, the VMware agents will automatically be added to them.

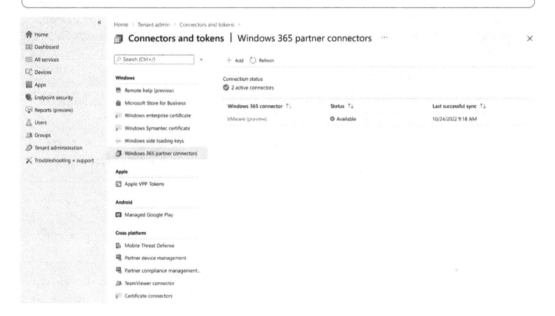

Figure 8.20 – Connector is successfully installed

Now that we have successfully installed the connector, we can start enabling the VMware Horizon service.

Signing up for the VMware Horizon Cloud Service – next-gen

In the following steps, you will learn how to sign up for the Horizon Cloud Service trial to enable its use together with Windows 365:

1. Sign up for a Horizon Cloud Service – next-gen free trial tenant via your sales representative or the VMware website – `https://www.vmware.com/horizon-universal-license-trial.html`.

2. You also need to request access for the VMware Horizon and Windows 365 preview via this website: `https://www.vmware.com/learn/1733900_REG.html`.

3.   You will receive a welcome email with instructions on the next steps:

   A.   You can schedule our onboarding team to do the remaining steps live with you to ensure accuracy.

   B.   The email has a button to launch CSP in your web browser.

   C.   You need to either use your existing CSP account or create a new one.

   D.   When asked, select **V2 (next-gen)** as your target Horizon Cloud Service.

   If you don't have a CSP account, you will need to create one using your email address (via VMware Cloud Services at `https://docs.vmware.com/en/VMware-Cloud-services/services/Using-VMware-Cloud-Services/GUID-92E04F0D-0A4E-4A14-BEE7-EE1E822FAE35.html`).

   You will need the following API configuration to finish:

   •   **CSP org ID**: Available from the **View Organization** page in (`https://console.cloud.vmware.com`).

   •   **CSP API key if not using OAuth**: Open `https://console.cloud.vmware.com`, click your org name in the top right, and then click on **My Account**. Navigate to **API Token** to create an API key.

4.   Follow the remaining steps until you are able to log in to the admin console.

5.   AD requirements for Horizon Cloud and Windows 365:

   A.   On-premises AD server is supported, as well as Azure AD.

   B.   Create a new Azure AD tenant by following this guide – `https://docs.microsoft.com/azure/active-directory/fundamentals/active-directory-access-create-new-tenant`.

   C.   Create a user on Azure AD and assign a Global Administrator role.

   D.   Follow these steps to sync your on-premises AD to Azure AD:

   •   Create a few users and groups on the AD server (make sure the users are members of some group).

   •   Install Azure AD Connect on the AD server so it can be linked to Azure AD. Here are the instructions to do that – `https://docs.microsoft.com/azure/active-directory/hybrid/how-to-connect-install-custom`.

   •   Once the Azure AD Connect setup is complete, go to Azure AD and check whether the AD users and groups are there.

Licensing for Microsoft Windows OSs: Horizon Cloud does not provide any guest OS (within the Cloud PC) licensing required for use of Microsoft Windows OSs that you use in the course of using the Horizon Cloud workflows. You, the customer, are responsible for having a valid Microsoft license that allows you to create and perform workflows, as well as operate the Windows-based desktop VMs and RDSH VMs that you choose to use in your Horizon Cloud tenant environment. The required licensing depends on your intended use.

In the next section, we will set up the connection from your Horizon Cloud tenant to Windows 365.

Configuring your Horizon Cloud Service tenant via the Windows 365 getting started workflow

In this section, we will be going over the steps to perform in the VMware portal:

> **Note**
>
> This section describes the detailed use of Horizon Cloud Service for integrating with Windows 365 based on the pre-release versions. Actual releases may vary slightly from the descriptions and screenshots shown here.

1. Go to the **Getting Started** page.
2. Click on **SELECT** under **Manage Windows 365 Desktops** to start configuring your Windows 365 inter-tenant connection:

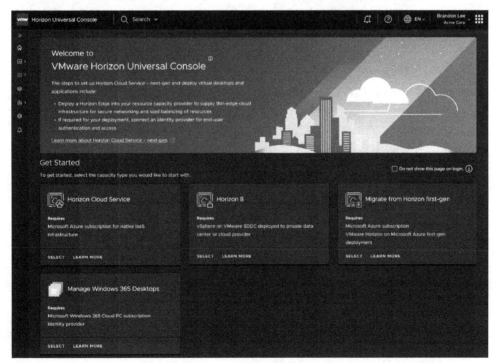

Figure 8.21 – VMware Horizon Console

3. From here, you can configure your identity and access or go ahead and provide permissions for Horizon Cloud Service to communicate with Windows 365.

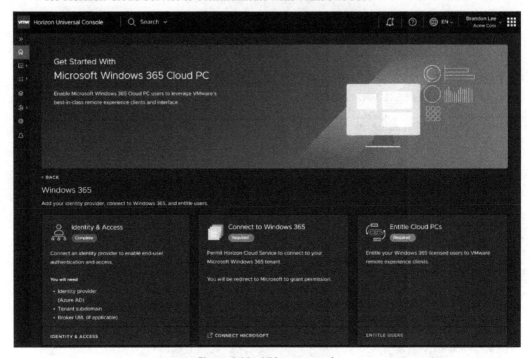

Figure 8.22 – VMware portal

4. To grant permissions, accept the dialog prompt presented:

Figure 8.23 – Permissions

5. Next, click on **ENTITLE USERS** on the final card on the right.

6. This will bring you to the **Desktop & Applications** section of the console, where you can select the **Windows 365 Cloud PC** entry from the table:

Figure 8.24 – Desktops & Applications

7.   Then, select **ENTITLEMENT** and then the **Entitle** sub-menu option:

Figure 8.25 – Entitlement

8.   Search for and select the users you want to entitle with user access to Cloud PCs through VMware's broker:

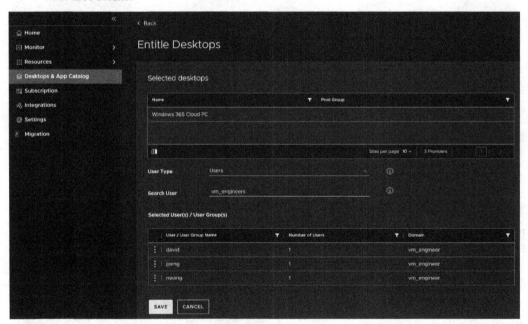

Figure 8.26 – Selected desktops

Once the entitlement is saved, you will be shown the entitlement window for all Windows 365 Cloud PC users. This window shows all users with their entitlement status, which includes the following:

- **Waiting for Agent Registration**: This means an entitlement instruction has been sent to the Microsoft Azure portal and the user is awaiting either a Cloud PC or the installation of the VMware agent

- **Registering**: This means the agent is installed and is pairing with Horizon Cloud Service – next-gen

- **Idle**: This means the agent is installed and functioning, ready to accept broker connections from Horizon Clients

- **Active**: The user is currently connected to their desktops

- **Pairing Failed**: The agent was not able to register

In addition, registered users will be displayed with their Cloud PC desktop names:

Figure 8.27 – Registered users

In the case of pairing failure, admins can attempt to manually pair agents by obtaining their pairing token and manually installing the agent on the Cloud PC. They can also retry the pairing:

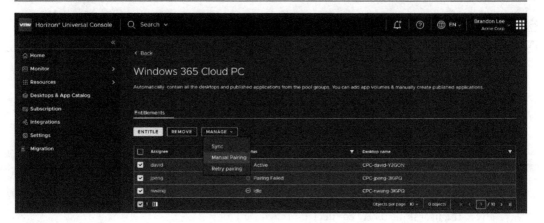

Figure 8.28 – Manual pairing

You can also remove a user entitlement by selecting the user and clicking the **Remove** button. Removing an entitlement will instruct Microsoft to uninstall the VMware agent.

End-user access

End users can access their Windows 365 desktops via several methods:

- **VMware Horizon web client**: To use VMware's Horizon web client, go to `cloud.vmware.horizon.com` and log in with your Windows 365 AD credentials

- **VMware Horizon native client**: If you've already installed a native client on your Windows or Mac device, launch the client with `cloud.horizon.vmware.com` and your AD credentials

- **VMware Workspace ONE Access portal**: If your company uses VMware's Workspace ONE Access portal for VDI and cloud desktop access, simply log in to your portal

- **Windows 365 end user portal**: You can go to `Windows365.microsoft.com` and log in using your AD credentials

Once logged in to any of the previously mentioned clients, you will be presented with the Windows 365 desktops you are entitled to access. You can simply launch the desktop by clicking on it. Each end user application is used slightly differently but all work essentially the same, enabling you to manage your remote session.

Figure 8.29 – Windows native Horizon Client showing Windows 365 Cloud PC

In the next section, you will learn how the IGEL partner enables you to connect to Windows 365 via a low-end OS.

Client partners – IGEL Technology

IGEL Technology is the developer of a third-party client for connecting to **Azure Virtual Desktop (AVD)**. The IGEL client, known as the **AVD remote desktop app for IGEL OS**, was the first ever Linux-based client built on Microsoft's Remote Desktop Client SDK. Because the core of the IGEL client is Microsoft technology, the client is jointly supported by Microsoft and IGEL, which provides users with a smooth user experience.

The IGEL Windows 365 app for IGEL OS is built using the same underlying technology as the IGEL AVD remote desktop app, but with additional features unique to a Cloud PC. Because users have a 1:1 dedicated relationship with their Cloud PCs, they can reboot, shut down, suspend, restore, and rename their cloud computers. These Cloud PC control features are built into the IGEL Windows 365 app.

Other features of the IGEL Windows 365 app include the ability to interact with multiple Windows 365 Cloud PCs at a time. Each of these machines can be displayed in a separate workspace using the paging feature of the base IGEL OS.

Of course, the IGEL Windows 365 app supports a media-optimized Teams experience. IGEL also extends the app to work with many third-party integrations, including Zoom, Imprivata, ThinPrint, Tricerat, ControlUp, and FabulaTech.

With IGEL, a device running IGEL OS boots directly to a Windows 365 Cloud PC. In such a scenario, users authenticate against Azure AD at the device level and they are immediately connected to their Cloud PC using single sign-on. Booting to the cloud effectively gives the user the experience of having a desktop PC except the PC is a Windows 365 Cloud PC.

To support the Microsoft Windows 365 Frontline experience, the IGEL Windows 365 client includes features to pre-start machines and notify users when no machines are available.

> **Important note**
> The IGEL Windows 365 app is only available on IGEL OS.

IGEL OS is a secure, read-only OS designed for connecting to cloud workspaces. As an OS, IGEL OS will run on most 64-bit x86 computers manufactured in the last 10 years. The system is completely configurable, allowing users to "shape" devices to meet unique operational requirements. In other words, users can configure a device to look and behave exactly as they want, thus creating an edge device that delivers a stable and predictable user experience.

To ensure devices are running the most current version of the IGEL Windows 365 app, IGEL OS is connected to IGEL COSMOS, which is a group of cloud-based services maintained by IGEL. Using the COSMOS platform, users and organizations can manage devices running using the IGEL Universal Management Suite, which is a management tool that scales to handle hundreds of thousands of devices.

Configuring the IGEL Windows 365 app

After you have installed IGEL OS on your endpoint and walked through the first boot wizard, you will have an IGEL OS desktop; however, before you can connect to Windows 365, you need to install and configure the Windows 365 app for IGEL OS. Click the IGEL App Portal icon in the lower-left corner of the IGEL desktop.

The IGEL App Portal icon can be found in the task bar of IGEL OS, and when connected, your screen will look as follows:

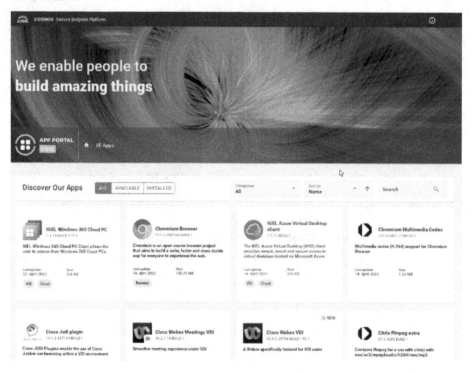

Figure 8.30 – IGEL App Portal

Locate the **IGEL Windows 365 Cloud PC** option in the APP PORTAL. Click on the panel and the following screen will be displayed:

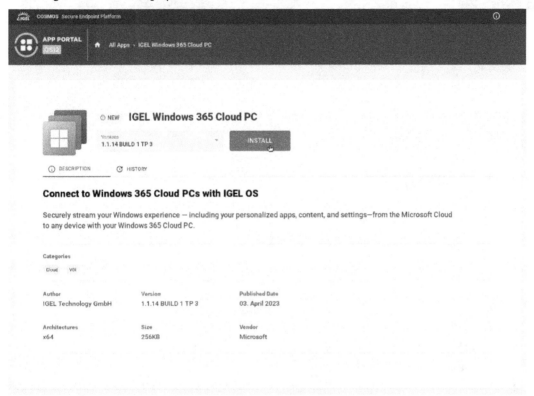

Figure 8.31 – Windows 365 Cloud PC app install

Using the drop-down menu, you may select the version of the Windows 365 app to install; however, Microsoft and IGEL recommend always using the latest version. Once selected, click the **INSTALL** button:

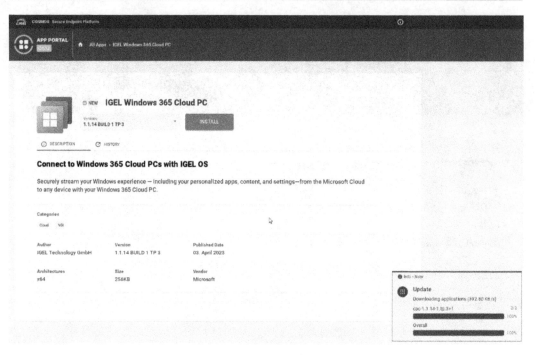

Figure 8.32 – Install in progress

After the **IGEL Windows 365 Cloud PC** app is downloaded or updated, you need to reboot your IGEL OS endpoint device to finish the installation. The system reboot will happen automatically unless you cancel the process. If you cancel the reboot process, the installation will finish the next time the device boots.

Follow these steps to connect to the Cloud PC after the reboot is done:

1. Open **IGEL Setup** and navigate to the **Apps** section, where you will find **Windows 365 Cloud PC**.
2. Click to expand and navigate to **Windows 365 Cloud PC Sessions**.
3. Click the + sign to create a new session.

> **Note**
>
> The default name for your session will be **Windows 365 Cloud PC session**, but you can give your session any name you like (this will be the name associated with the Windows 365 shortcut icon).
>
> Browse through the various configuration options and turn on/off features as you wish (for example, you could select **Autostart** to launch the Windows 365 app on boot).

4. Click **Save and Close**.

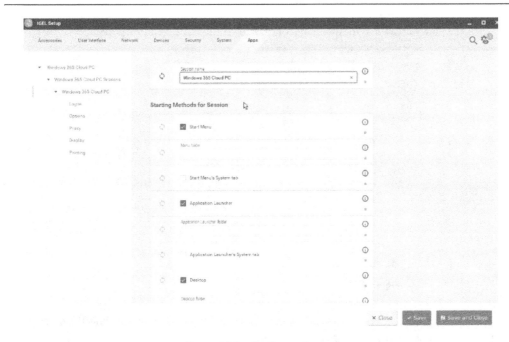

Figure 8.33 – Configure the app

5. A Windows 365 icon will appear on the desktop with the name you configured when creating your session:

Figure 8.34 – IGEL OS desktop screen

6.   Click the newly created Windows 365 icon to launch the IGEL Windows 365 app:

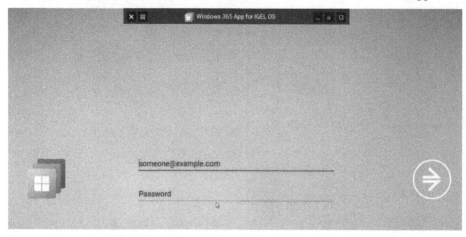

Figure 8.35 – Windows 365 app on IGEL OS client UX

7.   After entering your credentials, you will be presented with an MFA request; follow the on-screen process as required. After you are properly authenticated, you will be presented with one of two different access workflows. If you only have access to a single Windows 365 Cloud PC, then your connection will start automatically, and you will see your Windows 365 desktop displayed. If you have access to multiple Windows 365 Cloud PCs, then all your Windows 365 resources are presented, and you will be able to choose which Cloud PC to connect to.

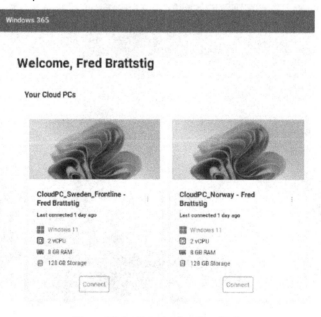

Figure 8.36 – Select your Cloud PC

8. If you have difficulty connecting to your Windows 365 Cloud PC, use the context menu to interact with your Cloud PC. Here, you will find options to restart, restore, rename, troubleshoot, and read the system information.

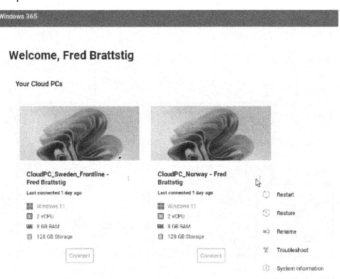

Figure 8.37 – Cloud PC user actions

9. You are now ready to connect to your Cloud PC. Choose a PC and click the **Connect** button:

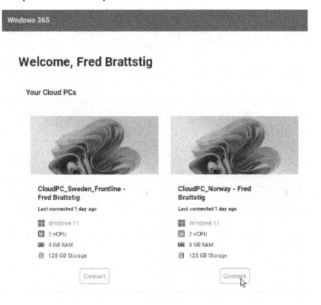

Figure 8.38 – Connect to your Cloud PC

10. The IGEL Windows 365 app initiates the connection and displays your Windows 365 Cloud PC:

Figure 8.39 – Active Cloud PC session

This concludes the section about Windows 365 on IGEL OS. Now, we'll move on to another exciting partner solution on offer: Rimo3!

Package modernization partners – Rimo3

Rimo3 modernizes your application estate. From migration to maintenance, Rimo3 is a solution that automates preproduction compatibility testing, package modernization, and migration of your Windows application estate. It is used to test and modernize applications for OS upgrades, patch updates, migrations from legacy to cloud workspaces, modern management planes, and ongoing maintenance for evergreen environments.

Rimo3 automates the entire modernization process, from migration to maintenance, with intelligent, unattended automation that eliminates the need for scripting, specific expertise, or complex configuration. The cloud-native Rimo3 platform integrates with industry-leading solutions and uses your uniquely configured and customized Windows images for testing.

Automating application import from ConfigMgr

Since **Configuration Manager** (**ConfigMgr**) was introduced by Microsoft nearly 25 years ago, customers have used the solution to store, deliver, and manage applications across their end user devices. During this time, application repositories have been updated with package scripts, custom actions, transforms, updates, and new packages.

Organizations moving to modern, cloud-based workspaces are accelerating and prioritizing their move to Intune to manage and control how all their organization's devices are used, including mobile devices and cloud desktop-as-a-service workspaces. Automated migration of legacy ConfigMgr packages to Intune will remove substantial time and labor hours in moving to a modern management platform.

The ConfigMgr Import feature enables customers to import application packages into an Azure subscription-linked Rimo3 Cloud tenant. Importing applications from ConfigMgr improves the onboarding experience by removing the limitations of package upload, such as maximum upload size, and ensuring that custom install switches and properties are used without having to be manually configured.

The feature will import applications from ConfigMgr with a deployment type of Windows Installer (MSI), App-V 5, as well as Script Installers.

The import also includes logic to automatically remediate install and uninstall commands that contain switches that would result in user interaction being required. This ensures that the automated processes can run completely unattended.

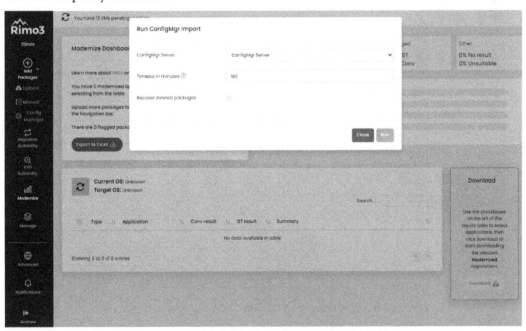

Figure 8.40 – ConfigMgr import

Once applications have been successfully onboarded from ConfigMgr, Rimo3 initiates the unattended automation pipeline to test and modernize the application in scope. The automation is broken out into individual sequences, outlined as follows:

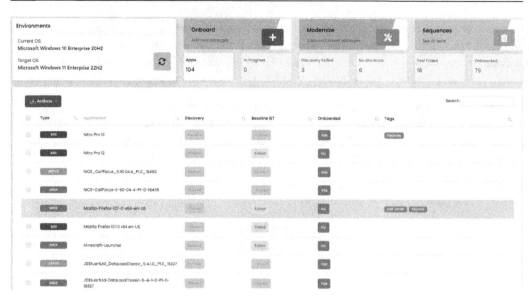

Figure 8.41 – Package onboarding

An activity runs as part of onboarding applications from ConfigMgr to automatically identify applications and executables to determine which should be tested as part of the Intelligent Smoke Test.

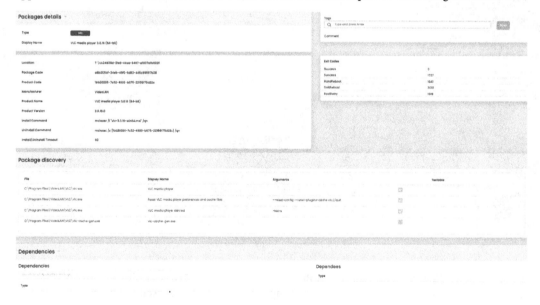

Figure 8.42 – Package details

Now we know how to pull the applications, we can move on to application smoke testing.

Rimo3 Intelligent Smoke Test

The Intelligent Smoke Test is Rimo3's "revolutionary" automated testing capability, designed to test any application for compatibility with Windows without requiring a predefined script or needing to know what the application is or does. The **Rimo3 Intelligent Smoke Test** is executed against the current OS, then against the target OS to analyze for any impact in your environment in regards to performance and stability of the application. This process is executed via automation with no user interaction.

Figure 8.43 – Smoke testing apps

Rimo3 automated conversion/capture for modern formats

Automated modernization for the following application package types:

- Bulk conversion to Microsoft MSIX for suitable applications (includes a global trusted root certificate as part of the conversion)

- Bulk capture to VMware App Volumes for suitable applications

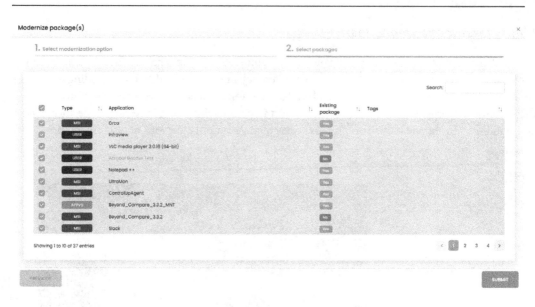

Figure 8.44 – Modernize packages

The following are the package formats supported by Microsoft Intune:

- Windows universal line-of-business apps
- MSI line-of-business apps
- Windows apps (Win32)

Post-packaging automated Intelligent Smoke Test

The post-packaging Intelligent Smoke Test validates a modern package against a specified operating environment. Now, we will go over the steps to export packages to Intune.

Export to Intune

The Export to Intune feature of Rimo3 Cloud completes the journey of applications that have been imported from Microsoft ConfigMgr and converted into modern MSIX packages by enabling these packages to be exported to Intune, where they can be deployed to modern cloud workspaces such as AVD and Windows 365.

Applications that have been successfully converted to MSIX packages and automatically tested for compatibility with the MSIX format and a modern OS can be exported to Intune in bulk from the **Modernize** dashboard:

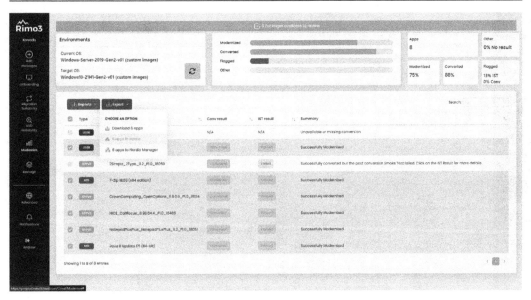

Figure 8.45 – Review your packages to export

Additionally, applications can be exported to Intune individually from the **Package Details** screen as either an MSIX or in their original package format. Based on the package type and where it was acquired from, the platform will automatically determine the appropriate application type to create in Intune:

- MSIX packages are exported as Windows universal line-of-business apps

- MSI packages with no command-line customizations or external files are exported as Windows MSI line-of-business applications.

- All other supported package formats, such as setup EXEs, script installers, and MSIs with command-line customizations or external files, will be automatically wrapped in the Intune wrapper format and exported as a Windows app (Win32):

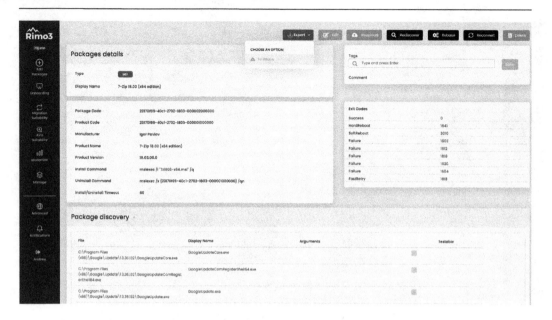

Figure 8.46 – Export to Intune

You can watch some demo videos for Rimo3 here: `https://www.youtube.com/@Rimo3Cloud`. For more information about Rimo3, go to `https://www.rimo3.com/`.

Client modernization partners – LG

Microsoft and LG have partnered to deliver the Windows 365 app on LG Smart TVs as part of their WebOS. All the new 2023 LG TV models will ship with a new Home Office app inbox that includes Windows 365 in the home menu.

Clicking on the icon will bring you to the Windows 365 app client experience, which is the same for Web and Windows desktops. You can use single sign-on to sign in from your TV to your Cloud PC. Adding a USB wireless receiver for a keyboard and mouse makes it a very convenient setup!

Figure 8.47 – LG Home Office app

In the next section, we will be going over the new Motorola ThinkPhone partnership.

Client modernization partners – Motorola/Lenovo

Microsoft and Motorola partnered to deliver a new unique Windows 365 Cloud PC streaming experience to their new Lenovo ThinkPhone. This new phone includes a new experience that allows you to directly connect to your Cloud PCs from the Android UI using a USB-C-to-HDMI cable.

Plugging in the cable unlocks the new Cloud PC UI integration and the user is asked to select the Cloud PC to connect to.

If the user has multiple Cloud PCs, all of them will be shown.

The credentials will automatically come from the Azure AD account registered on the phone.

Figure 8.48 – Motorola ThinkPhone – Windows 365

Once you are connected to your Cloud PC, you can also favorite it by hitting the toggle to start the Cloud PC session automatically the next time you plug in the USB-C-to-HDMI cable.

This makes it very convenient for frontline or hotdesking workers as it allows them to use a docking station. The moment you plug your phone into a docking station, it automatically boots you into the Cloud PC.

Figure 8.49 – Motorola ThinkPhone – favorite your Cloud PC

Summary

In this chapter, you've learned how partner solutions help Windows 365 to extend its native offering. We walked you through how Citrix brings the benefits of the protocol to Windows 365 and how both IGEL and Rimo3 deliver other great benefits to make the end user and onboarding experiences of applications easier.

In the next chapter, we will celebrate some people that have a passion for Windows 365 and other Microsoft technologies. These people are not just community experts, but they also help build great communities that are fun to be a part of.

Questions

1. Does Citrix HDX Plus support the onboarding and offboarding of Cloud PCs without re-provisioning?

2. Does IGEL OS run on Linux or Windows?

3. Do Citrix HDX Plus and Windows 365 still require Intune?

Further reading

Learn more about the different partner solutions via these links:

- *Windows 365 approved partners | Microsoft Learn* (`https://learn.microsoft.com/windows-365/partners`)

- *Troubleshoot Citrix HDX Plus for Windows 365 | Microsoft Learn* (`https://learn.microsoft.com/windows-365/enterprise/troubleshoot-citrix-hdx-plus`)

9

Community Experts
Hall of Fame

Writing a book takes a lot of dedication but it wouldn't be possible without the support of our amazing community. This chapter is a way to send love to all the community experts out there who share knowledge in any form. A heartfelt thank you from us!

Figure 9.1 – Microsoft MVP Summit 2023

Please join our Windows 365 Community group via www.w365community.com today. It includes information about new releases as well as technical information about fixing issues and implementing new features.

Microsoft MVPs for Windows 365

Microsoft **Most Valuable Professionals** (**MVPs**) are highly skilled technology experts who actively engage in sharing their knowledge with the community. They are constantly seeking out the latest cutting-edge technologies, such as Windows 365, with a fervent desire to explore and discover new ideas.

Figure 9.2 – Microsoft MVP logo

Their expertise in Microsoft products and services runs deep, and they are adept at bringing together a variety of platforms, products, and solutions to solve real-world problems. Through their unwavering commitment to technology and their passion for collaboration, MVPs play a critical role in driving innovation and advancing the field of technology.

Here are the current MVPs for Windows 365:

Name	Website/Social Channel
Anoop Nair	www.howtomanagedevices.com
Aresh Sarkari	askaresh.com
Davina Armstrong-Cruz	www.linkedin.com/in/darmstrongcruz
Dominiek Verham	techlab.blog
Doug Petrole	desktopsforeveryone.com
Jon Jarvis	practical365.com
Jitesh Kumar	www.linkedin.com/in/jiteshkumar8092
Jakub Piesik	www.piesik.me
Kevin Kaminski	checkyourlogs.net
Laurent Gébeau	devapps.ms
Mark O'Shea	intunedin.net
Mathieu Leroy	workplaceninjas.fr
Morten Pedholt	www.pedholtlab.com
Ola Ström	www.olastrom.com
Petri Paavola	intune.ninja
Ritsuko Nishibata	ictschool.jp
Rory Monaghan	www.rorymon.com
Sune Thomsen	www.osdsune.com

Sami Laiho	`www.adminize.com`
Soonman Kwon	`www.hakunamata2.net/`
Thomas Marcussen	`www.thomasmarcussen.com`
Yannick Plavonil	`www.msnloop.com/`
Yoojong Jeon	`blog.naver.com/jijonx`

Other community experts

We want to celebrate all community experts, regardless of their status as Microsoft MVPs or primary focus areas. One of the best things about working in IT is the feeling of togetherness and spending time with other people that share the same interest. Community experts do not just have incredible knowledge but also the desire to help others learn by sharing information and hosting community events.

Without community togetherness, the IT world wouldn't be so fun to be part of. Thanks to everyone for being awesome! We know there are more people than on this list; sorry to the people we missed.

Name	Website/Social Channel
Aaron Parker	`www.stealthpuppy.com`
Adam Gross	`intune.training`
Ben Whitmore	`www.msendpointmgr.com`
Bas van Kaam	`www.basvankaam.com`
Bryan Dam	`www.damgoodadmin.com`
Ben Reader	`intune.training`
Christiaan Brinkhoff	`www.christiaanbrinkhoff.com`
Donna Ryan	`www.TheNotoriousDRR.com`
Dean Cefola	`www.youtube.com/AzureAcademy`
Ed Baker	`www.ed-baker.com`
Freek Berson	`www.themicrosoftplatform.net`
Gerry Hampson	`www.gerryhampsoncm.blogspot.ie`
Jan Ketil Skanke	`www.msendpointmgr.com`
James Kindon	`www.jkindon.com`
Jesper Fütterer Bing	`www.linkedin.com/in/jesper-fütterer-bing-132ba86/`
Jörgen Nilsson	`ccmexec.com`
Kim Oppalfens	`www.oscc.be`
Mayunk Jain	`www.twitter.com/mayunkj`
Mirko Colemberg	`blog.colemberg.ch`

Mattias Melkersen	`www.msendpointmgr.com`
Maurice Daly	`www.msendpointmgr.com`
Michael Mardahl	`www.msendpointmgr.com`
Martin Bengtson	`www.imab.dk`
Marcel Meurer	`blog.itprocloud.de`
Martin Therkelsen	`www.cloudninja.nu`
Niall Brady	`www.windows-noob.com`
Nikolaj Andersen	`www.msendpointmgr.com`
Neil McLoughlin	`www.virtualmanc.co.uk`
Oliver Kieselbach	`www.oliverkieselbach.com`
Per Larsen	`www.osddeployment.dk`
Peter Daalmans	`www.peterdaalmans.com`
Peter van der Woude	`www.petervanderwoude.nl`
Peter Klapwijk	`www.inthecloud247.com`
Panu Saukko	`www.twitter.com/panusaukko`
Peter Dahl	`www.peterdahl.net`
Ronni Pedersen	`www.ronnipedersen.com`
Robin Hobo	`www.robinhobo.com`
Ronny de Jong	`ronnydejong.com`
Steven Hosking	`intune.training`
Sandeep Patnaik	`www.sandeeppatnaik.com`
Sandy Zeng	`www.sandyzeng.com`
Simon Binder	`www.kneedeepintech.com`
Thijs Lecomte	`www.365bythijs.be`
Thomas Kurth	`www.wpninjas.ch`
Tim de Keukelaere	`dekeukelaere.com`
Travis Roberts	`www.ciraltos.com`
Tim Hermie	`www.linkedin.com/in/timhermie/`
Tom Degreef	`www.oscc.be`
Tim Mangan	`www.tmurgent.com/TmBlog`

Microsoft resources

The following table details additional resources that you may find useful. The links provided include technical information, new releases, and information relating to fixes and implementing new features for Windows 365:

Name	Website
Windows 365 landing page	`aka.ms/w365`
Windows 365 roadmap	`aka.ms/w365roadmap`
Windows 365 documentation	`aka.ms/w365docs`
Windows 365 Tech Community	`aka.ms/w365TC`
Microsoft MVP program	`mvp.microsoft.com`
Windows 365 feedback	`aka.ms/w365feedback`
Windows 365 reports and whitepapers	`aka.ms/w365papers`

Windows 365 Learn modules	`learn.microsoft.com/training/modules/manage-windows-365`
	
	`learn.microsoft.com/training/modules/manage-virtual-desktops`

Microsoft Certification Exam MD-102: Endpoint Administrator	`learn.microsoft.com/certifications/exams/md-102`
Windows in the Cloud resources	`windowsinthecloud.com`

Fun stuff we did for the book

We've had lots of fun writing this book. Some moments stood out for us, which we would like to share with you.

Christiaan

This is one of Christiaan's memorable experiences:

Figure 9.3 – Christiaan writing chapters on his Cloud PC while working from the clouds

Morten

Here is one of Morten's memorable experiences:

Figure 9.4 – Morten on a visit to the Microsoft campus in building 121 (the Windows 365 building) with Christiaan Brinkhoff, Scott Manchester, and the APENTO team

Sandeep

Last but not least, this is one of Sandeep's memorable experiences:

Figure 9.5 – Sandeep testing the SpaceX Starlink connection to Windows 365 Cloud PCs

Everything must come to an end

We have now reached the end of this book. We can truly say it's been a journey for us. We started back in December 2022 with the first thoughts of writing a book that could help you master Windows 365. We hope you feel that goal has been achieved. It's been a fun and learning process along the way. We'd love to hear how this book has helped you, so drop us a note on LinkedIn with your inspiring stories. Let's spread the positive impact of this book together!

Thank you for reading this book; we wish you good luck in mastering Windows 365.

Christiaan Brinkhoff, Sandeep Patnaik, and *Morten Pedholt*

Index

C

N

O

Packtpub.com

Subscribe to our online digital library for full access to over 7,000 books and videos, as well as industry leading tools to help you plan your personal development and advance your career. For more information, please visit our website.

Why subscribe?

- Spend less time learning and more time coding with practical eBooks and Videos from over 4,000 industry professionals

- Improve your learning with Skill Plans built especially for you

- Get a free eBook or video every month

- Fully searchable for easy access to vital information

- Copy and paste, print, and bookmark content

Did you know that Packt offers eBook versions of every book published, with PDF and ePub files available? You can upgrade to the eBook version at packtpub.com and as a print book customer, you are entitled to a discount on the eBook copy. Get in touch with us at customercare@packtpub.com for more details.

At www.packtpub.com, you can also read a collection of free technical articles, sign up for a range of free newsletters, and receive exclusive discounts and offers on Packt books and eBooks.

Other Books You May Enjoy

If you enjoyed this book, you may be interested in these other books by Packt:

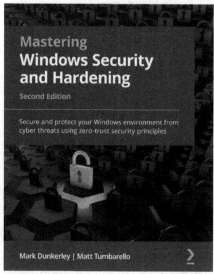

Mastering Windows Security and Hardening - Second Edition

Mark Dunkerley, Matt Tumbarello

ISBN: 978-1-80323-654-4

- Build a multi-layered security approach using zero-trust concepts
- Explore best practices to implement security baselines successfully
- Get to grips with virtualization and networking to harden your devices
- Discover the importance of identity and access management
- Explore Windows device administration and remote management
- Become an expert in hardening your Windows infrastructure
- Audit, assess, and test to ensure controls are successfully applied and enforced
- Monitor and report activities to stay on top of vulnerabilities

Mastering Microsoft 365 Defender

Ru Campbell, Viktor Hedberg

ISBN: 978-1-80324-170-8

- Understand the Threat Landscape for enterprises
- Effectively implement end-point security
- Manage identity and access management using Microsoft 365 defender
- Protect the productivity suite with Microsoft Defender for Office 365
- Hunting for threats using Microsoft 365 Defender

Packt is searching for authors like you

If you're interested in becoming an author for Packt, please visit `authors.packtpub.com` and apply today. We have worked with thousands of developers and tech professionals, just like you, to help them share their insight with the global tech community. You can make a general application, apply for a specific hot topic that we are recruiting an author for, or submit your own idea.

Share Your Thoughts

Now you've finished *Mastering Windows 365*, we'd love to hear your thoughts! Scan the QR code below to go straight to the Amazon review page for this book and share your feedback or leave a review on the site that you purchased it from.

`https://packt.link/r/1837637962`

Your review is important to us and the tech community and will help us make sure we're delivering excellent quality content.

Download a free PDF copy of this book

Thanks for purchasing this book!

Do you like to read on the go but are unable to carry your print books everywhere? Is your eBook purchase not compatible with the device of your choice?

Don't worry, now with every Packt book you get a DRM-free PDF version of that book at no cost.

Read anywhere, any place, on any device. Search, copy, and paste code from your favorite technical books directly into your application.

The perks don't stop there, you can get exclusive access to discounts, newsletters, and great free content in your inbox daily

Follow these simple steps to get the benefits:

1. Scan the QR code or visit the link below

https://packt.link/free-ebook/978-1-83763-796-6

2. Submit your proof of purchase
3. That's it! We'll send your free PDF and other benefits to your email directly

Printed in the USA
CPSIA information can be obtained
at www.ICGtesting.com
JSHW051121051123
51471JS00004B/9